The Literary Taylor Swift

The Literary Taylor Swift

Songwriting and Intertextuality

Edited by Betsy Winakur Tontiplaphol and
Anastasia Klimchynskaya

BLOOMSBURY ACADEMIC
NEW YORK • LONDON • OXFORD • NEW DELHI • SYDNEY

BLOOMSBURY ACADEMIC
Bloomsbury Publishing Inc, 1359 Broadway, New York, NY 10018, USA
Bloomsbury Publishing Plc, 50 Bedford Square, London, WC1B 3DP, UK
Bloomsbury Publishing Ireland, 29 Earlsfort Terrace, Dublin 2, D02 AY28, Irelan

BLOOMSBURY, BLOOMSBURY ACADEMIC and the Diana logo are trademarks
of Bloomsbury Publishing Plc

First published in the United States of America 2024
Paperback edition published 2026

Cover design: Louise Dugdale
Cover image © Kevin Mazur/TAS/Getty Images for TAS

Bloomsbury Publishing Inc does not have any control over, or responsibility for, any third-party websites
referred to or in this book. All internet addresses given in this book were correct at the time of going to
press. The author and publisher regret any inconvenience caused if addresses have changed or sites
have ceased to exist, but can accept no responsibility for any such changes.

Whilst every effort has been made to locate copyright holders the publishers would be grateful to hear
from any person(s) not here acknowledged.

Library of Congress Cataloging-in-Publication Data

Names: Tontiplaphol, Betsy Winakur, editor. | Klimchynskaya, Anastasia, editor.
Title: The literary Taylor Swift : songwriting and intertextuality / edited by Betsy Winakur Tontiplaphol
and Anastasia Klimchynskaya.
Description: [1.] | New York : Bloomsbury Academic, 2024. |
Includes bibliographical references and index.
Identifiers: LCCN 2024011866 (print) | LCCN 2024011867 (ebook) | ISBN 9798765104514 (hardback) |
ISBN 9798765104552 (paperback) | ISBN 9798765104521 (ebook) | ISBN 9798765104538 (pdf)
Subjects: LCSH: Swift, Taylor, 1989–Criticism and interpretation. | Swift, Taylor, 1989–Themes, motives. |
Music and literature. | Popular music–United States–History and criticism.
Classification: LCC ML420.S968 L58 2024 (print) | LCC ML420.S968 (ebook) |
DDC 782.421642—dceng/23/20240409
LC record available at https://lccn.loc.gov/2024011866
LC ebook record available at https://lccn.loc.gov/2024011867

ISBN: HB: 979-8-7651-0451-4
        PB: 979-8-7651-0455-2
        ePDF: 979-8-7651-0453-8
        eBook: 979-8-7651-0452-1

Typeset by RefineCatch Limited, Bungay, Suffolk
Printed and bound in the United States of America

For product safety related questions contact productsafety@bloomsbury.com.

To find out more about our authors and books visit www.bloomsbury.com
and sign up for our newsletters.

Contents

Introduction

Blank Spaces, Fresh Pages: Taylor Swift and/as Literature

Betsy Winakur Tontiplaphol and Anastasia Klimchynskaya

It would be an understatement to say that Taylor Swift has profoundly influenced the cultural landscape of the early twenty-first century. We could defend that position with financial or statistical evidence, since Swift's album sales, Grammy wins, Spotify streams, and tour revenue have broken records. However, since numerical data alone can't capture a creator's *cultural* significance, we could also note that in addition to putting up groundbreaking numbers, Swift's work has shaped the music, film, and other media of her age. From winning a Grammy for *Fearless*, an album dedicated to the experiences and tribulations of teenage girls at a time when such an emphasis was distinctly lacking in popular music, to placing her songs on multiple soundtracks, including *The Summer I Turned Pretty*, *Where the Crawdads Sing*, *Dickinson*, and *Killing Eve*, Swift has, in remarkable ways, defined this moment's Zeitgeist. In 2005, Swift released her first single "Tim McGraw," in which one of the biggest names in country music serves as an imaginary soundtrack to a teenage love story, and by 2019, she herself was identified as a musical mainstay when country singer Savannah Burrows released "What Would Taylor Swift Do?" ("[S]he'd write a song about it," the refrain tells us.) But on top of changing the numbers and the conversation, Swift has transformed her industry by, among other gestures and achievements, pulling her music from streaming services until artists were compensated fairly, producing a union-approved concert film during a writers' and actors' strike, and selling millions of CDs and vinyl records at a time when the music industry is moving almost exclusively toward streaming. Indefatigable, she's also scripted and directed short films, collaborated with musical legends such as Andrew Lloyd Webber and the Chicks, and challenged sexist media images of female celebrities in many quarters but most famously in her song "Blank Space," which *Billboard* named one of a hundred that defined its decade.

Put simply, Swift's effect—on *everything*, including, at the time of this writing, America's National Football League—is undeniable, and her outsized influence has been the subject of scholarship in a variety of fields, including musicology, psychology, popular culture studies, celebrity studies, and even economics. This collection, however, examines a facet of Swift, both artist and phenomenon, that hasn't received careful or sustained scholarly attention. The writers assembled here argue that Swift exhibits a distinctly *literary* sensibility that merits treatment in its own right and on its own terms—as, that is, a dimension of her artistry and persona as significant as her sound, her celebrity, or her business acumen. Permitted to determine the specific parameters of "the literary" for themselves, the contributors to this volume examine Swift's significance, timeliness, and power through the diverse lenses afforded by the broad discipline of literary studies. Some regard Swift as akin to a lyric poet, a writer interested in preserving discrete moments, images, and confessions; others treat her as something like a novelist or memoirist, a writer who returns again and again to narrative in order to capture human experience, her own and others': a crush on an unapproved boy becomes a "Love Story," wherein *Romeo and Juliet* gets a happy ending; a break-up becomes synonymous with the *tale* of a relationship when she confesses, "I used to think they'll tell the story of us" ("The Story of Us"); and a would-be boyfriend dating "the wrong girl" is reminded that "she'll never know your story like I do" ("You Belong With Me"). Indeed, very often in Swift's world, to know someone is to know their "story." In essence, then, *The Literary Taylor Swift* both explores Swift's engagements, intertextual and otherwise, *with* literature and treats her songbook *as* literature—as, that is, a body of stories, poems, and other textual forms to which literary-critical theories and methodologies can (and, given Swift's extraordinary reach and talent, should) be productively applied.

For us, the notion of a literary Swift is anchored in Swift's own words, in her lyrics' unusual (in a pop-musical context, anyway) emphasis on reading and writing. Books— stacked on bedside tables ("Paper Rings"), "covered in cobwebs" in "antique shop[s]" ("Timeless"), cited as status symbols ("I Bet You Think About Me"), and more—appear in song after song, and Swift alludes, both explicitly and obliquely, to a variety of English and American authors, among them Charlotte Brontë, Daphne du Maurier, F. Scott Fitzgerald, Nathanial Hawthorne, William Shakespeare, and William Wordsworth. In addition to those nods to the English-language literary canon, Swift's songbook manifests a nerdy enthusiasm for bookish terminology in its references to chapters ("The Story of Us") and footnotes ("tolerate it"), as well as the vagaries of literary categorization. In other words, Swift both specifies literary genres, from poetry ("you fit my poems like a perfect rhyme" ["Holy Ground"]) to history ("You held your head like a hero on a history book page" ["Long Live"]), and interrogates the concept of genre itself by highlighting the fungibility of literary types. She observes, for example, that romance often bleeds into "tragedy"—"the story of us looks a lot like a tragedy now" ("The Story of Us")—and that assumptions regarding generic stability can blunt one's critical judgment. As her avatar remarks in "White Horse," "I'm not your princess, this ain't our fairytale," and the unique instability of the "fairytale" persists as a special anxiety for Swift, who conjures enchantment-associated settings—castles, gated gardens, and the like—with blithe regularity while simultaneously impugning those sites' (and their flagship genre's) ethics and authority. In "Cruel Summer," to "[sneak] through the garden gate" is to "seal" a hellish "fate," and in "Look What You Made Me Do," a taunting reflection on some ill-defined but unquestionably modern-day "drama," Swift hints, if only metaphorically, at a Brothers Grimm-esque backstory in order to demonstrate how quickly "princess" status can be revoked: "You asked me for a place to sleep," she icily intones, then "[l]ocked me out and threw a feast." Fairytales, after all, are defined in part by their origins in orality, by their historical link to vocalization, and Swift arguably prefers the relative safety and certainty of writing—of, that is, the literary. Genre concerns notwithstanding, then, her lyrics ultimately portray a text-saturated world, a landscape in which wills ("Anti-Hero"), grocery store receipts ("marjorie"), and notes—on doors ("Holy Ground"), in lockets ("Run"), in pockets ("Sad Beautiful Tragic"), on the backs of Polaroids ("The Very First Night"), and passed in classrooms ("It's Nice to Have a Friend")—are both ubiquitous and potent.

That said, however, Swift's literary sensibility manifests thematically as more than an interest in realized texts—in, that is, finished stories, poems, notes, and other documents. Punctuated by images of paper and ink, her songs never let us forget that writing is an act, and Swift often lingers on accounts of in-progress or aspired-to—in other words, not yet complete—moments of inscription, composition, and even revision. The titular document in the early track "Our Song" is drafted in a car—"In the front seat . . . / I grabbed a pen and an old napkin / And I wrote down our song"—and in the much later "Sweet Nothings," Swift recounts a similar experience; however, by identifying the product of that act as a "poem" instead of a "song"—"On the way home / I wrote a poem / You say, 'What a mind'"—she underscores the literariness (as opposed to the musicality) of her speaker's on-the-go drafting. In the albums that intervene, the Swiftian "mind" remains, in a very literal sense, writerly. The acerbic Taylor of "Look What You Made Me Do" maintains, we're told, "a list of names"—"yours is in red, underlined," she warns—while her flirtier alter-ego croons elsewhere, "I've got a blank space, baby, / And I'll write your name." In the latter song, 2014's aforementioned chart-topper "Blank Space," Swift assures an appealing new acquaintance that she "can read [him] like a magazine," but by 2019's "Cornelia Street," voiced by a more mature lover, the central relationship's text becomes collaborative, an evolving joint narration: "We were a fresh page on the desk," she says, "[f]illing in the blanks as we go." Collaborative writing endures as a theme on 2020's *folklore*, which includes both "august"—"[y]our back beneath the sun / Wishin' I could write my name on it"—and "invisible string," wherein Swift, Ariadne-like, toys with the primal link between text and textile to spin a yarn about the gossamer threads that have always bound her own still developing story to her beloved's. "Bad was the blood of the song in the cab / On your first trip to LA," she reflects—the linguistic reference in those lines is to her own hit "Bad Blood"— before noting that "you ate at my favorite spot for dinner."

To sum up, then: Swift inhabits a text-full and text-*made* world, and it's no surprise that when she portrays that realm in her lyrics, she does so with a writer's appreciation for literary and rhetorical device. Humor writer Christian Tucci has minutely catalogued via Twitter thread Swift's deployment of a few particularly exotic devices, among them antanaclasis ("Devils roll the dice, angels roll their eyes" ["Cruel Summer"]), assonance ("Rosé flowing with your chosen family" ["the one"]), mesozeugma ("The moon is high / Like your friends were the night that we first met" ["Paper Rings"]), and epizeuxis ("We are never, ever, ever, ever getting back together. Like, ever" ["We Are Never Getting Back Together"]). But so-called "literary" writers typically demonstrate more than a taste for metatextuality and a facility with linguistic machinery—and there, too, Swift holds her own. In other words, the contributors to this volume assert that Swift, too often flatly characterized as the doyenne of the break-up song, in fact explores *many* aspects of experience and consciousness, including a few of English-language literature's perennial favorites: the exigencies of time, the pains of aging, the challenges of identity, the profundities of place, the cruelties of politics, the glories of the body, and, yes, the complexities of love. Put differently, the work presented here allows that Swift, an avid reader, understands literature as a *conversation* that, as writers respond to and take inspiration from the texts and genres that have preceded them, transcends the bounds of time and space.

Of course, no theme or issue is "universal," and it's important to acknowledge that the conversation into which Swift inscribes herself is, broadly speaking, both white and Western. As the above list of Swift's explicit literary references suggests, her touchstones are primarily the "Great Books" of the nineteenth- and twentieth-century Anglo-American canon, and to recognize that restriction is, we think, to encounter a valuable opportunity to ask who *isn't* included in Swift's notion of the literary, whose voices are amplified and whose are relegated to silence—and why. Swift's *folklore* track "the lakes" speaks disdainfully of a "namedropping sleaze" who would tell the singing subject what her "words [are] worth," but to catalogue the (necessarily) limited names and ideas that Swift "drop[s]" in her own writing is to raise bigger questions about our culture's attitudes regarding the "worth"—monetary and otherwise—of certain perspectives and ideas. In today's increasingly visual world, many would argue that reading *needs* compelling and well-positioned advocates, but when the immensely popular Swift is understood (and, maybe, *taught*) as an important reservoir of literary tradition, thematic and expressive diversity are undeniably at risk. As the scholars represented here conduct their analyses, they aim to admit and attend to that concern.

Those analyses are presented in four distinct sections, and the initial section explores Swift's participation in the literary conversation described above by reading her through, or examining her engagement with, a selection of English-language literary-historical voices and movements. When the speaker of *Lover*'s "Paper Rings" celebrates having gone from "stalk[ing]" her crush "on the internet" to having "read all of the books beside [his] bed," Swift associates intimacy with a shared reading list—with, that is, the community-establishing power of a common library—and the volume's first set of essays considers the direct literary references and subtler literary-historical echoes that appear in Swift's lyrics and shape her creative practice. Moving chronologically from the seventeenth century through the twentieth century, the section demonstrates Swift's debts to and bold revisions of such writers as John Donne, Jane Austen, and the aforementioned F. Scott Fitzgerald and includes a cluster of arguments that evaluate Swift's substantial interest in English Romanticism, to which *folklore*'s track "the lakes" explicitly refers in lines that pun on William Wordsworth's name and describe the unique landscape of his Lake District home. Scholars address, among other issues, Swift's relationships to Renaissance "self-fashioning"; to eighteenth-century negotiations between public and private expression; and to nineteenth-century "coterie" traditions.

Swift's identity as a woman figures in many of the first section's historical arguments, but her persistent interest in gender and sexuality, as well as her sometimes problematic engagements with race and her own whiteness, take center stage in the collection's second section. As "mirrorball" intimates—"I'll show you every version of yourself / Tonight"—Swift understands, at least intuitively, the often fractured and always intersectional nature of identity, and the second section finds scholars applying feminist theory, queer theory, and critical race theory to a range of Swiftian texts, both literal and metaphorical. Its first two essays treat Swift's "feminist politics of collaboration" and her contemporary reimagination of the Gilbert-and-Gubar "madwoman in the attic," who becomes, in Swift's oeuvre, the "crazy ex-girlfriend." The subsequent pair examines Swift's complex literary engagements with queerness, concentrating in particular on her lyrics' queer (or queer-coded) spaces and narratives, and the section's final essay grapples with Swift's whiteness and the questions about appropriation and privilege that that dimension of her identity necessarily raises.

Of course, identities, like artistic movements, mature and evolve, and the collection's third section reflects broadly on Swift's attentiveness to time, especially in her perennial (and traditionally literary) concern with memory. Time, Swift reflects in *folklore*'s quietly meditative "invisible string," is a "curious" blend of beneficence and malevolence—it's "cuttin' me open then healin' me fine," she writes—and the third section's assembled scholars acknowledge Swift's insinuation that memories can haunt and enervate as often as they affirm and energize. In addition to essays that deploy theories of memory to examine the ways in which Swift's habits of narrative recollection affirm her "agency" and even foster a uniquely Swiftian "mythology," the section includes two arguments that interrogate Swift's lyrical grapplings with grief and trauma.

The collection's final section foregrounds questions of style and form (as opposed to theme) in an effort to highlight Swift's always playful and sometimes subversive engagement with artistic categories and conventions—and the expectations that they engender. Its arguments portray Swift as a savvy craftswoman especially adept at destabilizing culturally inherited ideas about literary language and at challenging such notions as "originality" and "authenticity." Following treatments of Swift's disruption of the "show, don't tell" tradition and her mobilization of defamiliarization (*ostranenie*) in relationship to convention and cliché, the section affiliates Swift's work with two distinctive aesthetics/genres—excess and autofiction—and concludes with analyses of Swift's Benjaminian interests in "aura," intermediality, and technology.

There are, without question, additional literary-studies lenses through which to consider Swift, whose body of work has grown substantially during the relatively brief period between this anthology's conception and its completion—and whose body of work will continue to grow between the moment of this anthology's completion and the moment of its publication. In fact, as this volume heads to press, audiences eagerly await *The Tortured Poets Department*, the Grammys-announced 2024 album whose literature-focused title and published tracklist (which names such songs as "The Manuscript" and the *maybe* Coleridgean "The Albatross") suggest that Swift's eleventh collection will lend additional credence to the claims articulated here. But Swift's prolificacy is itself a viable area of examination—it's worth exploring, perhaps, which literary artists, past or present, she most resembles in her extraordinary productivity—

and as Swift's corpus further expands, questions about reception will inevitably arise. In other words, if Swift's future influence on popular music is for others to document, her appearance in and effect on more conventional (than pop music, anyway) works of literature—novels, poems, memoirs, and others—will, we imagine, become a rich field of exploration for literary-critical thinkers. Of course, *which* writers choose to engage Swift in their fiction or lyric will prove telling in itself. How, for example, might Swift's whiteness, combined with her ostensible commitment to white Western literary "classics," affect her reception—and ultimately her legacy—among critics and creatives alike? We trust that the numerous courses and conferences presently dedicated to Swift and her work will shape the discourse moving forward, but we are delighted to have played a role in highlighting the distinctiveness of Swift's voice relatively near the beginning of what we presume will become a long tradition of taking Swift seriously. When the academy, like the gaggle in "22," began to ask, "Who's Taylor Swift anyway?" it seemed, to paraphrase the same single, like the perfect time.

Works Cited

Tucci, Christian [@chrtucchi]. *Twitter*, 16 Nov. 2020.

Part One

All of the Books Beside Your Bed: Engaging the Literary-Historical Canon

"I haven't met the new me yet": *folklore/evermore* and Taylor Swift's Self-Fashioned Renaissance

Devori Kimbro

On the track "happiness" on Taylor Swift's *evermore*, the singer looks back on a failed relationship, wondering how someone beloved could become hateful. Central to the song's narrative is not just the singer's perception as she moves forward from the dissolution of the relationship, but how it impacts her identity. She has been blindsided by the break-up, telling her former partner, "in the disbelief, I can't face reinvention / I haven't met the new me yet." Swift goes on to reiterate this sentiment of identity-in-flux, lamenting that "no one teaches you what to do" in these situations, wanting the listener to know that her self is unstable at this moment. There is a new "me" emerging, but she is unsure who that will be.

While this is just one of the songs from *folklore* and *evermore* that deals explicitly with the issue of the (re)construction of identity, much of the content of the albums and the discussion surrounding it engaged that subject as well. For example, Swift reflects on how her career and personal life developed since her last original album, *Lover* (2019). Swift's fans, and even casual listeners, were unsurprised to hear these confessional tracks; Swift has used her music to shape her identity and public perception of that identity since her debut album released when she was sixteen. Nevertheless, *folklore* and *evermore* represent something more nuanced in this construction of self. In an interview with Zane Lowe, Swift revealed that due to the COVID-19 pandemic, she was largely unshackled from the influence of Republic Records during production. As a result, *folklore* and *evermore* feel like meaningful departures from previous offerings. While tracks like "no body, no crime (feat. Haim)" and "betty" evoke her country roots, Swift also offered up significant changes to what fans typically expected. For instance, Swift allowed fully fictional narratives and characters to occasionally take center stage. I posit that some songs that most concretely diverge from Swift's past compositions do work akin to that seen among early modern female authors undertaking their own self-fashioning as well as espousing common genres and tropes from the period. Swift's use of these genres—the country house poem as represented in "the last great american dynasty," and the sonnet sequence in the trilogy of songs "cardigan," "betty," and "august"—exemplify gendered self-fashioning, discussing female occupation of spaces not intended for them, and the complexities of veridical, or "truth-telling" frameworks in traditional sonnet sequences.

As a result, Swift's movement toward forms of songwriting that are novel in her oeuvre is a form of self-fashioning, drawn from Stephen Greenblatt's definition of the term in his *Renaissance Self-Fashioning: From More to Shakespeare*.

Early modern authors, Greenblatt argues, produced texts in a world where literary communities were simultaneously rigidly enforced and wildly expanding. Self-fashioning as an act arose from consolidations in the power structures that surrounded early modern authors, who experienced "a shift from absorption by community, religious faith, or diplomacy toward the establishment of literary creation as a profession in its own right" (8). What, then, do we make of the way that *folklore* and *evermore* feel like meaningful digressions from Swift's usual songwriting and production style, and how can they be read as forms of self-construction?

As a songwriter who has been keen to engage her personal life in her writing, Swift is exemplary of Renaissance self-fashioning, which, per Greenblatt, relies on a complex interplay between the author's literary self, the private self, and their merging in the public sphere. According to Greenblatt, "[self-fashioning] functions without regard for a sharp distinction between literature and social life" (3). Even someone with a casual awareness of Taylor Swift would be inclined to agree that her songwriting body *is* her social life. Although Swift is discreet when it comes to naming names, songs like "Dear John" from *Speak Now* evoke her past public, and sometimes messy, relationship woes. Greenblatt observes, however, that Renaissance self-fashioning also must push back on the boundaries of pure biography, otherwise running the risk of the texts "becom[ing] literary biography (in either a conventionally historical or psychoanalytic mode) and risks losing a sense of the larger networks of meaning in which both the author and [her] works participate" (4). Swift's sudden shift to prolonged engagement with fictional narratives on *folklore* and *evermore* render this distinction by Greenblatt more important as Swift signals a desire to no longer be seen as the subject of all her songwriting.[1] As a result, while much of Swift's discography expresses frustrations over her lack of control over her own public image while paradoxically seizing the power to *create* that public image, *folklore* and *evermore* use a more quintessentially Renaissance form of self-fashioning. In this mode, Swift negotiates an identity surrounding the power structures that made her feel so helpless for so long. Additionally, the releases of *folklore* and *evermore* were orchestrated, pointedly, without interference or machinations by Swift's label or management. These were truly self-fashioned works wherein there was no dramatic lead-up to release, and no single that shaped public expectation of the album.

Swift and Self-Fashioning

I here turn my attention to some of the tenets of Renaissance self-fashioning and how they may be ascribed to Swift in the scope of these two albums. Greenblatt notes that

[1] It should be noted that Swift has songs that are narratively framed around others in her oeuvre, not just around herself.

"self-fashioning ... involves submission to an absolute power or authority situated at least partially outside the self." In essence, the act of self-fashioning occurs when the author must find a way to live in some semblance of harmony with this outside power. Likewise, self-fashioning must be achieved "in relation to something perceived as alien, strange, or hostile ... [a] threatening Other [that] must be discovered ... in order to be attacked or destroyed." This placement of the author between an absolute authority and an alien who "is always constructed as a distorted image of the authority," embodies the experience of listening to *folklore* and *evermore*. Much of the diaristic work on the album is suffused with songs that explore Swift's relation to the powerful "authorities" that have governed her life as an artist. "my tears ricochet," "mirrorball," "peace," and "happiness" all recount to some extent her relationship with the music industry and the public. In "mirrorball," the singer compares herself to the well-known dance floor decoration, ending the first verse by cautioning that when she "break[s] it's in a million pieces." Still, she assures the listener that they are "not like the regulars" who are "drunk as they watch [her] shattered edges glisten," critiquing celebrity culture that requires one to strike a balance between public acts of "shattering" wherein one must be careful not to alienate fans. In "my tears ricochet," Swift seems to grapple with her split from Big Machine Records and public falling-out with former manager Scott Borchetta who notoriously sold Swift's master recordings of her first five albums to music executive Scott "Scooter" Braun, cutting her off from ownership of her own life's work. Swift accounts for her oftentimes rancorous public discussion of the matter in her Disney+ special *folklore: the long pond studio sessions* (2020), implying disdain and distaste for Borchetta by allowing that "[she] didn't have it in [herself] to go with grace." Of the song, Swift says that it represents betrayal on a visceral level: "It's a song about greed ... how somebody could be your best friend, and companion, and most trusted person in your life, and then they could go and become your worst enemy." Similar to Swift's songs about romantic entanglements, she discreetly avoids outright naming Borchetta and Braun, but lines like, "And when you can't sleep at night, you hear my stolen lullabies," are hard to interpret any other way.

However, Greenblatt's work, while compelling, neglects the female experience of early modern authorship—a viewpoint which is fundamental to understanding Swift's perspective. Unfortunately, early modern female authorship as a construct is rare and limited. According to Ulrike Tancke's work on how Greenblatt's notions of self-fashioning can be applied to the feminine sphere, early modern female authors "engaged in these processes only from the margins" (3). In general, women were far less likely to be encouraged to write as a means of self-expression and were even less likely to be able to find avenues for publication for their written works. Tancke's examination of early modern women's writing reflects something akin to Swift's *folklore* and *evermore*, asserting that these texts "do not recreate real experience, but only reveal its representation" (8). As her career has developed, Swift has become more diligent in protecting her private life from public scrutiny, so her construction of self is relegated primarily to her albums, "representations" that fans gleefully parse to attempt to get to Swift's "real experience." Much of Swift's public persona has been devoted to the complications that are inherent in being a powerful, lauded female singer-songwriter in an environment that still primarily caters to the desires and gazes of male fans, executives, etc. As a result, her self-fashioning on the albums *folklore* and *evermore*, achieved largely without input from her label or management team, constitutes a form of strictly feminine self-fashioning that at once mirrors that undertaken by Greenblatt's exemplars Thomas More and William Shakespeare, but is also unique and further complicated by issues of gender. Early modern female authorship is on one hand limited by "socio-cultural and material circumstances," but the act of deliberate creation allows us to "tease out the complex dialectic of structure and agency on which identity relies" (Tancke 8). This argument about female authorship in the early modern period mirrors strongly similar arguments about female pop stardom and agency over identity, as Paula Wolfe argues, that current female singer-songwriters are occasionally "allowed to voice [their] awareness of, and anger at, the subsequent limitations imposed" (155). These limitations have not altered significantly in the span of four centuries. Artists like Taylor Swift, like her early modern predecessors, utilize genre to develop content that is at once familiar and subversive—hence her attention to space and identity in the form of the country house poem, and the truth-telling constructs of the sonnet sequence. The role of women in public and private spaces along with their capacity to occupy a stance of truthfulness or believability in a public forum are integral to Swift's songwriting ethos.[2]

Holiday House and Country Houses: Swift and the Country House Poem Tradition

In *folklore*'s "the last great american dynasty," Swift employs a dual narrative structure. The bulk of the song tells the story of scandalous American socialite Rebekah Harkness, who married and outlived William Hale Harkness, heir to the Standard Oil fortune. Harkness failed to conform to societal expectations and was widely shunned as a result. Swift's song tells the story of Harkness's life through the lens of her ownership of Holiday House, the Rhode Island mansion that she owned until 1974. Swift acquired the property in 2013, and "the last great american dynasty" functions not just as an ode to Harkness, but a poetic exploration of Swift's relationship to the community around her—one illuminated by considering it through the lens of the country house poem.

    The country house poem emerged in the early sixteenth century. Like Swift's song, the form used the physical properties of the home as a means of identity-making.[3]

---

[2]   As Swift asks us in *Lover*'s "The Man," a discussion of gender and power, "When everyone believes ya – what's that like?"

[3]   There are a few other songs on both *folklore* and *evermore* in which space and place are intimately tied to Swift's exploration of other themes. "seven" references Swift's childhood exploits in Pennsylvania and her recollection of a friend who she realizes was suffering from parental abuse. In "coney island," a collaboration with producer Aaron Dessner's band The National, Swift allegorizes a failing relationship as an abandoned amusement park.

Such poems constituted an important discourse "that articulated a web of socio-economic concerns about the . . . social relationship that land engenders" (McBride 2). Central to Swift's exploration of Harkness's and her own relationship to Holiday House and the surrounding community is the "social relationship" of property. Country house poems focus on the needs and desires of the aristocracy. The poems were rarely authored by the actual homeowners, but instead were authored by poets desiring patronage. They idyllically described the home, the surroundings, and its peaceful day-to-day operations. While Swift engages in no such idealism in "the last great american dynasty," her approach to describing both her and Harkness's relationship to the house embodies a distinctly feminine approach to the country house poem.

Kari Boyd McBride observes that typical country house poems represented firmly gendered dividing lines. They demonstrate a patriarchal bent—the praise for the home's beauty and function heaped on the male landowner. In these works "the exercise of power depended on a distinction between masculinity and femininity . . . on the control of everything associated with the feminine by those who claimed the fullness of masculine privilege" (5). Women are typically silent figures but ever-present in the acclaim offered up for the beauty of the furnishings and the smoothness of the household operations. Passages singling out women in country house poems tend to only "occur when the woman in question is of some special importance to her husband or family, or in her own right" (Lewalski 261). One notable outlier in the genre is the first known female-authored offering of a country house poem—Aemelia Lanyer's "The Description of Cooke-ham," which first appeared around 1610. Lanyer dedicates "Cooke-ham" to her patron, Margaret Clifford, countess of Cumberland, and to Clifford's unmarried daughter, Anne, and includes herself in the narrative since she had lived at the estate previously. Like Swift's Harkness, Clifford was an independent sort of woman, even after the death of her husband. Margaret spent much of her life in litigation over her only daughter's right to inherit the family's wealth rather than having it entailed away on male relatives. Swift also seeks to depict an essentially feminine-over-masculine framing of Holiday House as a space. As with Lanyer's descriptions of the Cliffords, Swift reminds us that Harkness is, first and foremost, not one to bow to patriarchal pressure to conform. Ulrike Tancke reminds us how place and space operate in early modern female self-fashioning, arguing that texts that explored these ideas often examined how private and public intersected in such spaces, quoting Johnathan Goldberg's argument that "the individual derived a sense of self from largely external matrices, among which the family and its place in society was paramount" (161). Lanyer's poem to Cooke-ham is a public text evoking private sensibilities about the place so dear to her. Swift's description of Holiday House and its significance to both her and Harkness is a chimera of the public and the private. Both Harkness and Swift dwell privately in Holiday House, but their presence in the community surrounding the home is open for public speculation and derision.

Barbara Lewalski observes that "struggle against the male establishment develop in [Margaret and Anne] a very strong sense of family, self-worth, and female solidarity" (266). Lanyer's poem is a loving ode to Cooke-ham as an estate and the remarkable women with whom she spent time there. Lanyer thanks Clifford for her patronage, asserting that the poem itself would not exist since "from whose desires did spring this work of grace" (12). Lanyer's poem is a meaningful deviation from typical country house poems because it celebrates female agency, ownership of property, highlighting the importance of female friendship and patronage. To demonstrate this, Lanyer elides Clifford *with* Cooke-ham—as if the "great Lady" cannot be separated from her estate. They are one. Lanyer describes the foliage as protecting its mistress, saying, "The trees with leaves, with fruits, with flowers clad, / Embraced each other, seeming to be glad, / Turning themselves to beauteous Canopies, / To shade the bright sun from your brighter eyes" (lines 23–6). Unlike other poets, Lanyer foregrounds the female presence at Cooke-ham by continually shaping the interconnectedness of Clifford and her estate. The trees seek to shade the sun from their mistress's eyes, and "each plant, each flower, each tree / Set forth their beauties to welcome thee! / The very hills right humbly did descend, / When you tread on them did intend. / And as you set your feed, they still did rise, / Glad that they could receive so rich a prize" (lines 33–38). While a male-centered country house poem positions the wife as ornamental, for Lanyer, Clifford *is* Cooke-ham. The surrounding landscape is eager to pay her homage. Swift positions Harkness *as* Holiday House, much like a country house poem. Through the song, we learn little about Harkness's life prior to and after her leaving Holiday House. Swift's interest is not in Harkness's full biography, but rather how Holiday House is essential to understanding Harkness. In the bridge, Swift uses the physical surroundings of Holiday House to embody Harkness's state of mind: "They say she was seen on occasion, / Pacing the rocks staring out at the midnight sea." This calls to mind a lonely, contemplative phase after her husband's death, facing an ever-worsening financial situation. Lanyer similarly seeks to express the emotional comfort Cooke-ham provides to Clifford in times of trial, musing that an oak on the property was "seeming joyful in receiving thee, / Would like a palm tree spread his arms abroad, / Desirous that you there should make abode" (lines 60–3.) Like Swift's Harkness merging with the environs of Holiday House, Lanyer's Cooke-ham similarly suffers when Clifford must quit the estate, lamenting, "The trees that were so glorious in our view, / Forsook both flowers and fruit, when once they knew / Of your depart . . . As if they said, While will ye leave us all?" (lines 133–4, 140).

The initial voice in Swift's song is heavily inflected by mid-century Rhode Island "society," alternately surprised Harkness has been able to ascend from the middle class to Holiday House, critiquing her "new money" tastes. Her wedding is "charming, if a little gauche," and her parties are "tasteful, if a little loud." She is perceived as "mad" and "shameless" by those observing her lifestyle. After Bill's death, held against Rebekah since "it must have been her fault his heart gave out," the singer describes a woman who frees herself from the judgement of her "society" neighbors, fixating on fellowship with those who desire her company, flying in her "Bitch Pack friends from the city," and entertaining luminaries like Salvador Dali, losing the entire fortune she has inherited. Harkness defies what Tackne identifies as a quintessentially early modern feminine virtue—solitariness. The primary objection of the townsfolk is that Harkness will not shamefully hide her lifestyle, when "only a woman who keeps to herself, who does not venture beyond the confines of her home, can be considered virtuous" (162). The intersection of feminine virtue and space are on display in "the last great american dynasty" as it becomes apparent that it is not that Harkness and Swift "occupy" this space that is problematic; it is *how* they choose to occupy it—publicly and unapologetically.

While much of the last of "Cooke-ham" is focused on the estate bereft of its mistress, Swift's ode to Harkness strikes a more hopeful tone. Later in the bridge, Swift ties herself to Harkness by lamenting, "Fifty years is a long time / Holiday House sat quietly on that beach / Free of women with madness, their men and bad habits, / And then it was bought by me." Although she never existed at Holiday House with Harkness, Swift's revelation that she is the current owner of the mansion demonstrates a desire like Lanyer's in "Cooke-ham"—yoking her identity to Holiday House *and* the notable woman who lived there prior, herself also prone to scandal. Swift mirrors the earlier choruses where Harkness was declaimed as "mad" and "shameless" by evoking the voice of scandalized Rhode Islanders calling herself "the loudest woman this town has ever seen." At the core of the connections among Harkness, Swift, and Holiday House is the destabilizing influence of women with money, power, and no desire to behave "properly" to appease others. In the final lines, Swift returns to the sentiment expressed by Harkness's neighbors—"I had a marvelous time ruinin' everything."[4]

Unraveling the "cardigan" Sonnet Sequence

While "the last great american dynasty" is representative of Swift's reliance on biographical songwriting, *folklore* and *evermore* constitute her most marked engagement with fictional narratives. In interviews, Swift notes that several tracks on the two albums are not inspired by personal narrative. *folklore*'s "this is me trying" is a commentary on the rigors of recovery from addiction; *evermore*'s "no body, no crime" describes a woman seeking justice for a murdered friend. In *the long pond studio sessions*, Swift describes a trio of songs on *folklore* depicting a love triangle from three perspectives—"cardigan," "august," and "betty."[5] The narrative that unfolds over the

---

[4]   There are parallels between Swift's discussion of Harkness and Holiday House and *reputation*'s (2017) "This is Why We Can't Have Nice Things," wherein Swift scolds former friends' "shady" behavior, forcing her to revoke the perks of her lavish lifestyle. The opening lines recall Swift's frequent use of "Roaring 20s" references, detailing the decadence of "swimming in a champagne sea," and "feelin' so Gatsby for that whole year." Swift infers that losing access to the luxuries her friendship affords is punishment for bad behavior, lamenting, "This is why we can't have nice things, darlin'. / Because you break them, I had to take them away." Both songs are indicative of Swift's perception of power, property, and gender. Like Harkness, Swift uses her power and wealth to bestow favor on "good" friends and punishing them with the loss of those privileges should they betray her. Both songs are displays of conspicuous consumption, but I also believe that Swift's self-orientation as someone who no longer desires toxic relationships, friendships or otherwise, hinges a lot on her lifestyle. She demonstrates a self-awareness of the material elements she brings to relationships and does not hesitate to remind people that losing her goodwill is also losing the metaphorical "keys to the kingdom," saying "I'm shaking my head, I'm locking the gates."

[5]   *evermore* also contains a two-song sequence comprised of "'tis the damn season" and "dorothea." Swift has explained that the former song is told from the perspective of a young woman who has left her Midwest hometown to seek fame and rekindles a love affair upon returning for the holidays. The latter song is a wistful, upbeat tune from the point-of-view of Dorthea's lover, exclaiming that if she should ever tire of LA, he'll be waiting.

songs is that of high schoolers Betty, James, and a second young woman Swift dubs "August" or "Augustine." "betty," told from James's point of view, describes a teen romance gone awry. Betty, James's girlfriend, dances with another boy at the school dance. In revenge, he spends the remainder of the summer with Augustine. Betty is told of the affair by Inez, of whom James cautions, "You can't believe a word she says / most times, but this time it was true." A regretful James shows up at Betty's party asking forgiveness. "august" tells Augustine's side of the story. Betty's point of view appears earliest on the album, track two, but is set further in the future, representing an older woman looking back on a relationship that tested her. As Swift observes in her discussion of James and Betty's relationship in *the long pond studio sessions*, "he really put her through it."

Songs sequences of this nature are common on concept albums with strong narratives that link all or most songs together. For Swift, however, it is rare to devote such a significant portion of an album to fictionalized voices and rarer for those voices to tell a broader story. This inclusion represents a concerted effort by Swift to both self-fashion by expanding her songwriting methodology, but also to engage in a distinctly Renaissance form of the sonnet sequence popularized by the likes of Shakespeare. Many sonnet sequences from the period are set from a first-person perspective, wherein the poem's speaker is most often associated with the author. Others, such as Philip Sidney's notable *Astrophil and Stella*, exchange pseudonyms for the names of real lovers. While many early modern sonnet sequences are indeed veiled missives from the authors to those who do not return their affections, Danijela Kambasović-Sawers argues that "sonnet sequences . . . are mostly conceived of as philosophical and poetic explorations of erotic, usually unrequited, love from the perspective of a first-person speaker." This framing is at the core of what I call Swift's "song sequence." Betty laments James's infidelity. Augustine talks of a similar sorrow once James returns to Betty after their summer affair. James's story frames him as an unrequited lover as he woos Betty after his affair.

Sonnets are typically lyrical in nature, meaning that they express the emotional state of the speaker. As a result, they have long been relegated to the category of first-person narratives usually in the voice of the author him or herself. But as Danijela Kambasović-Sawers argues, there was sometimes more fiction to be observed in the traditional sonnet sequence—one that had a bearing on the development of other popular fictional literatures: the veridical or "truth-telling" frame. These poems are written in the first-person, and most importantly, in these frames "truthfulness is claimed or implied" (51). Together with the lyrical aspect of the poem, the veridical frame implies the trustworthiness of the narrative. Kambasović-Sawers notes, however, that the purpose of the veridical frame is to titillate the reader with the impression that the speaker may not actually be trustworthy. Early modern authors of sonnet sequences often "play games with their voice when they conceal their identity or proclaim themselves to be the editors," to further fictionalize the poems and engage readers. Essentially, veridical framing impresses upon the reader the truthfulness of the text while implying the opposite, intriguing readers by making them unsure of whose voices to trust. Such examples of veridical framing can be seen in Dante's *La Vita Nuovo* (*c.* 1293) up until

Jonathan Swift's satirical *Gulliver's Travels* (1726). Kambasović-Sawers explores veridical framing in English sonnet sequences to Anne Locke's *Meditation of a Penitent Sinner, upon the 51 Psalme* from 1560. Much like Swift's Inez, the "author" reveals that "he" is not in fact Anne Locke, but that he has received the sonnets from an acquaintance, publishing them on her behalf. However, the sonnets were likely published by a female sonneteer. As Kambasović-Sawers explains, "the frame protects its female author from accusations of frivolity or presumption" (53).

At the core of Swift's song sequence is such veridical framing, made more compelling by the fact that although the story is told from the points of view of three individuals, all the narratives are delivered in Swift's voice. The veridical element is encapsulated in how memory and forgetting are presented by all three speakers. "cardigan," Betty's song, comes earliest on the album, setting the tone for the others. This is an intriguing narrative structure, since "cardigan" represents Betty's view on the ordeal well after it has drawn to a conclusion. The lyrics are indicative of a woman who has the benefit of hindsight and has learned to contextualize the events of that summer, though painful. Her refrain laments, "When you are young, they assume you know nothing," exposing Betty's veridical framing. Betty is aware that the reception of her story is impacted by the belief that young women are unreliable in assessing the strength of their emotions. In a type of call-and-response, Swift counters the assertion "when you are young, they assume you know nothing," with Betty's retort, "But I knew you." Coming first on the album, Betty's voice begins the discussion of remembering and forgetting undertaken by our love triangle. By asking one another to remember that summer, they are reaching out across narrative lines to establish their truth-telling posture—as if to say, "This is how I remember it, and you should remember it similarly." Betty's contribution arrives in Swift's bridge for "cardigan," speaking *for* James: "I knew you'd miss me once the thrill expired / And you'd be standin' in my front porch light / And I knew you'd come back to me." As the wronged woman, Betty assures James, and the listeners, that even in her most heartbroken moments she knew, as well as she knows herself, that James would return.

Augustine is the next voice in the song sequence. In *the long pond studio sessions*, Swift explained "august" challenges the traditional framing of "the other woman" as a bad woman. "august," like "cardigan" is set after the summer of James's and Augustine's affair, as she looks back, trying to frame the context of the relationship and her own desires. Much like Betty's stance in "cardigan," "august" is about the slippage between memory and truth (and truth-telling), as Augustine asks if James recalls the affair with her same fondness, again from a first-person perspective. Swift is clearly unwilling to allow this narrative to be framed from any one participant's point of view, adding to the veridical framing. These narratives are truthful as each song's singer understands it. The line that opens the chorus of the song is, "But I can see us lost in the memory / August slipped away into a moment in time." Whereas Betty sings from a place of confidence in her assessment of the situation as it unfolded, Augustine sings from a place of doubt, as if she is trying to achieve Betty's self-assuredness. Rather than Betty's repeated "I knew" refrain, Augustine plaintively asks "Do you remember?" of her subject. There is a layer of irony to this plea of remembrance in this song since Swift points out in the above-mentioned interview that James's "other woman" is unnamed, forgotten—Swift just "calls" her August or Augustine because the affair takes place during the titular month.

Both songs bear resemblances to Petrarchan complaints, common fodder for sonnet sequences, wherein the poem's speaker addresses a recalcitrant lover and airs their grievances. Catherine Bates supports a reading of veridical framing in the lyric tradition, arguing that "[Petrarchan] lyric poetry is not seen as a simple outpouring of emotion but as an artful presentation, carefully contrived with an eye to audience and effect" (7). For Betty, she laments lost time and the pain she endured during James's absence despite "knowing" that he would return. Augustine, on the other hand, speaks of the loss of the love after the summer has ended, but her veridical framing challenges James's memory of the events to see if they are the same as hers. Whereas Betty knows that James will return to her, Augustine explores what she has come to understand since that summer—James would never stay. The song alternates between a memorial reconstruction of events, claiming that she can "see [them] lost in the memory," with "lost" implying that when she returns in her mind to these romantic moments, they are unmoored from reality, remaining in permanent summer existing only in her memory. However, the fond recollection is broken up by the repeated assertion that Augustine understands the relationship was doomed, grieving that "August slipped away like a bottle of wine / 'Cause you were never mine." The interpolation of veridical framing and Augustine's narrative means that the song's singer is not seeking to present a differing version of events from Betty or James, but instead seeks validation of her own memories. Fittingly, as the woman caught in the middle of the two narratives (literally and figuratively since "august" is the song that comes between Betty and James's songs), Augustine does not assert claim over James's affections or apologize for her "bad" behavior, but rather simply hopes that someone remembers the events the same way she does. As a result, her veridical framing presents a bridge between Betty's knowing and James's suppositions.

In true Swiftian fashion, James is allowed to share his story after the ladies have spoken. This feels like a validation of Swift's desire to avoid presenting Augustine as a "bad woman." James's perspective comes in the ironically titled "betty," demonstrating the single-minded focus of each song's singer's framing of their narratives—Betty reminds us of how James makes/made her feel like an old "cardigan," Augustine is fixated on the lost month of "august" she spent with James, and James titularly betrays himself as undeserving of Augustine's affections since his focus is "betty." While both "cardigan" and "august" are told from the perspectives of the women of the love triangle when older, James's narrative is tellingly fixed in the moment of his transgression, offering an intriguing reading of his veridical framing. Much like Betty's and Augustine's narratives, James's is rooted in remembering, but he is much closer to the event than the other narrators. "betty" takes place at the end of the summer that seventeen-year-old James has spent with Augustine instead of the titular character and, chagrined, has arrived on Betty's doorstep to ask forgiveness. James's veridical framing is rooted in his youth and his gendered position; while the two female narrators frame their knowledge internally—speaking only to what they personally know—James attempts to build a narrative *for* Betty without her input. He speculates on her emotions and reading of his infidelity despite opening the song saying, "Betty, I won't make assumptions." He then constructs a narrative that is largely assumed.

James attempts to break down the veridical framing of characters mentioned in the song, by reminding Betty, "You heard the rumors from Inez / You can't believe a word she says / Most times, but this time it was true." In this initial portion, James waffles in his ability to accept full culpability for Betty's heartache. James's narrative is comprised of two parts—the first is trying to parse the events of the past summer and how it "all went wrong." He evokes the language of youthful indiscretion by reminding Betty, "I'm only seventeen, I don't know anything / But I know I miss you." The second portion of James's narrative is largely speculative and places us in Betty's narrative initially explored in "cardigan." After he has reminisced about his affair with Augustine and the heartbreak it caused Betty, the listener arrives with him when he is approaching her to ask forgiveness. As Betty predicted James would be "standing in [her] front porch light," James says, "Betty, I'm here on your doorstep / And I planned it out for weeks now," as he ironically crashes a party to apologize. He imagines the potential outcomes throughout the song, but especially in this moment when he muses, "Will you have me? Will you love me? Will you kiss me on the porch in front of all your stupid friends?" Since these characters live outside of herself, Swift chooses to never give us resolution in this moment. Betty knew James would be there, and James arrived accordingly, but the fate of their relationship is left for listeners to ponder.[6]

Veridical framing is essential to Swift's ethos since the narratives surrounding her personal life were often used to denigrate and demean.[7] Unsurprisingly, "cardigan" and "august" represent similar, female-centered veridical framing rooted in assessing and asserting truthfulness. "betty," conversely, allows Swift to explore male-centered veridical framing in truly early modern ways, implying that such framing may be unreliable. James's truth-telling is complicated by his youth, but since his narrative is presented last, it is hard not to recognize the relative callousness toward Augustine when he assures Betty that upon leaving the dance he was "thinking of [Betty] when she [Augustine] pulled up like a figment of my worst intentions . . . Slept next to her, but / I dreamt of you all summer long." In "cardigan," Betty assures James of what she knew

---

[6] This is perhaps where we may read a more thoroughly gendered form of self-fashioning in these fictional narratives. Swift's use of veridical framing is not unique to these two albums; it is a tool Swift uses often in her biographical songs. Many of the songs about her past relationships are similarly framed as questions posed to lovers to determine whether they recall events the same way she does, asserting the validity of her recollections. In the ten-minute version of "All Too Well" on *Red: Taylor's Version*, Swift asks her lover in ironic confidence, "Just between us, did the love affair maim you too?" reiterating repeatedly that she "remember[s] it all too well." She reminds the song's object "you were there," as if testing to see if the memories align in accuracy. Swift frequently uses phrasing evoking truthfulness in memory and recollection in her songs, reminding all that doubt that her version of events is as valid and accurate as any other version.

[7] Director Lana Wilson deconstructs the negative aspects of Swift's public image in the 2020 Netflix documentary *Miss Americana*. The documentary features many conversations with Swift regarding how she is discussed in the media, as well as primary evidence derived from media clips.

about herself and him from the vantage point of the future. Likewise, "august" represents a hurt lover asking to be reassured that she meant something to James. In the aptly named "betty," however, James exposes his twice-limited veridical framing—temporally limited since he is without the benefit of hindsight, and conceptually limited since he is unwilling to take appropriate accountability. Any blame he ascribes to himself is undercut by criticizing the unreliable Inez, personifying Augustine as "worst intentions," and accusing Betty of neglecting him at the dance although James admits he was "nowhere to be found." Even with the benefit of youth, Swift uses veridical framing of her fictional James, Betty, and Augustine to mirror similar relationship traumas she explores on previous albums. James's narrative occupies a fraught space where we want to forgive him because of his youth, but because Swift allows Betty and Augustine to speak with experience and complexity, James's shallowness is glaringly evident. His veridical framing exposes another side of stories that Swift has been unable to tell previously since the content was biographical. Swift uses the sonnet sequence format and its veridical framing to finally give voice to past partners who have mistreated her, exposing mere "boys" locked in the moment of their bad behavior even as she matures, examining those relationships with newly discovered knowledge of the real "truth."

Conclusion

In conclusion, we return to Swift's "happiness." she notes in an interview that this song was the last one written and recorded from the two albums, completed just six days before *evermore*'s release. Compared to the vitriol expressed in songs like "my tears ricochet," which seethes with indignation and hurt, "happiness" is to some extent about release through self-fashioning. Swift acknowledges that after all the pain and heartache she has experienced at the hands of those she has trusted, ultimately there is a way through. "In our history, across a great divide / There is a glorious sunrise" on the horizon. The singer apologizes to those she has hurt in retaliation for hurts inflicted upon her, reminding all involved that "you haven't met the new me yet." The song's ability to elide invective with conciliation demonstrates self-fashioning *in situ*, almost as if the experience of writing these songs and working through these feelings have finally led her to a state wherein she can finally move past hurts and into that "glorious sunrise" of a new era. The song is conversational and as a result feels unedited. The song adopts that veridical framing described above and shifts rapidly from insult to apology: "I hope she'll be a beautiful fool / Who takes my spot next to you. / No I didn't mean that / Sorry, I can't see facts through all of my fury." It is unvarnished self-fashioning, rooted in Swift's public scandals and successes, reasserting her ability to frame the narrative however she chooses but opting this time to allow the glimpse of the unreliable narrator to shine through. In this moment, Swift counsels her listeners that these albums represent an identity that is shifting in new and exciting ways, permitting her to explore different modes of expression that can contain the multitudes of the old Taylor and the new.

Works Cited

Bates, Catherine. *Masculinity, Gender and Identity in the English Renaissance Lyric*. Cambridge University Press: Cambridge, 2009.

folklore: the long pond studio sessions. Directed by Taylor Swift, Big Branch/Taylor Swift Productions, 2020.

Greenblatt, Stephen. *Renaissance Self-Fashioning: From More to Shakespeare*. University of Chicago Press: Chicago, 1980.

Kambasović-Sawers, Danijela. "Fictional Elements in Sixteenth- and Seventeenth-Century Sonnet Sequences and Early Modern Fictions." *Parergon*, vol. 29, no. 1, (2012): 47–69.

Lanyer, Aemelia. "The Description of Cooke-ham (1611)." *The Norton Anthology of English Literature: The Sixteenth Century and the Early Seventeenth Century*. Norton: New York, 2000, 986.

Lewalski, Barbara K. "The Lady of the Country House Poem." *Studies in the History of Art*, vol. 25, (1989): 261–75.

McBride, Kari Boyd. *Country House Discourse in Early Modern England: A Cultural Study Of Landscape and Legitimacy*. Ashgate: Burlington, VT, 2001.

Tancke, Ulrike. *'Bethinke Thy Self' in Early Modern England: Writing Women's Identities*. Brill: New York, 2010.

Swift, Taylor. "Taylor Swift's Songwriting Process on 'evermore' y Apple Music." *YouTube*, Uploaded by Apple Music, December 15, 2020. https://youtu.be/CQacWbsLbS4.

Wolfe, Paula. *Women in the Studio: Creativity, Control and Gender in Popular Music Production*. Routledge: London, 2019.

2

Big Reputation: Reading Taylor Swift with Eighteenth-Century Women Writers

Bridget Donnelly

Taylor Swift's 2017 album *reputation* was styled as both comeback and clapback, responding to the post-*1989* backlash toward her infamous "squad" and public feuds with Kanye West, Kim Kardashian, and Katy Perry. The album, referred to by *Pitchfork* as "an aggressive, lascivious display of craftsmanship," provided Swift an opportunity to—once again—rewrite her image, highlighting the extent to which her success as a songwriter and performer required a consistently malleable public identity (Cox). By the release of her sixth studio album, Swift could brashly emphasize that the "old Taylor"—the public persona who had seamlessly evolved from country ingenue to pop princess—was dead, leaving in her wake a hardened, vengeful version of herself. Yet *reputation* does not only call for petty revenge against Swift's presumed enemies; it also tells a story of falling in love. As Swift claims in *reputation*'s prologue: "We think we know someone, but the truth is that we only know the version of them they have chosen to show us."

One's reputation, of course, matters immensely in the celebrity culture in which Swift has developed and sustained her enormously successful career. The notion of a public "reputation" that conceals an individual's private motivations, desires, and virtues can be traced back to the development of the novel—particularly novels written by women writers—in the eighteenth century. In works like Eliza Haywood's *Fantomina* (1725), it is possible to glimpse the origins of women's need to modulate their self-portrayals in response to public concerns about their reputations. The line between power, revenge, and love is always complicated for women writers. In this essay, I argue that by reading Taylor Swift's career alongside eighteenth-century women writers like Haywood and Frances Burney, we might better understand Swift's deployment of the concept of "reputation" at this decisive moment in her career as a strategic, gendered negotiation between public and private selves.

"The old Taylor can't come to the phone right now"

In the wake of Swift's immensely successful pivot to pop superstardom with the release of her fifth album *1989*, her public image experienced a drastic shift. Between the highly publicized Fourth of July parties with her "squad" of models, actors, and musicians; her debut of the "Bleachella" hairstyle; and her whirlwind romance with Tom Hiddleston immediately following a relationship with DJ Calvin Harris, Swift's media exposure was at an all-time high. In early 2016, however, her image took an immediate nosedive when, following a public reconciliation with Kanye West, headlines about a feud between West and Swift again began to circulate. After Swift publicly called out West for claiming responsibility for Swift's career success in his song "Famous," Kim Kardashian used Snapchat to release an audio recording implying Swift had lied about West gaining her permission to include the lines about her in the song. Kardashian also Tweeted, "Wait it's legit National Snake Day?!?!? They have holidays for everybody, I mean everything these days!" In response to the series of emojis accompanying Kardashian's tweet, fans bombarded Swift's social media channels with snake emojis (Holterman). In her 2020 documentary *Miss Americana*, Swift remarks: "When people decided I was wicked and evil and conniving and not a good person, that was the one that I couldn't really bounce back from, 'cause my whole life was centered around it. #TaylorSwiftIsOverParty was the number one trend on Twitter worldwide. Do you know how many people have to be tweeting that they hate you for that to happen?" (*Miss Americana*). These responses to Swift's public presence continued throughout the year, culminating with Swift's post encouraging followers to vote in the presidential election, in which she maintained "a carefully crafted image of neutrality" and did not endorse a candidate (Framke).[1] By the end of 2016, Swift's cultural capital was on the decline.

That Swift's public reputation had suffered was exemplified by a thinkpiece published by *Buzzfeed* author Ellie Woodward in early 2017, entitled "How Taylor Swift Played the Victim for a Decade and Made Her Entire Career." Positioning West as a victim of Swift's manipulative PR strategy, Woodward claims that Swift's career was built on chronically identifying as a victim. Woodward, capitalizing on articles alleging Swift's alignment with online white supremacist circles, claims: "The feud exposed the truth that white fragility is the most imperative component of Swift's success. [...] Swift propagating this narrative of fragile white womanhood to villainise a black man is 'ruthless' at best, and at worst, dangerous" (Woodward; Donnella). Certainly, Swift had acquired a reputation for staying silent on controversial issues, famously responding to a 2012 interviewer's question of whether she considered herself a feminist that "I don't really think about things as guys versus girls. I never have. I was raised by parents who brought me up to think if you work as hard as guys, you can go far in life" (Setoodeh). By 2016, however, Swift's political neutrality was no longer seen as an option, as the election backlash proved. While Woodward's assertion that the "positive perception of Swift is now in tatters" might not have been entirely true, it served as a harbinger for Swift's decreased public presence in the coming months.

---

[1] Swift's silence was newsworthy in itself, prompting media outlets to speculate on supposed "clues" regarding her voting record. See Baila.

Swift's deletion of all of her social media profiles in August 2017 culminated in this period of so-called "disappearance." While Swift returned only a week later to begin promoting the release of *reputation*—with the teasing of a wriggling snake, no less— she never reposted her earlier content, signaling a break from her previous media strategy. The lead single off *reputation*, "Look What You Made Me Do," sparked much controversy, particularly as the music video clearly references Swift's high-profile feuds through insinuations of karmic retribution that many viewers found insensitive or even cruel. Throughout the video, Swift sits in a bathtub filled with diamonds, gold, and cash, seemingly a visual reference to the armed robbery of Kim Kardashian in 2016, wherein over ten million dollars of jewelry were taken from her at gunpoint in her Paris hotel room (Jones; Soteriou). Swift, her hand draped in jewels, sings, "Is it cool? No, I don't like you," holding her fingers in the shape of a gun. Later in the video, Swift drives her car into a pole, dressed like Katy Perry in the promo for her album *Witness*. While Swift might muse that "all I think about is karma" (a revenge she characterizes more explicitly as fantasy in her 2022 album *Midnights*' tracks "Karma" and "Vigilante Shit"), these representations of imagined violence toward Swift's presumed enemies read, to some viewers, as a step too far.

Still, the campiness of "Look What You Made Me Do" suggests viewers are not meant to take the song—or Swift's manipulated public persona more broadly—too seriously. The video emphasizes the performative nature of Swift's career, as she dons costumes from previous music videos and media appearances. Referencing her continual self-reinvention, Swift's chorus victoriously announces: "Honey, I rose up from the dead, I do it all the time." During the bridge, as she sings, "I don't trust nobody and nobody trusts me," Swift stands on a pile of her old selves, all grappling toward the top, where *reputation*-era Taylor stands triumphant in her signature black glittery bodysuit. Ultimately, she declares, "I'm sorry, the old Taylor can't come to the phone right now / Why? Oh, 'cause she's dead!" This punch line culminates in responses to Swift's musical evolution with *1989*. The "old" Taylor, many fans argued, was the relatable country starlet who sang about unrequited love, baked her fans cookies, and interacted frequently with fans on social media.[2] With her pop star transition, she had begun to pull back from such public interactions, instead positioning herself as an early influencer, becoming one of the first accounts to crack 50 million followers on Instagram (Harrison). The opening of "Look What You Made Me Do" visually references this change, as a zombie Swift, wearing the dress from *1989*'s "Out of the Woods" video, digs up a grave marked "Here lies Taylor Swift's Reputation."

In retrospect, this line—and the song in general—also alludes to Swift's conflict with her record label, Big Machine Records, its CEO Scott Borchetta, and the fight over her contract and the right to own her master recordings. This dispute was not made public by Swift until 2019, when Scooter Braun's Ithaca Holdings acquired Big Machine,

---

[2]   See De Elizabeth and McKinney for references to Swift's country career as the "old Taylor," following her transition to pop.

thereby becoming owner of the masters for all six of Swift's existing albums. However, rumors of tension between Swift and Borchetta had circulated for years, including reports that he was displeased with the pop crossover success of "You Belong With Me" and Swift's continued work with pop producers Max Martin and Shellback.[3] While, of course, Swift had not yet begun the project of re-recording her first six albums until after signing a new contract with Republic Records in 2018, this acknowledgement of a split between the "old" and "new" Taylor implies a crossroads in her music career. "Look What You Made Me Do" marks the first of many instances in which Swift revisits her career trajectory, foretelling her move away from the autobiographical mode of lyrical storytelling. Conceptualizing each album as an "era," Swift's line of "old Taylors" at the end of the video reveals the extent to which each era necessitates developing a persona: not just a musical and stylistic aesthetic, but also a carefully crafted public character corresponding to the album's theme. These personas, Swift's self-satire suggests, are by definition "fake," even as the music itself contains her truth.

From this vantage point, then, audiences might begin to understand *reputation*'s thematic dissonance. While "Look What You Made Me Do" set the tone for the *reputation* era as one characterized by Swift's "bad girl" persona, critical responses to the album reveal the vulnerability of its second act, which tells a story of Swift falling in love. Songs like "Delicate" and "Dancing with Our Hands Tied" confess her anxieties that her position in the media will be too much for any potential partner. *Rolling Stone* referred to *reputation* as Swift's "most intimate album—a song cycle about how it feels when you stop chasing romance and start letting your life happen" (Sheffield). Yet some argued that Swift's reinvention of herself in *reputation* fell flat of the authenticity and access to her deepest self that the earlier albums promised: "The controlling and manipulative side of her persona has come into view to an extent that much of her audience is having trouble believing in the authenticity and intimacy of the other side" (Grady). Swift gave very few public interviews during the *reputation* era, instead relying upon the album and accompanying stadium tour to tell her story. After the release of her subsequent album *Lover* in 2019, Swift explained: "At the very beginning of the album I was pretty proud of coining the term, 'There will be no explanation. There will just be Reputation.' […] I didn't try to explain the album because I didn't feel that I owed that to anyone" (Lindsay). Ultimately, Swift conveys with *reputation* a divide between public and private selves, reminding audiences, fans, and critics alike that they will only ever have access to what she chooses to share.

"In the death of her reputation, she felt fully alive"

Eighteenth-century writer Eliza Haywood serves as a fascinating companion to Swift, not only because exploring the importance of women's reputations was a major subject

---

[3]   See Vargas and also Taylor.

of her fictions, but also because her public persona influenced critical responses to her work throughout her lifetime and even into the present. One of the most prolific writers of the eighteenth century, Haywood played a central role in the development of modern print culture and the novel. Kirsten Saxton stresses Haywood's significance in "explicitly defin[ing] her audience as female and present[ing] her texts as a means by which women readers can negotiate the dangerous waters of heterosexual romance"; like Swift, who has often been maligned for catering to an audience of predominantly young women, Haywood was denigrated for overtly writing to and for a female readership (4). Still, Haywood's contributions were noteworthy enough for Fielding to base a character named "Mrs. Novel" on her in his 1730 play *The Author's Farce*. Aleksondra Hultquist and Chris Mounsey note that Haywood "contributed substantially to making women's writing a locus of debate that had to be taken seriously by contemporary readers, as well as now by current scholars of historical, political, moral, and social enquiries into the eighteenth century" (1). Her writings, which included the genres of amatory fiction, scandal writing, and secret history, were the subject of much contemporaneous debate. The shocking nature of her subject matter was judged especially relative to Haywood's position as a woman who participated in spheres like the theater and writing for profit, which were deemed inappropriate for women, even as her writings remained wildly popular.[4]

To some extent, Haywood's thinly veiled satires of prominent figures and scandalous representations of upper-class life resemble the investments of contemporary audiences in Swift's music. In *reputation*'s prologue, Swift warns audiences against making assumptions about the subjects of her music: "When this album comes out, gossip blogs will scour the lyrics for the men they can attribute to each song, as if the inspiration for music is as simple and basic as a paternity test. There will be slideshows of photos backing up each incorrect theory, because it's 2017 and if you didn't see a picture of it, it couldn't have happened right?" Swift's desire for privacy, however, was always equivocal; although she insisted in interviews that she wouldn't drop names, the first five albums' liner notes include random capitalizations in the lyrics, which provided easily recognizable hints—e.g. "Tay" signifying Taylor Lautner as the addressee of "Back to December" and "Maple Lattes" in "All Too Well" referencing paparazzi photos of Swift on a date with Jake Gyllenhaal. Like Swift, Haywood's public position made her personal life subject to scrutiny, and as a result she seems to have intentionally obscured the circumstances of her own life. Still, she toys with giving audiences autobiographical hints; for instance, in the introduction to her anonymously published periodical *The Female Spectator*, Haywood coyly comments upon readers'

---

[4] John Richetti notes: "[T]he scandal novel or 'chronicle' of Mrs. [Delarivier] Manley and Mrs. Haywood was a successful popular form, a tested commercial pattern, because it presented an opportunity for its readers to participate vicariously in an erotically exciting and glittering fantasy world of aristocratic corruption and promiscuity. That fantasy world was, in the long run, more important in making the book popular than the specific scandals and libels in which Mrs. Manley dealt" (123–4).

desires to know authors intimately. Without revealing her identity directly, she teases: "My life, for some years, was a continued round of what I then called pleasure, and my whole time engrossed by a hurry of promiscuous diversion. [...] The company I kept was not, indeed, always so well chosen as it ought to have been, for the sake of my own interest or reputation" (8). Rumors of illegitimate children and affairs with prominent public figures, like the poet and playwright Richard Savage, circulated throughout her lifetime, leading Haywood to desire secrecy. Still, she plays with the tenuous nature of her public reputation, suggesting that women plagued by scandal might offer lessons to better the lives of their female readers.

Despite Haywood's prominence in both the literary and theatrical spheres throughout the early eighteenth century, therefore, much of her biography remains obscure. Her first biographer, David Erskine Baker, wrote:

> As to the circumstances of Mrs. Haywood's life, very little light seems to appear; for, though the world was inclinable, probably induced by the general tenour of her earlier writings, to affix on her the character of a lady of gallantry, yet we have never heard of any particular intrigues or connexions directly laid to her charge; and have been credibly informed that, from a supposition of some improper liberties being taken with her character after death, by the intermixture of truth and falsehood with her history, she laid a solemn injunction on a person who was well acquainted with all the particulars of it, not to communicate to any one the least circumstance relating to her. (321)

Haywood's success in keeping her private life relatively hidden emphasizes a primary difference between eighteenth- and twenty-first-century public figures: the speed at which gossip spreads. While eighteenth-century Europe saw a massive rise in proto-celebrity culture, with discussion of public literary, political, and theatrical figures circulating at a dramatically increased speed due to improvements in print technology, the relative difficulty of transporting gossip outside of cities made for more localized celebrity cultures, affording Haywood opportunities to minimize the public's access to her private self.[5]

One of the most infamous representations of Haywood is found in Alexander Pope's mock-heroic poem *The Dunciad* (1728–1743), which ridicules the perceived hack writers of his day by representing them as "Dunces" serving the goddess of "Dulness." Baker describes the extent to which *The Dunciad* paradoxically derided Haywood's skill while simultaneously magnifying her writerly reputation: "[C]ertain it is, that that great poet had taken some pains to perpetuate her name to immortal infamy" (320). He argues that, despite Haywood's complicated public reputation, Pope's critique ensured that her notoriety would not be forgotten. Christine Blouch argues:

---

[5] For more on the rise of celebrity culture in the eighteenth century, see Inglis; Jones and Joule; Lilti; Marcus; and *Intimacy and Celebrity*.

"Haywood's appearance in the *Dunciad* remains a singular example of how [biographical research, critical practice, and literary history] combine to constitute the politics of literary reputation, particularly since Pope's rhetorical strategies were designed to collapse the binary terms of personal and aesthetic judgment" (540). Although Pope's critique of Haywood stemmed primarily from her satirical representations of his friend Martha Blount in her scandal narratives, his representations of Haywood do critique her writerly ability.[6] Pope's attack on Haywood has become inextricable from the narrative about her life and works that has endured for over two centuries. Despite Haywood's prolific publishing record, it can be argued that Pope's memorializing ensured her continued notoriety. Similarly, Kanye West, in "Famous," establishes a claim to Swift's success, referencing the 2009 incident at the MTV Video Music Awards when he stormed the stage during her acceptance speech to protest Swift's victory over Beyoncé. According to West: "I made that bitch famous." Still, just as Swift's career was already on the rise in 2009, Haywood's popularity in her day predated *The Dunciad*, suggesting the extent to which both prominent male figures attempt to downplay the accomplishments of their female counterparts and take credit for the women's successes.

Pope's satire on Haywood fixates, however, not only on her perceived lack of skill as a novelist but also on her physical body. Characterizing Haywood as sexually licentious, with "Two babes of love close clinging to her waste," Pope figures her as "*Juno* of majestic size, / With cow-like udders, and with ox-like eyes" (172–3). Pope's implicit accusation that Haywood had two illegitimate children has persisted as part of her public reputation to this day, though some contemporary scholars question whether the "babes of love" were actually meant to represent her scandalous works of fiction.[7] Pope's vulgar characterization of Haywood's body, he argues, is justified because of her poor literary skill in addition to the lack of moral virtue implied by bastard children. West similarly desecrates Swift's body when he claims, "I feel like me and Taylor might still have sex," maintaining that he deserves access to her body because of his alleged role in making her famous. The objectification of Swift's body is further exacerbated by

---

[6] Valerie Rumbold notes: "Print is ... the medium which, by its unnerving power of multiplication, gives these women the power to project an arguably distorted version of the private into the domain of public embarrassment, and Pope's medium for revenge draws deeply on the gendered implications of such transgressive reproduction" (527).

[7] Kathryn King explains in her biography of Haywood: "The 'babes of love' are often taken to refer to actual children, but the image works just as well as a reflection upon her illegitimate textual offspring, specifically, the two scandal chronicles named in the Scriblerian footnote in which 'Eliza' is identified as 'authoress of those most scandalous books called the court of Carimania and the New Utopia.' David Oakleaf has observed that 'the prolific author' who wrote these books is caricatured as an offensively teeming and lactating woman,' but something of the opposite effect is achieved by placing the babes at her waist rather than her breasts. Waist suggests rubbish, discard and worthlessness, but it may carry a more specific print-world application in the sense of spoiled, wasted, or surplus sheets" (28). However, Rumbold argues that Pope wrote in an early draft: "She had 2 Bast: / tards, others say / three," suggesting that the "babes" were, in fact, references to her suspected illegitimate children (*Dunciad* 172). And Blouch affirms: "The two children assigned to Haywood by tradition have been confirmed in her own papers, and Pope had the number right" (540).

the music video, which features naked wax dolls of Swift alongside other celebrities, including Donald Trump, Kim Kardashian, Rihanna, Chris Brown, and Bill Cosby, lined up in a bed surrounding West. The tableau received critiques from prominent figures like Lena Dunham, who accused West of participating in rape culture: "While Bill Cosby's crimes are still being uncovered [... n]ow I have to see the prone, unconscious, waxy bodies of famous women, twisted like they've been drugged and chucked aside at a rager? It gives me such a sickening sense of dis-ease." Swift herself referred to "Famous" as "a revenge porn music video which strips my body naked." Under the pretense of satire, Pope and West suggest that the women they deride deserve to be stripped down to their naked bodies as a result of their public prominence. That male artists remain free to share their sense of entitlement to successful women's bodies reveals the latent misogyny running through public discourse from the eighteenth century to the present. It is no wonder, then, that artists like Haywood and Swift might choose to remove themselves from the public eye after such displays of male aggression.

Still, the importance of maintaining a public reputation was important for eighteenth-century writers like Haywood, who benefitted from the scandal associated with her life and works in order to continue publishing writings for profit. In an essay on Haywood's use of gossip in her 1725 work *The Tea-Table*, Bethany E. Qualls emphasizes: "If no one talks about you, you have *no* reputation; the trick is to have the 'right' people talking about you in the 'right' ways. Gossip is part of this important circulation process" (205). Swift proved the significance of gossip to the public understanding of her character in the intervening months between her so-called "disappearance" and her comeback with *reputation*. Swift's choice to delete her social media profiles marked the end of a period in which, Swift would later claim in *Miss Americana*, "Nobody physically saw me for a year." Fans have constructed thorough timelines of this period to dispute Swift's alleged "disappearance," although it is indisputably true that, compared to her overexposure during the *1989* era, Swift's public appearances dwindled to a minimum.[8] That this withdrawal from the public eye was newsworthy in itself was reflected in the extent to which media outlets ran with stories about whether or not Swift was hiding in a giant suitcase (Yapalater). Clearly, Swift's regression from the public eye felt significant to her, as she included a poem entitled "Why She Disappeared" in the *reputation* album booklet, which was subsequently used as a spoken-word interlude during her stadium tour. The poem acknowledges both her need to regain a sense of normalcy in her private life, dismissing her "fair-weather friends," and to step away from public critique. Swift recognizes that her success lies at the intersection of a delicate balancing act. Haywood, too, went through a period of disappearance, scaling back her publishing under her name in the 1730s following Pope's attack. Scholars have challenged representations of this decade as Haywood's "lost years," however, noting the extent to which Haywood remained

---

[8] See, for instance, a timeline posted on Reddit: "Nobody physically saw me for a year."

prolific, just in different arenas, as she shifted her focus from fiction to theatrical productions, periodicals like *The Female Spectator*, and political writings (Blouch 541).

Swift's poem ends triumphant: "And in the death of her reputation, / She felt truly alive." Swift concedes that her reputation will never remain spotless if she desires to continue attaining success as a public figure. In giving up her reputation, she creates a space between Taylor Swift the person and Taylor Swift the celebrity within which she can instead play with the identity she shares with the world. Haywood explores that same notion, though with the intention of emphasizing the means by which women in the eighteenth-century public sphere strive for power in the limited forms available to them, in her proto-novelistic *Fantomina; or, Love in a Maze* (1725). The protagonist leverages her sexuality and relative economic privilege to continuously acquire the upper hand over her inconstant lover, Beauplaisir, by adopting a series of disguises, tricking Beauplaisir into initiating sexual relationships with each subsequent identity she tries on. In so doing, Fantomina is forced to consider the distinction between "virtue" and "reputation" for a young woman of her ilk.

The elision between social and sexual "reputation" is emphasized when, shortly after first dressing as a courtesan to attract the attention of Beauplaisir, Fantomina finds herself coerced into sex to avoid revealing her true identity. The narrator explains: "She had Disernment to foresee, and avoid all those Ills which might attend the Loss of her *reputation*, but was wholly blind to those of the Ruin of her *Virtue*" (49). Haywood establishes a dichotomy between "virtue" and "reputation," suggesting that the latter may remain intact at the expense of the former. Fantomina, armed with financial autonomy and the lack of a chaperone in London, does not suffer any stain on her social reputation until she becomes pregnant toward the end of the narrative.

Throughout the text, Haywood establishes the divide between virtue and reputation as analogous to that of private versus public, or, as Kathryn S. Hansen describes: "the distinction between the *reality* of a woman's virtue and the *appearance* of a woman's reputation" (9). While the utmost importance was placed on women's virtue—what Samuel Richardson in his 1740 novel *Pamela* termed "the best Jewel"—novels throughout the eighteenth century impress upon their female readers the necessity of maintaining a spotless public reputation (190). It is striking that the reader never learns Fantomina's real name—only those identities she crafts. While readers might get a glimpse into Fantomina's inner thoughts, these, like Swift's confessional lyrics, still do not create a complete picture of an individual.

Haywood, of course, was not the only writer in the eighteenth century concerned with the importance of women's reputations. During this period, conduct literature written for women also emphasized the alliance between private (sexual) virtue and public (social) reputation. In countless didactic works of fiction and instruction manuals, young women are reminded to take heed to ensure that they behave in such a way that *both* their public reputations and private virtues remain unsullied. However, as virtue was often used euphemistically to describe virginity, such conduct literature frequently focuses on public-facing behaviors, like how young women should behave in the company of men. In tandem with conduct books, many novels written for young women readers attempted to use plots focused on women's entrances into polite society for didactic purposes: to simultaneously educate and entertain. For instance, in Frances Burney's *Evelina* (1778), the naïve young protagonist is reminded by her guardian: "Remember, my dear Evelina, nothing is so delicate as the reputation of a woman: it is, at once, the most beautiful and most brittle of all human things" (166). Evelina, however, consistently behaves in ways that endanger her reputation out of her guardian's fear of explicitly educating her about sexuality. She talks to the wrong men and frequently finds herself in compromising situations, such as riding in a carriage alone with the rakish Sir Clement Willoughby. The novel's rhetoric parrots one of the most popular works of conduct literature from Burney's day, James Fordyce's *Sermons to Young Women* (1766): "Remember how tender a thing a woman's reputation is, how hard to preserve, and when lost how impossible to recover; how frail many, and how dangerous most, of the gifts you have received; what misery and what shame have been often occasioned by abusing them!" (32). Fordyce closes the gap between public and private, claiming that virtue "to a woman is in effect nearly the same" as reputation (82).

Swift's teenage rise to fame, coming on the heels of the extremely public breakdowns of teen idols like Britney Spears, succeeded in part due to a carefully calibrated squeaky-clean image. Her public reputation was inextricably linked to the presumed "virtues" of this adolescent innocence; she was, according to Vanessa Grigoriadis, "the goodiest goody-goody in the nation." Therefore, when *reputation* divisively drew a line between that juvenile persona and the matured Swift, many listeners found the transition jarring and inauthentic. The extent to which *reputation*'s more adult themes and language (it was the first album labeled with a parental advisory for explicit content) shocked fans reveals the fact that, despite different moral sensibilities between the eighteenth and twenty-first centuries, virginal innocence is still deeply conflated with reputation for young women.

That the writers most concerned for eighteenth-century women's conduct were predominantly men cannot be understated. While female novelists like Burney and, later, Jane Austen (who references Fordyce after Lydia Bennet runs away with George Wickham in *Pride and Prejudice*) represent the dangers that may attend women who are careless with their reputations, the genre of conduct literature reveals its often misogynistic intent.[9] For instance, John Moir's 1786 "Female Tuition; or, An Address to Mothers, on the Education of Daughters" asks: "In a vortex of luxury, intemperance, and depravity, how shall female virtue be preserved? how shall the woman, whose mind is incessantly accosted by the grossest indelicacies, retain those nameless purities, on which her reputation and happiness in life depend?" (313). The sexual and behavioral double standards of the eighteenth century put the onus for acceptable conduct on women. Responses to *reputation* reflected similar concerns over Swift's attitude and self-presentation. One response chastises Swift for dismissing the importance of public opinion, accusing: "Taylor, you've portrayed yourself as CLASSLESS" (Farella). Similarly, Baker concludes that Haywood's writerly skill must be acknowledged in spite

---

[9] By contrast, one conduct book written by a woman, Jane West's *Letters to a Young Lady* (1806), discusses women's authorship as it relates to their *literary* reputations.

of, rather than because of, the scandalous content of her fictions: "although we should be far from vindicating the libertinism of her subjects, or the exposing with aggravation to the public the private errors of individuals, yet we think it cannot be denied that there is great spirit and ingenuity in Mrs. Haywood's manner of treating subjects, which the friends of virtue may perhaps wish she had never entered on at all" (320). Such a focus on women's propriety serves as a reminder of the inherent sexism that remains in the entertainment industry.

"Reputation" thus works as a defining concept throughout the content of eighteenth-century fictions as well as a vector by which both Haywood's contemporary audience and readers today might understand her work. Her muddled biography has consistently confounded scholars, leading many to recklessly assign autobiographical intent to her fictional writings.[10] The extent to which this incomplete biography still influences Haywood scholars mirrors the autobiographical readings that Swift's fans and critics insist upon performing, even when she explicitly instructs them not to. Although Swift had previously reminded her audiences that her songs were not all directly confessional—for instance, in countless interviews where she insists that "Blank Space" satirically responds to criticisms of her love life—*reputation*'s prologue does so unequivocally: "We may hear rumors about a person and believe those things to be true. We may one day meet that person and feel foolish for believing baseless gossip." Just as eighteenth-century secret histories and scandal narratives often satirized the royal court, politicians, and other public figures under thinly veiled classical or allegorical names, Swift's early albums reveled in dropping secret messages for her fans to decode.[11] *reputation* marked a definitive move away from Swift's early career marketing of herself as an open book. While she has, in recent years, altered her strategy to instead drop "Easter eggs" in social media posts, interviews, and music videos, fans still find it difficult to remember Swift's requests to stop reading everything as autobiographical.

Swift's prologue to *folklore* repeats *reputation*'s injunction, albeit through the lens of its own theme: "A tale that becomes folklore is one that is passed down and whispered around. Sometimes even sung about. The lines between fantasy and reality blur and the boundaries between truth and fiction become almost indiscernible. Speculation, over time, becomes fact. Myths, ghost stories, and fables. Fairytales and parables. Gossip and legend. Someone's secrets written in the sky for all to behold." Swift echoes *reputation*'s prologue, repeating that emotional truth in lyrical storytelling is not identical to private truth. Despite Swift's many warnings, fans still read *reputation* as a fully autobiographical record, especially after comments in the 2020 *Folklore: The Long Pond Studio Sessions*

---

[10] Earla Wilputte notes: "Past biographers of Haywood, like George Whicher, have tended to blur the writings with the woman, so that even Whicher's title—*The Life and Romances of Mrs. Eliza Haywood*—suggests a relation between the amatory works and the lifestyle of the author" (22).

[11] One of the most famous examples of these eighteenth-century narratives was Delarivier Manley's *The New Atalantis* (1709), a political satire of the Whig government that, despite leading to Manley's arrest for libel following publication, was so wildly popular that a key was published accompanying the second edition in 1713.

special, where Swift refers to *folklore* as the first album in which she "let go of that need to be one hundred percent autobiographical." The slideshows and paternity tests remain, just as Haywood's careful concealment of her biography couldn't keep twentieth-century scholars from attributing biographical intent to her fictions.

Reading Eliza Haywood and other eighteenth-century writers alongside Swift can teach contemporary listeners about the challenges of crafting public versus private versions of one's self, separating reputation from identity. Conversely, Swift might be used as a contemporary analogue for teaching Haywood in an undergraduate course. But even more importantly, Haywood offers a lens through which we might consider Swift's navigation of authorship as a problem that has particularly affected women artists throughout history. We will never, as readers or listeners, gain full access to the artist's own personal life, even—perhaps especially—when they purport to show it directly to us.

Works Cited

Baila, Morgan. "The Best Theories On Who Taylor Swift Voted For." *Refinery 29*, Vice Media Group, 8 Nov. 2016.

Baker, David Erskine. *Biographia Dramatica; or, A Companion to The Playhouse*. vol. 1, London, Longman, Hurst, Rees, Orme, and Brown, 1764.

Blouch, Christine. "Eliza Haywood and the Romance of Obscurity." *Studies in English Literature, 1500-1900*, vol. 31, no. 3. (Summer 1991): 535–52.

Burney, Frances. *Evelina*. Oxford University Press: Oxford, 2002.

Cox, Jamieson. "Taylor Swift: Reputation." *Pitchfork*, Condé Nast, 13 Nov. 2017.

De Elizabeth. "Taylor Swift Fans Leave Messages That They Miss the 'Old' Taylor on YouTube." *Teen Vogue*, Condé Nast, 25 Jul. 2016.

Donnella, Leah. "Taylor Swift, Aryan Goddess?" *NPR*, 27 May 2016.

Dunham, Lena. "Peeking From Between My Fingers." *Facebook*, 27 June 2016.

Farella, Marissa. "4 Things Taylor Swift Taught Me NOT To Do." *Society19*, 7 Sept. 2017.

Folklore: The Long Pond Studio Sessions. Dir. Taylor Swift, Disney+, 25 Nov. 2020.

Fordyce, James. *Sermons to Young Women*. Vol. 1, Cadell and W. Davies: London, 1814.

Framke, Caroline. "Who is Taylor Swift voting for? She'll never tell." *Vox*, Vox Media, 8 Nov. 2016.

Grady, Constance. "A unified theory of Taylor Swift's reputation." *Vox*, Vox Media, 7 May 2018.

Grigoriadis, Vanessa. "The Very Pink, Very Perfect Life of Taylor Swift." *Rolling Stone*, Penske Business Media, 5 March 2009.

Hansen, Kathryn S. "Dress as Deceptive Visual Rhetoric in Eliza Haywood's Fantomina." *ABO: Interactive Journal for Women in the Arts, 1640-1830*, vol. 11, no. 2. (2021).

Harrison, Lily. "Taylor Swift Beats Kim Kardashian and Beyoncé With 50 Millon Instagram Followers." *E! News*, E! Entertainment Television, 8 Oct. 2015.

Haywood, Eliza. *Fantomina and Other Works*, eds. Alexander Pettit, Margaret Case Croskery, and Anna C. Patchias, Broadview Press: Canada, 2004.

Haywood, Eliza. *The Female Spectator*. vol. 1, 5th ed., London, Printed for T. Gardner, at Cowley's-Head, near St. Clement's-Church in the Strand, 1755.

Holterman, Alexandra. "The History of Taylor Swift & the Snake." *Billboard*, Billboard Media, 21 Aug. 2017.

Hultquist, Aleksondra and Chris Mounsey. "Introduction: Spying on Eliza Haywood." *A Spy on Eliza Haywood: Addresses to a Multifarious Writer*, eds. Aleksondra Hultquist and Chris Mounsey, Routledge: London, 2022. 1–16.

Inglis, Fred. *A Short History of Celebrity*. Princeton University Press, 2010.

Jones, Emrys D., and Victoria Joule, editors. *Intimacy and Celebrity in Eighteenth-Century Literary Culture: Public Interiors*. Palgrave Macmillan: London, 2018.

Jones, Marcus. "Here's Why Some People Are Mad At Taylor Swift's New Video." *BuzzFeed News*, BuzzFeed, Inc., 27 Aug. 2017.

@KimKardashian. "Wait it's legit National Snake Day?!?!? They have holidays for everybody, I mean everything these days!" *Twitter*, 17 Jul 2016, 6:22 p.m.

King, Kathryn R. *A Political Biography of Eliza Haywood*. Routledge: London, 2012.

Lilti, Antoine. *The Invention of Celebrity, 1750-1850*. Translated by Lynn Jeffress, Polity Press: Cambridge, UK and Malden, MA, 2017.

Lindsay, Kathryn. "Taylor Swift's Low-Key Days Are Officially Over." *Refinery29*, Vice Media Group, 1 May 2019.

Marcus, Sharon. *The Drama of Celebrity*, Princeton University Press: Princeton, 2019.

McKinney, Kelsey. "The problem with Taylor Swift's new pop song: it's perfect." *Vox*, Vox Media, 19 Aug. 2014.

Miss Americana. Dir. Lana Wilson, Netflix, 2020.

Moir, John. "Female Tuition; or, An Address to Mothers, on the Education of Daughters." *Conduct Literature for Women, 1770-1830*, Vol. 1., eds. Pam Morris, Pickering and Chatto: London, 2005.

Pope, Alexander. *The Dunciad in Four Books*, ed. Valerie Rumbold, Routledge: London, 2011.

Qualls, Bethany E. "'I Have Such a Piece of News for You': Serving Gossip at Haywood's The Tea-Table." *A Spy on Eliza Haywood: Addresses to a Multifarious Writer*, ed. Aleksondra Hultquist and Chris Mounsey, Routledge: London, 2002. 194–218.

"reputation, n.s.1755." *A Dictionary of the English Language*, by Samuel Johnson, 1755. johnsonsdictionaryonline.com.

Richetti, John J. *Popular Fiction Before Richardson: Narrative Patterns, 1700-1739*. Oxford University Press: Oxford, 1969.

Richardson, Samuel. *Pamela: Or Virtue Rewarded*. Oxford University Press: Oxford, 2001.

Rumbold, Valerie. "Cut the Caterwauling: Women Writers (Not) in Pope's *Dunciads*." *The Review of English Studies*, vol. 52, no. 208. (November 2001): 524–39.

Saxton, Kirsten T. "Introduction." *The Passionate Fictions of Eliza Haywood: Essays on Her Life and Work*, eds. Kirsten T. Saxton and Rebecca P. Bocchicchio, The University Press of Kentucky: Kentucky, 2000, 1–19.

Setoodeh, Ramin. "Taylor Swift Dishes on Her New Album 'Red,' Dating, Heartbreak, and 'Grey's Anatomy.'" *DailyBeast*, The Daily Beast Company, 14 Jul. 2017.

Sheffield, Rob. "'Reputation' Review: Taylor Swift Ditches Tabloid Drama on Most Intimate LP Yet." *Rolling Stone*, Penske Business Media, 10 Nov. 2017.

Soteriou, Stephanie. "Kim Kardashian's Paris Robber Accused Her of 'Throwing Money Away' Before the Heist." *BuzzFeed News*, BuzzFeed, Inc., 22 Aug. 2022.

Swift, Taylor. "Prologue." *folklore*, Republic Records, 24 Jul. 2020.

Swift, Taylor. "Prologue." *reputation*, Big Machine Records, 10 Nov. 2017.

Swift, Taylor. "Why She Disappeared." *reputation*, Big Machine Records, 10 Nov. 2017.

Taylor. "9 Times Big Machine Interfered With Taylor Swift's Artistry." *The Fandomentals*, 11 Jan. 2021.

u/meddwannabe. "Nobody physically saw me for a year." r/TaylorSwift, *Reddit*, 14 April 2020.

Vargas, Alani. "Taylor Swift Refused Scott Borchetta's Request for '1989': 'This Is How It's Going to Be.'" *Showbiz CheatSheet*, 30 Mar. 2021.

"virtue, n.s.1755." *A Dictionary of the English Language*, Samuel Johnson, 1755. johnsonsdictionaryonline.com.

West, Jane. *Letters to a Young Lady: In which the Duties and Character of Women are Considered, Chiefly with a Reference to Prevailing Opinions.* Vol. 1, New York, O. Penniman and Co. Troy, and I. Riley and Co., 1806.

West, Kanye. "Famous." *The Life of Pablo*, GOOD Music and Def Jam Records, 14 Feb. 2016.

Wilputte, Earla. "Introduction." *Adventures of Eovaai*, by Eliza Haywood, ed. Earla Wilputte, Broadview Press: Canada, 1999.

Woodward, Ellie. "How Taylor Swift Played the Victim for a Decade and Made Her Entire Career." *BuzzFeed*, BuzzFeed, Inc., 31 Jan. 2017.

Yapalater, Lauren. "A Deeper Investigation Into Whether Taylor Swift Was Hiding In That Giant Suitcase or Not." *BuzzFeed*, BuzzFeed, Inc., 17 Jul. 2017.

3

"Just to break me like a promise": Taylor Swift as Ridiculous Romantic Heroine

Rita J. Dashwood

It all starts with a red scarf. In the first lines of Taylor Swift's "All Too Well," we find the speaker retelling her memories of a past relationship. The red scarf is described as having been left at the house of the love interest's sister, and in his possession. It thus becomes a symbol for the relationship; the belief that the love interest has maintained the red scarf in safe keeping denotes a desire to trust that, like the speaker, he has continued to cling to happy memories of their relationship. The song, about a young woman's relationship with an older man and her feelings of anger and sadness at its collapse, is rumored to have been inspired by Swift's relationship with actor Jake Gyllenhaal at the end of 2010. When in November of 2021, Swift rereleased her 2012 album *Red* as part of her process of re-recording her first six albums after she lost ownership of them, the new ten-minute version of "All Too Well" started nothing short of a media frenzy, centered around the potential real-life inspiration for Swift's song, including the precise whereabouts of the red scarf. The *Guardian* published an article entitled "Where's Taylor Swift's Scarf—Is It in Jake Gyllenhaal's Drawer?" (Khomani), whereas *Forbes*, in an attempt to enlighten its readers, published "Taylor Swift's Scarf Explained: Why Everyone Wants to Know Where It Is—And If Jake Gyllenhaal Has It" (Delatto).

Then came the videos of Swift's fans singing along to the song. A video in a club in Nottingham shows a crowd of mostly young women singing every line of the song at the top of their lungs as flawlessly and passionately as if they had written it themselves, hands reaching out to the skies and then clutching their hearts to convey the intensity of their emotion. They wrap their arms around each other and smile as they sing along, together in this shared expression of emotions. A video from Buenos Aires, Argentina, and another from Columbus, USA, show the same thing: the same joyfully out-of-pitch belting out of the lyrics, the same gestures to convey strong emotions, the same camaraderie, and the same self-aware, unapologetic, shared vulnerability. And it did not stop at clubs. Another video shows Swift visibly moved by her fans, who gathered outside the building in New York where the special screening of her short film "All Too Well" was taking place to serenade her with the song.

It is all a bit ridiculous. But I want to argue that that is precisely the point and to clarify that I mean this in the most positive way possible. As the co-author of *Reading the Romantic Ridiculous* (Routledge, 2024), and someone who had "Ridiculous" in her job title for over a year, I have had time to think about this concept. The Romantic period has predominantly been associated with the sublime, dealing with existential crisis by recognizing individual frailty but then super-imposing a poet or artist's superiority and mastery over their own human nature. The ridiculous, on the other hand, focuses on failure and finitude, finding funniness in existential crisis, which brings people together in shared laughter (McInnes and Dashwood). We use the "ridiculous" in a way that is distinct from "ridicule," which we see as often malicious humor directed outwards. Ridiculous laughter is, instead, simultaneously a release as well as a recognition of pain, a positive experience that joins one in laughter with other people, making them feel part of a community, recognized as ridiculous, together in their ridiculousness. We define the ridiculous, therefore, as something that can be inwardly experienced by an individual, but which can also draw groups of people together in joint laughter. The videos of the fans in Nottingham, Buenos Aires, Columbus, and New York perfectly encapsulate this potential the ridiculous has to bring people together, as one of the top comments on the New York video, with over ten thousand likes, expresses: "I've never felt so close to a community as I do to this one."

But what does all of this have to do with Romanticism? In the song "New Romantics" (2014), Swift identifies as a modern Romantic poet: "Baby, we're the New Romantics." In doing so, the song references the "New Romantics," the music movement of the 1970s and 1980s which defied conventional ideas on gender and identity through the androgyny and unashamed flamboyance of its members. Through this song, Swift references also a much older literary history, that of the Romantic movement—usually conceived as having begun in the last two decades of the eighteenth century and concluding in the mid-nineteenth century—which the New Romantic movement was itself inspired by. The Romantic movement developed as a counter movement to the Enlightenment, which valued reason, logic, and objectivity to the neglect of the individual, the subjective, and the irrational. The Romantics sought to rethink the role of the artist by reemphasizing the individual, including one's experience and expression of intense emotions, with the Romantic protagonist traditionally being characterized as deeply imaginative, sensitive, and emotional. The Romantic influence was not limited to literature but reached other forms of art, including music, characterized by an experimentation with musical forms that brought forth strong emotions from its audience.

With this self-identification as a starting point, I want to argue that "All Too Well" shows Swift self-portraying as a dejected Romantic heroine and to read this song through the prism of the Romantic tradition from the beginning of the nineteenth century of the heroine who is mistreated in love. In particular, I will be analyzing the parallels between Swift's "All Too Well" and Jane Austen's first published novel, *Sense and Sensibility* (1811). Like Swift's writing and subsequent re-recording of "All Too Well," Austen wrote *Sense and Sensibility* in her youth, when she was only nineteen, and re-wrote it in her adulthood. One of the heroines of the novel, seventeen-year-old Marianne Dashwood, is a representative of the Romantic movement's exploration of emotional intensity, an intensity that Swift also embraces in her work. Like Marianne, the speaker in Swift's "All Too Well" embodies the profoundly imaginative, sensitive, and emotional nature that characterizes the figure of the Romantic heroine. Both also personify the ridiculous in their simultaneous recognition and release of pain while in the midst of an existential crisis, demonstrating an emotional honesty that invites others in and draws them together in joint recognition, sympathy, and, ultimately, laughter. As with Austen, Swift's music is relatable to young audiences across the world due to her true-to-life portrayal of the difficulties of the coming-of-age process, something in which Romantic writers were also deeply interested. More specifically, Swift's songs, like Austen's novels, are concerned with the difficulty in navigating romantic relationships as a young woman living in a patriarchal society. In calling herself a "New Romantic," therefore, Swift establishes a link between her music and a Romantic literary tradition.

Others have noticed these links between Austen's and Swift's work. A BBC quiz "Who Said It: Austen or Swift?" notes that "Jane Austen's heroines tended to be strong, witty characters who spoke their own mind, not unlike global superstar and singer-songwriter Taylor Swift," and that "Romance is a major theme in both of these women's work." Similarly, the aptly titled "Swift and Sensibility" states that the "visceral connection to the emotional landscape of young women" in Swift's songs makes them "the perfect ... soundtrack for Austen's juvenilia" (Hill n.p.). Swift's expression of, and appeal to, strong emotions through her music also connects her to the cult of sensibility during the Romantic period. The cult of sensibility, usually considered to have originated in Britain in the mid-eighteenth century, characterized sensation as a moral and emotional capacity, and came to associate sensibility with "refined feeling, discrimination, and taste, as well as an intense sensitivity to the suffering of others" (Wickberg 665). However, excessive sensibility was also seen as dangerous for women, since "they would not then fit in with what was required of them or put up with what they had to endure" as they navigated a patriarchal society designed to disadvantage them (Doody xii). For this reason, feminist authors like Mary Wollstonecraft warned against the cultivation of sensibility, arguing that, far from being a source of power and protection, sensibility in a woman would leave her defenseless against a cruel world (Doody xiii).

In *Sense and Sensibility*, it may at first appear that Austen is putting forward such a view through the character of Marianne. After all, "the young female of sensibility is also a prime target for seduction," with the capacity for deep emotion and enthusiasm associated with sensibility being linked to sexual appetite and sensitivity, which make her at risk of being manipulated by a man who desires her for a sexual partner, without wishing to marry her (Doody xiv). And Marianne, as the woman of sensibility described here, does fall prey to Willoughby, who woos her with no intention of marrying her, making her vulnerable in the eyes of a society in which female desire and sexuality are taboo. However, through the depiction of Marianne's public admission and expression of her pain at having been wronged, Austen also shows the empowerment that can come from vulnerability and the honest expression of pain at a moment of existential crisis. Through this viewpoint, sensibility comes to signify power, rather than the relinquishment of it. Instead of a symbol of the perils of youthful innocence and naivete, sensibility becomes a way for the Romantic heroine to refuse to "fit in with what was required of them or put up with what they had to endure," to master her pain and remain quiet about it instead of expressing it. In her embracing of sensibility, Marianne embraces the ridiculous, as we define it, as an undercurrent in moments in which we lose control of ourselves, freely embracing her feelings in a way that makes her simultaneously vulnerable and powerful in her emotional honesty and potential for bringing people together in a shared experience.

The ridiculous is for us, therefore, a movement from individual abjection to collective action, building on three strands of theory: the silly (a term borrowed from Jordan Stein's "silly theory"), the low (in Jack Halberstam's "low theory") and the vulnerable (in Julietta Singh's "vulnerable reading"). Stein's "silly theory" takes the silliness of theory seriously, exploring "the queer material of which theory is made— that big, difficult idea which always threatens to turn into a puddle of soft and ridiculous goo" ("Silly Theory," n.p.). Ridiculous theory focuses on moments in literary and philosophical culture which make good on this threat: moments of failure and misunderstanding when big, difficult ideas seem about to turn into a puddle of soft and ridiculous goo. Halberstam's "low theory" also takes seriously the opportunities afforded by silliness, arguing that, while in doing so one runs the risk of not being taken seriously, this is very much his goal, as "Being taken seriously means missing out on the chance to be frivolous, promiscuous, and irrelevant" (6). Feeling silly and low, feeling ridiculous, in the academy runs the risk of "not being taken seriously," but this lack of seriousness comes with its own benefits: frivolity, promiscuity, irrelevance. The ridiculous allows us to explore the opportunities afforded by Halberstam's "low theory," especially what it means to resist mastery, including flirting with failure; privileging the naive and nonsensical; assembling eccentric texts; and challenging traditional hierarchies. Julietta Singh builds on Halberstam's reading of "failure as a queer refusal of mastery" to develop her own methodology of "vulnerable reading" in *Unthinking Mastery* (21, 22). Vulnerable reading is "an open, continuous practice that resists foreclosures by remaining unremittingly susceptible to new world configurations that reading texts—literary, artistic, philosophical, and political—can produce. Vulnerable readings resist disciplinary enclosure, refusing to restrict in advance how and where one might wander through textual engagement" (22). Singh affirms that "The practice of vulnerable reading can move us 'beyond' mastery, not in the sense of exceeding it but in the sense of surviving it in order to envision being otherwise in and for the world" (23).

To put it simply, when we feel ridiculous, we feel silly, low, and vulnerable. Silliness implies the embracing of moments in our lives of failure and misunderstanding. Lowness depends on accepting the risk of not being taken seriously, of being regarded as frivolous, promiscuous, or irrelevant. And the sharing of one's vulnerability comes with inevitable discomfort. In embracing all of these risks first through the relationship with Willoughby and then through the open expression and release of her pain at its breakup, Marianne embraces all of these elements. While certainly young and naïve, Marianne's sensibility allows her to also communicate her wisdom, namely her understanding of the unfair ways in which patriarchy demands silence and compliance from women, punishing them for being seduced but never punishing the seducers. Similarly, in her choice to write openly about her experiences as a young woman navigating romantic relationships within a patriarchal society, Swift also embraces all the elements we see as being encompassed by the ridiculous. As Lindsay Zoladz argues, Swift's music expresses the "oft-denigrated wisdom of teenagers," reminding us that "growing up doesn't automatically mean growing wiser—it can just as easily mean compromise, self-denial and growing numb to emotions we once felt with bracing intensity." In embracing her moments of failure through the writing of lyrics that express disappointment at the breakup of a relationship, Swift accepts the risk of not being taken seriously, her choice to allegedly write about her personal life potentially making her music be considered a lower form of art, and she herself as frivolous, an embracing of vulnerability and admission of failure that inevitably comes with a dose of discomfort. But it is this embracing of vulnerability that allows Swift to connect to her audience of predominantly young women, as evidenced by the videos of her fans singing along to "All Too Well." Similarly, it was Marianne's sensibility that made it possible for contemporary women readers to find a connection to the character, including famous ones such as Princess Charlotte of Wales (1796–1817), the only child of the Prince Regent. In 1812, at sixteen, and after reading Austen's novel, Charlotte compared herself to Marianne: "'Sence and Sencibility' [*sic*] I have *just finished* reading; it certainly is interesting, and you feel quite one of the company. I think Maryanne and me are very like in *disposition*, that certainly I am not so good, the same imprudence, &c., however remain very like. I must say it interested me much" (qtd in Le Faye, *Family Record* 168, emphasis in the original).

"All Too Well" and *Sense and Sensibility* are connected both by the characterization of their protagonists and their shared themes, namely those of easy attachment and obsessive memory. Marianne is described as a very emotional person, in similarity to her mother: "She was sensible and clever; but eager in everything; her sorrows, her joys, could have no moderation" (4). After the death of her father, she and her mother "encouraged each other in the violence of their affliction. The agony of grief which overpowered them at first, was voluntarily renewed, was sought for, was created again and again" (4). This behavior, with Marianne "voluntarily" embracing the full "agony of grief" and "wretchedness," can be seen as representative of the cult of sensibility, and the celebration of a response to life charged with high emotion that is traditionally associated with it. By contrast, Elinor, Marianne's more pragmatic sister, fights hard to hide her grief, receiving her brother, the new owner of her home, and his wife with a politeness that they do not deserve, as they take over the house immediately after the funeral, revealing a lack of consideration towards the grieving family.

This disposition for feeling emotions intensely, as feared by critics of sensibility, means that Marianne easily forms a strong attachment to Willoughby despite having just met him, making herself vulnerable and thus embracing one of the elements of the ridiculous. Their courtship period is described as "a dream of felicity" for Marianne, who, unaware of the dangers, goes through all of the typical steps that engaged couples would be expected to experience, but without the safety of an actual offer of marriage. Marianne begins to spend a great deal of time with Willoughby, drives around in his carriage with him, and even visits the family home he expects to inherit. Willoughby does not only express a romantic interest in her but actively encourages her to imagine a future in which she is his wife. The most significant moment in their relationship is that in which Willoughby takes Marianne on a tour of Allenham, the house that he is to inherit from his aunt. When Elinor admonishes her for visiting the house by saying that "you would not be justified in what you have done" even if the house were one day to be her own, "Marianne blushed at this hint; but it was even visibly gratifying to her" (52–3). Marianne's blush intimates that, as Elinor has guessed, she is already mentally inhabiting that future time in which she will be able to take possession over the space of Allenham. Her reaction to Elinor's use of the pronoun "your own" also indicates that she has begun to think of Allenham not only as Willoughby's house but also as her own. Marianne's confession that Willoughby introduced the topic of potential refurbishments indicates that, through the visit, Willoughby attempted to encourage these feelings of emotional attachment towards the property. As Amanda Vickery's analysis of courtship correspondence indicates, "only betrothed couples mere weeks, sometimes days from the altar, have conversations of this practical intimacy" (84). By introducing this topic, Willoughby is encouraging Marianne to mentally inhabit a future in which she is mistress of Allenham, thereby implying that he wishes to marry her. In doing so, he places Marianne in a precarious situation, since their status as an unengaged couple means that she has not received a promise from him that the affection she has begun to establish towards this potential future will ever be legitimized through marriage.

In Swift's "All Too Well," a young woman also makes herself vulnerable by easily and quickly becoming attached to an older man, who takes advantage of her naivete. Like Marianne and Willoughby, they go through the usual steps of courtship. They drive around together in his car, the protagonist describing the love interest almost driving through a red signal because he is distracted looking at her, and the feeling of the wind in her hair as they zoom past the streets of his small hometown. In similarity to Marianne's visit to Willoughby's family estate, the protagonist visits his family home and meets his family. There, she becomes close with his mother, who makes the love interest blush by showing photos of him as a young boy with glasses and sharing some of his childhood stories. Like with Marianne, the house is associated with this prospective future to which the heroine becomes emotionally attached. Even though Swift's heroine is visiting her love interest's sister's house for the first time, she describes it as feeling "like home somehow," the word "home" denoting the establishing of this feeling of affective ownership not just to the place but to a life with this man. Like Marianne, she becomes emotionally attached to a prospective future with him by being allowed access to his past. Believing that the love interest could only be sharing moments of such emotional significance because he feels as strong a romantic connection for her, and as deep a belief in the feasibility of them sharing a future together, the heroine becomes fully entranced by this prospective future: "You told me 'bout your past thinking your future was me."

The same melancholic tone that pervades *Sense and Sensibility* characterizes "All Too Well." It is made clear to us, from the very beginning, that these relationships are doomed to failure. The love interest's charisma in "All Too Well" means that he is welcomed into the protagonist's family circle with little consideration as to what his real values or intentions towards her might be. While Willoughby's "manly beauty and more than common gracefulness were instantly the theme of general admiration" (33), the speaker of "All Too Well" also mentions that the love interest "charmed" her dad through his confidence and self-effacing sense of humor. Already in debt with an income of £600 a year and no wife to support, however, it is true to character when Willoughby puts an end to the relationship with Marianne and marries a young heiress. Similarly, the love interest in "All Too Well" also leaves the protagonist, claiming their age difference as the reason, but continuing to date women of the same age as her.

Both protagonists embody another element of the ridiculous, silliness, by embracing their full emotions during the moments of failure and misunderstanding that they experience as the relationship begins to collapse. Marianne finds an opportunity to confront Willoughby about his disappearance from her life when they coincidentally attend the same ball in London. Excited to see Willoughby, Marianne makes herself vulnerable by expressing her feelings for him in front of other people, "pronouncing his name in a tone of affection" and extending her hand to him upon first seeing him (131). When Willoughby rejects this demonstration of affection, Marianne's mental state is expressed fully through her physicality, with her suddenly "looking dreadfully white, and unable to stand" (132). Struggling to comprehend the change in Willoughby's manner towards her, Marianne openly acknowledges her misunderstanding of Willoughby's actions and the limits of her forbearance, instead of concealing this existential crisis from others and performing mastery over her own human nature, as her more rational sister Elinor does various times throughout the novel. Similarly, the speaker in "All Too Well" also runs the risk of being perceived as silly by releasing the pain she feels when her relationship ends. On one hand, this is done through her description of a party she attended, where she is found crying in the bathroom by an actress, who asks her what has happened, to which she responds, retrospectively, addressing not the actress but the love interest directly: "That's what happened, you." Like Marianne, the speaker here feels keenly the unfairness of being set up for failure and dismissed by the love interest for not conforming to unrealistic expectations that he always knew she would never be able to fulfil. While Marianne would never be able to inherit the fortune that would tempt Willoughby into marrying her, the protagonist of "All Too Well" could also never be the idealized concept of passive and submissive femininity that the love interest apparently always expected her to be, the "never-needy, ever-lovely jewel whose shine reflects on you." On the other hand, the speaker in "All Too Well" also embraces silliness by writing the song and making her mistake, her finitude, and, ultimately, her failure, public, a much larger extension of her behavior at the party, where others were able to witness her moment of existential crisis.

This relationship, like the one between Marianne and Willoughby, ends with the speaker making herself vulnerable by admitting to having been gaslighted by this older man, who took advantage of her naivete and, like Willoughby, seemingly never having had any intention of making the relationship last. Willoughby never has the courage to admit to Marianne the reason behind his decision to end their relationship, namely Marianne's lack of fortune. The same is true for the love interest of "All Too Well," who tells the protagonist that the reason he decided to end the relationship was the age gap between them. In doing so, he conceals his lack of belief in the longevity of the relationship, which he held from the beginning. Being told that something so beyond her control, and of which the love interest was aware from the start, is the reason for the end of the relationship makes the heroine "want to die." With this emotionally intense description of a subject's moment of existential crisis, "All Too Well" once again continues a Romantic ridiculous tradition by describing the speaker as embracing the third aspect of the ridiculous: lowness, the acceptance of the risk of not being taken seriously, of being regarded as frivolous, promiscuous, or irrelevant. The emotional intensity the speaker feels at the breakup of this relationship is perfectly encapsulated here. This intensity continues throughout the rest of the song, with the speaker describing herself at the end of this relationship as "a soldier who's returning half her weight." There is a clear connection between mind and body here, as the speaker describes the relationship and its collapse as a war she has fought in, the emotional pain she has experienced being reflected in her now fragile body. This emotional intensity and its expression through bodily exhaustion has its parallel in Marianne's near-deadly illness after she is informed by Willoughby himself that he is engaged to another woman: "in restless pain of mind and body she moved from one posture to another, till growing more and more hysterical, her sister could with difficulty keep her on the bed at all" (143).

After the breakup of the relationship, both Marianne and the speaker in "All Too Well" engage in obsessive memory, remembering the relationship and embracing the feelings of pain and disappointment long after it has ended. Both protagonists take this risk by continuing to mourn the loss of the love interest long after their relationship is over. Their mutual emotional attunement, sensibility, and imagination mean that Marianne continues to wonder about Willoughby even after she hears of his engagement, while Swift's speaker still continues to imagine what the love interest is doing nine years after the last time they saw each other. For Marianne, this obsessive memory culminates in her walk through the rain at Cleveland to try to see Willoughby's estate, which is a few miles from the house where she is staying. This very physical expression of grief, which almost causes Marianne's death, represents, for her, the acceptance of the risk of being seen as promiscuous, as it is an admission of an emotional attachment to a man to whom she was not married. While she is between life and death, Willoughby comes back, insisting on telling his side of the story, but offering no better justification for his actions than that he desired his fiancée's money and would have done anything to secure it, including hurting Marianne (249). Ultimately, Willoughby reveals his selfish and mercenary spirit, saying nothing that makes him any more sympathetic to the reader. Once again, this sounds awfully similar to what the love interest does in "All Too Well," described by the speaker as disturbing her process of grief to try to tell his version of events, making it all the worse for her: "And you call me up again just to break me like a promise / So casually cruel in the name of being honest." Similar to Willoughby, his reasoning for the breakup of the relationship may make the love interest feel better, but it inevitably contributes to the suffering of the heroine.

For Swift's speaker, on the other hand, the obsessive memory culminates in her writing of the song, through which, like Marianne, she embraces lowness. By engaging in a self-dramatization of her own life through her lyrics, Swift takes the risk of being perceived as promiscuous, which she has certainly incurred, a sexist bias in the media becoming painfully obvious in its reporting of Swift's relationships, a sexism Swift has addressed in such songs as "Shake It Off" (2014) and "The Man" (2020). In the latter, Swift criticizes the bias of a patriarchal society that would view multiple relationships in a man as something commendable and, simultaneously, as reprehensible and promiscuous in a woman. Her choice of themes for her music, namely personal relationships, also exposes her to accusations of irrelevance, as their lack of obtuseness may see them dismissed as a lesser form of art. In the end, however, ridiculousness provides women like Swift and Austen (through Marianne) with methods of resistance to and exposure of the inherent sexism of a patriarchal society that blames women for the failure of relationships and judges them harshly for the communication of their feelings on them. Another indication that Swift is thinking in these terms is the mention of the speaker being tossed a "Fuck the Patriarchy" keychain by the love interest in "All Too Well," a symbol of the opportunity he has granted her to, through the recognition of the failure of their relationship and the reasons that led to it, openly condemn a patriarchal system that actively seeks to disadvantage women like her.

Marianne and Swift are united in the gendered criticism they receive for their open expression of their emotions. Elinor tries to convince Marianne to hold onto her pride and go out into society pretending that nothing has happened, to which Marianne retorts: "No, no … misery such as mine has no pride. I care not who knows that I am wretched. The triumph of seeing me so may be open to all the world" (141). While Elinor considers keeping up appearances to be more important, Marianne places a higher value on emotional honesty. As Thomas Keymer argues, we are not meant to think that Elinor's opposite approach, of pretending to not care when confronted with the fact that, much like her sister, she has been persuaded to fall in love with a man who turns out to be engaged to someone else, is the commendable one. While Elinor shows an "acquiescence in codes of behaviour that work to entrap her, … Marianne's habit of causing stirs and making scenes … serves to disrupt social mechanisms that empower rank, wealth, and especially masculinity at the expense of both sisters" (66). Like Marianne, Swift is routinely mocked for the ways in which she expresses her feelings through her music, this willingness to make herself vulnerable routinely depicted in the media as ridiculous (and here it is very much meant in the negative sense I talked about before). While Marianne is thought of by her sister as being blamable for her own misfortune, as she refuses to conceal her emotions, this in fact constitutes the only form of resistance she possesses against the patriarchal society in which she lives. Ultimately, it is precisely this willingness to be vulnerable, even ridiculous, that makes Marianne such a relatable character to readers, and Swift so relatable to her fanbase, which is disproportionally made up of women.

Feeling ridiculous can be a negative thing if experienced in the context of someone laughing at us, much like the media laugh at Swift and society laughs at Marianne. But if others join in with my ridiculous laughter, I might instead feel part of a community, recognized as ridiculous, together in our ridiculousness. In this way, we move from individual abjection to collective action. Swift may have called "All Too Well" "One of the saddest songs I've ever written," but there is a bite to it, a laughter that comes through that is in itself a form of defiance. The speaker tells her experience of being gaslighted by this older man, who took advantage of her inexperience, embracing vulnerability and resisting this treatment through laughter. While describing herself as not particularly good at telling jokes, the speaker offers as a punchline the comment that, while she gets older, the lovers of the love interest remain the age she was when they were romantically involved. In doing so, she references the love interest's dishonest attempt to blame the end of their relationship on their age gap, while he continues to date women who are much younger than he is. With this line, Swift exposes a contemporary society that is quick to judge a young woman for having been taken advantage of in a relationship but never the older man who mistreated her in the first place.

Swift has been consistently ridiculed by the media for, in similarity to Marianne, not hiding her sadness at having been mistreated by men. Even with the advantage of two hundred years, this open expression of her emotions continues to be, like with women in Austen's time, her only available means of resistance. And it is precisely because this self-expression "serves to disrupt social mechanisms that empower ... masculinity" that Swift has received such mean-spirited criticism from the media and the general public. Instead of fearing accusations of ridiculousness, however, Swift embraces this tradition of the Romantic ridiculous by fully embracing obsessive memory in "All Too Well" and its short film, which, by featuring Swift herself playing the character of the protagonist at the end, further reinforces the idea that the song is based on her personal experiences. As the videos of her fans singing along to "All Too Well" so vividly demonstrate, by continuing a tradition of the Romantic heroine who has been mistreated in love, and embracing ridiculousness, Swift's music has the undeniable ability to bring people together in a shared experience of silliness, lowness, and vulnerability, that altogether constitute an excellent basis for collective action. Much like Austen with *Sense and Sensibility*, Swift's music brings people together, inviting its listeners to question and defy gender biases within our patriarchal society that seek to oppress women.

It ends with a red scarf. The "All Too Well" short film concludes with Swift, acting in the role of the speaker of the song now years after the breakup of her relationship, walking into a book signing. As the camera pans out, the love interest is shown standing outside the window observing her, the red scarf around his neck, a sign that he too is engaged in obsessive memory long after the breakup of the relationship. Here, the heroine makes the choice to dramatize the story of her relationship into a novel, reading it before a crowd of mostly young women whose ability to relate to the emotions conveyed is clear through their engaged and sympathetic expressions. This engagement with literary history is further reinforced by the first frame of the video, which contains a Pablo Neruda quote from his 1924 poem "Tonight I Can Write (The Saddest Lines)": "Love is so short, forgetting is so long." Through the music video, Swift aligns herself with a literary tradition, classing herself as, above all else, a storyteller, and demonstrating an awareness of how music, like literature, through the expression of human experience, has the potential to bring people together.

In the same "All Too Well" music video, the male love interest invites the protagonist for dinner with his friends, proceeding to ignore her throughout the evening. As the protagonist shows that she's upset at this treatment, he says: "Why are you so pissed off? ... It's ridiculous." Exactly.

Works Cited

Austen, Jane. *Sense and Sensibility*. Oxford University Press: Oxford, 2008.

BBC, "Who Said It: Austen or Swift." https://www.bbc.co.uk/bitesize/articles/zmtrbqt [Accessed: 20 July 2023].

Delatto, Marisa. "Taylor Swift's Scarf Explained: Why Everyone Wants To Know Where It Is—And If Jake Gyllenhaal Has It." *Forbes*, 16 November 2021.

Doody, Margaret. "Introduction." in Austen, J. *Sense and Sensibility*, Oxford University Press: Oxfrod, 2008.

Halberstam, Jack. *The Queer Art of Failure*. Duke University Press: Durham, 2011.

Keymer, Tom. *Jane Austen: Writing, Society, Politics*. Oxford University Press: Oxford, 2020.

Khomani, Nadia. "Where's Taylor Swift's Scarf—Is It in Jake Gyllenhaal's Drawer?" *The Guardian*, 15 November 2021.

Hill, Jennifer. "Swift and Sensibility." *Jane Austen Summer Programme Blog*, 21 October 2022.

McInnes, Andrew and Rita J. Dashwood. *Reading the Romantic Ridiculous*. Routledge: London, 2024.

Singh, Julietta. *Unthinking Mastery: Dehumanism and Decolonial Entanglements*. Duke University Press: Durham, 2018.

Stein, Jordan Alexander. "Silly Theory." *Avidly*, 20 November 2012.

Swift, Taylor. "All Too Well: The Short Film." *YouTube*, uploaded by Taylor Swift, 13 November 2021.

Wickberg, Daniel. "What Is the History of Sensibilities? On Cultural Histories, Old and New," *The American Historical Review*, vol. 112, no. 3. (2007): 661–84.

Zoladz, Lindsay. "Taylor Swift and the Wisdom of Youth." *The New York Times*, 9 March 2021.

4

"What are my 'Wordsworth'?": Taylor Swift's New Romanticism

Brittany Reid and Taylor Mckee

In summer 1816, a group of writers found themselves stuck inside amidst a global cataclysm.[1] The volcanic eruption of Mount Tambora in 1815 produced unseen climate change, leading to crop devastation and starvation. For the young men and women staying together at the Villa Diodati near Lake Geneva, the "year without a summer" meant that they were forced to shelter in place and keep themselves occupied during what they imagined could be the beginning of the end times. This party included many figures who are now associated with the movement known as "Romanticism": an artistic tradition characterized by an emphasis on revolution, imaginative pursuits, expressions of individual experience, and the revelation of the divine through nature. For these Romantics, months of anxious cohabitation led to an efflorescence of artistic outputs. Their works were informed by their present circumstances, as their apocalyptic nightmares birthed twin monsters: Mary Shelley's *Frankenstein* (1818) and John Polidori's *The Vampyre* (1819). But they also recast their modern isolation through the poetic lens of their literary predecessors, with Percy Shelley turning to one writer in particular: William Wordsworth. In 1816, Wordsworth was no longer considered a young revolutionary, but he remained a living monument to Romanticism's first generation. As the group of young writers experienced fear of global ruin and pangs of isolation, Percy Shelley found solace in Wordsworth's visions of enduring nature in the possible end times, so much so that Lord Byron recalled that he "used to dose me with Wordsworth physic even to nausea" (Medwin 194).

In 2020, as the world again feared potential destruction through the COVID-19 pandemic, those fortunate to shelter in place found themselves in a context not unlike that of the Romantics in 1816. Perhaps surprisingly, one artist further extended this Romantic practice of creating art at the *fin de siècle*. It was July 2020 when Taylor Swift emerged out of the pandemic haze with the surprise release of *folklore*,[2] her eighth studio album. Those expecting her to replicate the same beats of her past forays would

---

[1] For more on the "Year Without a Summer" and Romanticism, see A. Collett and O. Murphy (2019), *Romantic Climates: Literature and Science in the Age of Catastrophe*, London: Palgrave Macmillan.

[2] *folklore* and its song titles are styled in lower-case.

have been surprised to encounter a distinctly Romantic collection that explored themes of haunting and heartbreak, youth and maturation, and frequent returns to the "golden years" of a nostalgic past. For this reason, Swift emulated the Romantics by writing in response to a changing world, and her thematic preoccupations directly aligned with their own. As she posted online to accompany the album's release, "Picking up my pen was a way of escaping into fantasy, history, and memory," and *folklore* marks her own imaginative excursion. For the English Romantics, the experience of the individual in the face of an increasingly alien and industrialized world was a key preoccupation, made even more urgent through ensuing global revolutions or environmental crises. Often expressing that they felt like outsiders in this new world order, Romantic writers longed for the simplicity of the past, whether their own youth or a collective state of innocence. In *folklore*, Swift brings new vitality to these Romantic themes. Her approach is both distinctly modern and achingly nostalgic; she frequently references the trappings of fame, technological intrusions, or pandemic horrors, while also returning to her childhood or the Romantic Age as a form of imaginative escape. It is this referencing of Romanticism as a creative tradition, and especially one Romantic author, that makes *folklore* Swift's most extensive and exceptional engagement with literary history.

This study explores Taylor Swift's New Romanticism as both an implicit and explicit creative undercurrent in her *folklore* era. The term "New Romanticism," which has been previously applied to Romantic-era revivalism in the 1980s, is used here to convey Swift's own unique interpolation of this literary historical moment. Furthermore, the term itself is a nod to Swift's song "New Romantics" off her album *1989* (2014). Through this study, we look at how Swift's New Romanticism entails recalling Romantic themes, imagery, and ideas, and resuscitating them for a modern context and audience. Specifically, we consider how questions of authorial attribution, temporality, the individual in nature, and collaboration gain new resonance through *folklore*. While we cover examples from throughout *folklore*, as well as Swift's own public persona, we chiefly treat her song "the lakes" as an explicit proclamation of her Romantic influences. "Is it romantic?" Swift asks us at the start of "the lakes." Throughout this study, we not only argue in the affirmative but further assert that Swift's revival of Wordsworth's literary identity constitutes what can be read as a New Romanticism.

Romanticizing *folklore*

The release of *folklore* shocked the music world in 2020. Certainly, much of that collective surprise derived from the LP's rollout plan, since Swift opted to forgo the traditional beats of making an announcement, followed by unveiling an album cover, lead single, track listing, merchandise, and music video(s). Instead, a series of thirteen Instagram posts on July 23 heralded her return as one of popular music's most significant figures. Within these posts, Swift took the exceptional step of simultaneously announcing the album's existence and same-day delivery. But while such an unusual debut would be sufficient cause for surprise, fans and critics alike found Swift's message to be just as intriguing as her chosen medium. Swift's immense popularity, and *folklore's* album rollout, meant that millions of eager listeners were especially ready and receptive to analyze her latest musical offering.

Pivoting from the glittery populence of 2019's *Lover*, Swift's Instagram preview posts collectively conveyed that *folklore* would represent yet another pivot in a career defined by reinvention. More than most contemporary singers, Swift and her career have been marked by mutability. As Fogarty and Arnold describe in their introduction to a special issue of *Contemporary Music Review*, entitled "Taking Taylor Seriously": "Via her varied personas—girl-next-door, cheerleader, heartbreaker, nerdy girl, businesswoman or cottagecore explorer—Taylor Swift is both a monument to the past and a modern megalith, toppling the music industries" (2). With *folklore*, yet another form of reinvention had taken place. Swift reimagined herself as a woodland wanderer: a poetic vision from an idealized past. But rather than committing herself to historical cosplay, Swift used *folklore* to contend with distinctly modern anxieties, including the trials of fame and living in the COVID-ridden world. Cottagecore to her core, this new Swift persona reframed the contemporary artist as a sylvan songwriter, inviting us into the woods with her to seek shelter during our own personal or global tempests.

Following the album's release, responses to *folklore* suggested that its distinctive aesthetic carried through into the music as well. Critics were quick to acknowledge that Swift, an artist long associated with genre-shifting, had again transformed. In his album review for the *New York Times*, music critic Jon Caramanica described the album as a "rebaptism" for Swift and "the first attempt at a post-pop Swift, and it is many things that Swift albums generally are not: rough-edged, downtrodden, spacey." Through *folklore*, she disposed of the musical confectionary that had recently defined her, instead making the singer-songwriter album for which so many fans had been clamoring. To accompany this major turn, the language used by critics to characterize *folklore* was also distinct from her previous albums. One fascinating word was commonly used to convey the unique ethos of Swift's latest project: Romanticism.[3] There is much to *folklore* that encourages this Romantic categorization, including the album art's visual evocation of Caspar David Friedrich's Romantic-era paintings of individuals in nature. But nowhere is this connection more explicitly underscored than in her bonus track from the deluxe edition: "the lakes."

The Lake District and "the lakes": From Wordsworth to Swift

As part of her unconventional album release, Swift released the deluxe edition of *folklore* alongside the standard album. Her de facto seventeenth track, "the lakes," was thus included and featured as part of *folklore's* initial rollout. The result is that "the lakes" occupies a unique and unusual position on *folklore*. It is not a single, yet it was

---

[3] This includes the descriptors "fuzzy romanticism" from *Slate* and "abiding Romanticism" from *The Guardian*.

rendered more precious through its "deluxe" designation. The speaker in "the lakes," a presumed stand-in for Swift herself, expresses the desire to be taken to "the lakes where all the poets went to die." For listeners not immediately familiar with Swift's historical referent, these fatal lakes conjure both mystery and melancholy. Swift provides enough context clues in the song to indicate that these fateful lakes are not merely fantasy. Instead, she is referencing England's famous Lake District: a region in northwest England that was home to several historical Romantics.

In the late eighteenth century, the Lake District emerged as an important site of creative collaboration for one of Romanticism's first artistic circles. Jones offers a description of the Lake District that highlights how often the environment served as a poetic retreat: "the Lake District was not necessarily a desirable place to live in ... the privations of life in so remote and barbaric a region—its rocks and 'torrents roaring'— could also induce a shudder of horror" (xiii). For this reason, it was perhaps an unusual choice of residence for three young friends who met at Cambridge and went on to shape the course of English literary history. William Wordsworth, Samuel Taylor Coleridge, and Robert Southey moved to the Lake District with aspirations of living and writing in peaceful commune. The group later became known as the "Lake Poets": a sardonic moniker intended to mock their unusual environs and frequent depiction of the landscape (Wheatley 64). The Lake Poets transformed their home into a mythical enclave, a mecca for Romantics and Romanticists alike. Consequently, for well over two centuries, the Lake District has been an English tourist destination, offering visitors the chance to experience the place that inspired these authors. Importantly, this group of faithful pilgrims to the Lake District even includes Taylor Swift.

This background on the Lake District makes Swift's first line in "the lakes" even more puzzling: "take me to the lakes where all the poets went to die." With an air of Gothic Romanticism, she reframes the lakes as a site of both artistic retreat and demise. As previously discussed, the Lake Poets themselves did not move to the eponymous district "to die." On the contrary, it is where they went to start a new life, one defined by the Pantisocratic vision they hoped to create through a new society.[4] Swift's re-casting of the Lake District as a terminal destination is thus entirely novel to her characterization and requires further exploration.

In her concert documentary for Disney+, entitled *folklore: the long pond studio sessions*, Swift provides additional context on her understanding of the Lake District that perhaps sheds light on the song's first line:

> There was a poet district, these artists that moved there. They were kind of heckled for it and made fun of for it as being eccentrics. I remember when we went, I thought, "Man, I could see this. You live in a cottage, you've got wisteria growing up the side of it, of course they would escape like that."

---

[4] For more on the Lake Poets and Pantisocracy, see S. Tedeschi (2018), *Urbanization and English Romantic Poetry*, Cambridge, Cambridge University Press.

Swift introduces the Lake Poets as subjects of mockery, reading them as refugees from societal judgment. Swift's reading thus offers greater insight into her creative point of entry, perhaps explaining why she casts this Romantic setting in a darker light. Throughout the song, Swift references "eulogies," "sad prose," "insurmountable grief," "the perfect place to cry," and the image of foliage growing over her feet "'cause I haven't moved in years." These images align with her characterization of the lakes as sanctuary.

Throughout "the lakes," outside dangers take the form of preternatural entities that both haunt and hunt our speaker. The speaker positions herself as distinct from these "cynical clones" and "hunters with cell phones," remarking that they are not "cut out for" these pursuing figures. Notably, the definite article "these" lends specificity and immediacy to the invaders. For the speaker, the threat is not indistinct or imagined. It represents an invasion of the technological into the natural, modernity into the nostalgic past, which necessitates their furtive escape. Later, the speaker describes how "a red rose grew up out of frozen ground / with no one around to tweet it," again highlighting the sense of discord and difference between the speaker's perception versus those around them. Forgarty and Arnold observe that during the *folklore* era, "Taylor is an artist somehow now on the outskirts of American society" (5). Despite her landmark success and overwhelming popularity, Swift employs Romantic framing, and the perceived "eccentricities" of the Lake District, as historical antecedents for her own feelings of being "heckled," pursued, and "hunt[ed] with cell phones." The speaker in "the lakes" may feel isolated from a life they are not "cut out for," but the visit forges a kinship between likeminded individuals across time.

When "the lakes" was released for the deluxe edition of *folklore*, Swift's eighth studio album, fans were quick to notice the explicit allusions to the Lake Poets. But one writer among them stood out through Swift's explicit reference: William Wordsworth. Although it has been more than 150 years since he lived and wrote, the English poet continues to influence readers and writers today. During his life, Wordsworth rose to early prominence with *Lyrical Ballads* (1798), a collection of poems co-authored with Coleridge that ushered in a new epoch of English poetry. Throughout his literary life, Wordsworth built on this early renown to achieve societal regard and artistic legitimacy, including his role as England's Poet Laureate in 1843. Commenting on Wordsworth's persisting popularity in 1905, Charles Harold Herford observed that up until that point "Wordsworth's fame has never undergone any real relapse," which he credited to the fact that he had been "appreciated from widely different points of view." Still today, Herford's conviction that Wordsworth is a poet for all times and all places holds true in the twenty-first century. Through both artistic and critical modes, Wordsworth continues to be re-read, reinterpreted, and reimagined by a broad array of global readers. But perhaps few among this faithful throng have had a more pronounced impact on Wordsworth's current cultural legacy than Taylor Swift.

In "the lakes," Swift treats her listeners to a lyrical pun on Wordsworth's name: "what are my Wordsworth." In referencing Wordsworth by name, even visually highlighting her joke in her official lyric video with cascading letters, Swift caused many of her devoted fans, or "Swifties," to gather on message boards and groups chats looking to learn more. Throughout much of her career, Swift has demonstrated a penchant for hiding clues and references in her communication, fostering a close-reading culture among her passionate fanbase. Had Swift simply included the play on words here, the homophone of "words worth" and "Wordsworth," it is likely that the reference would have been considered one of her more rarified "easter eggs": a treat for only the most voracious of Swiftian folklorists. However, in the broader context of "the lakes," the namecheck becomes a skeleton key to unlocking her broader project of legacy building, artistic renown, and the commercial value of creative labor.

"Please Picture Me in the Trees:" Reading Swift Through Wordsworth

But why Wordsworth and, moreover, why does it matter for our reading of *folklore*? Of the many authors and artists now grouped under the umbrella term "Romantic," Wordsworth is among the most foundational and broadly associated with the movement, as already seen in 1816 with Percy Shelley's voracious reading of the elder poet. Bergren describes the continuing impact of Wordsworth, especially among younger readers around the world: "Wordsworth was described as a poet capable of inculcating taste in his young readers, and this association with taste proved durable, clinging to Wordsworth as his poetry travelled beyond England" (23). Bergren describes how Wordsworth's monolithic presence in English literary history extended well beyond the borders of his homeland to similarly enchant a global readership. Moreover, she asserts that for readers outside of England, which would include the American-born Swift, he has become synonymous with our external perceptions of "Englishness" (23). Swift's professed Anglophilia has been seen across her recent albums, as epitomized by the cheeky "London Boy" on her album *Lover* (2019). Her evocation of Wordsworth in particular, a poet who has become synonymous with England and "Englishness," is thus notable in the context of Swift's larger musical project. But even beyond serving as a symbol of his nation, Wordsworth is an exceptionally apt antecedent for Swift's New Romanticism.

For example, like Swift, Wordsworth engendered intimacy with his readers through his writing's perception as autobiographical and deeply vulnerable. Bergren argues that this familiarity was forged "thanks to his particular lyric 'I,' which often has the effect of collapsing the distinction between poet and speaker, the line between him and his poetry could often be faint" (27). This interiority is best captured through his extensive project *The Prelude or, Growth of a Poet's Mind; An Autobiographical Poem*, composed from 1798 until his death in 1850. This same blurring between distinct personae extends to popular conceptions of Swift and her songwriting. As with Wordsworth before her, Swift employs narrative arcs, characters, and imagery that seem plausibly germane to her own documented life. More than any other contemporary artist, this conflation of her fictionalized and lived realities has collapsed the traditional poet/speaker divide in her catalogue. Fogarty and Arnold identify the resulting triumvirate as "Taylor Swift, the trilogy: singer, songwriter, and persona" (4). Much like when readers encountered Wordsworth, Swift's listeners perceive herself as the true subject behind her art.

From a thematic standpoint, Wordsworth's lyrical treatment of nature is a fitting historical antecedent to Swift's *folklore*. Among the Lake Poets, Wordsworth was especially transfixed by the natural beauty of his surroundings. He was not only inspired by the Lake District, but he immortalized it through his poetic meditations on his surroundings. Because of this, Willard Spiegelman notes that Wordsworth "made famous the geography of his main regions and . . . granted fame to those who inhabit that geography" (12). In their Broadview edition of *Lyrical Ballads 1798 and 1800*, editors Gamer and Porter include a map of the Lake District that indicates how twenty-two different poems from the collection directly reference or derive from twenty-two distinct locations in the region (544–5). In so many ways, the later renown of the Lake District was because of Wordsworth's thorough depiction of its natural diversity.

Dubbed the highest "Priest of Nature" by Victorian author Matthew Arnold, Wordsworth is still directly associated with the natural landscapes he depicted through his writing (Gottfried 38). For him, nature took on diverse attributes: the holy and haunted, the sacred and scarred. He thus bandied between considering nature as alternatively foe or familiar. Writing about the Lake District, Wordsworth depicted nature as a humanized, and even personalized, entity that encompassed these many dualities. As Wordsworth writes in "Lines Written a Few Miles Above Tintern Abbey" (1798), "Nature never did betray the heart that loved her," and he spent his entire career expressing his adoration of nature. When he wrote about nature, it was not distant or distinct from his speaker. It was the physical embodiment of his own interior landscape. Oerlemans notes that for Wordsworth, "his 'nature' is a blank canvas, an illusory (though perhaps necessary and worthwhile) space free of received meaning, against onto which the individual poet paints an idealized version of himself" (34). This view led fellow Romantic John Keats to criticize Wordsworth's approach as self-centered. He negatively referred to Wordsworth's view of the natural world as the "egotistical or Wordsworthian sublime"[5] because he treated his surroundings as an expression of himself (Potkay 208). Despite Keats's derogatory view, it is this intimacy between Wordsworth and nature that defined his poetic voice and conveyed a rich subjectivity to his readers, many of whom were young, female, and looking for themselves in their own environments.

While *folklore* is not the first time Swift integrated natural imagery into her lyrics, it is certainly her most extensive engagement with the theme. Beyond the album artwork, which depicts the singer embedded in natural settings, *folklore* lyrically depicts nature as an alternative to the urban, the modern, and the false. In direct opposition to the cityscapes' problems and inhabitants, the speakers throughout *folklore* are attuned to nature and see themselves within it. Throughout the album, Swift's speakers are transported to the past through meditations on nature. In a study entitled "Quantifying the Nature of Taylor Swift," Opperman conducted a quantitative analysis of *folklore*,

---

[5]   First used by Keats in an 1818 letter to Richard Woodhouse.

and its spiritual sister album *evermore* (2020), to determine how Swift's lyrical references to nature stacked up against those of her peers (2021). His study concludes that across both albums, Swift "uses nature-themed words seven times as frequently as the other pop songs do." Reflecting on his study for the *New York Times*, Opperman observed that for both *folklore* and *evermore*, "nature has primacy of place from the beginning: their cover art, with photography that shifts with the seasons like the menu of a farm-to-table restaurant. Recorded in the spring, 'Folklore' finds Ms. Swift dwarfed by trees in a foggy vernal forest." Opperman further elucidates that nature is not an abstract or distant concept in *folklore*, since "in Ms. Swift's lyrics, nature is not remote." Like Wordsworth before her, Swift employs nature as a mirror to her present state and a catalyst to be drawn back to her distant past.

The speaker in "seven," for example, asks the listener to "Please picture me / In the trees" before stating that "I hit my peak at seven."[6] The speaker returns to her past self and environment, associated with the purity of wild youth: "Please picture me / In the weeds / Before I learned civility / I used to scream ferociously / Any time I wanted." Opperman explains that in "seven," Swift "packs in nature references at a dizzying clip while evoking the landscape of the state where she grew up . . . nature, childhood and friendship are all intertwined and seared deep in memory." Written from an adult perspective, "seven" transports the speaker through both time and place. Although the speaker has since changed, admitting that she no longer remembers her friend's appearance, eternal nature serves as a reminder of her former innocence.

The dichotomy between youthfulness and knowledge is a key preoccupation of the Romantics that is fully realized through encounters with nature.[7] Through nature, they were often pulled back into the simpler experiences of their past selves, especially in the poetic works of Wordsworth. His poetic oeuvre is filled with examples of past and present in conversation. This allegorical juxtaposition of innocence and experience is sometimes literalized through his conversational lyrics, including the "Matthew Poems," which bring a younger poet-speaker into dialogue with a much older schoolmaster.[8] But while the Matthew Poems position Wordsworth's speaker as the younger mentee, his iconic "Tintern Abbey" enables him to relive his past youth through the experiences of his younger sister, Dorothy. Not unlike Swift's evocation of her childhood friend in "seven," Dorothy's innocence reminds Wordsworth of his own former state.

Throughout the poem, Wordsworth emphasizes the twin sensations of pain and pleasure he experiences while visiting a familiar spot with his sister. Beginning with a lamentation, he then expresses gratitude for what his memories of the location have

---

6   This title recalls Wordsworth's poem "We Are Seven" (1798), which tells the story of a young girl's childlike response to her siblings' death.

7   Beyond Wordsworth, William Blake published his twin collections, *Songs of Innocence* (1789) and *Songs of Experience* (1794), which explored human growth and maturation.

8   Wordsworth's "Matthew poems" include "Lines Written on a Tablet in School," "The Two April Mornings," and "The Fountain," all of which were included in Volume II of the 1800 edition of *Lyrical Ballads*.

provided—"How often has my spirit turned to thee!"[9]—and the heartsick realization that "That time is past, / And all its aching joys are now no more." Just as Swift implores her listener to "please picture me / In the trees" because "I hit my peak at seven," Wordsworth elegizes the man he was when he last visited this hallowed ground, admitting that "I cannot paint / What then I was" because "I have learned / To look on nature, not as in the hour of thoughtless youth." But again, while both Swift and Wordsworth acknowledge that they cannot recover these earlier selves, they are unified in their belief that nature will enable them to transcend time. For Swift, "seven" ends with her defiant rejection of memory's limitations: "And though I can't recall your face / I still got love for you" and "Passed down like folk songs / Our love lasts so long." Wordsworth similarly thwarts time's constraints by endowing his environment with greater meaning for him and his sister: "And this green pastoral landscape, were to me / More dear, both for themselves and for thy sake!" For both Swift and Wordsworth, although they begin with nostalgic recollection, their time-slip narratives reveal a path to immortality through shared experience, even across time.

Finally, one of the most salient connections between Wordsworth and Swift is also one of the least acknowledged aspects of Wordsworth's modern legacy: his commitment to artistic copyright reform. Throughout his career, Wordsworth fought to achieve credit and compensation for authors. Eilenberg explains that Wordsworth lobbied for copyright reform "to right these wrongs, to improve the writer's lot and put him in a better position to write" (351). She further characterizes his efforts as "extraordinary," remarking that he was motivated in part by his "altruistic belief that the law should recognize the right of genius to receive the fullness of its reward, partly by his belief that an extension of the term of copyright might improve his family's finances" (351–2). Writing on the topic in 1819, Wordsworth boldly asserted that when it came to authors, "It appears to me that towards no class of his Majesty's Subjects are the laws so unjust and oppressive" (844).[10]

Any discussion of artist copyright disputes of the last ten years must include Taylor Swift. For this reason, the lyric "what are my Wordsworth," a pun Swift underscored in both her album liner notes and official lyric video for "the lakes," gains particular poignancy in this context. In 2015, Swift wrote an open letter to Apple Music explaining her decision to hold back her new album *1989* from their streaming platform. The decision was informed by Apple's announcement that they would be offering customers a three-month free trial to sign up for the service. However, this promotion meant that artists would not be paid royalties during that period. Swift concluded her letter by stating, "We don't ask you for free iPhones. Please don't ask us to provide you with our music for no compensation." The letter was both symbolically and materially important for artist rights; Apple quickly reneged, restoring royalty payments to all artists.

---

[9] This recalls Wordsworth's poem "I wandered lonely as a cloud" and his description of fondly remembered daffodils: "For oft, when on my couch I lied / In vacant or in pensive mood, / They flash upon that inward eye / Which is the bliss of solitude."
[10] Wordsworth's hyperbole, all the more ridiculous prior to the 1833 Slavery Abolition Act, does highlight his conviction regarding artist rights.

Beyond the Apple Music letter, Swift has also been involved in other notable examples of artist rights disputes. Most prominently, Swift's decision to re-record her previous albums, a direct response to the contentious sale of her masters in 2019, caused a seismic shift in the music industry.[11] Writing about the legal dimension of Swift's major undertaking, Tilghman explains that "her decision to re-record her albums is not for money, but instead to move the needle in the direction of artists rather than the recording label in terms of ownership and ownership rights of the music" (406–7). It is therefore not an exaggeration to suggest that Swift has irrevocably changed the landscape of artist-label relations.

In juxtaposing Swift and Wordsworth, we therefore see two artists working in different centuries and countries, yet united by several key features. Swift's conjuring of Wordsworth by name in "the lakes" invites comparisons between the writers, calling forward the latter and his literary legacy. They are united by their early appeal to female audiences, their perceived vulnerability and subjective lyrical mode, their view of nature as a highly personalized reflection, and even their dogged commitment to copyright reform. However, a comparative reading of *folklore* and Wordsworth's Romanticism requires acknowledgement of each artist's commitment to their collaboration and what that entailed for their respective collaborators.

"Not Without You": Towards Swift's New Romanticism

As we have already explored, Swift's evocation of Romantic themes and tropes places her in line with this important literary tradition. But although Swift imports much of Wordsworth's characteristic style into "the lakes," we argue that she ultimately subverts his ethos through her willingness to give agency to her own key collaborators.

The Romantic movement relied on the premise that authors were singular talents in commune with nature. Their works were often framed as divinely inspired and entirely original, leading to a shared belief in Romantic "Genius." Higgins thus argues that, for the Romantics, "the essence of genius is its claim to distinctiveness" (8). Although most of them participated in artist communes and coteries, it was also important for them to be perceived as distinct from their collaborators. Wolfson captures this popular characterization of Romantic texts as "generative, even revolutionary, literature of single perspectives" (1). Similarly, Stillinger termed this long-held belief "The Myth of Solitary Genius": a pervasive fiction regarding Romantic authorship based on individual exceptionalism and isolation.

Wordsworth himself was a key figure in the creation and perpetuation of this Romantic lie. For him, his status as an individual genius was essential to his reputation. As Bergren explains, "Wordsworth's literary productions could be seen as of a piece with his persona, capable of producing a monolithic figure who represented the

---

[11] Beginning in 2021, Swift began re-recording her previous albums, with the stated intention of producing a "Taylor's Version" of each. In 2021, she released her versions of *Fearless* (2008) and *Red* (2012), followed by *Speak Now* (2010) and *1989* (2014) in 2023.

developing norms of good taste" (27–8). Although he is often treated as a singular talent in English literary history, this reputation overlooks the shared efforts of his collaborators, including Coleridge[12] and his younger sister, Dorothy.[13]

In re-evaluating Wordsworth's history of silencing his collaborators and denying them credit, one cannot help but be reminded of his determination to secure rights for artists, a cause that Swift herself has fiercely championed. Here we find the crux of Taylor Swift's "New Romanticism" and one of her key differentiators from Wordsworth. While she references Wordsworth by name in "the lakes," and her poetic treatments of nature throughout *folklore* recall his poetic ethos, her crediting of Joe Alwyn as a co-writer on the album reflects a genuine commitment to collaboration, especially regarding her loved ones.

As the chorus continues, the speaker shares that she is going to leave for the lakes but, importantly, "not without my muse." Swift ultimately thwarts our expectations by assuring us that the speaker is no Romantic hero venturing out on her own. What initially feels like a declaration of independence settles into an expression of romantic contentment. The song concludes with the speaker again recalling her beloved: "I'm setting off, but not without my muse / No, not without you." In reading "the lakes" in the broader context of *folklore*'s history and production, this commitment to collaboration was further literalized through Joe Alwyn's song writing credits.[14] As a co-writer on two *folklore* tracks, Alwyn received due credit and compensation for his participation, sharing in the album's critical acclaim, including the 2021 Grammy for Album of the Year. In this way, Swift went beyond poetic memorialization of her "beloved" by elevating her collaborator from passive muse to credited contributor.

*   *   *

In 2020, in the face of global pandemic, one of the world's most famous musicians wrote a song indebted to the English Romantics. More specifically, in "the lakes," Swift renewed popular interest in the Lake Poets and the Lake District by looking back in time to the Romantic Age and recalling many of the themes and features central to Wordsworth's artistic project. But ultimately, Swift does not simply replicate these Romantic tropes. She reimagines them for her modern context by providing her collaborator with autonomy and credit. Resultantly, although Swift's Romanticism emerged in response to different circumstances, and an entirely different global cataclysm, it is at once familiar and entirely novel. By forging an intergenerational collaboration across time and place, Swift elevated *folklore* into a work of New Romanticism and, in turn, demonstrated her words' profound worth.

---

[12] For example, although *Lyrical Ballads* was co-authored by both Wordsworth and Coleridge, Wordsworth secured full rights in 1798.

[13] Modern readers of Dorothy's texts, including the *Grasmere Journals* from 1799 (1897), argue that she is "the most famous case of William singularizing his sister out of poetic agency" (Wolfson 175). Unfortunately, as Jones explains, "Wordsworth was to deny Dorothy's contribution entirely" (114).

[14] During *folklore: The long pond studio sessions*, Swift revealed that William Bowery was a pseudonym for her long-term partner at the time, Joe Alwyn.

Works Cited

Bergren, Katherine. *The Global Wordsworth: Romanticism Out of Place*. Bucknell University Press: Lewisburg, 2019.

Blake, William. *Songs of Innocence and Songs of Experience*. Dover Publications: Mineola, 1992.

Caramanica, Jon. "Taylor Swift's 'Folklore' Review: A Pop Star Done with Pop." *The New York Times*, 26 July 2020.

Coleridge, Samuel Taylor and William Wordsworth. *Lyrical Ballads 1798 and 1800*. eds. Michael Gamer and Dahlia Porter. Broadview Press: Peterborough, 2008.

Collett, Anne and Olivia Murphy. *Romantic Climates: Literature and Science in the Age of Catastrophe*. Palgrave Macmillan: London, 2019.

Eilenberg, Susan. (1989), "Mortal Pages: Wordsworth and the Reform of Copyright." *ELH*, vol. 56, no. 2. (1989): 351–74.

Fogarty, Mary and Gina Arnold. "Are You Ready For It? Re-Evaluating Taylor Swift." *Contemporary Music Review*, vol. 40, no. 1. (2021): 1–10.

folklore: the long pond studio sessions. Directed by Taylor Swift, Disney, 2020.

Gamer, Michael and Dahlia Porter. "Appendix H." *Lyrical Ballads 1798 and 1800*. eds. Michael Gamer and Dahlia Porter. Broadview Press: Peterborough, 2008. 544–5.

Gottfried, Leon. *Matthew Arnold and the Romantics*. London: Routledge, 2016.

Herford, C.H. *The Age of Wordsworth*. London: Bell, 2008.

Jones, Kathleen. *A Passionate Sisterhood: Women of the Wordsworth Circle*. New York: St. Martin's Press, 2000.

Medwin, Thomas. *Conversations of Lord Byron*, ed. Ernest J. Lovell Jr., Princeton University Press: Princeton, 1966.

Oerlemans, Onno. *Romanticism and the Materiality of Nature*. University of Toronto Press: Toronto, 2002.

Opperman, Jeff. "Quantifying the Nature of Taylor Swift." *WWF*, 12 May 2021.

Opperman, Jeff. "Taylor Swift Is Singing Us Back to Nature." *The New York Times*, 12 May 2021.

Polidori, John. *The Vampyre and Other Tales of the Macabre*, ed. Robert Morrison and Chris Baldick. Oxford University Press: Oxord, 2008. 1–24.

Potkay, Adam. "The British Romantic Sublime." *The Sublime: From Antiquity to the Present*, ed. Timothy M. Costelloe. Cambridge University Press: Cambridge, 2012. 203–16.

Shelley, Mary. *Frankenstein*. Paper Mill Press: Thorold, 2018.

Spiegelman, Willard. *Wordsworth's Heroes*. University of California Press: Berkeley, 2021.

Stillinger, Jack. *Multiple Authorship and the Myth of Solitary Genius*. Oxford University Press: Oxford, 1991.

Swift, Taylor. "Liner Notes." *folklore*: Sony, 2020.

Swift, Taylor. "Taylor Swift – the lakes (Official Lyric Video)." *YouTube*, uploaded by Taylor Swift, 18 August 2020, https://www.youtube.com/watch?v=tOHcAc3r2kw.

Swift, Taylor. "To Apple, love Taylor." *Stereogum*, https://www.stereogum.com/1810310/read-taylor-swifts-open-letter-to-apple-music/news/. Accessed 16 April 2024.

Tedeschi, Stephen. *Urbanization and English Romantic Poetry*. Cambridge University Press: Cambridge, 2018.

Tilghman, Justin. "Exposing the 'Folklore' of Re-Recording Clauses (Taylor's Version)." *Journal of Intellectual Property Law*, vol. 29, no. 2. (2022): 403–17.

Wilson, Carl. "Taylor Swift's New Album Reveals That Social Distancing Has Served Her Well." *Slate*, 24 July 2020.

Wolfson, Susan J. *Romantic Interactions: Social Being & The Turns of Literary Action*. Johns Hopkins University Press: Baltimore, 2010.

Wordsworth, Dorothy and William Wordsworth. *Home at Grasmere*. Penguin Classics: London, 1979.

Wordsworth, William and Dorothy Wordsworth. *The Letters of William and Dorothy Wordsworth; The Middle Years*, ed. Alan G. Hill and Ernest De Selincourt, Oxford University Press: Oxford, 1937.

Wordsworth, William. 'The Fountain: A Conversation.' *Lyrical Ballads 1798 and 1800*, eds. Michael Gamer and Dahlia Porter. Broadview Press: Peterborough, 2008. 352–4.

Wordsworth, William. "I Wandered Lonely as a Cloud." *Poetry Foundation*, https://www.poetryfoundation.org/poems/45521/i-wandered-lonely-as-a-cloud. Accessed 16 April 2024.

Wordsworth, William. 'Lines Written a Few Miles Above Tintern Abbey, on Revisiting the Banks of the Wye During a Tour, July 13, 1708.' *Lyrical Ballads 1798 and 1800*, eds. Michael Gamer and Dahlia Porter. Broadview Press: Peterborough, 2008. 282–6.

Wordsworth, William. 'Lines Written on a Tablet in a School.' *Lyrical Ballads 1798 and 1800*, eds. Michael Gamer and Dahlia Porter. Broadview Press: Peterborough, 2008. 349–50.

Wordsworth, William. *The Prelude or, Growth of a Poet's Mind; An Autobiographical Poem*. Penguin Classics: London, 1996.

Wordsworth, William. 'The Two April Mornings.' *Lyrical Ballads 1798 and 1800*, eds. Michael Gamer and Dahlia Porter. Broadview Press: Peterborough, 2008. 350–2.

Wordsworth, William. 'We Are Seven.' *Lyrical Ballads 1798 and 1800*, eds. Michael Gamer and Dahlia Porter. Broadview Press: Peterborough, 2008. 213–14.

Wheatley, Kim. *Romantic Feuds: Transcending the "Age of Personality."* Routledge: London, 2016.

@taylorswift13. "In isolation my imagination has run wild and this album is the result. I've told these stories to the best of my ability with all the love, wonder, and whimsy they deserve. Now it's up to you to pass them down. folklore is out now." *Twitter*, 24 July, 12:08 a.m., https://twitter.com/taylorswift13/status/1286513561553047557.

5

Baby, We're the Late Romantics: Taylor Swift and the English *Biedermeier*

Betsy Winakur Tontiplaphol

Taylor Swift's Romanticism is, by now, old news. In "the lakes," *folklore*'s lush meditation on melancholia and England's Lake District, Swift puns on William Wordsworth's name—"I've come too far," she sings, "to watch some namedropping sleaze / Tell me what are my words worth"—and in the aftermath of the track's release, institutions as different as *Rolling Stone* and the British Association for Romantic Studies (BARS) were eager to inform audiences about Swift's interest in and knowledge of British Romantic poetry. Brittany Spanos, writing for *Rolling Stone*, observed that "the lakes" "goes deep on the Romantic poetry references" and offers a "clever reference to . . . Wordsworth"; meanwhile, Zoë van Cauwenberg, in the inaugural essay for the BARS Blog's "Romanticism Now" series, underscored the degree to which the song signifies "the resonance of Romanticism in our modern world," especially in the (post-) pandemic years: "In the opening lines of 'the lakes,' [Swift] wonders: 'is it romantic how all my elegies eulogize me?' . . . [T]he lyric suggests a particular form of self-expression that combines melancholy with praise, as though sadness ought to be celebrated." Other writers, both journalists and scholars, have continued to explore Swift's engagement with literary Romanticism—many note that "in the Disney+ documentary *folklore: the long pond studio sessions*," Swift references John Keats as well as Wordsworth, suggesting that both "retreated to [the Lakes] 'hundreds of years ago'" (van Cauwenberg)—and several contributors to this collection endeavor to lend additional depth to that still developing discourse. I am certainly among those.

But if Swift's Romanticism is old news, might it also be old Romanticism? As an adjective, "old" can convey both earliness—one might say, for example, that Swift's oldest album is her self-titled debut—*and* maturity, a lateness in some temporal trajectory. It's the second sense of "old" that interests me as I approach the question articulated above, since Romanticism itself is perhaps best understood as a movement that *aged*, a movement whose later adherents retained the values of its original revolutionaries but evolved in their manner of expressing and pursuing them. Some critics might even suggest that Romanticism, like the speaker of Swift's literarily titled "Anti-Hero," "[got] older but just never wiser," and my object here is to explore the resonances between Swift's lyrics and the work of those English writers associated with late Romanticism, especially the Victorian poet Alfred Tennyson. By acknowledging Swift's interest in canonical high Romanticism—that is, in voices like Wordsworth and Keats—Romanticists encounter an opportunity to examine their movement's contemporary afterlives and, of course, to introduce their critical subjects (to students and to the public) via an accessible and timely lyrical voice. By framing Swift's Romanticism as an afterlife of *late* Romanticism, however, Romanticists gain purchase on their focal movement's unique transformations and surprising longevity, not to mention Swift's extraordinary popularity in the twenty-first century.

I'm keen to acknowledge upfront that literary periodization is a kind of fiction, a framework imposed *post hoc* by the critics of the present on the voices of the past. The so-called late Romantics certainly wouldn't have identified themselves as such; when, for example, Arthur Henry Hallam dubbed Tennyson a "poet of sensation," he meant, as Jayne Thomas explains, to distinguish his friend from Wordsworth but to *link* him to the likes of Keats and Percy Bysshe Shelley, who "trembled into emotion at colours, and sounds, and movements, unperceived … by duller temperaments"—and who are universally categorized as both "Romantic" and, in some important ways, even Wordsworthian today (in Thomas). Put simply, neither Hallam nor Tennyson was aware of (let alone interested in) the labels that contemporary students and scholars apply, with encouragement from academic institutions like W.W. Norton and their ubiquitous anthologies, to the major literary voices of the nineteenth century. But if periodization is a fiction, it's often a useful one, an heuristic aide that inspires would-be decoders to foreground questions about creative relationships, artistic trajectories, and contextual influences. Swift's decision to conceptualize her own career as a series of "eras"—a word essentially synonymous with *periods*—suggests that she's attuned to the interpretive benefits that accrue to the reader or listener who aims to think (sensitively and judiciously, of course) in terms of historical units, and I approach this argument with a similar optimism, a literary historian's confidence that late Romanticism, in all of its definitions and associations, is/was an "era" that can help to illuminate *all* of Swift's.

But when was "late Romanticism," and how did the literature of that moment differ, aesthetically or otherwise, from earlier Romantic productions? It's tough to say, and Thomas Ford acknowledges that some readers "have argued that Romanticism never came to an end in its European homelands … and that we all still dwell in the era it opened up." "It is certainly true," he concedes, "that many contemporary philosophical structures of aesthetic evaluation remain deeply indebted to Romantic formations. Perhaps this is why literary historians have struggled to describe the end of Romanticism. They have been haunted by the possibility that they are still inside it" (187). Undaunted by that prospect of eerie inescapability, however, other scholars have posited concrete endpoints for the Romantic movement. Ford's own suggestions are more experiential than temporal—"computers, communism and climate change," he asserts, "sharply [distinguish] contemporary intellectual life from its Romantic pasts" (188)—but Virgil Nemoianu, in *The Taming of Romanticism*, proposes a specific date range. Adopting the terminology established by scholars in "the German-speaking center of Europe" to "describe the opposition between high romanticism and its later, moderate stages," Nemoianu suggests that "approximately 1815–1845" constituted, throughout Britain and continental Europe, the Romantic movement's terminus, or *Biedermeier* period (1). The term *Biedermeier*, Nemoianu notes, "might be translated as 'John Simpleton'" and "carries a connotation of nostalgic smiling benevolence" (4); in essence, then, *Biedermeier* writers are Romantic in their *wish* for Romanticism, in their earnest desire to sustain the movement's fading zeitgeist by trafficking in its most easily recognizable and reproducible features and thus tempering (or, in Nemoianu's parlance, "taming") its once disruptive energy. As Nemoianu puts it, "the foremost dichotomy within romanticism is the opposition between the great fantasies and visions of the revolutionary age (high romanticism) and the more perplexed and disappointed musings, sentimentalities, aspirations, and ironies of the post-Napoleonic era" (2)—of, that is, the *Biedermeier* era. "The grand tour of the Alps," for example, "ceased to be the property of the intense, lonely, and sublime poet and became the object of organized tourism" (Nemoianu 11), and those touristy mountain jaunts, those "diminutive prettifications" (Nemoianu 6) of their arguably more authentic predecessors, became their *own* brand of Romantic. *Biedermeier* artists generated resonant "new combinations" and "practical solutions" when they operated from "splintered or reduced interpretations of the high-romantic model" (Nemoianu 6).

It's in this context that I wish to consider Swift, who opens the melodically buoyant single "Shake It Off" by both wincing and winking at her status in the public imagination as a kind of Jane Simpleton, and "late" to boot: "I stay out too late / I got nothin' in my brain / That's what people say." To my mind, Swift's "late" "nothin[gness]"—and the combination of nonchalance and anxiety with which she embraces it—embodies the "new" "reduc[tions]" to which Nemoianu refers, and to consider Swift's Romanticism is to see a *Biedermeier* artist capturing in her music not Romanticism's ideological core but rather its distinctive surfaces, the frayed but still moving leftovers of its once "high" fabric. Even a casual student of English Romanticism's best-known poetic voices will likely recognize that Swift's lyrics afford a veritable catalogue of high Romantic tropes, each polished to a fresh simplicity, an accessible non-sublimity. For example, memory for Swift is *always* textbook-Wordsworthian, ubiquitous and self-immortalizing; in "All Too Well," for instance, shifting tenses neatly capture the degree to which her past animates her present: "'Cause there we are again on that little town street," she sings, "You almost ran the red 'cause you were looking over at me / Wind in my hair, I was there, I remember it all too well." In "Wildest Dreams," meanwhile, she imagines-*cum*-commandeers her interlocutor's future memories. Just like Wordsworth, who, near the close of the archetypally Romantic "Tintern Abbey," instructs his sister Dorothy to "remember [him]" with "tender joy," and "these [his] exhortations" (148–9), Swift makes explicit demands. "Say you'll remember me," she sings, "standing in a nice dress / Staring at the sunset, babe / . . . Say you'll see me again / Even if it's just in your wildest dreams." And although the "babe[s]" who inhabit Swift's universe are themselves quintessential Romantic types, as Byronic as they come, her lyric speakers are overreachers, too. In "Wildest Dreams," the object of the speaker's affection recalls the titular hero of George Gordon Byron's *Childe Harold's Pilgrimage*—"he's so bad, but he does it so well," she purrs—but the women Swift voices are, as she puts it in "Blank

Space," "nightmare[s] dressed like . . . daydreams," women with their own purchase on darkness and danger. Their capacious desire, we gather, is at the heart of the threat that they pose to themselves and to others, but at the end of the day, Swift's lyrics are typically more sensual than sexual, often distinguished by a Coleridgean or Keatsian synaesthesia. "You're so gorgeous it actually hurts," she insists in "Gorgeous," while "Welcome to New York" finds her fusing sight, sound, and touch in "a kaleidoscope of loud heartbeats under coats" that seems almost overtly to echo the "light in sound" and "sound-like power in light" that Samuel Taylor Coleridge imagines in the Romantic touchstone "The Eolian Harp" (28). Put simply, Swift's vaunted Romanticism is, in fact, more *Biedermeier* than high Romantic in its dependability, its reliable *recognizability*. Like the *Biedermeier*-era essayist William Hazlitt, whose theory of artistic "gusto" is "most notable for that which it doesn't contain, namely the element of transfiguration" (Nemoianu 53), Swift appreciates the labor that attends aesthetic-crafting and the consistency of product that accompanies it, and that earthly pragmatism animates her work. Hazlitt, Nemoianu notes, "spoke about genius as quantitative and methodic [rather than] irrational, mysterious, and divine" (53), and eight years after "Shake It Off," "nothin' in my brain" Swift rebranded herself a "Mastermind," asserting in the final track of *Midnights*[1] that she "laid the groundwork and then just like clockwork / The dominoes cascaded in a line." Although the ostensible subject of "Mastermind" is amorous gamesmanship, references to "plan," "design," and (perhaps most notably) a "strategy [that] sets the scene for the tale" evoke artistic *craftsmanship*, and I submit that Swift wields her favored Romantic tropes, types, and figures—her "diminutive prettifications"—with the practiced gusto of Hazlitt's *Biedermeier* maker-artist rather than the transcendent virtuosity of the revolutionary poet-creator mythologized in the story of high Romanticism.

It's vital to emphasize, however, that *Biedermeier* gusto isn't inherently *lesser* than Romantic "transfiguration," than "the great fantasies and visions of the revolutionary age"—and that a poetics anchored in "organized tourism" isn't necessarily a lesser poetics than one inspired by unmediated encounters with the Alps. The emotional incongruities that shaped the "peaceful yet nervous" *Biedermeier* age, a "period that managed to avoid major wars but was riddled with outbursts of agitation and rebellion" (Nemoianu 6), arguably birthed a generation uniquely interested in the pleasures of *placedness* and exceptionally skilled at cultivating immersive, moody tableaux. In other words, the schematic literary Romanticism purveyed by *Biedermeier* "masterminds" often depicted or otherwise manifested as solid-seeming environments, locations defined by the material surety that their creators' anxious historical moment couldn't provide—and that their Romantic aspirations couldn't, in themselves, secure. Although Romantic "atmosphere[s]" possessed some "properties of permanence," they also, Ford explains, "always . . . involved drift, turbulence, transience, change and erasure"; the transition *away* from Romanticism proper, then, involved attempts to "sever

---

[1]   I refer to the standard edition of the album.

[atmosphere] from this heritage of loss" (192), to generate real and imaginary spaces that evoked immovability. In fact, as Nemoianu explains, "time seemed to be replaced by space as a dominant category" in the *Biedermeier* period—"local landscapes, familiar objects, home and hearth, animals and plants, woods and gardens were fervently sought" (14)—and the poetry of Alfred Tennyson furnishes a useful English example of that phenomenon. Though conventionally identified as a Victorian poet, Tennyson has been productively reconsidered in the context of the *Biedermeier*, as a figure who embodies late Romanticism's taste for "reduction and assimilation" rather than "denial and opposition" (Nemoianu 55). The man who eventually became Queen Victoria's Poet Laureate, Nemoianu writes, embodied a "tempered" and "more realistic romanticism [that] may well be understood as the answer to the needs of a Biedermeier age": "[Tennyson] continued Keats by divesting him of all visionary grandeur, but preserving the magic, the nostalgia, and the doubts" (76). In *Tennyson and the Doom of Romanticism*, Herbert Tucker identifies Tennyson as "the most finished, the most inevitable of the English poets, at least in the Romantic tradition" (23), and the double meaning of Tucker's "finished"—the term conveys not only a quality of definitive end but also the accumulation of detail—captures both Ford's and Nemoianu's differently phrased assertions ("permanence" and "preservation," respectively) regarding late Romanticism's preoccupation with *dwelling*, with those spaces in which people stay and those objects on which their senses linger. Even "[w]hen undertaking an actual story," Tucker elaborates, Tennyson "consistently opts for descriptive over narrative effects" and "gives atmospheric or local description priority over physical description of characters or analysis of their minds" (17).

Swift is undeniably an artist who dwells. Literal dwellings, from Holiday House ("the last great american dynasty") to a rented "place on Cornelia Street" ("Cornelia Street"), crowd her lyrics, and much to some critics' chagrin, she dwells *on* teenage drama, failed relationships, her industry's inequities, and more. In "Death by a Thousand Cuts," dwelling in and dwelling on merge when a former passion is figured in the song's chorus—a lyrical moment, by definition, *returned to*, dwelled upon—as an abandoned house: "I look through the windows of this love / Even though we boarded them up / Chandelier still flickering here." Swift herself acknowledges her commitment to return and rumination in *folklore*'s opener "the one," whose speaker sings in another apt chorus, "In my defense, I have none / For never leaving well enough alone." Most interesting, however, is the fact that by that chorus's latest iteration, the abstract, aphoristic language in the second line above becomes spatial and tactile—"In my defense, I have none / For digging up the grave another time"—and thereby more typical of Swift's ruminative habits, which are more Tennysonian-material than Wordsworthian-philosophical. Tennyson's "Mariana," spun from a fragment of Shakespearean setting,[2] affords a useful illustration and point of comparison. Abandoned by "the one" in her own life, Mariana yearns for a traditional grave—"He cometh not," she exclaims at the close of every stanza, "I would that I were dead!"—but

---

[2] The poem's epigraph reads, "'Mariana in the moated grange.' —*Measure for Measure*."

instead finds herself entombed alive, so to speak, in an environment that churns with the shovelfuls of evocative materio-sensory detail that Tennyson extracts from every square inch of her tableau. There's much that's *superficially* Romantic about "Mariana," including its rustic location, its heroine's brooding intensity, and even the diction in its final stanza, which, according to Tucker, "attempts a point-for-point reversal of Keats's ['To Autumn']" (76). The poem's literary power, however, derives primarily from its *Biedermeier* "descriptive ... effects," not its engagement with Romantic values. Nothing develops or, to invoke Nemoianu, "transfigur[es]" in "Mariana," but in the "lonely moated grange" where its title character perpetually waits (8), "flower-plots" stand "thickly crusted" "[w]ith blackest moss" (1–2), a "mouse" "shriek[s]" "behind the moldering wainscot" (63–4), "clustered marish-mosses" "[creep]" about "[a] sluice with blackened waters" (40, 38), and "[t]he shadow of [a] poplar [falls] / Upon her bed, across her brow" (55–6). As Tucker puts it, "the temporality of Mariana's grange attains a curious suspension" through which "the objects that fill its space take on a life of their own" (73), and that statement accurately characterizes Swift's dominant mode, too. "[C]urious," in fact, is the descriptor that Swift applies to "temporality" in the first chorus of her track "invisible string"—"Time, curious time / Gave me no compasses, gave me no signs"—and that piece eschews traditional narration in favor of accumulating "clues," of cataloguing meaningful places (Centennial Park, a yogurt shop, a cab in LA, a restaurant "down by the lakes," a "dive bar") and particular things, both literal and metaphorical: green grass, a teal-colored shirt, golden leaves, chains, barbed wire, and a "cold" "steel" "axe," among others. And if there's a crystalline clarity to "invisible string"—a sense of tying up life's loose ends, as it were—it's because the track articulates what Swift *herself* has been doing, in the words of the song, "[a]ll along." To look backwards from *folklore* is to recognize that Swift's Wordsworthian memorializing, Byronic overreaching, and Coleridgean/Keatsian synaesthestic experimentation have consistently manifested in and as Tennysonian environments, as works in which, to borrow Tucker's account of "Mariana," "scenery ... exhibits a cumulative permanence that makes each scenic feature preternaturally vivid" and "discrete details, for all their individual sharpness, conspire in a common atmosphere" (73).

Strangely, many of the "discrete details" in "Mariana" appear in Swift's writing, too. In Tennyson's poem, "rusted nails fell from the knots / That held the pear to the gable wall"; Swift describes rust accumulating "on your door" ("august"), on once "[shiny]" "wheels" ("this is me trying"), and "between telephones" ("Maroon"). In Tennyson's "Mariana," the "thickest dark [does] trance the sky" (17–18), while in Swift's "You're Losing Me," "the air is thick with loss and indecision"; later, when Tennyson describes "hinges" that "creak" (62) and "[o]ld faces glimmer[ing] through ... doors" (66), one might recall the "creaks in the floors" that the lovers "memorize" in Swift's "Cornelia Street" and the insomnia-induced visions recounted in her "Anti-Hero": "All of the people I've ghosted stand there in the room." There are additional correspondences— both "Mariana" and Swift make evocative reference to clocks, footsteps, the moon, and the wind—but my primary aim isn't to identify "Mariana" as a Swiftian source, even if it is one. Rather, my object is to suggest that Swift is *broadly* Tennysonian in her "vivid[ness]," late Romantic in her atmospherics. In Swift's lyric world, precisely observed details abound: a cat "flex[es] like a Vegas acrobat" ("Karma"), an emotionally distant man "hang[s] [his] head low in the glow of the vending machine" ("Cruel Summer"), and an anxious caretaker "pray[s]" nightly to the "holy orange bottles" that cluster (like "marish-mosses," perhaps) in her patient's space ("Soon You'll Get Better"). Polaroids, wine bottles, jackets, scars, headlights, refrigerators, cosmetics, gates, Christmas trees, keychains, and more pile up in what Rob Sheffield terms Swift's "one-of-a-kind songbook," a textual realm in which a scarf in a drawer ("All Too Well") and a cardigan under a bed ("cardigan") possess uncanny material permanence, utterly unlosable and never divested of the odors that matter. Swift's accumulative, materio-sensory instinct certainly shapes individual songs—Sheffield notes, for example, that in "The Other Side of the Door," "Tay" includes not just *another* slamming door but also, "pouring rain, photo albums, a little black dress . . . , [and] a guy throwing pebbles at her window"—but it is indeed the consistency of the "songbook," the steadiness of Swift's lyric vision, that solidifies her kinship with the purposefulness of the *Biedermeier* writers' mature, *crafted* Romanticism. As emotional as Swift's lyrics often are, there's no Wordsworthian pretense that they represent a "spontaneous overflow of powerful feelings" (Preface to *Lyrical Ballads* 246); rather, the songs' emotionality is *cultivated* through Swift's careful place-making and scene-setting, and just as, according to Tucker, there exists a "deeply satisfying correspondence between Mariana and her surroundings [that] arises from a projection of self onto environment" (71), there's pleasure and comfort in watching Swift curate, over and over again, the "environment[al]" details that capture her songs' nuanced consciousnesses, many of them versions of Swift's own. It's notable, for example, that in the songbook's bedrooms[3] alone, a would-be lover awakens when her "phone lights up my nightstand in the black" ("Delicate"); an established lover crows that "now I wake up in the night and watch you breathe" ("Paper Rings"); and an ambivalent lover shrugs because, "head on the pillow, I could feel you sneaking in" ("willow").

But to characterize Swift as both *Biedermeier* artist-dweller and, when we assume an autobiographical dimension to her lyrics, a Mariana-esque character-dweller is to recognize that Tennyson's "The Lady of Shalott" is an even more useful touchstone in a discussion of Swift's late Romantic aesthetic. The titular figure in Tennyson's iconic ballad is doomed to dwell alone in a tower on the outskirts of King Arthur's bustling Camelot, whose denizens occasionally hear her "song that echoes cheerly" (30). Per the terms of an undefined "curse," she's forbidden to look directly out the window but must weave a never-ending tapestry that portrays the material richness of the outside world—"the river eddy," "the surly village churls," "the red cloaks of the market girls," and more (51–3)—as it's reflected in "a mirror clear / That hangs before her all the year" (46–7). In other words, the Lady of Shalott is, like Swift, both an accomplished, detail-oriented artist—she tirelessly and with "delight" "weave[s] the mirror's magic sights"

---

[3] Sheffield highlights a different recurring room, writing that Swift seems "on a mission to have emotional experiences in every square inch of the kitchen."

(64–5)—and, it turns out, a woman who broods, "half sick of shadows" (71), on her own isolation, which ultimately proves unsustainable. When "bold Sir Lancelot" and his shining accoutrements ("gemmy bridle," "bridle bells," "blazoned baldric," "silver bugle," and others [82, 85, 87, 88]) flash into her mirror, the Lady turns to look out the window, thus triggering the curse—"[t]he mirror cracked from side to side" (115)—and initiating her own demise. In its broad outline, there's much in that story that calls to mind the circumstances of Swift's lyrical avatars, who often experience unique forms of isolation—"Sometimes I feel like everybody is a sexy baby / And I'm a monster on the hill," Swift muses in "Anti-Hero"—and therefore fall fast for potential lovers, the predictable consequences be damned. In "Blank Space," Swift even welcomes those consequences with breathless, albeit tongue-in-cheek, enthusiasm: "Nice to meet you, where you been? [...] Saw you there and I thought / 'Oh, my god, look at that face / You look like my next mistake ...'" But if the circumstances of Tennyson's Lady evoke those of the prototypical Swift protagonist, the poem's language, its very diction, is significant, too. Medievalist environmental trappings—castles, towers, gardens, kings— enchant both the author of "The Lady of Shalott" and the voice of "Today Was a Fairytale," "Look What You Made Me Do," and numerous other works defined by their fairytale-evocative imagery, and there are some especially surprising similarities between Tennyson's account of Lancelot and Swift's account of the relationship chronicled in her early hit "State of Grace." Tennyson's hero enters the poem like "a bowshot from her bower eaves," and when "the sun came dazzling through the leaves," it "flamed upon [his] brazen greaves" and, "in the blue unclouded weather," made "helmet and ... helmet-feather / [Burn] like one burning flame together" (73, 75–6, 91, 93–4). Although the speaker in "State of Grace" figures *herself* as the knight—"You come around and the armor falls"—the object of her affection, who "pierce[s] the room like a cannonball," is still the weapon; the union of the two is all fire and blueness— "Twin fire signs, four blue eyes"—and seems, to a woman who had "loved in shades of wrong," an Arthurian "golden age" of the "good and right and real." "I never saw you coming, / And I'll never be the same," Swift sings, before concluding that, despite the cracks in their "mosaic broken hearts," "this is a state of grace." In the closing lines of Tennyson's ballad, Lancelot hopes that "'God in his mercy [will] lend her grace, / The Lady of Shalott'" (171–2).

But there's still more: As substantial as they are, the circumstantial and imagistic similarities between "The Lady of Shalott" and Swift's songbook are less consequential, I think, than those texts' similar *positioning* with regard to Romanticism. Always alone and, since she weaves whatever happens to appear in a mirror, bound to an artform limited by both reflection and "spontane[ity]," the Lady of Shalott has long been read as a stand-in for the quintessential Romantic poet, a Wordsworth-esque "writer"[4] whose

---

4   Tucker notes that the Lady of Shalott's song "is a 'song that echoes,'" a detail which "should alert us to the multiple echoes of Romantic poetry in [the] introductory portion of the poem" (102). The presence of those "echoes," those *reduced* references to the poetry of high Romanticism, is in itself a *Biedermeier* feature.

textile-text proves difficult to sustain in a new politico-historical movement that privileges collective authority (as represented by the famous Round Table) over individual power. Indeed, as Tucker explains, the Lady of Shalott "has just enough in common with ... Wordsworth's cuckoo to throw into relief" what's missing: the "Wordsworthian or Shelleyan power to make the earth over" (104). It follows, therefore, that when the image of King Arthur's most distinguished advisor hits the solitary Lady's mirror, her Romantically conceived tapestry simply disintegrates—"[o]ut flew the web and floated wide," Tennyson writes (114)—in a manner that also illustrates Ford's claim, cited above, that Romanticism proper "always ... involved drift," never solidity or permanence. But where the Lady of Shalott dies, the "The Lady of Shalott," composed by a *Biedermeier* artist, survives; what endures, in other words, is a poem that testifies to Romanticism's fast-fraying dominion while simultaneously attempting to *locate* and thereby preserve some semblance of its energy within the material certainty of "[f]our gray walls, and four gray towers" that "[o]verlook a space of flowers" (15–16)—and, of course, within other place-, sense-, and materials-saturated lines. In "The Lady of Shalott," then, Tennyson is a new *kind* of Romantic—wistful but practical, more seeing than visionary—and in "New Romantics," Swift figures herself similarly. Although its lyrics allude to the American Nathaniel Hawthorne ("our different scarlet letters"), Swift captures in broad strokes both the feverish revolutionary joy of English Romanticism's first generation and the agonized urgency of its second; at the same time, she works to ground those experiences in a distinctly *Biedermeier* series of environments and objects, both literal and figurative. The young folks "too busy dancing to get knocked off [their] feet" recall, affectively, Wordsworth's famous *Prelude* reflection on the French Revolution's earliest moments—"Bliss was it in that dawn to be alive, / But to be young was very heaven!" (10.108–9)—and the invitation in Swift's chorus is Byronically seductive, an echo of the exhortation near the close of "On This Day I Complete my Thirty-Sixth Year." In that piece, Byron, afire for Greek independence, asks, "If thou regret'st thy youth, *why live*? / The land of honourable Death / Is here—up to the Field! and give / Away thy Breath" (33–6); Swift, playing with a lexicon that also evokes nationalism and political liberty, makes a similar case in "New Romantics": "Baby, we're the new romantics," she cries, "Come on, come along with me / Heartbreak is the national anthem / We sing it proudly ... / The best people in life are free." But if the vibe of "New Romantics" is Wordsworthian-slash-Byronic, its atmosphere is Tennysonian, earthy and vivid. "[T]ired" and *late*—"we wait for trains that just aren't coming," Swift sings—the song's speaker and her compatriots "cry tears of mascara in the bathroom," and although they "hang back" at the club when "the lights and noise are blinding," they eventually *become* the machine that makes the music: "We team up / Then switch sides like a record changer." Obstacles and criticism are reimagined in Swift's chorus as the raw materials for an Arthurian dwelling—"[b]aby, I could build a castle / Out of all the bricks they threw at me"—and the song's bridge defines the new "romantic" as corporeal rather than ideal, as a place to be "take[n]" and "[left]" rather than a series of emotions to be felt or notions to be upheld: "Please take my hand and / Please take me dancing, and / Please leave me stranded / It's so romantic."

In *The Words and Music of Taylor Swift*, James Perone identifies in "[t]he best people in life are free" an homage to Elvis Costello's wordplay in "I'm Not Angry" ("There's no such thing as an original sin," Costello says) and, in "New Romantics" more broadly, an homage to the New Wave music of the 1970s and 1980s, some of whose affiliates and inheritors came to be known in the media discourse as the New Romantics. "The sense of fashion that was at the core of new wave rock can clearly be seen in the characters that Swift counts among her cohort," Perone argues (66), and although I wouldn't deny the logic or usefulness of that pop-historical analysis, I would quarrel with its completeness. There's no doubt that Swift purposefully engages pop's history on *1989*, which, Perone notes, was named for Swift's birth year and was clearly "inspired by the music of [that] decade" (66). As "New Romantics" asserts, however, "it's all in the timing," and Perone's commentary predates the release of "the lakes," in which the term "romantic" becomes an indisputable reference to the *literary* tradition associated with Wordsworth and his inheritors. I would suggest that "the lakes" finds Swift doubling down on—or, perhaps, finally recognizing and naming—the late Romantic vision that subtly informs her whole corpus, "New Romantics" included. Like "New Romantics," "the lakes" appeared as its album's final "bonus track," and although the songs' shared belatedness seems significant in its own right, more meaningful, maybe, is the fact that the term "romantic" appears *only* in "New Romantics" and "the lakes,"[5] notwithstanding Swift's longstanding interest in so-called romantic relationships and the trials that attend them. In other words, "romantic" appears to function for Swift as an aesthetic label that carries particular implications, and notably, it's not until the last movement of "New Romantics" that "romantic" becomes an adjective. The word functions as a noun—a kind of person—until the song's bridge, in which Swift sighs, "It's so romantic." Given the adjacent references to dancing and hand-holding, it would be natural enough, I think, for listeners to understand *that* "romantic" as small-r, as a judgment or characterization offered by a lovesick teen or, worse, an arrested adolescent, and I would argue, then, that "the lakes" functions as a kind of corrective coda to "New Romantics," simultaneously picking up where the earlier song leaves off and critically reexamining its central term.

By opening with the adjectival "romantic" embedded in a question—"Is it romantic how all my elegies eulogize me?"—Swift embarks in "the lakes" on a quintessentially *Biedermeier* quest to locate and then "preserve" (I borrow Nemoianu's term, cited above) the essence of Romanticism, the distillate of the movement. And in gesturing toward self-centered poems—that is, "elegies" that "eulogize me"—the question itself functions as the first in a series of references to easily identifiable high Romantic tropes (and, in the obvious Wordsworth pun, easily identifiable high Romantics): a distaste for urbanity ("I'm not cut out for all these cynical clones / These hunters with cell phones"),

---

There is no authoritative, searchable digital archive of Swift's lyrics. I turned for support to "Taylor Swift Lyric Searcher" (https://shaynak.github.io/taylor-swift/) and "Taylor Swift Lyrics: Search and Explore" (https://ts-lyrics.netlify.app/). The term "romance" does appear frequently in Swift's songbook.

a penchant for intense emotionality ("What should be over burrowed under my skin /
In heart-stopping waves of hurt"), and a deep appreciation for a nature's "peaks,"
"rose[s]," "auroras," and "cliffside pools." As that last catalogue intimates, however, the
Biedermeier—as opposed to high Romantic—quality of "the lakes" also lies in the
track's Tennysonian obsession with objects and environments, with a placedness so
intense as to render the senser indistinguishable from what she senses. "I want to watch
wisteria grow right over my bare feet / 'Cause I haven't moved in years," Swift writes,
and as the very title of "the lakes" suggests, place is everything in this meditation, which
reframes Romanticism as an immersive collection of sensory riches that includes,
ultimately, a lover. "Take me," Swift's speaker begs in choruses that recall the bridge in
"New Romantics," and although that phrase might, in isolation, evoke something like a
prayer or incantation, "the lakes" keeps the context earthy and, if not quite carnal,
distinctly companionate: "I don't belong, and my beloved, neither do you / Those
Windermere peaks look like a perfect place to cry / I'm setting off, but not without my
muse / No, not without you." This trip, those lines declare, will be an almost literal
version of Nemoianu's "organized tourism," since the place "where all the poets went to
die" will function for Swift and her travel partner as "a perfect place to *cry*." That line
about not moving for years is aspirational—"I want"—rather than practical, and having
sobbed at Windemere, Swift will return, alive and well, to the anxious modernity from
which, as her casual reference to "tweet[ing] it" suggests, her psyche and artistry cannot
be severed.

   I close, then, with my own bonus track (so to speak), in the form of a superadded
claim: Although contemporary literary critics have repeatedly evaluated Romanticism's
ties to rock music, I submit that they have attended insufficiently to Romanticism's
relationship to pop, the very soundtrack of anxious modernity. That lacuna is due in
part to a limiting definition of rock but also, I would suggest, a limit*ed* definition of
Romanticism—a definition that excludes the movement's *Biedermeier* finale and "the
more perplexed and disappointed musings, sentimentalities, aspirations, and ironies"
that it purveyed (Nemoianu 2). Consider, for instance, the introduction to *Rock and
Romanticism*, in which James Rovira articulates the Janus-headed vision that guides his
volume. The book, Rovira writes, "seeks not only to demonstrate the influence of
Romantic literature on rock . . . but to argue that rock itself is a late-twentieth-century
expression of Romanticism—an extension, continuation, partner, or doppelgänger of
this eighteenth- and nineteenth-century phenomenon" (xi-xii). In addition, then, to
proffering essays such as Jaaneke van der Leest's, which "studies the implications of
Mick Jagger reading portions of *Adonais* at the Hyde Park concert held just days after
the death of Rolling Stones's founder Brian Jones" (Rovira xviii), *Rock and Romanticism*
includes pieces that evaluate its title phenomena from the *other* direction—that argue,
in other words, that Romantic-period writers were, for all philosophical and practical
purposes, rockers in their own right. That rocker affect is anchored, Rovira suggests, in
what Robert Sayre and Michael Löwy describe in *Romanticism Against the Tide of
Modernity* as the Romantics' "'opposition to capitalism in the name of pre-capitalist
values'"—in, that is, "a 'collective mental structure' . . . characterized by a sense of loss
and a longing for unity . . . [experienced] in response to the interpellation of a capitalist

subjectivity" ([in] Rovira xiii). Like the post-World War II expressive mode that we call rock, Rovira explains, nineteenth-century Romanticism was a response to "[p]ervasive industrialism, widespread global trade, and the spread of . . . colonial enterprises" that generated "almost continuous" international political conflict (xv), and although he acknowledges that "'rock is every bit as . . . difficult to define as Romanticism," he observes that "most contributors" to his volume "[write] about artists who fall within the groupings of musical styles originating in the 1960s and 1970s known as 'classic rock.'" Rovira gestures to the book's breadth by listing those artists, a group that includes Bob Dylan, Mick Jagger, Leonard Cohen, Kurt Cobain, and others (xvii); essayists, he notes, were "allowed to define rock for themselves," and the rock "subgenres" (xvii) represented in his prefatory catalogue include folk, post-punk, grunge, and more.

And yet, Rovira's ostensibly flexible parameters and lengthy inventories of both artists and genres ironically capture the narrowness of the existing conversation regarding Romanticism's afterlives in twentieth- and twenty-first-century music. In addition to (largely) excluding female musicians, *Rock and Romanticism*—due, presumably, to a framework that *defines* Romanticism as a critique of global capitalism—essentially excludes pop, the subgenre of rock that, according to Nick Sloan and Charlie Harding in *Switched on Pop*, critics too often "dismiss" as irredeemably "corporate, a Marxist's nightmare" (7). Real rock, the argument goes, constitutes an authentic and durable response to modern subjective experience; pop music, in contrast, is "commercial fluff" designed to sell *now*, a "product of corporate strategy sessions and focus groups" (Sloane and Harding 7)—and therefore, some Romanticists might suggest, a mode at odds with Romanticism's anti-capitalist origin story. As scholars of late Romanticism have demonstrated, however, Romanticism did, indeed, go up for sale, its markers exchanged for and *as* currency in a variety of economic and social contexts. Put differently, Romanticism became *popular*, and in his overview of critics' recent treatments of late Romantic literature and culture, Brecht de Groote puts it thus:

> If late Romanticism marks the decline of one strand within Romanticism, it also names the growth of several others. The explosion of periodicals and para-literary publications—biographies that commodified literary lives for public consumption; florilegia of poetry marketed to previously underserved audiences; guidebooks to sublime and picturesque locations—demonstrate that Romanticism found new channels: a Romanticism may be seen to emerge that is perhaps best described as remediated.

"[C]ommodified," "public consumption," "marketed," "guidebooks": *Biedermeier* Romanticism is, perhaps, productively regarded as *pop* Romanticism—and Tennyson regarded as the Swift to Dylan's Wordsworth, to Jagger's Byron. The reality, as Swift's case demonstrates, is that notwithstanding its corporate affiliations and energies, pop music (like popular journalism, popular biography, and, yes, popular poetry) is neither easy to produce nor unengaged with contemporary (and, often, historical) aesthetic and political discourses. As a result, much of it is produced, Sloan and Harding argue, not by "[o]ppressive, reductive" mass-media functionaries who "[prize] commercial success over artistic integrity" but by "genuine artists" (7). High Romanticism aged into the *Biedermeier*, and anti-capitalist rock, in birthing "commercial" pop, arguably matured similarly. Swift, one of sixteen "genuine artists" evaluated in Sloan and Harding's redemption-minded book, embodies both the richness of the pop tradition and the fullness of historical Romanticism's paradoxical and "dichotom[ous]" life cycle. For those reasons and others, her work proves pretty hard to shake off.

Works Cited

Byron, George Gordon. *Byron's Poetry and Prose*. ed. Alice Levine. Norton and Company: New York, 2010.

Coleridge, Samuel Taylor. "The Eolian Harp." *Romanticism: An Anthology*. 3rd. ed.. ed. Duncan Wu. Blackwell: Oxford, 2006. 601–5.

De Groote, Brecht. "Change time: Timing and placing late Romanticism." *Literature Compass*, vol. 19, no. 6. (2022): n.p.

Ford, Thomas. "Atmospheric Late Romanticism: Babbage, Marx, Ruskin." *Romanticism*, vol. 27, no. 2. (2021): 187–200.

Nemoianu, Virgil. *The Taming of Romanticism: European Literature and the Age of Biedermeier*. Harvard University Press: Cambridge, 1984.

Perone, James. *The Words and Music of Taylor Swift*. Praeger: Santa Barbara, 2017.

Rovira, James. "Introduction: Rock and Romanticism." *Rock and Romanticism: Blake, Wordsworth, and Rock from Dylan to U2*. ed. James Rovira. Lexington Books: Lanham, 2018. xi–xxiv.

Sloane, Nick and Harding, Charlie. *Switched on Pop: How Popular Music Works, and Why it Matters*. Oxford University Press: Oxford and New York, 2020.

Spanos, Brittany. "Taylor Swift Channels Romantic-Era Poetry With 'The Lakes.'" *Rolling Stone*, 18 Aug 2020, n.p.

Sheffield, Rob. "All 237 of Taylor Swift's Songs, Ranked." *Rolling Stone*, 8 Jul 2023, n.p.

Tennyson, Alfred. *Alfred Tennyson: A Critical Edition of the Major Works*. ed. Adam Roberts. Oxford University Press: Oxford, 2000.

Thomas, Jayne. "'Echo and allusion': Tennyson and Wordsworth." *Wordsworth Grasmere Blog*, 9 Jul 2019, n.p.

Tucker, Herbert. *Tennyson and the Doom of Romanticism*. Harvard University Press: Cambridge, 1988.

van Cauwenberg, Zoe. "'Take me to the Lakes where all the poets went to die': Romantic Escapades in Taylor Swift's *Folklore*." *BARS Blog: Romanticism Now*, Series 24 Sept 2021, n.p.

Wordsworth, William. *Selected Poems*. ed. Stephen Gill. Penguin: London, 2004.

Wordsworth, William. *The Prelude: 1799, 1805, 1850*. ed. Jonathan Wordsworth, M.H. Abrams, and Stephen Gill. W.W. Norton and Company: New York, 1979.

6

Modernist Intertextualities in *folklore* and *evermore*

Jennifer Smith

Taylor Swift loves an allusion. Her 2008 single "Love Story" builds a narrative around a modern-day Romeo and Juliet, weaving a story of star-crossed lovers, complete with balconies, clandestine meetings, and scolding parents. Swift even manages to include a reference to Nathaniel Hawthorne's *Scarlet Letter* in the same song. Her 2017 album *reputation* repeatedly alludes to F. Scott Fitzgerald's *The Great Gatsby*; in "This Is Why We Can't Have Nice Things" she muses that "throwing big parties" and "swimming in a champagne sea" left the speaker "Feeling so Gatsby for that whole year," and in "Don't Blame Me," she plays with floral themes to invoke Daisy Buchanan in a song about a woman who used men for her "playthings" until she sincerely and *madly* (in all meanings of the word) fell in love: "I once was poison ivy, but now I'm your daisy." Swift's engagement with the Western canon is longstanding.

What is new with the release of the 2020 albums *folklore* and *evermore*, however, is Swift's move from allusion to intertextuality. More than merely referencing J.M. Barrie, C.S. Lewis, William Wordsworth, and the Lake District poets, these new albums usher in a sustained, complex engagement with literature that exceeds mere reference. Intertextuality describes "the *wovenness* of texts, their *interconnectedness*, their *web* of discourse" (Cheney 717). For Gérard Genette, intertextuality means "the copresence between two texts or among several texts: that is to say eidetically and typically as the actual presence" through quoting, plagiarism, or allusion "of one text within another" (1–2). And indeed, the power and appeal of *evermore* and *folklore* often depend upon meaning mediated through other texts. Specifically, Swift weaves direct quotations and oblique allusions to modernist figures including E.E. Cummings, Robert Frost, F. Scott Fitzgerald, Ernest Hemingway, and Jean Rhys. This constellation of modernist touchpoints imbues the albums with the alienation and fragmentation that so pervade modernist literature. Modernist writers loom large in these albums, and this essay explores the myriad ways in which they add meaning to her oeuvre. More than just referencing Gatsby's pool parties, Swift embraces the ironic reversals that inhere in modernist texts to build ambiguity into her songs. Modernist literature provides a productive *web* because our current moment has so much in common with the sea changes of the early twentieth century. The context of the pandemic and the rise of

#MeToo in the early twenty-first century resonates with the collective trauma and gender dynamics that permeate modernist literature. Specifically, she constructs anthems celebrating female authorship and ownership against the gaslighting that continues to diminish women a century after the modernist literature she so often cites.

The Stories We Tell Ourselves: Drawing on Ambiguity in Cummings and Frost

Swift's music holds broad popular appeal even as it explores how language can invite experimentation. In this, she has much in common with a poet she often references directly and alludes to obliquely: E.E. Cummings. As early as 2014, Swift was referencing the poet via Instagram—"For whatever we lose (like a you or a me), / It's always ourselves we find in the sea" (@ThrowbackTaylor). The caption accompanies a photo of Swift looking backwards across her shoulder, her body facing a grey-blue ocean scene. These lines conclude the 1958 poem "maggie and milly and molly and may." Cummings's poetry embraces idiosyncratic lowercase spellings and syntax, even as he often wrote in traditional poetic forms. Swift too embraces typographical play and traditional forms. Her 2017 album title, *reputation*, was similarly stylized, but the song titles within retained typical capitalization. The lowercase representation of both album and song titles in 2020 signals that the two albums are "sister records," a term she used to describe them in the Instagram post that announced *evermore*'s imminent release. The cursive lower case of the song titles creates aesthetic continuity across the albums and mirrors how she styles her name on these albums. Modernist poets loom large in her aesthetic rolodex.

Swift's allusions to Robert Frost's "The Road Not Taken" in "tis the damn season" from *evermore* and "illicit affairs" from *folklore* clearly show how Swift invokes modernist works to build ambiguity. Frost's poem is, perhaps, one of the most misread in all of literary history. It is a poem teachers and professors everywhere love to use to show the importance of close reading. In popular culture, the phrase and poem are often said to signify that taking unknown, unpopular, or risky paths leads to personal or social reward. The phrase has become synonymous with trailblazing individualism. The poem, however, tells a much more complex story. The speaker stands in a forest at a literal fork: "Two roads diverged in a yellow wood" (1). The speaker stands at the crossroads for a long period lamenting they cannot take both and reasons that the one they do take is better "having perhaps the better claim, / Because it was grassy and wanted wear" (6–7). However, within the same stanza, the speaker confesses, "that the passing there / Had worn them really about the same" (9–10). The speaker repeatedly considers why they took the road they did, only to recant that the other was its equal. In the third stanza, the speaker even consoles themselves that they will return and take the other path, only to immediately acknowledge that life gets busy, and we rarely return to such sites. All of this leads to the poem's final stanza:

I shall be telling this with a sigh
Somewhere ages and ages hence:
Two roads diverged in a wood, and I—
I took the one less traveled by,
And that has made all the difference. (16–20)

The speaker recognizes that the paths are really not much different at all and yet, with the passage of time, he will convince himself they were different and that the speaker is smart and bold enough to take the less popular route, which changed the course of their lives. The poem is not so much a celebration of trailblazing individualism as it is a melancholy reflection on the stories we tell ourselves about our own intention, agency, and boldness.

The poem suggests that our choices matter little, but we tell ourselves they matter greatly, a theme central to *folklore and evermore*. In "illicit affairs," the figure is working hard to cover her tracks. She masks her affair by telling her friends that she'd gone for a run, which explains why she returns "flushed." The road less traveled is the choice to have an affair; running serves as cover for the encounter. Here, the line refers to both the road she says she is running on and the choice to defy convention. The power of the stories we tell ourselves recurs when the speaker consoles herself that she has the power to stop at any time, even as an affair that began in "beautiful rooms," a metonym for romantic possibility, ends in "parking lots," symbolic of the mundane realities of an affair that cannot be sustained. The repetition of "tell yourself" resonates with Frost's speaker who consoles that their choice in path mattered. Here, it does matter, just not in the ways the figure in the song hopes for initially, as the chorus reveals that such an affair is "born from just one single glance" even though, ultimately, "it dies, and it dies, and it dies." The repetition of death invokes the popular notion of the orgasm as a little death and also the end of the affair. Frost's "The Road Not Taken" is about the impossibility of going back; the choice does make a difference in so far as return is elusive.

Within this context, the reference to Frost in "'tis the damn season" is even more poignant. Co-written with Aaron Dessner, the song is built on playful and partial verbal metonymy. The title subverts the conventional tone of the holiday season to create a melancholy mood. She sings, "the holidays linger like bad perfume." In the use of this simile and in the title, the songwriters' work is similar to Frost's, which often invokes homey and pastoral settings and images only to reverse readers' expectations. Much like Frost's "Mending Wall" or the window at the staircase in "Home Burial," those settings become the sites of intense alienation. The song follows a girl who returns home for Christmas, reuniting with a former love. The chorus repeats, with some variation in wording and repetition, four times, ending in, "And the road not taken looks real good now." The speaker laments the loss of this relationship, and, as she takes up her old bedroom, parks her car by their old school, and sleeps in like a teenager, she wonders about the path she did not choose, waxing nostalgic and longing for a romantic return to a more innocent time. The sincerity of their relationship comes through in her statement that his is the "the only soul who can tell which smiles I'm fakin,'" in contrast to her life now in Los Angeles with opportunistic, insincere friends. The song replicates a classic modernist move: juxtaposing the fake city life of its young adult protagonist (think Nick Adams, Nick Carraway, George Willard) and the sincerity of the hometown from which they emerged—only to reveal that life in the small town was just as alienating. By alluding to Frost, Swift and Dessner convey that the speaker is telling herself a story about her past life and choices. Their love is sincere, but it was never a love that would last, stating, "Time flies, messy as the mud on your truck tires." They have just this short time together, but she will be leaving again. The nostalgia does not lead to an easy or lasting homecoming. The ending is already written. Just as in Frost's poem, though, the song suggests that the stories we tell about our past decisions matter much more than the decisions themselves.

"Can't face reinvention": Fraught Love in Fitzgerald and Swift

The stories we tell ourselves about the past fuels Fitzgerald's *The Great Gatsby*, and Swift and her co-writers draw on the novel's recurring motifs and key scenes to imbue the albums with the same theme. In "This Is Why We Can't Have Nice Things," the allusions are clever but surface-level—appropriate for the 2017 album, which concerns the gaps between appearance and reality. In the 2020 albums, the lyrics build a more complicated intertextual relationship to the iconic novel. She invokes key scenes from the 1925 classic to construct ambiguity and comment on gender dynamics.

For instance, "happiness" is about a failing relationship in which the speaker must reconcile that she had been happy in this relationship; the song is about the paradoxes of a once happy, now doomed relationship. Happiness is possible "after you" and "because of you," claiming "Both of these things can be true." In many ways, Fitzgerald's novel is about this same paradox. Gatsby wants Daisy to leave Tom, and he even more desperately wants her to say she never loved her husband whose once "winning smile" had "become a smirk," as it does for the former love in "happiness." In the novel, Gatsby confronts Tom: "'Your wife doesn't love you,' . . . She's never loved you. She loves me.'" He tells Tom that "'She only married you because I was poor and she was tired of waiting for me. It was a terrible mistake, but in her heart she never loved any one except me!" (137). Daisy cannot console Gatsby with any confidence:

> "I never loved him," she said, with perceptible reluctance.
> "Not at Kapiolani?" demanded Tom suddenly.
> "No." . . .
> "Not that day I carried you down from the Punch Bowl to keep your shoes dry?" There was a husky tenderness in his tone. . . . "Daisy?"
> "Please don't." Her voice was cold, but the rancor was gone from it. She looked at Gatsby. . . .
> "Oh, you want too much!" she cried to Gatsby. "I love you now—isn't that enough? I can't help what's past." She began to sob helplessly. "I did love him once— but I loved you too."

Gatsby's eyes opened and closed.

"You loved me *too*?" he repeated.

"Even that's a lie," said Tom savagely. "She didn't know you were alive. Why—there're things between Daisy and me that you'll never know, things that neither of us can ever forget." (141)

This is a powerful scene, because Tom—although a reprehensible, racist, sexist, classist philanderer—is right: he and Daisy share a history that Gatsby cannot understand or erase.

Their child, Pamela, is the physical manifestation of that shared history and a reminder of what could have been but is not, a sentiment expressed across these albums but punctuated in "happiness." Earlier in that same chapter, Gatsby meets Pamela and Nick reflects, "Afterward he kept looking at the child with surprise. I don't think he'd ever really believed in its existence before" (123). Gatsby seeks a simple narrative—one he's been telling himself these last five years—that he and Daisy have been pining for each other. The girl, whom Nick calls "it" as if to reflect Gatsby's perception, disrupts that narrative. Just like the lovers in "happiness," Daisy and Tom have loved each other and made memories. Even though Daisy is furious with Tom for his affairs and his callous treatment of her, she cannot "make it go away by making [him] a villain" as the speaker says in "happiness." Swift uses alliteration and anaphora, "Past the blood and bruise / Past the curses and cries," to crescendo to her point: she "would've loved you for a lifetime," which, of course, does Jay of Daisy. Yet, Daisy stays with and even loves Tom. Nick explains, "They were careless people. Tom and Daisy—they smashed up things and creatures and then retreated back into their money or their vast carelessness or whatever it was that kept them together" (188). Their love is built on selfishness and antipathy, but it is a love that is theirs.

At two points in the song, Swift and Dessner directly reference *The Great Gatsby*. In this, the albums align with Genette's idea that intertextuality relies on the eidetic presence of one text in another. The first is "I hope she'll be a beautiful fool." The speaker is referencing her former love's next love. She immediately recants, "Sorry I can't see facts through all of my fury / You haven't met the new me yet." The song is about the revision of self required to leave an unhappy relationship and the speaker who cannot yet "face reinvention." This is Daisy's bind, too; she cannot really leave the money, status, and comfort Tom offers, because she desires these things, too. Daisy's faults, which are many, do not mean that she lacks self-awareness. Upon finding out that she gave birth to a girl, Daisy wishes that her daughter will "be a fool—that's the best thing a girl can be in this world, a beautiful little fool" (21). In a world where beauty, position, and wealth dictate women's opportunities, Daisy knows her world to be cruel to smart women; a century later, so too does Swift, as she makes explicit in the 2019 song "The Man." In "happiness," for one lover to wish it onto another signals that the best chance for happiness is obliviousness, which is what Daisy wishes for her Pammy. On the night she was born, Tom was "God knows where" as she "woke up out of the ether with an utterly abandoned feeling" (21). The birth of their child is not a moment of transcendent connection but confirmed alienation. Retelling it to Nick years later, she comments,

"Sophisticated—God, I'm so sophisticated" (22). Swift's song similarly treats the cynicism and alienation that attend such a relationship; by referencing Fitzgerald's novel, Swift and Dessner underscore this bitter acknowledgment in "happiness."

The second direct allusion to *The Great Gatsby* in "happiness" is the invocation of the green light on Daisy's dock beckoning Gatsby. The green light captures all that Daisy represents: love, purity, whiteness, status, and acceptance. Seeking it out from his own shore, he "believed in the green light, the orgastic future" (189). Just as the light in the book proves untouchable and ever elusive, forgiveness remains so in this song. The enchantment has worn off their relationship and, with it, her old self. Nick contemplates how much Gatsby loses when the dream of the green light shatters: "Possibly it had occurred to him that the colossal significance of that green light had now vanished forever. Compared to the great distance that had separated him from Daisy it had seemed very near to her, almost touching her. It had seemed as close as a star to the moon. Now it was again a green light on a dock. His count of enchanted objects had diminished by one" (98). This revelation occurs early in their reunion, as Gatsby walks Daisy around his home, with her admiring his shirts, views, and photographs. The reality of Daisy in his space could never live up to his dreams as he looked across the shore; in the song, the speaker cannot give him "the green light of forgiveness," but she hopes his new love will. Readers of the book must have their doubts, though.

The references to both Frost and Fitzgerald are about the ways in which women delude themselves—about their agency in situations that have spun out of their control. "The road not taken" underscores the intractability of the past, and "The green light" offers only empty promises. Bittersweet and ironic reversals suggest that the women at the center of these songs cannot, in fact, return and re-make their lives.

(Gas)Lighting the Match: Brontë, Rhys, and Swift

Swift and Dessner draw on a pair of interconnected texts—*Jane Eyre* (1846) by Charlotte Brontë and *Wide Sargasso Sea* (1966) by Jean Rhys—to dramatize how control and authorship are denied women. Through an allusion to an urtext of feminist literary history, Swift and Dessner construct a lineage that connects the plight of twenty-first-century women to nineteenth-century gender dynamics. In Brontë's novel, on the cusp of Jane Eyre's departure to Ireland, Mr. Rochester laments that she is leaving. He confesses, "I have a sometimes have a queer feeling with regard to you . . . as if I had a string somewhere under my left ribs, tightly and inextricably knotted to a similar string situated in the corresponding quarter of your little frame . . . I am afraid that cord of communion will be snapt; and I've a nervous notion that I should take to bleeding inwardly. As for you—you'd forget me" (215). Jane is in anguish over leaving Thornfield and Rochester, because, as she explains through sobs, with him she has "lived in it a full and delightful life,—momentarily at least" (215). This moment appears unquestionably romantic. Rochester professes his profound connection to Jane, and Jane states her happiness with him; however, his own positioning of himself as devoted and her as indifferent suggests the ways he fails to understand her. The violent imagery portends his mercurial nature. Moreover, the context for why Jane is leaving undercuts his romantic appeal. Jane thinks Rochester soon to be engaged to Blanche Ingram, but he insists it is Jane he loves and cannot live without. He implores her to marry, even though he is already married—not to Blanche but to Bertha, the "madwoman in the attic." Feminist literary scholars Sandra Gilbert and Susan Gubar took this formulation, in their seminal book of the same title, to explore how so much of nineteenth-century literature and culture only allowed women to be angels or monsters, a dichotomy that too often persists to this day and which Swift debunks by showing the range of female identification and expression. The tense gender dynamics of this invisible string play out in Swift's song.

In "invisible string," the chorus conjures Rochester's famous metaphor for their attachment, but the invisible string appears here as a question, rather than an emphatic statement. The chorus begins with a meditation on destructive and healing properties, asking, "Were there clues I didn't see?" Each time the chorus repeats, the adjective in front of time changes—from "curious" to "mystical" to "wondrous." The theme of the song seems to be how our experiences and mistakes lead us, ultimately, to the right person. The writers allude to Swift's own past songs—"Bad was the blood of the song in the cab," a reference to *1989*'s "Bad Blood"—and to her past loves—"For the boys who broke my heart / Now I send their babies presents," a reference to the birth of Joe Jonas and Sophie Turner's baby. The song seems like the surface-level reading of Rochester's invisible string—a romantic way to understand how past losses lead to current love. But the context of Rochester's quote and his person complicate any easy romantic sentiment in this song, a vivid illustration of the way intertextuality adds meaning to Swift's lyrics.

An interjected reference to Ernest Hemingway's 1926 novel *The Sun Also Rises* further reinforces the ambiguity. *The Sun Also Rises* ends with Jake Barnes reunited with his unrequited and unconsummated beloved, Lady Brett Ashley, who has been many times married and has recently been left by a young bullfighter. Jake and Brett seem to have an invisible string; they always find their way back to each other. At the end of the novel, seeking comfort, Brett says, "we could have had such a damned good time together." Jake responds, "Yes . . . Isn't it pretty to think so?" (251), and the novel ends. Jake knows that it is sweet to think they might have been happy together—had the war and its traumas not rendered their union physically and emotionally impossible. The story she is imagining is far from the reality; more than likely, they would have fought, cheated, and drunk too much, but Jake knows that it is "pretty to think" and so they ride on. This is the line that directly precedes Swift's reference to the "invisible string." Interestingly, the song also alludes to Centennial Park in Nashville and apparently refers to a trip she took there with Joe Alwyn in 2017. As such, fans read optimism and hope into the song, but the intertextual significations hint at something more ambivalent. She sings that "Gold was the color of the leaves," referencing back to the "single thread of gold" that concludes the previous verse and also suggesting the temporal setting of autumn, signifying the beauty that blazes before dying out. Swift and Alwyn's separation in the spring of 2023, after six years together and co-writing six songs across three albums, adds a bittersweet sundering of the string.

This ambivalence introduced in "invisible string" shifts to ominous foreboding in the song that immediately follows: "mad woman." If "invisible string" is Jane's song, "mad woman" is Bertha's response, exploring how mad women are created by those who call them mad, which is a theme Swift also explores in "last great American dynasty." According to Elena Nicolaou:

> In "Mad Woman," Swift identifies the cycle of how perception can alter a person's sense of self—as if perception were, itself, a form of gaslighting. The chorus of "Mad Woman" goes: "No one likes a mad woman / You made her like that." Then, once she's finally broken, she can be blamed, controlled, or hidden away in an attic: "And you'll poke that bear 'til her claws come out / And you find something to wrap your noose around."

Nicolaou explains how a woman's descent into madness is often narrated in advance and then justified by that script. In her recent albums, Swift has been interested in women who defy the labels that get ascribed to them. This is an interest Swift shares with *Wide Sargasso Sea*, which is a reclamation of Bertha Mason, *née* Antionette Cosway, from the ashheap of Thornfield Hall. Rhys's novel traces how madness was ascribed to Antoinette, through her mother's mental illness and through Rochester, who renames her and calls her mad, taking her from her home and locking her away in isolation. Christophine, the family's longtime servant, calls Rochester on his hypocrisy: "You want her money but you don't want her. It is in your mind to pretend she is mad. I know it. The doctors say what you tell them to say. That man Richard he say what you want him to say—glad and willing too, I know. She will be like her mother. You do that for money? But you wicked like Satan self!" (96). Christophine identifies that madness provides an easy excuse for a man to separate from his wife, and she rightly recognizes the ways in which doctors and her stepbrother—themselves patriarchal forces—cede to the authority of her husband, the rich Englishman. Antoinette is racialized, and there are implications in both novels that her mixed-race ancestry is seen as the source of her madness. Further, she sees that this is history repeating, stating of Antoinette's mother that "They drive her to it. When she lose her son she lose herself for a while and they shut her away. They tell her she is mad, they act like she is mad. Question, question. But no kind word, no friends, and her husban' he go off, he leave her. They won't let me see her. I try, but no. They won't let Antoinette see her. In the end—mad I don't know—she give up, she care for nothing" (94). Isolation, abuse, and the denial of their experiences all lead to Antoinette's fate. Madness is, to be frank, the only reasonable response.

The words "mad" and "crazy" repeat in various iterations in the above passages, showing how language brings madness into being. Here too, listeners and critics identify autobiographical dimensions to the song, as Big Machine characterized Swift as calculated and obstinate in her battle with Scooter Braun and Scott Borchetta over the rights to her masters, which Braun bought from Borchetta without Swift's consent or knowledge, for $330 million (Wang). She wrote the songs and initiated the wealth that generated from them but then was not originally permitted to play those songs at the 2019 American Music Awards or use past footage for the documentary *Miss*

Americana. In the framing comments before the song on *folklore: the long pond studio sessions*, Swift explains, "I was thinking the most rage-provoking element of being a female is the gaslighting. There have been instances of this recently with someone who is very guilty of this in my life, and it's a person who tries to make me feel like I'm the offender by having any kind of defense. I feel like I have no right to respond, or I'm crazy, or I'm angry. How do I say why this feels so bad?" Not being able to own and control her artistic legacy was infuriating, and yet when she expressed that anger, she was rebuked. Writing in a 2019 Tumblr post, Swift stated, "The message being sent to me is very clear. Basically, be a good little girl and shut up. Or you'll be punished." The conditions of Swift's artistic production—signing a long-term contract while still young and then not being able to control that property—echo Antoinette's crisis. The plots of both *Jane Eyre* and *Wide Sargasso Sea* hinge on women not being able to control their wealth, property, or legacy. Antoinette is a wealthy heiress who cannot inherit because of the laws and customs that pre-dated the Married Women's Property Acts of 1870 and 1882. Prior to that, married women forfeited all rights to property ownership, copyrights, and the ability to forge contracts and sue (Rhys 41 and 66).

The right to own and claim their creative work connects women artists from Brontë to Swift, dramatized in their adoption of pseudonyms. In the 1850 preface to *Wuthering Heights* and *Agnes Grey*, Charlotte Brontë explains the sisters' decision to publish under the androgynous pseudonyms of Currer, Ellis, and Acton: "we did not like to declare ourselves women, because—without at that time suspecting that our mode of writing and thinking was not what is called 'feminine'—we had a vague impression that authoresses are liable to be looked on with prejudice." Swift, too, has written under pen names, most publicly as Nils Sjöberg, which derives from two of the most popular male Swedish names. In a conversation with Paul McCartney published in *Rolling Stone*, she explains that she chooses to write under pen names occasionally to evade scrutiny: "when a pseudonym comes in is when you still have a love for making the work and you don't want the work to become overshadowed by this thing that's been built around you, based on what people know about you" (Doyle). Control over how and by whom women's art is produced and profited from is the backdrop for "invisible string" and particularly "mad woman." Swift responded to this lack of control over her artistic property by re-recording her earlier albums, rendering the original masters largely obsolete, thus stripping Big Machine of their power over her catalog.

Rhys's novel began from a similar desire to reclaim the narrative. In a 1958 letter to her editor, Rhys describes how, after re-reading *Jane Eyre* for the first time in years, she found that Bertha is a mere plot device and largely a disembodied voice off stage: "For me (and for you I hope) she must be right *on stage*. She must be at least plausible with a past, *the reason* why Mr Rochester treats her so abominably and feels justified, *the reason* why he thinks she is mad and why of course she goes mad, even *the reason* why she tries to set everything on fire, and eventually succeeds" (136–7). For Rhys, Antoinette must be fully human with agency, and she must be, ultimately, triumphant. So too with the woman at the center of "mad woman," who confesses, "Now I breathe flames each time I talk." In *Jane Eyre*, the women echo and mirror each other, splintering the idea of an autonomous self. The novel as a genre, especially *Bildungsroman* such as

Jane Eyre, is often thought to be a vehicle by which individualism is culturally defined and reinforced. The genre of the novel tends to flourish in places and periods that celebrate individualism; however, in *Jane Eyre*, the eponymous protagonist has a double, Bertha, who represents a threat to the novel's notion of the singular self. In Brontë's novel, Thornfield Hall must burn, and Bertha must perish for Jane to achieve selfhood. For Rhys and others, it is too high a cost. Rhys signals this by reclaiming the name she had, Antoinette, before Mr. Rochester anglicized and entombed her. *Wide Sargasso Sea* explicitly traces how Antoinette becomes a divided self, showing how, over time, Antoinette narrates as if she were not also the person doing the action. The traumas Rochester and her family enact upon her warp her memory and impulse control. Antoinette's alienation and fragmentation are hallmarks of of this modernist re-telling of Brontë's novel, and it's that sense that looms over both "invisible string" and "mad woman."

Swift's Modernist Era

The particular conditions of Swift's fight over her artistic legacy, combined with the conditions wrought by the global pandemic, made modernist works the most poignant intertexts for these albums. In 2021, *The Great Gatsby*, originally published in 1925, entered the public domain and spawned many editions, being not only a classic often taught but also addressing the disillusionment of our moment. In the explanatory interludes between songs in the documentary *folklore: the long pond studio sessions*, Swift describes how "epiphany" came to be. She had wanted to write a song unlike her others, rich with string instruments. She had been researching her grandfather who fought in the Second World War in Guadalcanal and who was never able to talk about what happened there. In living through lockdown, she realized that there were hospital workers, experiencing untold trauma, who would also never be able to speak of it. This inability to communicate loss isn't unique to modernist literature, but it is a heightened and pervasive feature of it, especially those texts that arose after the First World War. To treat the ways the pandemic made all of us witness to previously inconceivable loss, Swift and Dessner turned to writers who knew such loss well—whether it be from war, as it was for Hemingway and Cummings, both ambulance drivers in the First World War, or Rhys, who volunteered in the war effort, or from personal loss, as it was for Brontë and Frost, who experienced profound family losses. The ambiguity and irony that saturate their most famous works made it possible for Swift and Dessner to comment not just on the alienation that arose from loss and isolation but also on the very idea of what it means to make meaning of a life. From Frost to Fitzgerald, the modernists were curious about the production and consumption of art in moments of cataclysmic change, as is Swift. And by invoking fraught female characters from Daisy Buchanan to Bertha Mason, Swift places her 2020 albums in a "*web* of discourse" (Cheney 717) about trapped women whose experiences of reality are denied and whose choices are foreclosed. Intertextuality gives Swift a way to map these frustrations onto the sister albums at a moment of personal artistic turmoil and massive cultural upheaval. However, unlike Antoinette Cosway, she does not just burn the house down; she builds a new one.

Works Cited

Brontë, Charlotte. *Jane Eyre*. ed. Richard J. Dunn. Norton: New York, 2001.

Cheney, P. "Intertextuality." *The Princeton Encyclopedia of Poetry and Poetics*. Princeton University Press: Princeton, 2012. 716–8.

Doyle, Patrick. "Musicians on Musicians: Taylor Swift & Paul McCartney." *Rolling Stone*, 13 Nov. 2020.

Fitzgerald, F. Scott. *The Great Gatsby*. Scribner: London 1995.

folklore: the long pond studio sessions. Directed by Taylor Swift. Taylor Swift Productions, 2020.

Frost, Robert. "The Road Not Taken." https://www.poetryfoundation.org/poems/44272/the-road-not-taken. *Poetry Foundation*. Originally published 1916.

Genette, Gerard. *Palimpsests: Literature in the Second Degree*. Translated by Channa Newman and Claude Dubinsky. University of Nebraska Press: Nebraska, 1997.

Gilbert, Sandra and Susan Gubar, *The Madwoman in the Attic: The Woman Writer and the Nineteenth-Century Literary Imagination*, Yale University Press: New Haven, 2020.

Nicolau, Elena. "Taylor Swift's New Album *folklore* Is Teeming with Subtle Literary References." *Oprah Daily*, 24 July 2020.

Swift, Taylor. *Tumblr*. 30 Jun. 2019. @taylorswift. "I'm elated to tell . . ." *Instagram*, 10 Dec. 2020.

@ThrowbackTaylor. "8 years ago today, taylor swift via instagram: 'For whatever we lose (like a you or a me), It's always ourselves we find in the sea.' E.E. Cummings april 1, 2014." *Twitter*, 1 Apr. 2022, 10:01 p. m.

Rhys, Jean. *Wide Sargasso Sea*. ed. Judith L. Raiskin. Norton: New York, 1999.

Wang, Stephanee. "Taylor Swift Calls Alleged Live Album from Former Label 'Tasteless.'" *Nylon*, 23 Apr. 2020.

Part Two

Every Version of Yourself Tonight: Examining Gender, Sexuality, and Race

7

The Death of the Pop Auteur: Taylor Swift's Feminist Politics of Collaboration and Revision

Stephen Grandchamp

The late 1960s witnessed the articulation of two influential challenges to the privilege traditionally conferred upon the author: Roland Barthes's "La mort de l'auteur" and Michel Foucault's "Qu'est-ce qu'un auteur?" Whereas Barthes argues, "[t]o give a text an Author is to impose a limit on that text" (147), Foucault challenges the "author-function" to "imagine a culture where discourse would circulate without any need for an author" (138). Over the ensuing decades, these ideas would transform literary theory and criticism, with the line of inquiry initiated by Barthes and extended by Foucault wielding "a significant influence upon literary and philosophical theories of authorship" (A. Wilson 343). No longer could literary studies take authorship for granted, instead being forced to confront cultural and historical assumptions surrounding the concept at every juncture.

At the same historical moment, journalistic and scholarly discourse surrounding popular music began to solidify while privileging individual authorship through the category of pop auteur. And this concept—centrally influenced by cinematic auteur theory imported from France—continues to maintain cultural currency in writing about popular music to the present day. Its discourse centrally celebrates producers and artists for overseeing the songwriting and recording process. However, eminent pop auteurs overwhelmingly tend to be male, whereas female popular musicians who do not present the illusion of total control within the recording studio are criticized or pushed out of discourse surrounding authorship altogether.

This essay will examine the work of one of today's most popular recording artists, Taylor Swift, as a case study in challenging the notion of the pop auteur. I will explore Swift's work as a significant counterbalance to undertheorized canonization of male genius grounded in rockist concepts. By close reading Swift's lyrics, which tend toward metacommentary on songwriting and its critical reception, while also analyzing her open creative process—including many collaborations, as well as the release of demos, rerecordings, and voice memos—I will argue that she mounts a feminist challenge to the dominant discourse of the pop auteur. Swift reimagines the mainstream definition of the recording artist and, like Barthes and Foucault before her, insists that her audience no longer accept the concept of authorship as a stable construction. Instead,

Swift posits a process-based model of artistry in which auteur status is secondary to the joy of writing, performing, and collaboration. In doing so, she follows through on what Ron Moy identifies as a Foucauldian strand within contemporary popular music to "reflect upon the concept of authorship and ask us to reappraise our own individual value systems" (xii–xiii). For literary studies students, this analysis will additionally demonstrate the ways close reading and literary theory can be meaningfully applied in a context outside of works traditionally designated as literature.

There exists no single concept-defining text about the pop auteur that exerts overarching influence like François Truffaut's "Une certaine tendance du cinéma français" in the context of film. Rather, the concept creeps into the discourse of popular music journalism in the late 1960s and early 1970s to establish the auteur status of male singer-songwriters and producers. In analyzing popular music authorship roles in context of Barthes' problematization of authorship, Emma Mayhew underscores a crucial issue: "in the everyday world of the music industry and commercial profit, authorship is normally defined with little reference to the problematic and contested nature of the role" (152). In the following brief historical overview, I will sketch the contours of this uncritical application of auteur terminology with particular consideration of how the term "auteur" and the phrase "pop auteur" originate and retain male-skewing valuation in journalism and scholarship.

Though Keith Negus highlights writing from the early 1970s on Buddy Holly and Bob Dylan as early applications of auteur theory to popular music (611), and Gestur Gudmundsson, Ulf Lindberg, Morten Michelsen, and Hans Weisethaunet identify rock writer (and later Bruce Springsteen manager) Jon Landau in 1972 as having "advocated clear criteria of artistic authenticity that mixed the auteur perspective of film criticism with the folk and blues emphasis on roots" (51), the circulation of auteur theory within the realm of pop music has earlier—and, indeed, more haphazard—origins. A heretofore unnoticed early usage in a 1967 piece by Geoffrey Cannon in the British weekly publication *The Listener* concedes, "[r]ock music is in such a state of creative flux that, so far, any monolithic *auteur* theory seems inappropriate" (681). Yet, in a move representative of the concept's always-already-present—and therefore rather hollow—theoretical core, Cannon goes on to concede "that some rock producers . . . can be assessed in the same way as film directors" before ending with a final comparative gesture: "Like Jean Luc-Godard, Brian Wilson is a good reason to be alive in 1967" (682). If the auteur concept is "inappropriate" in the context of popular music as Cannon originally suggests, he nevertheless assumes a 1967 readership will appreciate more fully the work of male producers like The Beach Boys' Brian Wilson by comparing their artistic output with celebrated cinematic auteur Jean Luc-Godard.

Subsequently, in a context in which "authorial genius" becomes prominent in popular music marketing (Toynbee 30), journalists begin to deploy the term with high frequency. For instance, Steve Simels's 1974 review of Bruce Springsteen's *The Wild, the Innocent & the E Street Shuffle* proclaims Springsteen "a highly individual *auteur*," further praising him as "the first big American rock talent since John Fogerty" (92). It comes as little surprise that Fogerty of Creedence Clearwater Revival becomes the reference point for establishing Springsteen's pop auteur credentials because, as Roy

Shuker demonstrates, auteur status tends to be ascribed to male artists of the 1960s (69). Such references to auteur theory in popular music criticism also have an immediate and demonstrable impact on a readership in the early 1970s. A letter by Dennis Wilen published in a 1974 issue of *Stereo Review* stridently asserts Phil Spector's importance not merely as a producer but also in terms of his status as a "pop *auteur*" who "taught the world that records could, and should, have a unique sound" (15). This letter not only leverages the paternalistic language of pedagogy in establishing its claim of Spector's auteur status; it also posits an elusive artistry "that no one else" can recreate.

The term is also used to denigrate female recording artists and, in particular, Black women, with Dave Marsh deploying the term in 1972 while describing a compilation release as "thoroughly anti-auteur" (35). He at once celebrates the inclusion of "Locomotion" [*sic*] while belittling the song's Black female artist (Little Eva) in judging "the next dozen records she did were terrible, she'll never do another one that's any good at all" with the explanation, "she'll never matter any more or any less than her song does. She'll never be a heroine" (35). This backhanded compliment demonstrates critics withholding from women—particularly Black women—the ability to reach artistic heights. It further encapsulates a tendency toward expecting female artists to be the "heroine" of their lyrics, a trend still prominent in the later reception of Taylor Swift that interprets her lyrics as personal statements rather than as critically distanced and multidimensional.

More recently, Beyoncé's emergence as a celebrated auteur shows how this label continues to function as an undertheorized designation that is particularly problematic for Black female artists. Whereas Beyoncé's reception in scholarship of the early 2010s tended to neglect her artistry while criticizing her along economic lines for encouraging "her fans to buy all manner of commodities" (Cashmore 142) and for participating in "corporate-produced and -distributed media products" (Pullen 145), more recent work has tended toward acknowledging her as "an auteur—performer, songwriter, director, businesswoman" (Vernallis), or as someone who actively avoids the "lone genius auteur" designation and instead "thrives because and through a community of diverse women" (Li 107). Popular journalism has also mirrored this shift. Take, for instance, reviews of *B'Day* published in 2006, which sharply critique her songwriting (Finney), erase her work as a co-producer (Hiatt; Robinson; Mayers), or both (witness a review advocating, "One suggestion from me is that Beyonce take a songwriting class" [Joseph], while incorrectly crediting production on "Get Me Bodied" solely to Swizz Beatz). Contrast these write-ups with journalists' takes on Beyoncé from the 2020s: "pop's premier auteur" (Weinbender), "a conceptual auteur" (C. Wilson), a "pop auteur" (Richards). The fact that Beyoncé, a popular musician now nearly universally recognized for her control over her art, was withheld auteur status demonstrates the arbitrary application of the designation and how these fickle standards disproportionately critique Black women.

Such male-skewing auteur theory in the context of popular music also extends to scholarly analyses going back decades. In 1971, John G. Cawelti encapsulates the always-already-present core of auteur theory in a popular music context: "The methods of the *auteur* approach ... should prove a fruitful method for defining those patterns which mark the [*sic*] Beatles as *auteurs*" (267). Curiously, here The Beatles are already assumed to be auteurs, with the application of auteur theory merely reaffirming this fact. More recently in 2005, Virgil Moorefield places the concept of the auteur as one of the "three central developments in production" (xiii), arguing unambiguously that "the contemporary producer is an *auteur*" (xiii). At the same time, Moorefield's study also disproportionately highlights male producers. Such historical lineages typically overlook the work of female producers such as early pioneers like Anita Kerr (whose production and arrangement work in Nashville in the 1960s "has been given relatively little public credit" [Stimeling 158]) as well as modern artists like Björk, whose production tends to be ignored at the expense of male co-producers like Nellee Hooper or Matmos—a fact even Björk herself highlights in a 2015 interview (Hopper). Miles Parks Grier's explanation of rockism, "the jurisdiction straight white men exercise over matters of taste in popular music" (31), is informative in this context. While recognizing that "rock's archetypes have been race- and gender-specific" (32), he explains "that these raced and sexualized characters have incited visceral desires to purify, protect, and strengthen rock in relation to competing genres" (32). As a result, artists who are not straight white men and work outside of the narrow confines of the rock genre become critically marginalized.

As a female artist who participates in the songwriting and production process of recordings outside the narrow confines of rock, the question of authorship and, more particularly, the auteur label has long been a vexed issue in the reception of Taylor Swift. Laura Ahonen argues that the auteur designation in a pop context "requires that fellow artists, the media and audience members regard the would-be auteur's vision as unique and original" (81). At the same time, because of the auteur designation's male privilege, female artists like Swift have often been withheld such status in each of these contexts. For example, Mary Fogarty and Gina Arnold identify the popular doublethink in interpreting Swift's shift from country to pop, which "simultaneously heightened attention to the co-production of her songwriting and solidified her auteur status" (4). Whereas some journalists leverage the auteur designation to champion Swift's artistry and ability to collaborate successfully (for instance, Steacy Easton's judgment that "As much of an auteur as Swift is, she can mold her voice to a producer"), others deploy the term to denigrate her recordings (such as Jordan Sargent contrasting Swift's use of a "brand-assisted mass media campaign" with her "peers" who are "pursuing their own aesthetic visions as auteurs") or to disparage implicitly her commercialism (a 2011 profile by Lizzie Widdicombe judges, "Swift professes a kind of auteur approach to marketing"). Meanwhile, John Seabrook extends the auteur mythos by explaining that (overwhelmingly male) "hit makers" are "enormously influential culture shapers—the Spielbergs and Lucases of our national headphones" (8). In this register, Seabrook erases Swift's role in her collaborations by noting that producer and songwriter Max Martin has "become Taylor Swift's magic man" (8). Seabrook further provides a backhanded compliment in explaining that Swift is "an artist strong enough to stand up for her vision, but canny enough to appreciate his genius" (306) while judging, without elaboration, that Swift's collaborations with Martin "sound like anyone could have sung them" (306). Perhaps most telling of all, Vaughn Schmutz, Sarah H. Pollock, and Jordan

S. Bendickson's scholarly comparative analysis of journalistic responses to both Taylor Swift's 2014 album *1989* and Ryan Adams's song-for-song cover album released the following year reveal "the differences in the discourse used to assess the two versions of the album limit her aesthetic legitimacy by questioning her creative autonomy, her authenticity, and her artistic value" (211). Even when Swift's songcraft forms the entire foundation of a male musician's cover songs, he receives more positive artistic credit. A 2010 mixed-methods discourse analysis on popular music writing by Vaughn Schmutz and Alison Faupel provides a glimpse into the backdrop of such sexism: "gender significantly affects a performer's likelihood of consecration, leaving female artists significantly underrepresented in the popular music canon" (703).

Swift first deploys her lyrical resistance to this privileging of male auteurs in popular music, one which she will revise and expand on future releases, on her 2006 self-titled debut album. Tara Chittenden notes that while Swift's lyrics can "reinforce" idealized heteronormative dynamics, they can "also highlight the complexity of relationships" (187). Pushing this observation one step further, I contend that Swift's lyrics leverage surface narratives of romantic relationships to comment on the complexity of being a female popular musician. The debut album includes such coded gestures that form the basis of her career-long rethinking of authorship and gender within popular music. Most notably, "Our Song" embeds a final assertion of her artistry within a rural romance. The lyric begins with the narrator in a passive role within a frame narrative, riding as the passenger in the male love interest's truck and pondering "how we don't have a song." Later, the song ends with a twist emphasizing the narrator's artistry in the largely patriarchal context. Returning to the subservient position of "ridin' shotgun" in the boyfriend's truck, the lyric no longer passively laments the lack of "our song" but instead constructs a new one: "I grabbed a pen and an old napkin, and I wrote down our song." Here, the lyric celebrates the narrator's shift from passive girlfriend to active artist with the added irony that *this* song, the one the listener is hearing, is the one she wrote. Here, "Our Song" establishes the motif that Swift subsequently revises and expands of coding a romantic relationship narrative as broader commentary on the relationship between popular music authorship and gender.

At the same time, these feminist gestures of *Taylor Swift* take place on the terrain of the auteur, not so much destabilizing the category and its privileging of male authorship as attempting to accommodate herself to it. Swift begins to expand this approach on her sophomore release, 2008's *Fearless*, which intimates a politics of collaboration—an artistic practice typically obscured by the façade of male genius. Particularly noteworthy is "Breathe," a song cowritten and performed with another female recording artist, Colbie Caillat. "Breathe" sets up a scenario in which a relationship ends (whether platonic or romantic is left to the listener's inference). The repeated chorus, "I can't breathe without you, but I have to," expresses a painful paradox of the impossibility and inevitability of carrying on without the song's central relationship. Yet the inclusion of a second voice (Caillat's) enacts female solidarity in face of abandonment wherein the writing and performance of the duet instantiates a healing moment, making the "I have to" just a bit easier. Lyn Mikel Brown and Dana Edell's recent discussion of feminism in popular music with young female activists locates a critical element of Taylor Swift's effect on her audience in crafting tales that allow them to "feel connected" through the invocation of "empathy and solidarity" (70). In this respect, "Breathe" functions as an opening salvo for Swift's career, her first recording remaking the artistic process to celebrate the empathetic power of community and collaboration.

If *Fearless* begins to express Swift's implicit critique of the male pop auteur, 2010's *Speak Now* asserts her traditional auteur credentials. Featuring 14 songs composed solely by Swift without co-authors, *Speak Now* also features her as co-producer on every track. In addition to these credits that signal Swift's auteur qualifications, the album features the single "Mean," a veiled counterattack at male critics of her work that, like "Our Song," presents a superficial relationship narrative with an embedded critique of sexism. Most notably, it decries critics' tendency toward unfair assessments of female artists, or "picking on the weaker man." Indeed, while reviews at the time frequently note her songwriting credits on the album (sometimes with implicit surprise: "Its 14 songs were, *apparently*, all written by the 20-year-old herself" [Pearlman, emphasis mine]), they also incorporate gendered judgments of her "often angry, spiteful tone" (Ritchie) or for "indulging in such overt nastiness" (Hyden). Even reviews that celebrate her "mastery of song structure" (Keefe) sneeringly lament her inability to "write authoritatively about anything other than how great boys are or how much boys suck or how dreams about boys will take her somewhere better than where she is now" (Keefe). Such reviews tend to miss that Swift's relationship narratives like "Mean" are multilayered ruminations on the reception of female authorship in a popular music context rather than merely confessional lyrics in which Swift herself is the heroine.

Following this gendered rejection of her auteur credentials on *Speak Now*, Swift expands the lyrical approach of "Mean" to enact a sustained metacommentary on the reception of her lyrics in 2012's *Red*. For instance, "Begin Again" develops a relationship in which the narrator's male partner criticizes her inability to understand lyrics: "He always said he didn't get this song, but I do, I do." Swift's repetition of "I do" becomes a self-affirming statement of assertive feminism contradicting the partner. In the process, "Begin Again" sharpens the narrator's perspective of "Our Song" by not merely presenting the female narrator as uniquely capable of artistic acts but also highly aware of the gender politics of popular music reception. Elsewhere, the album's lead single, "We Are Never Ever Getting Back Together," presents a similar dynamic wherein the narrator declares to her partner, "I'm really gonna miss you picking fights," before explaining how he would "hide away and find [his] peace of mind" and assert his superiority in taste ("with some indie record that's much cooler than mine"). In these lines, the narrator first sarcastically laments her inability to remain above the fray by noting she will "miss" the partner "picking fights." Next, she flatly documents the partner's tendency to self-isolate to find "peace of mind." These lines set up the listener's expectations that the narrator has moved away from sarcasm to provide clarifying explanations. The final quoted line, however, reasserts the sarcasm of the opening by miming the partner's derision of female taste while listening to "some indie record that's much cooler" than the narrator's. This nested structure with a sarcastic frame heightens its power through contrast; indeed, by virtue of being forced to parse sentiment through multiple clarifying statements, the critique of the final line increases its impact by catching the listener, lulled into a sense of comfort by the preceding line, unawares. The final line also embeds a double meaning wherein the "indie record that's much cooler than mine" enacts a winking critique of popular music critics' tendency to dismiss Swift's own recordings as less "cool" than her indie counterparts.

In addition to expanding the relationship song as industry metacommentary, *Red* initiates a crucial new aspect of Swift's exploding of the auteur's status: the inclusion of early demos in the "Deluxe Edition." Whereas the mythos of the male pop auteur hinges on a belief that their genius is fundamentally inaccessible, these demos open the artistic process by emphasizing the work of revision. The listener can compare official versions with demos to analyze how songs evolved. Of particular note is "Red," the album's title track, of which Swift is the sole composer and co-producer, with its shifts in instrumental shading providing a glimpse into her revisions during the recording process. Although celebrated pop auteurs have released demo recordings (for instance, Bob Dylan's long-running *Bootleg Series*), they are typically made available decades after their genius mythos has solidified. By contrast, *Red*'s demos were made available on the album's original release date and therein provide a view of the artistic process simultaneous with the standard version. As a result, these demos aim not to bolster the distant inaccessibility of Swift's pop auteur status but rather to emphasize, even celebrate, an open process of revision.

The subsequent inclusion in 2014 of voice memos on the "D.L.X." version of *1989* deepens this emphasis on revision by decentering the credited performer and instead focusing on collaboration. Like *Red*'s demos, these voice memos offer early versions of tracks featured on the album, albeit with an added twist: Swift's commentary about the development of the songs. This commentary celebrates the joy of collaboration, hearkening back to "Breathe" while further launching an implicit challenge to the singularity of male auteur mythology. For instance, the voice memo for "I Wish You Would" traces the origin of the song to one of Swift's collaborators, Jack Antonoff:

[S]o we're hanging out and he pulled out his phone and goes, "I made this amazing track the other day. It's so cool, I love these guitar sounds." And, um, he played it for me and immediately I could hear this finished song in my head, and I just said, "Please, please let me have that! Let me play with it, like send it to me."

This process is notable for not only foregrounding collaboration but also in tracing the initial origin of the song to Antonoff rather than Swift. Myles McNutt interprets *1989*'s voice memos "as paratexts explicitly focused on Swift's labor, and on her place within gendered hierarchies operating within the music industry" (73). At the same time, McNutt holds that "the performative intimacy of these paratexts is part of a longer reclamation of authorship" (74) wherein the memos "unquestionably function as a rejoinder in an ongoing conversation about her authorship" (80). That may be, but also of clear significance is how these memos willingly share credit—even, as in the case of "I Wish You Would," for the origin of the song—and thereby call into question the qualifications of auteurhood. Swift does not fashion herself in the model of the producer-auteur or songwriter-auteur; rather, she brushes aside concern with these classifications entirely and instead celebrates the excitement of collaboration. In a cultural landscape in which "[c]ollaboration with other (usually male) producers, writers or performers often undermines a female performer's musical credibility" (Mayhew 155), these voice memos rethink the creative process in terms of collaboration outside the confines of the pervasive male-dominated auteur discourse. As Nate Sloan puts it, "Swift's exaltation of collaboration" demonstrates how "[c]o-writing does not have to mean the degradation of self-expression and artistry" but rather "can be a source of collective joy and discovery" (20). In a context in which "[t]he precise input of composers, producers, engineers, and back-up musicians is, most of the time, unclear to us" (Straw 200), Swift's voice memos provide an introductory step in offering greater clarity in these areas by decentering the credited performer and instead presenting pop music as a revision-based, collaborative process.

Swift's subsequent releases build upon this methodology to disrupt further the mythos of the male pop auteur. The deluxe version of the 2017 follow-up, *reputation*, transplants this approach into a new genre: a mock magazine that lampoons the sexism of music journalism. In the opening piece of this text (as well as in the liner notes of the standard version) entitled "Here's Something I've Learned About People," Swift laments the gender-based criticism of her work by noting that her "songwriting has been trivialized as 'oversharing'" before anticipating that "gossip blogs will scour the lyrics for the men they can attribute to each song." These defensive gestures against the sexist expectation that Swift is the heroine of her own songs underscore the combative lyrical posture of the album, which blurs the line between relationship narrative and feminist commentary. Indeed, while a listener could miss the declaration of female artistry in "Our Song" or the critique of male disregard for women's lyrics in "Begin Again," Swift's assertion "If a man talks shit, then I owe him nothing" on "I Did Something Bad" is such a direct response to critics that it actually threatens to subsume the superficial relationship narrative. Two years later, *Lover* continues *reputation*'s lyrical assault with "The Man," an update of the response to sexist critics embedded within "Mean." Like "I Did Something Bad," "The Man" features an outward relationship gesture ("They'd say I played the field before I found someone to commit to") that Swift pushes aside in favor of a critique of music industry double standards. In this dynamic, being a woman requires "running as fast as I can" while critics "shake their heads and question how much of this I deserve," whereas male artists' behavior is routinely treated in isolation from their musical "good ideas and power moves." Elsewhere, "You Need to Calm Down" addresses male critics in the business of "comparing all the girls who are killing it" with the rejoinder that female musicians now "all got crowns" so male writers "need to calm down." This lyric humorously reverses the common sexist command that women should "calm down" and instead emphasizes the sexist hysteria of male music writers.

Elsewhere, *Lover*'s "Deluxe Album" edition includes voice memos that squarely place focus on the process of songwriting, albeit with a novel confession of Swift's apprehensions surrounding collaboration. For instance, Swift prefaces the voice memo of "I Forgot That You Existed" with an account of the anxiety of creative partnerships, wherein she "wanted to come in with an idea that was pretty much all there" while collaborating with "two writers I hadn't ever worked with before" (Louis Bell and Adam King Feeney, also her co-producers on the song). In a different register, Swift's preface to the voice memo of "Lover" recounts "one of those magical experiences that you sometimes get to have as a songwriter," consisting of her composing the song "really quick in the middle of the night" and therein getting excited about playing it with Jack Antonoff, whom Swift "knew who would be the perfect person to produce it." Like the *1989* voice memos, these recordings make public the typically obscure intricacies of songwriting collaboration, not falling back into the mystique of the pop auteur but rather sharing credit and revealing the joys, and sometimes anxieties, of the creative process.

Swift's recent studio albums of new material continue to privilege the joy of collaboration rather than the public recognition of individual artistry. In fact, her pair of releases from 2020, *folklore* and *evermore*, each feature only one song credited solely to Swift. Provocatively, these albums sometimes feature songwriting in tandem with William Bowery, later revealed (in the 2020 documentary directed by Swift, *folklore: the long pond studio sessions*) to be a pseudonym for Swift's then-partner Joe Alwyn. By intentionally obscuring the collaboration in this manner, Swift playfully—and preemptively—strikes back at likely criticism of working with a non-musician who happens to be her boyfriend while also reaffirming the centrality of collaboration to her creative process. These releases, along with her 2022 album of new material, *Midnights*, also continue her work with Jack Antonoff, who variously serves as her cowriter and co-producer. *Midnights* further features "Snow on the Beach," a duet with Lana Del Rey, who emerged as a popular recording artist in the 2010s. Notably, the song (cowritten by Swift, Del Rey, and Antonoff) leverages its collaborative power to celebrate a Black woman typically withheld auteur status, Janet Jackson, with "Now I'm all for you like Janet" (referencing Jackson's 2001 recording "All for You"). This collaborative invocation of Janet Jackson as a reference point suggests a novel strategy in which direct allusions to underappreciated female artists both pay homage and direct younger listeners to formative influences who exist outside the biased critical framework of auteurhood. Elsewhere, "Mastermind" uses Swift's lyrical structure of relationship-as-authorship-allegory to poke fun at the very concept of auteurhood. With a narrator recounting that she is a "mastermind" who enacted all the supposed chance encounters of a relationship "all by design," the lyric crescendos at the revelation that the partner actually "knew the entire time" of this machination. Swift's narrative structure here playfully suggests the futility of auteur-fueled self-regard, revealing it to be a self-deceptive fantasy masking a process that was, in fact, collaborative.

Whereas these albums of new material from the early 2020s provide consequential revisions of Swift's previous explorations of auteurhood and collaboration, her recent turn toward rerecording and, indeed, expanding her previous albums under the guise of "Taylor's Versions" exposes the intricacies of the revision process from a new angle. Thus far releasing "Taylor's Versions" of *Fearless*, *Red*, *Speak Now*, and *1989*, these reinterpretations feature rerecordings of the albums' original tracklistings in meticulously recreated detail. These new versions also contain several previously unreleased "From the Vault" songs, some of which revise and deepen these albums' engagement with female collaboration. Take, for instance, the inclusion of "You All Over Me" on *Fearless (Taylor's Version)*, a duet with fellow songwriter and producer Maren Morris. Like "Breathe" with Colbie Caillat on the original 2008 release of *Fearless*, "You All Over Me" enacts a triangulated dynamic in which the lyrics directed at a past boyfriend ("I lived, and I learned, had you, got burned") become infused with feminist comradery when sung in harmony with Morris. More than that, the song's release in 2021 serves as a metacommentary on the difficulty of working in a male-dominated domain back in 2008, with "Held out, and held on, God knows, too long, and wasted time" standing in for Swift's efforts toward auteur recognition. This new version of *Fearless*, then, does more than merely magnify the listener's focus on collaboration by actually rethinking the original album's relationship narratives through "From the Vault" songs that speak to the futility of long-term efforts to receive recognition from men—whether in relationships or from critics. So while "the vault" as a concept is suggestive of sharing hoarded personal riches, these "vault" recordings actually reveal a wealth of shared ownership in the form of duets and creative partnerships.

 Red (Taylor's Version) builds on this unusual approach of recording previously unreleased songs with new collaborators. Swift duets with Phoebe Bridgers, a singer-songwriter and producer who emerged in a popular context during the nine years since *Red*'s initial release on "Nothing New." The song features a lyric enacting female comradery in the face of male critique and, as such, stands as another of Swift's metacommentaries on songwriting using narratives superficially about relationships. The lyrics also capitalize on the dramatic irony of the nine years between writing and recording as a means of exposing music industry misogyny. "Nothing New" speaks to a narrator's fears that her youthful "soaring through the sky" will later be tempered by sexist comments on her aging ("she looks like she's been through it") and reception ("what will become of me once I've lost my novelty?"). The inclusion of Bridgers, five years Swift's junior, as a duet partner meaningfully underscores how little reception of female artists has changed since *Red*'s release in 2012. The lyrics of "Nothing New" stridently demonstrate the ways then, as in 2021, artistic recognition—and, indeed, auteur status—is typically withheld from young female artists. At the same time, it functions as an encapsulation of Swift's feminist politics: first, using collaboration to push aside traditional notions of authorship and auteur status, and, second, revising previous works, in this case a demo from the early 2010s, to demystify the artistic process.

 If these new versions of *Fearless* and *Red* demonstrate a willingness to augment original tracklistings with "From the Vault" songs that underscore and complicate the feminist dynamics of the original albums, then *Speak Now (Taylor's Version)* goes one step further by directly revising the lyrics of previously released recordings. "Better Than Revenge," as originally featured on the 2010 original release of *Speak Now*, features a conspicuous instance of woman-on-woman sexual shaming. In the chorus, the narrator addresses her boyfriend to negate another love interest who is "better known for the things that she does on the mattress." The 2023 rerecorded "Taylor's Version," by contrast, revises these lyrics with the sexual shaming replaced by a well-worn metaphor: "He was a moth to the flame / She was holding the matches." Here the new version exhibits a novel tendency toward overhauling canonical lyrics as an act of feminist self-critique. Elsewhere on *Speak Now (Taylor's Version)*, the "From the Vault" track "Castles Crumbling" continues Swift's emphasis on duets (like "You All Over Me" and "Nothing New") to critique women's place in the recording industry. Singing with Paramore's Hayley Williams, "Castles Crumbling" comments on the perception of female artists as they age. Swift's verse observes, "They used to cheer when they saw my face," before anxiously admitting, "Now, I fear I have fallen from grace." This critique of the tendency to dismiss female artists as they age, nested within a lyric characterized by shame and anxiety, is lent further poignancy by the intertwined vocals of two women in their mid-30s who emerged in a sexist popular music context as young women nearly two decades earlier.

In each "Taylor's Version," as in the lyrical metacommentary and voice memos that preceded them, Swift's work exposes auteur theory's cultural blind spots in respect to gender. Rather than accommodate her reception to this sexist formulation, Swift's recordings rethink the assumptions of popular music authorship by positing a model in which collaboration supplants the mythos of the auteur and revision highlights the cultural mutability rather than timelessness of lyricism. Her body of work functions as not so much a counterpoint but rather a complete rethinking of authorship in a popular music context. In this way, her recordings follow through on the promise of applying Barthes's and Foucault's theories of authorship from the late 1960s in a popular music context, thereby undoing decades of solidification of the mythos of the auteur. But whereas Barthes hypothesizes the "birth of the reader" (148), and Foucault calls for "historical analysis of discourse" (137), Swift's approach is novel and idiosyncratic: she defines a model of artistry in which process takes precedence over finality, in which collaboration is preferable to the accolades of individual credit, in which the act of artistic creation is exposed, demystified, and celebrated. As we can see through close reading her lyrics, voice memos, and "Taylor's Versions," more than only arguing for the auteur designation for herself or other female recording artists, Swift sets aside the category entirely. Such a model of artistry can be crucial for students of literature and creative writing, providing them with a model in which their own work can thrive through collaboration and revision rather than be thwarted through contesting authorship or feeling the pressure of building an artistic persona. Instead, Swift's work imagines productive artistic spaces in which auteur status need no longer be a desired outcome.

Works Cited

Ahonen, Laura. *Mediated Music Makers: Constructing Author Images in Popular Music.* Finnish Society for Ethnomusicology: Finland, 2007.

Barthes, Roland. *Image-Music-Text*, edited and translated by Stephen Heath. Hill and Wang: New York, 1977.

Brown, Lyn Mikel, and Dana Edell with Montgomery Jones, Georgia Luckhurst, and Joneka Percentie. "'I Love Beyoncé, but I Struggle with Beyoncé': Girl Activists Talk Music and

Feminism." *Voicing Girlhood in Popular Music: Performance, Authority, Authenticity*, ed. Jacqueline Warwick and Allison Adrian. Routledge: London, 2016. 56–74.

Cannon, Geoffrey. "California!" *The Listener*, 23 Nov. 1967, 681–2.

Cashmore, Ellis. "Buying Beyoncé." *Celebrity Studies*, vol. 1, no. 2. (2010): 135–50.

Cawelti, John G. "Notes Toward an Aesthetic of Popular Culture." *Journal of Popular Culture*, vol. 5, no. 2. (1971): 255–68.

Chittenden, Tara. "In My Rearview Mirror." *Journal of Children and Media*, vol 7, no. 2. (2013): 186–200.

Easton, Steacy. Review of *folklore*, by Taylor Swift. *Parton and Pearl*, 25 July 2020.

Finney, Tim. Review of *B'Day*, by Beyoncé. *Pitchfork*, 7 Sept. 2006.

Fogarty, Mary, and Gina Arnold. "Are You Ready for It? Re-Evaluating Taylor Swift." *Contemporary Music Review*, vol. 40, no. 1. (2021): 1–10.

Foucault, Michel. *Language, Counter-Memory, Practice: Selected Essays and Interviews by Michel Foucault*, ed. Donald F. Bouchard. Translated by Donald F. Bouchard and Sherry Simon. Cornell University Press: Ithaca, 1977.

Grier, Miles Parks. "Said the Hooker to the Thief: 'Some Way Out' of Rockism." *Journal of Popular Music Studies*, vol. 25, no. 1. (2013): 31–55.

Gudmundsson, Gestur., et al. "Brit Crit: Turning Points in British Rock Criticism, 1960–1990." *Pop Music and the Press*, ed. Steve Jones. Temple University Press: Philadelphia, 2002. 41–64.

Hiatt, Brian. Review of *B'Day*, by Beyoncé. *Rolling Stone*, 21 Sept. 2006.

Hopper, Jessica. "The Invisible Woman: A Conversation With Björk." *Pitchfork*, 21 Jan. 2015.

Hyden, Steven. Review of *Speak Now*, by Taylor Swift. *The A.V. Club*, 2 Nov. 2010.

Joseph, Mike. Review of *B'Day*, by Beyoncé. *PopMatters*, 11 Sept. 2006.

Keefe, Jonathan. Review of *Speak Now*, by Taylor Swift. *Slant Magazine*, 25 Oct. 2010.

Li, Stephanie. "Introduction: Who Is Beyoncé?" *Black Camera*, vol. 9, no. 1. (2017): 106–13.

Marsh, Dave. "Looney Toons." *Creem*, May 1972, 34–5.

Mayers, Norman. Review of *B'Day*, by Beyoncé. *Prefix*, 18 Sept. 2006.

Mayhew, Emma. "Positioning the Producer: Gender Divisions in Creative Labour and Value." *Music, Space and Place: Popular Music and Cultural Identity*, ed. by Sheila Whiteley, Andy Bennett, and Stan Hawkins, Ashgate: Burlington, 2004. 149–62.

McNutt, Myles. "From 'Mine' to 'Ours': Gendered Hierarchies of Authorship and the Limits of Taylor Swift's Paratextual Feminism." *Communication, Culture & Critique*, vol. 13, no. 1. (2020): 72–91.

Moorefield, Virgil. *The Producer as Composer: Shaping the Sounds of Popular Music*. MIT Press: Cambridge MA, 2005.

Moy, Ron. *Authorship Roles in Popular Music: Issues and Debates*. Routledge: London, 2015.

Negus, Keith. "Authorship and the Popular Song." *Music & Letters*, vol. 92, no. 4. (2011): 607–29.

Pearlman, Mischa. Review of *Speak Now*, by Taylor Swift. *Yahoo! Music UK & Ireland*, 28 Oct. 2010.

Pullen, Kirsten. "If Ya Liked It, Then You Shoulda Made a Video: Beyoncé Knowles, YouTube and the Public Sphere of Images." *Performance Research*, vol. 16, no. 2. (2011): 145–53.

Richards, Chris. "Beyoncé's *Renaissance* Was Made to Last Forever." Review of *Renaissance*, by Beyoncé, *The Washington Post*, 29 July 2022.

Ritchie, Kevin. Review of *Speak Now*, by Taylor Swift. *NOW*, 4 Nov. 2010.

Robinson, Peter. Review of *B'Day*, by Beyoncé. *The Guardian*, 16 Sept. 2006.

Sargent, Jordan. "Taylor Swift Won't Let Go of Pop's Big Machine." *Spin*, 1 May 2019, spin. com/2019/05/taylor-swift-pop-music-me-essay. Accessed 3 Aug. 2022.

Seabrook, John. *The Song Machine: Inside the Hit Factory*. W. W. Norton: New York, 2015.

Shuker, Roy. *Understanding Popular Music Culture*. 3rd ed., Routledge: London, 2008.

Simels, Steve. Review of *The Wild, the Innocent & the E Street Shuffle*, by Bruce Springsteen. *Stereo Review*, (Apr. 1974): 92.

Sloan, Nate. "Taylor Swift and the Work of Songwriting." *Contemporary Music Review*, vol. 40, no. 1. (2021): 11–26.

Smith, Tracey. "Taylor Swift on 'Lover' and Haters." *CBS Sunday Morning*, 25 Aug. 2019, cbsnews.com/news/taylor-swift-on-lover-and-haters. Accessed 27, Sept. 2022.

Stimeling, Travis D. *Nashville Cats: Record Production in Music City*. Oxford University Press: Oxford, 2020.

Schmutz, Vaughn, and Alison Faupel. "Gender and Cultural Consecration in Popular Music." *Social Forces*, vol. 89, no. 2. (2010): 685–707.

Schmutz, Vaughn, Sarah H. Pollock, and Jordan S. Bendickson. "Gender and Critical Evaluation in Popular Music." *Gender and the Media: Women's Places*, ed. Marcia Texler Segal and Vasilikie Demos. Emerald: Bingley, 2018. 197–216.

Straw, Will. "Authorship." *Key Terms in Popular Music and Culture*, ed. Bruce Horner and Thomas Swiss, Blackwell: Oxford, 1999. 199–208.

Toynbee, Jason. *Making Popular Music: Musicians, Creativity and Institutions*. Arnold: London, 2000.

Vernallis, Carol. "Beyoncé's Overwhelming Opus; or, the Past and Future of Music Video." *Film Criticism*, vol. 41, no. 1. (2017).

Weinbender, Nathan. "As Pop's Premier Auteur, Beyonce [*sic*] Turns *Black Is King* Into a Gorgeous Platform for Up-and-Coming Artists." *Inlander*, 6 Aug. 2020.

Widdicombe, Lizzie. "You Belong With Me: How Taylor Swift Made Teen Angst Into a Business Empire." *The New Yorker*, 3 Oct. 2011.

Wilen, Dennis. "Auteur! Auteur!" Letter. *Stereo Review*, (August 1974), 15.

Wilson, Adrian. "Foucault on the 'Question of the Author': A Critical Exegesis." *The Modern Language Review*, vol. 99, no. 2. (2004): 339–63.

Wilson, Carl. "Can Beyoncé Go Back to Just Being a Pop Star?" *Slate*, 1 Aug. 2022.

.

8

"No one likes a mad woman": The Crazy Ex-Girlfriend Trope and/as Feminist Resistance in Taylor Swift's Music and Mythology

Ryanne Kap

Introduction (Taylor's Version)

In August of 2019, Taylor Swift confirmed her plan to re-record her first six albums. Following the sale of Swift's former record label to Scooter Braun, which made him the owner of her original masters, Swift explained via Tumblr post that she was a victim of Braun's "incessant, manipulative bullying" and lamented the loss of her musical legacy to "someone who tried to dismantle it." Since she still owns the publishing rights to her songs, Swift decided to reclaim her legacy through the re-recordings under her new label, Republic Records, beginning in 2021 with *Fearless*. Each re-recorded album has been released with the suffix "Taylor's Version," clearly demarcating the records as an assertion of her ownership and self-possession; they also include previously unreleased "From the Vault" tracks. From "Mr. Perfectly Fine" to "All Too Well (10 Minute Version)," these songs have provided new insights into past relationships as well as Swift's personal and public image.

In addition to emphasizing the importance of artists' rights to their own work, Swift writes that when Scott Borchetta sold her back catalogue to Braun, "He knew what he was doing; they both did. Controlling a woman who didn't want to be associated with them. In perpetuity." Throughout her career, Swift has shared the difficulties of being a woman in the music industry through public speeches and interviews. She is also outspoken about the importance of writing her own songs; when critics claimed she was too dependent on cowriters, Swift wrote the entirety of *Speak Now* alone. Swift's music is her "life's work," her legacy—a medium in which she articulates the inner workings of her personal life and grapples with her positionality both as a woman and as a world-famous singer. The reality of two powerful men threatening her legacy echoes the timeless struggle of women fighting for the rights to their own self-definition and self-assertion.

Such was the essential conflict staged in the work of women writers in the Victorian era. As Sandra M. Gilbert and Susan Gubar argue in *The Madwoman in the Attic*, the literature of this time represented a concerted effort by women to resist the patriarchal structures which sought to limit their self-expression. Women found themselves restrained by male writers to either side of the angel-monster binary, which posited that a woman was either a pure, virginal, selfless angel who existed only to please and placate men, or else an irreverent, promiscuous monster who dared to express her own desires rather than exhibit the "angelic humility . . . for which she was designed" (28). Swift herself became monstrous in the public eye due to the personal nature of her songwriting and the intimate details she revealed about former boyfriends. As hits like "Forever and Always" and "Back to December" shed light on her past romantic relationships, Swift became known as a crazy ex-girlfriend obsessed with airing her exes' dirty laundry. In 2014, Swift released "Blank Space," a song that challenged the image of the crazy ex-girlfriend through satirical lyrics and an equally hyperbolic music video. In several interviews beforehand, she spoke out against the label and its sexist connotations:

> For a female to write about her feelings . . . and then be portrayed as some clingy, insane, desperate girlfriend in need of making you marry her and have kids with her, I think that's taking something that potentially should be celebrated—a woman writing about her feelings in a confessional way—that's taking it and turning it and twisting it into something that is frankly a little sexist. ("Taylor Swift's Telltale Heart")

Of course, a woman being demonized for outwardly expressing her emotions is hardly unique to the present day. The trope of the crazy ex-girlfriend descends from the Victorian trope of the madwoman in the attic, in the sense that it suggests women are inherently hysterical and their emotions are either overreactions or symptoms of psychosis. Investigating the trope of the crazy ex-girlfriend is, then, an investigation into femininity, as it has been conceived from the Victorian era to today—what is a woman allowed to be? Why is the crazy ex-girlfriend such a betrayal of this ideal? What kind of freedom can be found in embodying her?

This chapter analyzes Swift's attempts to (re)construct her image through her songwriting, particularly concerning her reputation as a crazy ex-girlfriend and the representation of female hysteria and rage. What does it mean for Swift to write herself in this way, especially as she extends an invitation for listener/fan analysis? Specifically, I position Swift's methodology as a singer-songwriter in relation to the women writers of the Victorian era, specifically in the context of reacting to and against the demonization of mad women/crazy ex-girlfriends. In their discussion of the creative process from a woman's perspective, Gilbert and Gubar argue that before a woman writer can gain literary autonomy, she "must examine, assimilate, and transcend the extreme images of 'angel' and 'monster' which male authors have generated for her"; she must "kill the aesthetic ideal through which [she herself has] been 'killed' into art" (17). I aim to explore how Swift, as a modern analogue of these women writers, strives toward the same kind of autonomy by engaging with the angel-monster binary and renegotiating the boundaries of femininity in the public sphere.

"No One Likes a Mad Woman": Victorian Literature and the Crazy Ex-Girlfriend

To situate the "crazy ex-girlfriend" in a historical context, I turn to the nineteenth-century figure of the madwoman, which emerged as a feminist critique of male writers' representations of women. As men dominated the literary landscape of the 1800s, they had free rein to create and perpetuate their own reductive images of women. Without the ability to write against these alternative fictions, women became "reduced to *mere* properties, to characters and images imprisoned in male texts [and] generated solely . . . by male expectations and designs" (Gilbert and Gubar 12). Bolstered by literary precedents which established men as the creators of women (i.e. Adam's creation of Eve), male authorship became synonymous with male ownership over women. As women writers sought to free themselves from the constraints of the male imagination, they employed the trope of the madwoman to mirror their own natures; by "projecting their rebellious impulses not into their heroines but into mad or monstrous women," they could "come to terms with their own uniquely female feelings of fragmentation" (Gilbert and Gubar 78).

The "madness" of the madwoman is rooted in the nineteenth-century categories of mental illness, which "encompassed purportedly functional disorders like hysteria, hypochondriasis, and neurasthenia and permanent conditions like insanity and senile dementia" (Conti 144). However, the diagnosis of mental disorders was inordinately gendered by Victorian physicians into apparent "male and female mental illnesses," to the extent that "in the mid-1800s, the public face of insanity morphed from the raging, combative male to the emotionally vulnerable but sexually aggressive female" (146). Combined with literary representations of mad female characters, women became pathologically emotional in the cultural imagination. Thus, it is no great leap to view the crazy ex-girlfriend as a modern manifestation of the madwoman.

As Samantha Pergadia demonstrates in her article "The Manic Pixie Dream Girl in the Attic: On Netflix's *Love is Blind*," the crazy ex-girlfriend is one of many pop culture tropes that take their cues from the Victorian era. Pergadia explores how reality dating television shows adhere to the famous marriage plot represented in novels such as Charlotte Brontë's *Jane Eyre* (1847), Jane Austen's *Pride and Prejudice* (1813), and George Eliot's *Middlemarch* (1872). In doing so, she also traces the origins of the crazy ex-girlfriend to the Victorian era, citing Bertha Mason, Rochester's wife in *Jane Eyre*, as "the exiled 'crazy ex-girlfriend' . . . kept as a 'madwoman in the attic.'" Bertha haunts the romance between Jane and Rochester, appearing apparition-like in Jane's room in the weeks leading up to the couple's wedding. The strange woman proceeds to rip Jane's veil in two, her machinations made clear when Rochester reveals her as the scorned woman whom he was "cheated" into marrying (Brontë 340).

When Jane finally meets Bertha in the light of day, the other woman blurs the line between human and animal. As she watches the monstrous figure run back and forth, Jane narrates, "What it was, whether beast or human being, one could not, at first sight, tell: it grovelled, seemingly, on all fours; it snatched and growled like some strange wild animal: but it was covered with clothing, and a quantity of dark, grizzled hair, wild as a mane, hid its head and face" (341). When Bertha finally emerges into full humanity, it is as "a big woman, in stature almost equalling her husband, and corpulent besides"; when Rochester wrestles with her, she "show[s] virile force" and "more than once ... almost throttle[s] him" (342). Bertha's unruliness presents a threat not only to Jane but to Rochester and the gendered status quo—consequently, she is kept locked away in the attic, although she escapes her confines and sets fire to the house. Yet her escape is not triumphant; she jumps to her death from the roof, with the innkeeper callously confirming she is as "dead as the stones on which her brains and blood were scattered" (492). This brutal end is the cost of madness, of breaking the code that dictates how women must behave. Bertha is the monster to Jane's angel, the punished wife rather than the happy wife, yet Gilbert and Gubar also suggest that she is Jane's "truest and darkest double," an expression of the latter's repressed anger and emotionality (360).

The movement toward resisting male definitions of womanhood began with a different kind of internalization, with women writers such as Mary Elizabeth Coleridge "alternately defining themselves as angel-women or monster-women," thus falling into either self-imprisonment "in the glass coffins of patriarchy" or "fiery and suicidal tarantellas out of the looking glass" (44) not dissimilar to Bertha's grisly end. Yet as the eighteenth century drew to a close, women writers turned to "conceiving fictional worlds in which patriarchal images and conventions were severely, radically revised" (44). I argue that Swift, through her engagement with the modern trappings of the crazy ex-girlfriend, demonstrates a similar model of writing first within and then against reductive stereotypes; here, it is songwriting that enables the same kind of autonomy and self-representation by acting as a form of healing and resistance.

"Darling I'm a Nightmare Dressed Like a Daydream": The Swiftian Spectrum of Angel to Monster

Regarding the anxieties of women writers in the nineteenth century, Gilbert and Gubar ask, "What does it mean to be a woman writer in a culture whose fundamental definitions of literary authority are, as we have seen, both overtly and covertly patriarchal?" (45–6). Part of the answer lies in the reactionary writing with which women writers strove to represent themselves. Yet, as Gilbert and Gubar caution, "the images of 'angel' and 'monster' have been so ubiquitous throughout literature by men that they have also pervaded women's writing to such an extent that few women have definitively 'killed' either figure" (17). The angel-monster binary is often internalized rather than fully escaped, since "for the female artist the essential process of self-definition is complicated by all those patriarchal definitions that intervene between herself and herself" (17). Similarly, Swift's early career marks an uncritical engagement with and reflection of the angel-monster binary. However, by tracing the evolution of her representation of femininity, and in particular female rage, it becomes evident that Swift's lyricism seeks to actively redefine herself on her own terms.

In an article investigating Swift's representation of "authentic" American girlhood, Adriane Brown discusses the construction of her persona pre-2012, observing that Swift "cultivated a visual image of sweet wholesomeness by wearing soft dresses and pastel colours—often white—in real life, in images on her website, and in her music videos, bolstering her image of demure white femininity, frequently in opposition to other girls" (166). In "Fifteen," Swift describes how her best friend Abigail "gave everything she had to a boy who changed his mind"; meanwhile, Swift establishes herself "as a 'proper girl', one who achieves popularity and happiness through avoiding 'inappropriate' influences (such as parties or sexually active boys) and through maintaining an image of ultra-feminine innocence" (Brown 167). Yet this innocence quickly came into question after her breakup with Joe Jonas in 2008. Swift infamously exposed Jonas on *The Ellen DeGeneres Show* as "the guy who broke up with [her] over the phone in 27 seconds" (Lindsay). Although Swift later regretted "put[ting] Joe Jonas on blast," the intentional stoking of her own breakup drama cemented her reputation as a crazy ex. An entry in Urban Dictionary from 2009 defines "Taylor Swift Syndrome" as "a syndrome [which] girls can get after being recently dumped by their boyfriends." According to the user, symptoms include "wanting revenge," "being clingy," and "talking non-stop about your [e]x on a tv show."

"Better Than Revenge," released on 2010's *Speak Now*, also targeted Jonas's girlfriend, actress Camilla Belle. The chorus declares, "She's not a saint and she's not what you think, she's an actress / She's better known for the things that she does on the mattress." Swift paints herself as a victim whose boyfriend was "stolen" by this new woman, whom she shames for her promiscuous behavior, her apparent ego, and even her vintage dresses. "Better Than Revenge" has since been criticized for its misogynistic tone, earning a reputation as Swift's "slut-shaming" song (Tinubu). Her portrayal of the other woman echoes the more subtly sexist "You Belong With Me," in which Swift reinforces her image of purity by defining herself in opposition to promiscuity. Whereas her crush's brunette girlfriend "wears short skirts," the blonde Swift "wear[s] T-shirts." Notably, in the music video Swift plays both the innocent speaker of the song (Blonde Swift) as well as the antagonistic girlfriend (Brunette Swift). Blonde Swift is wholesome, down-to-earth, and approachable; she literally lives next door to her love interest. Conversely, Brunette Swift is self-obsessed, cold, and openly sexual—in one scene, Brunette Swift interrupts a tender moment between Blonde Swift and the love interest; after he gets into Brunette Swift's car, she grabs his head and kisses him while making direct eye contact with the dejected Blonde Swift. In doing so, she weaponizes her sexuality against the chaste protagonist of the song.

Swift may be performing both roles, but the character of the other woman is obviously meant to be the real act. Outfitted in tight-fitting clothes and an ill-fitting wig, she is the monster to Swift's angel. Thus, in both "You Belong With Me" and "Better Than Revenge," Swift uncritically reproduces the very patriarchal dichotomies that have perpetuated the trope of the crazy ex-girlfriend. But rather than protecting her from sexist labels, this early work only created a higher pedestal from which she eventually fell.[1] For younger female fans, Swift's continual positioning of herself as the subject of her own songs created a comforting sense of relatability and authenticity, as enabled by "her status as a white, middle class, heterosexual, normatively feminine girl" (Brown 162). But as Swift's music and rising fame continually invited speculation about her love life, her confessional style was often criticized for being attention-seeking, petty, and ultimately crazy.

"Blank Space" emerged as Swift's response to the media's increasingly critical view of her as a serial dater who, as she summarizes in an interview with *People*, "only writes songs to get emotional revenge on guys" (Maslow). The speaker of the song is a fictional persona based on the qualities the media ascribed to her; referring to the music video, Swift explained, "I created this whole character, and I had fun doing it." Thus, "Blank Space" and its accompanying music video are notable as Swift's most intentional performance of/as the crazy ex-girlfriend, exposing her deliberate deconstruction of her public image—an image which, notably, had already evolved from the innocent teen girl-next-door to a more mature, slightly more (openly) sexual woman in her twenties. As the boy-crazy serial dater, Swift's speaker addresses a potential love interest as her "next mistake," calls herself "a nightmare dressed like a daydream," and declares, "Got a long list of ex-lovers / They'll tell you I'm insane / But I've got a blank space, baby / And I'll write your name" ("Blank Space").

Swift does not split herself into the good girl or the bad girl but rather creates a character to inhabit, one which shields her from critiques of her femininity but also pokes fun at the version of womanhood deemed socially acceptable. This creation echoes Gilbert and Gubar's conceptualization of the madwoman as a creature conjured by female authors to "come to terms with their own uniquely female feelings of fragmentation, their own keen sense of the discrepancies between what they are and what they are supposed to be" (78). Accordingly, over the course of the music video, Swift shifts from appearing poised and "ladylike" as she and her love interest engage in picturesque activities (i.e. riding horses, picnicking) to "screaming, crying," burning clothes, stabbing a cake, smashing a car, and smiling devilishly as a new love interest appears and the cycle begins again. By figuratively and literally embodying the crazy ex-girlfriend on her own terms, Swift establishes agency and autonomy by satirizing the outsized criticisms of her dating life. Rather than merely identifying with a patriarchal ideal, Swift actively challenges and undermines it.

Here, I suggest a resonance between Swift and another iconic female figure portrayed as a calculating man-eater—Rebecca "Becky" Sharp of William Makepeace Thackeray's *Vanity Fair* (1847). Becky's scheming and manipulations earn her the comparison to "fiendish marine cannibals" (Thackeray 619); by the novel's conclusion, her husband is dead under suspicious circumstances, and she is wealthy but socially

---

[1] from *evermore*'s "long story short": "And I fell from the pedestal / right down the rabbit hole / Long story short, it was a bad time."

isolated. As Ana Moya notes, her desire for power, "within Victorian identity politics, turns her into a monstrous creature" (80) who naturally must be punished. Moya links this monstrousness to Becky's assumed masculinity; as a woman who "is ambitious, independent, clever, self-made, and uses her body to meet her ends," she "subverts the Victorian ideal of femininity to impersonate what Judith Halberstam refers to as the female masculine, a man (in cultural terms) in a woman's body" (80).

While not written by a woman, the character of Becky—and the demonization she endures for daring to be as ambitious as a man—clarifies the struggle of a woman fashioning her own identity in the world of men, one which Swift addressed head-on in 2019 in "The Man." Swift literalizes the double standards for men and women by doubling herself, but this time as a man. The conceit of the song sees Swift exploring the life of this alternate self; alluding to criticisms of her dating life, she notes, "They'd say I played the field before I found someone to commit to / And that would be okay for me to do / Every conquest I had made would make me more of a boss to you." Male Swift, portrayed by Swift in prosthetics in the music video, is fairly monstrous—he smokes and manspreads on a crowded subway car, urinates in the station, and throws a fit on the tennis court upon losing to an opponent. As the song ends and he walks off the tennis court, Swift appears as the director and faces her double of a different nature. Over the credits, mirrored images show her transformation into "The Man." In a variation on the looking glass which traps women into the roles that men demand they inhabit, Swift literally inhabits a male subjectivity to mirror herself in/through the monstrousness of toxic masculinity and reflect its horrors back to us. Through the conventions of pop music, she makes her message ubiquitous. As Swift explained in an interview with *Billboard*, "I wanted to make it catchy for a reason—so that it would get stuck in people's heads, [so] they would end up with a song about gender inequality stuck in their heads. And for me, that's a good day" (Lipshutz).

In 2020, Swift took a much different approach to representing her experiences of sexism. "mad woman," a stripped-down ballad with scathing lyrics sung in a menacing lower register, explores the emotional toll of gaslighting and allows Swift to express a level of rage previously expressed through ironic humor ("The Man") or petty vengeance ("Look What You Made Me Do"). In her analysis of the *reputation* tour performances, Gina Arnold notes a frustrating dichotomy within Swift's public persona, arguing that while Swift "appears to enact the perfect model of feminine behaviour ... her songs themselves often express deep personal dissatisfaction, a sense of invisibility, and at times, a boundless anger" (32). Arnold suggests that "the performance of female rage and female loneliness is both dangerous and unmarketable—which is exactly why we don't see it. Instead, what is performed, by Swift, is safety: safeness" (32). In "mad woman," that rage is brought directly to the surface, with the directness of the lyrics stepping away from a veneer of safeness.

Viewing Swift through the lens of Victorian literature, I return briefly to the figure of Bertha, that prototype of the madwoman in the attic. Whereas Jane is restrained by her Christian morals, Bertha is "driven by emotion—predominantly anger—and eager for vengeance"; she "represent[s] the uncontrolled—the spirited individual reduced to pure emotion and the pleasures of the flesh—and the uncontrollable—the spirit made flesh" (Russell 144). While Gilbert and Gubar include Bertha as an example of "a mad character ... created only to be destroyed," they also note that "even when a figure of rage seems to function only as a monitary image, her (or his) fury must be acknowledged not only by the angelic protagonist to whom s/he is opposed, but, significantly, *by the reader as well*" (78). I read Swift's embodiment of the mad woman/madwoman as a desire to similarly center her anger and demand the acknowledgement of her fury.

In the documentary *folklore: the long pond studio sessions*, Swift discusses the making of the track with co-writer and producer Aaron Dessner. She explains:

> I was thinking the most rage-provoking element of being a female is the gaslighting that happens when [...] for centuries we've been just expected to absorb male behaviour silently [...] There's been situations recently with someone who is very guilty of this in my life, and it's a person who tries to make me feel like I'm the offender by having any kind of defense [...] I have no right to respond, or I'm crazy. I have no right to respond, or I'm angry. [...] How do I say why this feels so bad?

As Gilbert and Gubar clarify, the freedom of mad or monstrous characters is that they have their own voices and desires; while from a male perspective that framed them as "terrible objects ... from a female point of view the monster woman is simply a woman who seeks the power of self-articulation" (79). "mad woman" features Taylor Swift speaking as directly as she ever has. In the pre-chorus, Swift sings, "Every time you call me crazy, I get more crazy / how about that? / And every time you say I get angry, I get more angry." The cycle of gaslighting and female rage is perpetual, with the former endlessly fuelling the latter. In the opening verse, Swift sings, "Do you see my face in the neighbor's lawn? / Does she smile, or does she mouth, 'Fuck you forever'?" As Giselle Au-Nhien Nguyen notes in her review of *folklore*, this lyric contains "the first-ever 'f-bomb' in [Swift's] decade-plus career, suggesting that, despite the softness of this album, she's developing her own steel." Gone is "the perfect model of feminine behaviour" (Arnold 32); in its place is vulgarity, pain, and unapologetic rage.

Notably, Swift also references internalized misogyny in her critique of patriarchal structures. Aligning herself with victims of the Salem witch trials, she sings, "women like hunting witches too / Doing your dirtiest work for you / It's obvious that wanting me dead has really brought you two together." Rather than performing a stereotype for an audience that may or may not understand she's in on the joke, she invokes historical contexts and imagery to firmly place herself in a feminist genealogy. The result is a different type of embodiment; there is no joy or winking self-awareness as she writes herself into the role of mad woman/madwoman. Instead, she directs her rage directly at the listener: "But no one likes a mad woman / What a shame she went mad / You made her like that."

Making Space for Madness: Revisions and Revelations in Taylor's Versions

In their discussion of the anxiety of authorship faced by women writers, Gilbert and Gubar gesture to "the uniquely female process of revision and redefinition" exhibited by authors such as Jane Austen, Mary Shelley, Emily Brontë, and Emily Dickinson, who "achiev[ed] true female literary authority by simultaneously conforming to and subverting patriarchal literary standards" (73). Considering her many eras and evolutions, Swift is no stranger to revision and redefinition, as demonstrated by her Eras Tour. As I have sought to demonstrate, she has also established herself both within and against patriarchal standards. Swift herself may even feel an affinity with Victorian-era writers; her so-called "Quill" lyrics were inspired by reading Charlotte Brontë (Shutler), while in her prologue to *1989 (Taylor's Version)*, she describes her demonization "by a culture that claimed to believe in liberating women but consistently treated [her] with the harsh moral codes of the Victorian Era." The success of Swift's career places her on a different path, in the sense that pop music is a genre in which women artists such as Whitney Houston, Madonna, Beyoncé, and Swift herself are universally recognized as major players. But while women in pop wield sizeable influence, inequalities in the music industry and beyond still present obstacles in terms of achieving true recognition and authority in their storytelling.

While some of her lyrics offer a shallow version of pop feminism (i.e. "ME!", "You Need to Calm Down") and others are obscure in much less productive ways (the music video and lyrics of "Look What You Made Me Do" require familiarity with nearly a decade of Swiftian lore), Swift is able to encode the more nuanced and difficult experiences that women often share, as exemplified by the representation of gaslighting in "mad woman." While "Blank Space" garnered significant critical and commercial success, I argue that a more permanent and successful deconstruction of the crazy ex-girlfriend trope lies not in Swift's ironic performance of it, but rather in the larger cultural shift that occurred in the wake of the #MeToo movement, one which led to more nuanced understandings of the actual trauma of the breakups themselves.

"All Too Well (10 Minute Version)," released as a vault track on *Red (Taylor's Version)*, extends one of her most acclaimed and beloved songs and aptly demonstrates the value of revision. With two extra verses and a lengthy outro, the sizeable age gap between Swift and actor Jake Gyllenhaal is given significant focus. At the time of their relationship, Swift was nineteen and Gyllenhaal was twenty-eight. While the original "All Too Well" does not clearly reference this age gap, in the ten-minute version Swift sings, "You said if we had been closer in age maybe it would have been fine / And that made me want to die." She also explicitly gestures to her ex's pattern of dating significantly younger women, noting, "I'll get older but your lovers stay my age." Whereas the original's most evocative image was Swift as "a crumpled piece of paper," here she is "a soldier who's returning half her weight"; she asks, "Did the twin flame bruise paint you blue? / Just between us, did the love affair maim you too?" By hyperbolizing the grief of this imbalanced relationship through haunting, violent imagery, "ATWTMV" rehabilitates

Swift's "crazy ex-girlfriend" image into that of a young woman attempting "to find retroactive equilibrium in a relationship that was based on a power imbalance that she was not at first able to perceive" (Zoladz). As Lindsay Zoladz argues:

> ["ATWTMV"] parallels the emotional work that many women have been privately undertaking in the wake of the #MeToo movement: Looking back on past encounters or relationships that left them with a seemingly outsize feeling of unease; wondering what exactly constitutes exploitation or emotional abuse; wishing they could go back and extend some compassion or wisdom to their vulnerable younger selves.

In this way, Swift's vault tracks not only offer unexpected revelations through their revisions of her past (at least as it was made available to the public) but also revelations: this is what it means to reshape your narrative, to reach back to the past and tell the story differently. If the old Taylor is truly dead, then the new Taylor is one that asserts herself and makes space for her hurt—whether in four minutes or ten—and invites us all to listen.

Conclusion

In the broadest sense, Taylor Swift's music is for people who feel things and feel them *intensely*. Swift's primary fanbase is young women, who as a demographic are constantly mocked and undermined for their interests. Women's emotions, both in the nineteenth century and now, have been dismissed as too loud, too demanding, too much. Yet Swift shares her emotions unapologetically. Whether it's the wistfulness of "Teardrops on My Guitar" or the regret of "Afterglow," Swift has never, in all her evolutions, made her feelings the punchline of the joke. Even "Blank Space," in its satirical mode, is not a mockery of the pain of relationships, but rather a mockery of the conditions that criticize the expression of that pain.

However, in considering the kind of women who are upheld as figureheads of the pain and trauma of female experiences, it is vital to consider the dimensions of femininity that Taylor Swift embodies. She may be mocked and undermined as a woman, but she also possesses enormous privilege as a white woman. For example, far more damaging than the trope of the crazy ex-girlfriend is the trope of the angry Black woman, which frames Black women as "aggressive, ill tempered, illogical, overbearing, hostile, and ignorant without provocation" (Ashley 27). Furthermore, Swift's feminist praxis is significantly limited; as Myles McNutt notes, "her personal articulation of her feminized star text has evolved not as a fully developed feminist identity, but rather as a neoliberal co-opting of feminist values" (73). For example, while Swift often critiques the gender imbalances in a male-dominated industry, she fails to consider the intersections of race and class, nor has she managed an "explicitly activist framing of her authorship or an extended partnership with female producers" (87). While Swift's negotiating of her image allows us to critically analyze broader social forces that condemn women and their emotional interiority, these negotiations still exist within a small, privileged space and fail to radically deconstruct patriarchal structures.

Nevertheless, Swift remains a distinct and powerful voice in the music industry and pop culture more broadly. By reading her as a descendant of the women writers of the nineteenth century, her identification with and eventual resistance of patriarchal ideals can be understood as her own form of feminist resistance, one which attempts to critically engage with and revise gendered scripts. While its effects may benefit her most directly, her songs provide a notable public platform for women to recognize and refute the ways in which their emotions have been similarly pathologized and dismissed. In her 2019 acceptance speech for Billboard Music's first-ever Woman of the Decade Award, Swift describes the hypercriticism that women artists face and concludes, "I've learned that the difference between those who can continue to create in that climate usually comes down to this: who lets that scrutiny break them and who just keeps making art."

For all there is to critique about Taylor Swift, one must admit to the strength of her work ethic. Through every feud, controversy, and high-profile heartbreak, Swift has kept making art. Just as contemporary women writers can "now attempt the pen with energy and authority" because of the foundational work of "their eighteenth- and nineteenth-century foremothers" (Gilbert and Gubar 51), Swift's art has inspired a new generation of women in pop such as Olivia Rodrigo, Maisie Peters, and Gracie Abrams; the latter cites Swift as "one of the blueprints for vulnerability as a young woman" (Blanchet). Indeed, this appears to be one of the singer-songwriter's greatest legacies. In her vulnerability, Taylor Swift suggests that to feel deeply and openly is far from crazy. In fact, it may be the best thing we do.

Works Cited

Arnold, Gina. "I Don't Give a Damn About Your Bad Reputation: Taylor Swift, Beyoncé Knowles, and Performance." *Contemporary Music Review*, vol. 40, no. 1. (2021): 27–40.

Ashley, Wendy. "The Angry Black Woman: The Impact of Pejorative Stereotypes on Psychotherapy with Black Women." *Social Work in Public Health*, vol. 29, no. 1: (2014): 27–34.

Au-Nhien Nguyen, Giselle. "Taylor Swift's new album is a fever dream you won't want to wake up from." *The Sydney Morning Herald*, 24 July 2020.

Billboard. "Taylor Swift Accepts Woman of the Decade Award." *YouTube*, 13 December 2019.

Blanchet, Brenton. "Gracie Abrams on Taylor Swift, Strength, and New Project "This Is What It Feels Like." *Teen Vogue*, Condé Nast, 12 Nov. 2021.

Brontë, Charlotte. *Jane Eyre*. E-book ed., Duke Classics, 2012.

Brown, Adriane. "'She isn't whoring herself out like a lot of other girls we see': Identification and "Authentic" American Girlhood on Taylor Swift Fan Forums." *Networking Knowledge: Journal of the MeCCSA Postgraduate Network*, vol. 5, no. 1. (2012): 161–80.

Conti, Meredith. "The Madwoman in the Theatre: Normalizing the Disordered Female Mind in Ellen Terry's Lyceum Repertoire." *Playing Sick*, 1st ed., Routledge: London: 2019. 143–74.

folklore: the long pond studio sessions. Directed by Taylor Swift, performances by Taylor Swift, Jack Antonoff, and Aaron Dessner, Disney+, 2020.

Gilbert, Sandra M. and Gubar, Susan. *The Madwoman in the Attic: The Woman Writer and the Nineteenth-Century Literary Imagination.* 2nd ed., Yale University Press: New Haven, 2020.

Lipshutz, Jason. "Taylor Swift Discusses 'The Man' & 'It's Nice to Have a Friend' In Cover Story Outtakes." *Billboard,* Billboard Media, 12 Dec. 2019.

Lindsay, Kathryn. "Taylor Swift Regrets Publicly Dragging Joe Jonas After Their 2008 Breakup." *Refinery29,* Vice Media Group, 15 May 2019.

Maslow, Nick. "Taylor Swift Reveals Her Inspiration for 'Blank Space': It's Like a 'Crossword Puzzle.'" *People,* Dotdash Meredith, 9 Oct. 2015.

McNutt, Myles. "From 'Mine' to 'Ours': Gendered Hierarchies of Authorship and the Limits of Taylor Swift's Paratextual Feminism." *Communication, Culture & Critique,* vol. 13, no. 1. (2020): 72–91.

Moya, Ana. "The Politics of Re-Presenting Vanity Fair: Mira Nair's Becky Sharp." *Atlantis* (Salamanca, Spain), vol. 32, no. 2. (2010): 73–87.

Pergadia, Samantha. "The Manic Pixie Dream Girl in the Attic: On Netflix's 'Love is Blind.'" *Los Angeles Review of Books,* Los Angeles Review of Books, 1 March 2023.

Russell, Danielle. "Revisiting the Attic: Recognizing the Shared Spaces of *Jane Eyre* and *Beloved.*" *Gilbert and Gubar's the Madwoman in the Attic after Thirty Years,* edited by Annette R. Federico, University of Missouri Press, 2009. *ProQuest Ebook Central.*

Shutler, Ali. "Taylor Swift organises her lyrics into three "dorky" pen-themed categories." *NME,* NME Networks, 9 October 2022.

Smith, Tracy. Interview with Taylor Swift. *CBS Sunday Morning,* CBS, 22 August 2019.

Stiegman, Kelsey. "All the Hidden Meanings Behind Taylor Swift's 'Mad Woman' Lyrics." *Seventeen,* Hearst Digital Media, 24 July 2020.

"Taylor Swift Syndrome." *Urban Dictionary,* Urban Dictionary, 19 Mar. 2009, https://www.urbandictionary.com/define.php?term=Taylor+Swift+Syndrome.

Thackeray, William Makepeace. *Vanity Fair.* E-book ed., Project Gutenberg, 2010.

Tinubu, Abeni. "Taylor Swift Critics Wonder if She'll Ever Apologize to Camilla Belle." *Showbiz Cheatsheet,* Endgame360 Inc., 1 Mar. 2021.

Zoladz, Lindsay. "Taylor Swift's 'All Too Well' and the Weaponization of Memory." *The New York Times,* The New York Times Company, 15 Nov. 2021.

9

Female Millennial Rage: The Weaponization of Cottagecore

Katherine Murray

Millennial women internalized the Spice Girls' messages about female empowerment and Elle Woods's promise that we could achieve anything. When Mulan reached the top of the pole, she brought honor to us all. On Myspace, we listened to pop and country songs that valorized female revenge ("Goodbye Earl," "Before He Cheats," "Gunpowder and Lead"), internalizing a new kind of empowerment: if our partner betrayed us, we could humiliate him at Harvard or wallop his windshield. When Lisbeth Salander tattooed "I am a sadistic pig, a pervert, and a rapist" on her abusive guardian, we celebrated violence against men who deserve it and hoped that these spectacles would serve as a warning. Empowerment, we reckoned, meant that you were finally allowed to express rage; destruction as a result of this rage, as long as it was directed at evil men, had no repercussions. We were allowed and encouraged to dream of spectacular vengeance. An eye for an eye makes the whole world blind, but a tattoo carved into a rapist's belly hopefully inspires potential rapists to consider another career path.

But we began to dream of vengeance against not just abusers and philanderers. The world let us down: recessions, ever-growing student loans, racial violence, the necessity of and backlash against #MeToo, a never-ending pandemic, NRA-funded politicians refusing to concede that shootings at elementary schools can be prevented, articles shaming us for renting forever because our avocado toast addiction prevented us from buying a house. In simpler times, millennial women found solace in revenge tales that targeted a specific bad person who deserved their comeuppance, but in 2020 our rage ballooned like a long-suppressed and now uncontained gas. The Trump presidency had already shattered the myth of gender progress, but the feelings of hopelessness evinced by both institutional and individual experiences forced millennial women to question their place in the world and consider who was actually invested in their well-being. The cottagecore aesthetic exploded in popularity during the pandemic—not because it encouraged violence against Trump or Ted Cruz or Mitch McConnell, but because it enabled escapism from doomscrolling and anti-maskers and Mitch McConnell. Millennial women's exhausted anger was validated by Swift's pandemic texts, *folklore* and *evermore*. The albums evoke more than just the aesthetic pleasure associated with the cottagecore spaces of whimsical gardens and charming libraries and the tent from *The Great British Bake Off*. Swift's particular brand of cottagecore advocates for liberatory potential from unrealistic, demeaning male expectations and creates a space where female rage may be expressed, celebrated, and mediated through solidarity. There is catharsis in expressing rage; there is catharsis in aiding and abetting with Olive Garden as an alibi. The expectation of perfection is exhausting, but the expectation of perfection for women when the bar for men seems to lower every day is just insulting.

As a necessary disclaimer of my own subject position, I am a casual Swift fan who, with friends and strangers on Instagram, Reddit, Tumblr, and Twitter, found that others had a similar emotional reaction to this album and its surprise sister. In this pre-vaccine, post-stimulus-checks-and-*Tiger King* era of the pandemic, many of us were desperate for both distraction and female community-building, and *folklore* provided emotional vindication.[1] The albums remind us that outside of the bounds of the heteronormative digital landscape, we do not have to rely on men who will betray us. Swift's cottagecore texts create a quiet, feminized space that acts as a pretty, genuine, queer alternative to the harsh outside world.

Millennial Nostalgia as Rejection of Capitalism

Millennials loathe the boomer misconception of our generation as lazy; cottagecore promotes industry free from the bounds of capitalism, celebrating meaningful labor and rejecting hustle culture and the perceived necessity of the gig economy. Enabling both female community-building and enjoyable labor, cottagecore is often regarded by critics as charming but ultimately too delicate to be taken seriously, as if our nostalgic desire to return to a simpler, pre-pandemic time ("the mall before the internet") renders us weak. For people who watched the fall of the Twin Towers in our elementary school classrooms and graduated high school and college during recessions, we welcome anything that promises some respite: "As a generation forever caught in a state of change given the utter lack of societal stability, it stands to reason that Millennials have a constant yearning for when things were just simpler" (Franco). However, critics also point out that mainstream cottagecore presents a curious paradox as it celebrates freedom from capitalism while relying on the ever capitalistic digital space.[2] Can aspiring homesteaders and gingham-clad curators of cute actually reach cottagecore nirvana if they require Wifi to do so?

Absolutely. Part of what differentiates cottagecore from its aesthetic predecessors is its community-building within digital spaces. The pragmatic return to gardening and

---

[1] As demonstrated by Evan et al.'s study, domestic violence rates skyrocketed during the early days of the pandemic. "seven" depicts the experience of living with an abusive father and the desire to escape a violent home: "I think your house is haunted / Your dad is always mad and that must be why."

[2] For instance, the "cardigan" video portrays an ethereal, dreamy forest that we'd like to think is untouched by capitalism, but the eponymous sweater is available for $55 in Swift's online shop.

home-bound crafts arose as a common-sensical response to living during lockdown: "idle homemaking became less escapism and more like an inescapable reality. Cottagecore under lockdown, then, became a way to spin the terror and drudgery into something adorable—and interest in it directly correlated to how bad it became outside" (Jennings). Jennings invokes Amanda Brennan, a trend expert at Tumblr, who noted that from March 2020 to April 2020, "the cottagecore hashtag jumped 153 percent, while likes on cottagecore posts were up 541 percent" (Jennings). Cottagecore hobbies became a way of making our small living spaces more pleasant and livable, and millennial practitioners used baking, gardening, sewing, knitting, and decorating as a means of keeping sane. We found solace in exchanging recipes and in sharing images of our succulent propagation; the aesthetically pleasing amalgamation of the millennial female desire for independence enables self-reliance and also happens to be cute.

Seeking comfort in aesthetically-pleasing-but-still-practical activities helped distract from the realities of a global pandemic, economic crash, and general feeling of hopelessness as we mourned a future whose dreams had once seemed attainable. As Swift explains in "peace," "Our coming-of-age has come and gone." In typical millennial fashion, we approach this with resigned existential dread and marvelous memes. The three memes below widely circulated in 2020 and 2021 because they encapsulate the desperate desire to retreat from capitalism and the need to recalibrate our hopes and dreams:

- "Plants are the new pets, pets are the new kids, and kids are like exotic animals: only rich people can afford them, and crazy people have them."
- A *McSweeney's* article, "I Have Decided to Live the Remainder of My Life as a Simple Woodland Creature," ponders, "I have not thought about the bathroom situation, or what to do in inclement weather, or how to tell if a berry is poisonous or not if I don't have my phone with me (and I definitely will not have my phone with me, because I'm going to throw it into the first babbling brook I see). And yes, I understand that aspect of my plan raises several additional questions, but preemptive counterpoint: What if you never had to open an email again for the rest of your life?" (McEly).
- A particularly delightful family of 2021 memes whose caption urges, "Stop glamorizing 'the grind' and start glamorizing whatever this is" over a stereotypically cottagecore image, i.e. Frog and Toad riding a bike or a cozy-looking mouse drinking tea.

The last example in particular demonstrates the imbrication between the cottagecore aesthetic and the 2021 r/antiwork movement. The subreddit gained popularity as it showcased the realities of late-stage capitalism, connected exploited workers with resources to help them navigate labor policies, and shared startling statistics (for instance, that the current wealth gap is greater than that of 1789 France [Ullman]). (The conversations started by this subreddit enabled the discussion of "quiet quitting" in 2022). As spectacles of the wealth gap (the cringey "Imagine" video, Kim Kardashian's assertion that "nobody wants to work anymore," Bezos's recreational space travel, dangerously misguided recreational submarine travel) fueled frustration with out-of-touch one-percenters, millennials sought relatable role models.

folklore and *evermore* initially seemed to confirm Swift's status as charmingly relatable; unlike the Sam Smiths and Ellen DeGenereses of the celebrity world who complained about quarantining in massive homes, Swift shared in the millennial pandemic fantasy of fleeing to the woods to live unbothered by people and technology. Her perceived relatability was jeopardized in August 2022, when a report released by the sustainability firm Yard showed that Swift topped the list of celebrities whose private jets are responsible for the largest amount of global emissions (Burga). In 2012, she had the luxury of "lying on the cold hard ground," but now she is lying on the rapidly warming ground. Swift's environmental failures felt like a betrayal for fans who identify as sustainability advocates. It is unsurprising that someone whose meteoric career has occupied a global microscope for over half her life struggles with maintaining relatability. Of course, Swift is an imperfect person, and it would be unfair to expect perfection of her. However, given her cultural capital and expansive worldwide fanbase, it is fair to expect that she should accept not just the privilege but the responsibility of being considered a role model. Perhaps it was the fallout from this egregious publicity that inspired the historic Eras Tour food bank donations; perhaps she would have made these generous donations anyway. As she (and her private plane's emissions) reach new heights, she becomes further removed from the sweetly naive character portrayed in "Our Song": "Via her varied personas—girl-next-door, cheerleader, heartbreaker, nerdy girl, businesswoman or cottagecore explorer—Taylor Swift is both a monument to the past and a modern megalith, toppling the music industries through her appeal to people that historically and culturally have been told that their musical tastes are invalid (like country fans and teenage girls)" (Fogarty and Arnold 2). As the Eras Tour has highlighted, Swift's successful embodiment of so many relatable, resonant personas demonstrates the privilege of the potential capacity for reinvention.

The Privileged Traditions of Cottagecore

For the purpose of this paper, I am less interested in pointing out Easter eggs that eagle-eyed fans have already identified, but rather in approaching the songs as texts that may be illuminated in a new way through considering them as literature and considering how these were defined and redefined by the cultural circumstances in which they were written and received. Like Swift herself, the cottagecore genre encompasses both the wholesome and the problematic, reflecting a history of criticism as too privileged, too white, too colonizing. Indeed, it is easy to see how it could be argued that the cottagecore aesthetic imposes an essentially colonial gaze if one is viewing "quaint" settings only through the lens of a phone's camera in search of the most Instagrammable babbling brook or blackberry bush. While Instagram and similar social media platforms do possess the potential to unify cottagecore practitioners around the world, they also make it very easy to promote a kind of reductive, extractive tourism by cherrypicking the most aesthetically pleasing aspects to share.

Swift's albums expand upon Romantic, Victorian, and Edwardian literary cottagecore traditions, but resonate more with recent cottagecore texts that offer similar aesthetic pleasure while positing these spaces as ready to be claimed by a more diverse protagonist. Texts such as *Heidi, A Little Princess, Anne of Green Gables*, and *The Secret Garden* established the outdoors as an acceptable space for little (white) girls who craved the same escapism offered by their brothers' adventure books. Charlotte Perkins Gilman's *Herland* elevated the notion of outdoor space as untapped female potential, suggesting that all-female utopias that emphasized women's engagement with nature would thrive without male interference. Reflective of the eras in which they were written, these once-radical texts achieved the same kind of gatekeeping as first-wave feminism, advocating for the elevation of middle- and upper-class white women at the expense of all other women.

The twenty-first-century literary cottagecore genre opts instead for a more inclusive examination of untapped female potential. Cottagecore tropes (exploration, self-discovery through engagement with nature, near-transcendental epiphanies in untamed woodland spaces) resonate through the genre lenses of gothic, dark academia, fantasy, and speculative thrillers. Texts such as Sayaka Murata's dystopian Bildungsroman *Earthlings*, Kim Liggett's feminist speculative dystopian thriller *The Grace Year*, Joanna Ruth Meyer's YA dark fantasy *Into the Heartless Wood*, and Kate Alice Marshall's thriller *What Lies in the Woods* highlight the potential for reclamation of female identity, and texts such as Rory Power's futuristic YA *Wilder Girls*, Rivers Solomon's gothic thriller *Sorrowland*, and Victoria Lee's dark academia gothic fantasy *A Lesson in Vengeance* depict the potential of these untapped spaces to be claimed as queer utopias. Indeed, Showtime's *Yellowjackets* and HBO's *The Last of Us* depict dystopian circumstances as bursting with queer potential. Thrust into terrifying scenarios that require self-sufficiency and sustainable survivalism, girls who are now free from heteropatriarchal capitalism achieve a new level of both independence and community-building, allowing them to achieve a kind of authenticity that would not have been possible pre-plane crash or pre-apocalypse.

Though free from wolves, zombies, and cannibalism, Swift's cottagecore texts show the progression from *fin-de-siècle* western literature's then-progressive depiction of outdoor spaces as places where little white girls were allowed to feel empowered. Pleasant spaces full of "small animals, calico tea cozies, and not a lot of men" are to be celebrated as relaxing, safe spaces for women, where " .... men are not consciously excluded; they are simply an afterthought" (Slone). However, Swift's version of cottagecore led to allegations of cultural appropriation. Some critics suggest that engaging with the cottagecore aesthetic for her albums was only further proof of her privilege and performativity; one Tumblr user claims that "[c]ottagecore romanticizes the legacy of settler colonialism and frontier living that relies on the stolen land of indigenous people" (Baix). However, some view her deliberate engagement with cottagecore as proof that she is actively trying to cultivate a more liberal image for herself: "What separates cottagecore from other nostalgia-based subcultures, too, is that despite its reverence for stories about and images of heterosexual white people, it's become nearly synonymous with queer people and progressive politics" (Jennings).

Swift and her publicity team have always been very aware of her image and its criticism, and from each trough of fatigue with her latest misstep springs a new incarnation, a new aesthetic and color palette, a new wardrobe, a new haircut, a new digital overhaul of her platforms, and, sometimes, a new beau. She has become the queen of reinvention, inspiring in her fans the notion that they too are capable of such instant evolution—but is this capacity for constant growth actually accessible? There is considerable privilege in possessing the material circumstances that enable reinvention and escapism; as the narrator of "happiness" considers, "I haven't met the new me yet," confident that there will be an opportunity to welcome a "new [her]."

All artists walk a fine line between accessibility and unrelatability, and fans' engagement with them vacillates between escaping into the vision offered by the artist and recognizing that this reprieve cannot always offer solace from the fan's less-than-glamorous life. Both texts occupy this awkward liminality, feeding into an aesthetic without acknowledging its real-world presence. Paul Quinn, Director of the Chichester Center for Fairy Tales, Fantasy, and Speculative Fiction, notes, "Taylor Swift is wearing a chunky knit on the cover of her album, but that's Irish, and most people can't wait to get off the island ... These rural settings, you want to go to them, but then you want to leave" (Jennings). As Jennings points out, "cottagecore ignores the fact that rural areas have always been unattainable for some and inescapable for others" (Jennings). Poets have long romanticized the rural, but it is irresponsible to present "the countryside" as idyllically free of all problems. As Slone indicates, "While cottagecore could easily be mistaken for an escapist fantasy, its proponents insist it is a form of self-care." There absolutely is merit in the self-care of fresh air and taking a break from the chaos of urban spaces, but it is condescending to those who live there to suggest that rural spaces are always-already transgressable leisure spaces designed only for bucolic respites from the "real world." The explicitly less-autobiographical-than-their-predecessors albums still achieve Swift's brand of creating heroes to root for: "She has capitalized on that universal appeal of rap: centering the underdog, the underappreciated, the hated, the disenfranchised. She has taken this narrative and spun it on herself and those in her ilk: the young, white, wealthy and beautiful" (Donnella). As she reminds us in "cardigan," "when you are young, they assume you know nothing," but she capitalizes on others underestimating her in songs like "champagne problems" and "no body, no crime." The Swift of *folklore* and *evermore* is world-weary and wise, but she still gains knowledge from stepping in the shoes of characters different from herself and is not above cleaning houses to enable a friend's revenge. Swift employs cottagecore tropes of self-discovery in nature in order to sustain a pleasing escapist fantasy: we can redefine ourselves whenever we choose.

Cottagecore Regendering

The feminine nature of the cottagecore does not prevent it from achieving feminist capital, and the rise of cottagecore enabled by the pandemic invited us to reconceptualize feminine and feminist labor. Cottagecore presents an interesting tension between the subservience associated with domesticity and the agency of using this domesticity as a means of escapism or fulfillment. The pandemic highlighted the contradictions to which millennial women are subject: self-sufficiency is admirable, but we have been conditioned to view self-sufficient, traditionally feminized tasks (gardening, sewing, baking) as regressive for the feminist cause. The pandemic assigned value to these skills. As Emily Matchar asks in "Why I can't stop reading Mormon housewife blogs," "So why, exactly, are these blogs so fascinating to women like us—secular, childless women who may have never so much as baked a cupcake, let alone reupholstered our own ottomans with thrifted fabric and vintage grosgrain ribbon?... With the rise of DIY culture across secular America, all of a sudden those skills have become trendy, even bankable." I agree with Matchar's claim that "... women of my generation are looking to the past in an effort to create fulfilling, happy domestic lives, since the modern world doesn't offer much of a road map. Our parents—divorced, stressed-out baby boomers—are hardly paragons of domestic bliss." In the dreamscapes of *folklore*'s and *evermore*'s "hikes in the woods; flowing, feminine clothing; freshly homemade bread; needlepoint kits, and writing a letter by a fire while drinking a warm beverage from a tea set," DIY culture indeed seems a happy reprieve from modern expectations, abusive partners, and a devastating news cycle (Munzenrieder). The pandemic granted millennial women permission to enjoy, engage with, and create visual pleasure for the sake of visual pleasure — but with ourselves as the intended audience rather than men. In *Our Aesthetic Categories: Zany, Cute, Interesting*, Sianne Ngai defines "cute" as "an aesthetic disclosing the surprisingly wide spectrum of feelings, ranging from tenderness to aggression, that we harbor toward ostensibly subordinate and unthreatening commodities." The desire to achieve cuteness occupies the center of the Venn Diagram of millennial cottagecore feminists and conservative trad wives. As Slone notes, cottagecore "offers a vision of domestic bliss without servitude in the traditional binary framework." Within this tension of superficially conservative but potentially liberatory gendering, cottagecore is not so much anti-male as it is pro-feminine. Female millennial rage is reserved for the misogynists and incels who spew hateful vitriol, but cottagecore celebrates non-toxic, empathetic masculinity.

In interviews, Swift conceptualizes *folklore*'s lyrics as inspired by "escapism and romanticism," and it makes sense that in a turbulent post-Trump era of gender policing, a prerequisite of an escapist fantasy would be an understanding of gender fluidity (Gibson). It also makes sense that breaking down toxic binaries was an essential first step towards envisioning more inclusive modes of masculinity. The Bon Iver collaboration "exile" on *folklore* of course provoked memes about the 2012 Tumblr "Bon Iver Erotica," a delightful blog that shares fictional vignettes about life with "Bon Iver," a character amalgamated from the band's lyrical personas. A gentle, creative feminist lumberjack devoted to female pleasure, Bon Iver epitomizes the dreamy skillset of a cottagecore lady's ideal partner: "Bon Iver insisted on washing my hair, and afterwards he braided it, weaving in fresh lavender and pussy willow buds" ("Bon Iver Erotica"). Alternate modes of masculinity can be celebrated without declaring all men are terrible, just as *folklore* and *evermore* can celebrate a particular kind of femininity without suggesting that all other types of femininity are invalid. While fans agree that the cottagecore albums celebrate the brand of non-toxic masculinity that we are trying to promote in 2023, fans are divided over the extent to which the albums actually celebrate diverse sexual identities. Swift has faced several allegations of queerbaiting, with critics suggesting that she performs nonheteronormativity only when trendy and convenient. Long accused of being too quiet about her personal politics when she holds such a position of visibility, Swift finally appeared to take a stance on LGBTQ rights when she publicly advocated for the Equality Act in 2019. However, suspicious fans and critics maintained that this was purely performative, and the murky sexuality of her cottagecore albums has not done much to dissuade them. One such critic maintains that Swift is not actually an ally, but rather abuses "the language of social justice for her personal gain, and even went as far as using queer people as props of sorts in her music video for last album's 'You Need to Calm Down,' which features LGBTQ pop-culture staples" (Venturo). Venturo maintains that *folklore* "is a jewel in Swift's crown of inauthenticity," critiquing those who laud "betty" as "queer-canon" when the song "portrays a heterosexual relationship with Swift singing from the male's perspective" (Venturo).[3] I agree with Venturo's assertion that "[q]ueerness is counterculture and Taylor Swift is the definition of establishment" as well as her conclusion that "as a queer consumer of pop-culture, this incarnation feels like a way to capitalize on the thematic concepts that were popularized by other artists without any personal risk that is tied to identity" (Venturo). Just as Swift benefits from white privilege and its ability to grant her access to most spaces (for instance, the "Wildest Dreams" video features an all-white cast in colonial garb frolicking around exoticized African landscapes), Swift flirts with portraying queer narrators because her heterosexual privilege allows her to do so. Indeed, queer critics have long wondered about Swift's potential appropriation of queer culture:

> Examples of behavior that could be perceived as queerbaiting include: switching the pronouns of lyrics in live performances, a bisexual flag-colored wig in the aforementioned music video, and according to a review in the Vermont Cynic, the overall "queer" feeling of *folklore*. Out of the blue, Swift shared a new single from gay singersongwriter girl in red, calling to mind the coded question, "Do you listen to girl in red?", a way to covertly ask about a woman's sexuality .... [S]he teased the release of news on April 26th of 2019, also known as Lesbian Visibility Day which turned out to be a single drop rather than a widely speculated coming out. This all begs the question–is Taylor queer herself? Does she simply resonate with the experience of queer women as an ally? Or is there something more nefarious going on in the name of album sales? (Holmes)

Given the speculation and criticism surrounding the albums' gender policies, it is essential to consider if Swift's cottagecore phase actually represents the more liberal

---

[3] The romantic relationship between Betty and James is oddly complicated by the fact that the song's characters were named after the daughters of Blake Lively and Ryan Reynolds, Swift's friends. Since the inspiration for James is a girl, diehard Swifties maintain that the song is actually "queer-canon"; critics wonder if a song can actually be queer canon if it is only implicitly queer.

persona that we would like to believe it does. Her entire career has been plagued with accusations that she is a white singer for white people, and it is not hard to see how her country roots led to allegations of racism. It is absolutely essential to consider how both Swift and cottagecore owe much to white privilege. The gatekeeping of whitestream feminism is one of the most powerful deterrents to feminism as a whole in 2024; by willingly avoiding an intersectional lens and prioritizing only themselves, white women who advocate for a monolithic female identity detract from the goals and positionality of progressive feminism. As Fogarty and Arnold demonstrate, "Taylor Swift's believable innocence is tied to white privilege. And, for women in the pop industry, it's always a tough sell to convince audiences that they are the producers of their words, images, and sounds, especially when they are young" (Fogarty and Arnold). Swift's well publicized tensions and feuds with Beyoncé, Kim Kardashian, and Nicki Minaj fueled conversations about the media's tendency to pit women against each other and present the white(r) woman as always-already innocent.[4] When she was a fledgling fourteen-year-old in the music industry, such perceived innocence was more palatable, but now that she is in her thirties, many fans hope that she will demonstrate more self-awareness in future ventures.

Millennial Mourning

While *folklore* and *evermore* do celebrate Swift's evolution from the "pick me" days of *Fearless*, the albums also use cottagecore landscapes and imagery as a vehicle for mourning simpler times. Pandemic fatigue cost us so much, but it also granted a curious freedom as things that once seemed important became laughably insignificant, heralding a wartime-esque recalibration of goals and relationships. In "invisible string," "Cold was the steel of my axe to grind / For the boys who broke my heart," but there is no sense in wasting rage towards the unchangeable past; now, the narrator "send[s] their babies presents." "Hell was the journey but it brought [the narrator] heaven," as granting herself the grace to be free of the past ultimately enables more mindfully living in the present. Swift makes peace with herself during a turbulent time to be alive. "I'm a soldier who's returning half her weight" resonates with the experience not just of a spurned woman who was kept like a secret when she kept him like an oath, but with the experience of any exhausted woman who agrees that those Windermere peaks look like the perfect place to cry. As the narrator of "happiness" reminds us, "No one teaches you what to do / When a good man hurts you"; being hurt by someone who was confirmed as a "good man" initiates a process of self-gaslighting. Swift's albums rage against the "good men" who enabled this self-doubt and the institutions that caused us to doubt that people we trust are genuinely invested in our well-being. When we reflect

---

[4] "In African American contexts, for example, black femininity has often been represented as vexed by the idealization of white femininity on the one hand and the cultural stereotyping of black women as strong, physical, and tough on the other" (Halberstam 117).

on pre-COVID days, as well as on past relationships, we mourn the ability to trust people who were supposed to protect us and care about our well-being. Swift delicately tackles portrayals of trauma, beautifully depicting the journey to freeing herself from toxic relationships with the same gravitas as describing how images of death lingered in all of our minds in 2020 (for instance, *folklore*'s "epiphany" used images from her grandfather's Second World War experiences at Guadalcanal to represent the battles of frontline ER workers). For millennial women, the pandemic showed how many institutions that we took for granted could no longer be trusted; we could not assume that people who say they are invested in our well-being actually care about us, just like we cannot assume that anyone will wear a mask to prevent someone else's potential death. We mourned not just the people and experiences that we lost to COVID, but also the trust that we used to have in humanity. We mourned the privileged idealism of assuming others recognized a baseline of basic decency.

As we mourn our hopeful younger selves and accept that there are more terrible people than we thought, we gain freedom in no longer caring what people think, since this grants us the freedom to express rage that previously felt forbidden to us. Read together, "exile," "the last great american dynasty," and "mad woman" create an anthem of rage against the gaslighters. The ethereal escapism of the Narnia vibes of the "cardigan" and "willow" videos are sharply juxtaposed by the images of this trinity of liberating anger: things that we once felt obligated to protect have revealed themselves to be unworthy of our loyalty. "exile" invites us to wonder why we help maintain institutions that do not prioritize us (toxic relationships? capitalism? American healthcare?): "You're not my homeland anymore, so what am I defending now? / You were my town, now I'm in exile." However, this feeling of placelessness and dissatisfaction is rarely validated when expressed from a female perspective. "mad woman" depicts the tautological futility of female rage never being taken seriously. "No one likes a mad woman," and women lose credibility when they are unlikeable, but "you made her like that," because it creates an advantage for men to divide women. "the last great american dynasty" depicts the story of Rebekah Harkness, an eccentric heiress whose home Swift purchased in 2013. The "maddest woman this town has ever seen" "had a marvelous time ruining everything, free of . . . their men and bad habits." Harkness emerges from *folklore* as the ideal woman who, though she obviously occupies a privileged position from which to fill her pool with champagne, encourages a greater emphasis on female friendship and less reliance on heteronormative romance. It is crucial to remember that these feminist anthems do not encourage hating men, but rather critique a mode of toxic masculinity that does not hold men accountable for their actions.

Emerging as perhaps the most quintessentially cottagecore selection from the albums, "the lakes" uses cottagecore tropes to mourn a simpler past through escaping to bucolic settings. The song is immediately established as one of mourning when the first line asks, "Is it romantic how all my elegies eulogize me?" In interviews, Swift revealed the inspiration for the song: "In the 19th century, you had a lot of poets like William Wordsworth and John Keats who would spend a lot of time there. There was a poet district, these artists that moved there. They were kind of heckled for it and made fun of for it as being eccentrics . . . You live in a cottage, you've got wisteria growing up the side of it. Of course they would escape like that" (Warner). The Lake District has come to represent a bucolic haven for poets and travelers alike, and the Lake Poets— among them, siblings William and Dorothy Wordsworth, siblings Charles and Mary Lamb, Samuel Taylor Coleridge, Thomas de Quincy, and Robert Southey— immortalized the District. Swift's narrator eagerly embraces the opportunity to unplug and escape, continuing the Lake Poets' tradition of celebrating the space as one that enables introspection and eschews technology. It is easier to be authentic and access inspiration when there is "no one around to tweet it" and no "cynical clones, these hunters with cell phones." Indeed, it is implied that the tech-obsessed cannot access or would not bother trying to access the Lake District, as they are incapable of understanding what makes it special. Free to be herself in this empowering, enchanting space, Swift's narrator celebrates her physical and emotional distance from a villain who bears a striking resemblance to Scooter Braun. He has lost his power over her, and she uses wordplay to laud her empowering Romantic hero while criticizing the man who is trying to engineer her downfall: "I've come too far to watch some namedropping sleaze tell me what are my words worth." The architect of "I Wandered Lonely as a Cloud" and *The Prelude* would surely be more sympathetic to Swift's introspective quest than to Braun's attempts to control and monetize her. Unfortunately, even Swift's narrator's enriching journey must come to an end; she "want[s] to watch wisteria grow right over [her] bare feet," but she is only a traveler to this beautiful place and not a resident of it. To allow herself to remain in the "ice frozen ground" would only grant her enemies power through her absence; this space is hers for recharging, but not for permanent habitation. To stand still too long is to risk succumbing to Ozymandian collapse. Because she recognizes the need for responsible tourism, she will be allowed to return to this healing site.

Conclusion

In this chapter, I argue that Taylor Swift's recent albums align with the ideals of the cottagecore aesthetic to create a feminized space free from the heteronormative demand that rage be suppressed. Examining how female rage is so frequently negatively portrayed in the media allows us to consider why any public expression of female emotion feels like trying to guide a bull through a china shop. The 2016 presidential debates highlighted the extent to which female emotion is scrutinized and used to deem us irrational. The subsequent presidency and insurrection proved that toxic masculinity is inextricably imbricated with not just violent misogyny, but also with white supremacy, racism, homophobia, and a terrifying sense of entitlement. When the Trump-enabled Supreme Court began to treat *The Handmaid's Tale* like a playbook, millions of Americans who do not benefit from antiquated prejudices felt genuine fear and rage. Many of us wondered for how long we would be allowed to express this fear and rage on public channels.

Social media became an essential space for cottagecore practitioners to connect and share during the pandemic; through an intersectional framework, commiserating over the indignities and injustices of the lived experience of womanhood can strengthen feminist spaces. While Elon Musk's collaboration with white supremacists and proud misogynists has, as of December 2023, virtually signaled the end of former Twitter as a potential space for female solidarity, female-identifying and female-allying creators are turning to Instagram, TikTok, and YouTube to combat the noxious morass of the manosphere by educating audiences about toxic masculinity and weaponized incompetence. Andrew Tate and his ilk are poisoning the minds of young men, but young feminists are toiling to create an antidote. Greta Gerwig's *Barbie* and the concurrent Eras Tour reaffirmed celebrations of girlhood and unapologetic femininity. Through the aforementioned channels, global fans found joy in videos of friendship bracelets, well planned outfits, and viral proposals during "Love Story." Much has been made of Swift's veritable ability to command a global army, but many of these critiques, gleeful and condescending alike, fail to consider that the Eras Tour enables expressions of rage as much as it enables expressions of love and comfort. Within a space of Swift fans, whether it be a movie theater or stadium or simply two friends listening to music in a car, no one is required to "take your indiscretions all in good fun" ("tolerate it"), and listeners are encouraged to gain the confidence to "call you out on your contrarian shit" ("gold rush"). Taylor Swift is an imperfect person, but in a tumultuous time to be a woman in America, her music provides a sense of much-needed solidarity, and that is absolutely something to celebrate.

Works Cited

Baix, "Time to stop tagging cottagecore along with solarpunk." *Tumblr*. 2 December 2019.
"Bon Iver Erotica." *Tumblr*. 2012.
Burga, Solcyre. "From Private Jets to Superyachts, Here's the Climate Impact of the Rich and Famous." *Time*. 25 August 2022.
Donnella, Leah. "Taylor Swift Is The 21st Century's Most Disorienting Pop Star." *NPR*. 26 September 2018.
Fogarty, Mary and Gina Arnold. "Are You Ready for It? Re-Evaluating Taylor Swift." *Contemporary Music Review*, vol. 40, no. 1. (2021): 1–10.
Franco, Angelo. "The Early Onset Millennial Nostalgia." *Highbrow Magazine*. 23 June 2022.
Gibson, Kelsie. "Taylor Swift Reveals the True Meaning of 'Peace,' and I Love the Song Even More Now." *Popsugar*. 13 November 2020.
Halberstam, Jack. "Gender." In *Keywords for American Cultural Studies*, Second Edition, eds. Burgett Bruce and Hendler Glenn. NYU Press: New York, 2014. 116–18.
Holmes, Alex. "Is Taylor Swift Engaging in the Appropriation of LGBTQ+ Culture?" *SCAD Radio*. 3 May 2021.
Jennings, Rebecca. "Once Upon a Time, There was Cottagecore." *Vox*, 3 August 2020.
Matchar, Emily. "Why I Can't Stop Reading Mormon Housewife Blogs." *Salon.com*. 15 January 2011.
McEly, Maureen. "I Have Decided to live the Remainder of My Life as a Simple Woodland Creature." *McSweeney's*, 1 October 2021, https://www.mcsweeneys.net/articles/i-have-decided-to-live-the-remainder-of-my-life-as-a-simple-woodland-creature

Munzenrieder, Kyle. "Taylor Swift Has Discovered Cottagecore." *W Magazine*. 23 July 2020.

Ngai, Sianne. "Zany, Cute, Interesting: Sianne Ngai on Our Aesthetic Categories." Asian American Writers Workshop. 7 February 2013.

Slone, Isabel. "Escape Into Cottagecore, Calming Ethos for Our Febrile Moment." *The New York Times*. 10 March 2020.

Swift, Taylor. "All Too Well: The Short Film." *YouTube*, uploaded by Taylor Swift, 12 November 2021.

Ullman, Harlan. "America's wealth inequality is a domestic IED, ready to ignite." 18 July 2022.

Warner, Denise. "11 Things We Learned From Taylor Swift's 'Folklore: The Long Pond Studio Sessions.'" *Billboard*. 25 November 2020.

Venturo, Sophia. "'Folklore' is market motivated 'queerbaiting.'" *The Vermont Cynic*. 9 October 2020.

10

"She would've made such a lovely bride": Queer Anxieties on *folklore* and *evermore*

Erin Geary

Swift's work has long been associated with heteronormativity: fairytales, Romeo and Juliet, straight weddings. However, the dual releases of *folklore* and *evermore* offer a lyrical shift away from ideas that have long been Swift's tried and true inspiration. Using theories of queer anxiety, I argue that these two records provide a continuous narrative about a young person struggling to fit available molds, a subject with inescapable queer resonances The speaker—be it Swift or not—is perplexed by how difficult normality feels to attain—always beyond reach, close enough to see, but not to touch. "Civility" is something the speaker has to learn. They "try, try, try," until they are pained by the feeling of performance. Swift's songs are carnal, lived-in, and full of unspoken desire. The relationships detailed are half-bloomed. There is a sense of failure running through the work.

Swift's obviously fraught attachment to her public image is a product of a music industry that has contained her since she sky-rocketed to success with 2006's "Tim McGraw." Since that time, the dominant narrative of her romantic life has been limited and sanitized, causing fans to search, like detectives, for more complex information about the star's relationships. At the same time, Swift herself has invited queer readings of her work by leaning into lesbian aesthetics (e.g. *folklore*'s cottagecore) and placing her songs in the hairs of queer media (e.g. *Dickinson*). These intentional and subtle stylistic choices stand in contrast to her explicit song and music video, the white feminist-leaning "You Need to Calm Down," which has been derided by LGBTQ+ fans and critics alike as performative, cynical, and self-interested (Avdeef; Smialek). My analytical scope, however, is focused on queer readings of Swift's sibling 2020 releases rather than her outspoken advocacy. Queer themes run through Swift's entire discography, with the most direct ones coming to fruition on her latest work. Swift is brave on *folklore* and *evermore*, saying overtly what she's long fit in the subtext.

In an effort to create robust queer representation, media tends to accidentally other and isolate this work when, in reality, it has natural wide appeal. Queer people want to hear their own stories, but queer stories are also broadly interesting; the segregation of media causes queer stories, while present, to be marginalized. Reading Taylor Swift as a queer storyteller proves that work with queer themes is not only relevant but beloved by the general public. It strengthens the bonds between different groups of people who otherwise have little in common.

As a fan and a scholar, I have the ethical obligation to avoid forcing labels onto unlabeled celebrities. However, I will argue that Swift's insistence on breaking ideas of perfection, subverting happy endings, and finding faults in what's expected of her represent a type of queer failure. On *folklore* and *evermore*, she sounds freer than ever, unbound from the confines of big-budget pop architecture, embracing a roomy indie-rock playground. She's introspective, critical, and nostalgic. It's the voice of someone remaking a childhood they couldn't have. It's the voice of someone questioning everything they know. One of the reasons why Swift's LGBTQ+ allyship prior to the "sister albums" felt subpar was because she inserted herself into the equation far too often, even stating in her 2020 Netflix documentary *Miss Americana*, "Gay pride is what makes me me," a confusing and bold claim from someone who only spoke publicly in solidarity one year before, petitioning for the Equality Act and quickly accruing half a million signatures as part of the trendy rollout for her single "You Need To Calm Down." However, Swift, as it turns out, is skillful at constructing queer stories with tact, respect, and breadth, earning praise and embrace from the queer community, especially from lesbian and bisexual women who previously felt iced-out from her written narratives.

Queer Failure as a Lens

folklore begins in a major key, signifying a contentedness, on the self-assured track "the 1." Off the top, Swift reminds audiences that "the greatest films of all time are never made," prompting us to wonder what she hasn't been sharing with the public. "We were something; don't you think so?" she asks, as if trying to convince herself. It's clear that there are relationships in Swift's life that she remembers as real, even if they didn't come to fruition, even if they were not legible to her audience or the press. Swift's personal sexual identity becomes beside-the-point, since a film that hasn't been made is hidden, scrapped, sidelined. It has failed. Queer failure is a concept coined by theorist Jack Halberstam, who argues, "Failure . . . offers more creative, cooperative, and surprising ways of being in the world." When Swift reminds us that these narratives are not fully real, at least in the way her earlier narratives were, she releases desire that has been trapped, and it runs, freely, chaotically, in all directions.

Later in the opening track, Swift wonders, "If one thing had been different, would everything be different today?" It's not uncommon for same-gender friends to say things like, "If you were a boy, I would totally date you!" Queer people feel frustration at the boundaries and roles of friendship that feel so solid and immovable in youth. Queerness brings down those walls and allows more malleability. In queer friendship, one isn't left pondering upon what could be but is given room to explore the hearty density of what is. Once again, the failure of these friendships to morph into anything beyond is what's special and creative here. Who's to say that friendship is of lower importance than romantic relationship? "The reason [celebrity friends get paired together romantically] is because our culture strips us of the vocabulary to understand something like that outside of the context of romance. . . . Friendships [of all kinds] do not get cultural weight, because our culture places all of the value in a single romantic relationship that is supposed to sustain you over time" (Romano). These links and bonds are ranked on a scale that is irrelevant to and exclusionary of the queer community.

Swift goes on to make reference to a "chosen family." LGBTQ+ youth have historically surrounded themselves with others who empathize with their experiences rather than their blood relatives, who—at best—don't *get* them and—at worst—disown or harm them. Developing a "chosen family" is a survival/coping mechanism. This phrase is not used outside of this context, so Swift's usage of it is intentionally queer (Damante). Even if the speaker's friendships are bound in unacted-upon desire and, thus, unfulfilling, they are safer than other friendships. When she is with people who are similar to her, she is affirmed. She gets to be fluid and complex.

Swift's most overtly queer song, "betty," uses feminine pronouns and a feminine name while discussing the narrator's love interest. In an interview with Zane Lowe of BBC Radio 1 following the release of *evermore*, Swift stated that her way of writing songs in her younger days was "not sustainable," so she pivoted away from diaristic storytelling toward something more flexible and imaginative. She realized she could "make up characters and project [her] own thoughts and feelings onto them." "betty" features a utopian place: the titular character's garden. Swift croons, "In the garden, would you trust me?" prompting listeners to consider the implications of that setting on the relationship occurring within it. Gardens are eclectic and varied. They are private and fenced in but hold an entire world, an entire ecosystem. When somebody is inside a garden, they feel natural. It's only in the garden where this speaker is able to let her guard down and let herself fail the way her body and brain are telling her to.

This isn't the only track where Swift cultivates the pastoral. On "the lakes," Swift waxes poetic about wanting to ditch the material world and live off-the-grid in nature: "Take me to the lakes where all the poets went to die." This can be read as a nod to the lesbian aesthetic cottagecore, a style of dress and mindset shared by Generation Z girls and millennial women online, who bond over a common fantasy of escaping capitalism, men, and fast-paced tech to create a life without money, war, and violence (Saxon). This life will take place in the woods, tucked away. It is cozy, romantic, and candlelit. It is rugged and bodily. On "the lakes," Swift even mentions wanting to watch "wisteria grow over [her] bare feet," a lavender-colored plant symbolic of the early queer rights movement.

"Meet Me Behind The Mall": Fear, Hiding, and Secrecy

The speaker of "mirrorball" tries desperately to reconcile her internal and external identities. At her center, she is beginning to come together and solidify, which can be a joyous moment in the life of LGBTQ+ youth, but at the same time, she feels tension and conflict. Swift sings, "I can change everything about me to fit in." There is desperation in her plea. The instrumentation is fuzzy and dreamy, but Swift's lyrics, anxious and insecure, chafe against it. Her inside and outside *should* gel nicely, but they don't. Juggling multiple versions of oneself is something many in the LGBTQ+ community deal with, since queer people must "pass" in certain settings as straight or cisgender, for safety or employment reasons. There is a similarity between this and the way Swift's speaker performs identity. It goes beyond just trying to fit in. It feels painful and compulsive.

A particularly interesting lyric here is "I know they said the end is near / but I'm still on my tallest tiptoes / spinning in my highest heels." It is oft asserted that we have passed through the age of homophobia and arrived at its other side, especially after the Supreme Court's legalization of marriage equality in 2015 (*Obergefell v. Hodges*). Actual queer people know this isn't the case, as there are lived experiences that say otherwise. Regardless of how much progress was or will be made, we are living in a time when violent oppression is in our immediate rearview mirror, lurks beneath our every move, and is still a very legitimate reality for people in most parts of the world. That's not even to mention casual microaggressions and assumptions of heterosexuality/cisgenderism. The speaker in "mirrorball" still has to perform, regardless of alleged progress. In fact, she's "never been a natural." What seems so easy for other people to achieve is awkward and foreign to her. Passing is a dance.

On the following track, "seven," the speaker describes her first childhood love who, though no pronouns are used, is coded as female ("Your braids like a pattern"). The two share a gentle, outdoorsy summer together. This is before the speaker "learned civility," a time when she could behave exactly as she wanted without worrying about the world's judgment. "Learning civility" might equate to learning to pass as heterosexual. As a child, there was no need to hide because she didn't perceive anything as wrong yet.

During the second verse of this song, the speaker reveals her love interest lives in a dangerous home environment: "And I've been meaning to tell you / I think your house is haunted. / Your dad is always mad and that must be why. / I think you should come live with me. . . . Then you won't have to cry / or hide in the closet." The speaker's view of the situation is innocent and imaginative—perhaps in order to process it and bear its weight; as theorist Kathryn Bond Stockton has suggested, many queer people remember their childhood as "maudlin, earnest, melodramatic," due to being on the precipice of danger before they were able to fully conceptualize of it.

What's most beautiful about this moment is when Swift reassures her partner that their "love will be passed on." Throughout history, queer people have looked to who's come before them in order to make sense of their own reality; at the same time, queer history has often been erased and rewritten. Swift understands that her childhood relationship, which hinges upon providing mutual respite and survival, will be part of that lineage, a powerful form of affirmation.

Similarly, on "august," Swift also describes youthful summer romance. Despite the song's straightforward, bubblegum feel, it plays out like a confession. There are lines that seem to be about burgeoning sexuality. For instance, the speaker "whispers" when she confesses what she wants, from whom, and how. There are other allusions to secrecy, too, like, "Meet me behind the mall." This romance is not one that's blossoming in typical teenage social settings like parties or school. It's covert. Hiding and secrecy, although born from necessity, often establish intimacy. Fear is a core tenet of LGBTQ+ relationships that adds to their fullness. Swift sighs, awestruck, and claims, "wanting was enough." Queer love can be so mysterious and unheard of that many LGBTQ+ youth think there's something wrong with them, that they're "broken" when they are not feeling desire the way their peers are. This speaker found joy living "for the hope of it all." She reveres potential, permission. These are lifesaving buoys.

As Swift's speaker gets older, as on "illicit affairs," the hidden relationships she had growing up are now even more shameful, perhaps because they are explicitly sexual. In public, she relies on "longing stares" with her partner to assure her that the romance is alive. Anything more than that would risk exposure. It's unfortunate, because the speaker mentions that her partner "taught [her] a secret language [she] can't speak with anyone else." She is risking a loss of that language and an erasure of self. All of this has queer undertones because of a historic need for queer people to hide due to prejudice, oppression, and violent legislature.

On "ivy," a song frequently linked to the queer poetry of nineteenth-century Emily Dickinson (O'Mearns), Swift details a deft, deep relationship between two women, which is occurring in the shadow of one woman's husband. "What would he do if he found us out? . . . / He's gonna burn this house to the ground," the speaker mutters midway through the track, defeat in her voice. Swift's tone sours as she spits her frustrations. The relationship's coming-to is underscored by fear from its conception. The husband's presence ("He's in the room") is always a factor. Of course, he likely represents a threat much more ever-present, like the patriarchy and cisheteronormativity in general. Regardless, the chorus of "ivy" erupts in joy: "Oh! Goddamn!" The passionate moments between the two women are so truthful that they outweigh all threats. The chorus even confirms the relationship is sexual in nature: "Your ivy grows, / and now I'm covered in you," Swift writes, a physical, sensuous image with a mature understanding of the body. There is no shame in this image.

Fathers and Control

Aside from themes of secrecy and hiding, there are other queer undertones in this work. For instance, *folklore*'s "cardigan" centers around a refrain of "When you are young they assume you know nothing," which is evocative of the way queer people's identities are denied if they are revealed early on. Many people go back into the closet, so to speak, until they are of age because their early admissions of identity are stifled or passed off as "a phase" by parents or guardians. It can be painful to be labeled or discussed in a way that feels at odds with who you are. Swift continues working with the motif of familial disappointment later in the song, describing a love interest who leaves "like a father." This simile works on multiple levels. When a father leaves, it's especially painful, emphasizing how difficult the breakup or falling-out felt. However, on a more important note, a father leaving is a queer trope. Fathers leave queer children for whom they feel disapproval, disgust. Patriarchs tend to uphold a typical, traditional hierarchy in the family, and a child's queerness disrupts the institution that they spearhead. The speaker has been "left," literally or figuratively, by her father *and* her love interest. It is no wonder she feels so lost and unsteady.

A father figure is also mentioned on "tolerate it," an anxious masterpiece that can be read as being about vying for a parent's love. We look to fathers to know best, to lead us, to bolster our confidence. The speaker on "tolerate it" says, "I sit and watch you. / I notice everything you do or don't do. / . . . I wait by the door like I'm just a kid." She is waiting for affirmation of the identity she revealed, but he won't give it. He is intentionally giving her the silent treatment, holding back. Still, she cares. She's doing everything to impress him, to butter him up. It's a relatable dynamic that many queer people have experienced—putting effort into a relationship that's doomed due to "ideological differences." What is just a fleeting political opinion to the other person is personal and harmful, and Swift's speaker wonders, "where's the man who'd throw blankets over my barbed wire?" She can't pretend years of love didn't exist prior to her coming out. What is she supposed to do with all that? However, is it worth it? "What would you do if I break free and leave us in ruins? / Take this dagger in me and remove it? / . . . Believe me, I could do it": She toys with cutting him off, almost says it as a threat. However, her testy attitude feels hollow and nervous. Severing ties with someone who provides for you, be it financially or spiritually, can cause a groundless feeling.

Breaking Free from Compulsory Heterosexuality

"champagne problems," a sprawling ballad plucked on a creaky piano, follows its speaker through a years-long journey of suppressing her queerness. From the earliest revelation of her true feelings, the speaker gets pushback. After she "told [her] family" because she "couldn't keep it in," "no one celebrat[ed]." She goes so far as to indulge in compulsory heterosexuality, entering into a relationship with a man and forcing herself to perform the role of "girlfriend" to him. However, when he finally proposes, she wakes up: "Sometimes you just don't know the answer, / 'til someone's on their knees and asks you," Swift writes. It's a moment that could be empowering for her, finally taking a stance against the life she is expected to live, rather than the one she truly desires, but it's followed by talk amongst the community. Swift sings, "she would've made such a lovely bride. / What a shame she's fucked in the head, they said." For a woman, becoming a wife is a step toward becoming a mother. The world says this is the perfect trajectory for a young lady. Queerness suggests another path (Muñoz). It's a path that feels liberating, but, to a world embedded in homophobia and transphobia, that path feels deviant. Taking it means queer people are "fucked in the head." Swift's sparing use of obscenities on this album puts more emphasis on this particular moment; it stands out and feels especially cutting.

Once again, Swift points out the hypocrisy of a country performing tolerance and acceptance of queer identities while failing to love its own. She writes, "Soon they'll have the nerve to deck the halls that we once walked through," which, in context, recalls the decadence of Pride parades, which are becoming more commonplace. In recent years, cis-heterosexual people have attended Pride events to dress up, party, and take pictures, while failing to accompany their attendance with any civil action or concrete support to the community. Swift is right to point out that this takes a lot of "nerve." Queer people, unfortunately, must always be thinking of their safety, and a rainbow flag doesn't always signify an actual ally. On "peace," Swift sings that danger is "just around the corner, / . . . cause it lives in me." The speaker is so reluctant to engage in a queer relationship in fear of making someone else a target for prejudice that she begins reinforcing that prejudice herself.

Conclusion

"I don't belong and, my beloved, neither do you," Swift sings on "the lakes." How does Taylor Swift, of all people, not "belong?" How do her wealthy, white, straight male partners not "belong?" Inserting queer meaning into Swift's discography is a way of injecting it with life, connections, and edges.

Swift's *folklore* and *evermore* have garnered immense success since their respective releases. The general public enjoys and resonates with this music. While there are other A-list pop acts that write about queer themes, very rarely are the lyrics as varied, nuanced, and vast as Swift's. This is proof that queer media is universal through its specificity. This is a lesson that teachers of writing and storytelling can pass along to their students.

Rumors about Swift's sexual orientation have been floating around the internet for years. Some of these rumors surface from tabloids and blogs, while others come from well-meaning fans who feel connected to their favorite singer and wonder why. We have siphoned off queer artists so much so that queer fans might not feel capable of being "seen" by the music of a heterosexual artist. Do straight people yearn? Do straight people comprehend internalized homophobia? Do straight people feel uniquely othered, like an alien amongst their surroundings? There are questions that can't be answered definitively, and the speculation about Swift's personal life is futile, reducing queerness to something square and clean-cut, when, by definition, it is not. Sexuality and gender are spectrums we all constantly negotiate. Swift is simultaneously a symbol of heterosexuality and a symbol of queerness, depending upon which lens her listeners employ. Her canon expands rapidly to encompass all the stories she holds; it is almost bursting at the seams.

Works Cited

Avdeeff, Melissa K. "TikTok, Twitter, and Platform-Specific Technocultural Discourse in Response to Taylor Swift's LGBTQ+ Allyship in 'You Need to Calm Down.'" *Contemporary Music Review*, vol. 40, no. 1. (2021): 78–98.

Damante, Becca. "All of the Lesbian Easter Eggs Taylor Swift Left Us in *folklore*." *The Advocate*, 25 Jul. 2020.

Halberstam, Judith. *The Queer Art of Failure*. Duke University Press: Durham, 2011.

Muñoz, José Esteban. *Cruising Utopia: The Then and There of Queer Futurity*. New York University Press: New York, 2009.

O'Mearns, Riley. "Taylor Swift's *evermore* (Emily Dickinson's version)." K-State English, 20 January 2022, https://englishkstate.org/2022/01/20/taylor-swifts-evermore-emily-dickinsons-version/.

Romano, Aja. "The Queering of Taylor Swift." *Vox*, 30 Jul. 2020.

Saxon, Katherine. "What is Cottagecore? The Fanciful Aesthetic Explained." *The VOU*, 2 August 2023.

Smialek, Eric. "Who Needs to Calm Down? Taylor Swift and Rainbow Capitalism." *Contemporary Music Review*, vol. 40, no. 1. (2021): 99–119.

11

What It Means to Shake It Off: Taylor Swift, Race, and Citizenship

Shaun Cullen

At least since W.E.B. Dubois's 1903 analysis of what he called "the problem of the color line" in *The Souls of Black Folk*, many U.S. musicologists have sought to understand popular music—its lyrics, its sounds, its performers—as a confluence of musical cultures. Another critic, Albert Murray, would later characterize this confluence, in 1970, as "omni-American." For critics like DuBois and Murray, omni-American music, perhaps more than any other artistic form, represents the apotheosis of the cultural crossings, sometimes voluntary, often forced, that occurred when Black laborers were kidnapped from Africa and brought to the New World in chains. Thus, even in the musical expressions of U.S. performers whom listeners might identify as white, like Taylor Swift, analysts may arguably detect the remnants of what these critics and others, like Toni Morrison in her influential book *Playing in the Dark*, might identify as an "Africanist presence" (6), even if these remnants only manifest themselves as what Morrison (or Jacques Derrida, in another key text) described as ghosts, specters, haints. Among the white U.S. authors Morrison identifies most closely with this tendency is the great Southern modernist William Faulkner, who despite his personal prejudices, articulated for Morrison, and for other authors like the Colombian Gabriel Garcia-Márquez, a stark vision of the post-colonial encounter that is rooted in racial conflict but also generative of new progressive identities.[1]

In this essay, I analyze the racial meanings of Taylor Swift's lyrics within this global Southern context of cultural borrowings, theft, trauma, and transcendence, a context previously articulated most notably by Eric Lott in his book *Love and Theft* on blackface minstrelsy.[2] I begin with a discussion of Swift's lyrics' specific Southern origin in the genre of what is called in the U.S. "country" music. I then discuss the ways in which tropes of light and darkness have played out in her lyrics throughout her career, focusing especially on her rivalry with the African-American performer Ye (more

---

[1]   In his 1982 Nobel Lecture, Marquez described Faulkner as "his master."
[2]   See in particular the chapters on white ethnic music and the whiteness of film noir in Lott's *Black Mirror* (63–118). Coincidentally, one of Swift's earliest songs "Hey Stephen" was written about a member of the country group Love and Theft, Stephen Liles, who, perhaps ironically, borrowed their name from Lott's book via Bob Dylan's 2001 album of the same title.

commonly known as Kanye West). I close with a coda that seeks to understand the significance of Swift's most recent, mature lyrics within the context of the contemporary social justice movement in the U.S. that has been described by some supporters as "antiracist." The intent of this piece is not to claim that Swift's lyrics themselves are racist or antiracist in the sense that might be suggested by commentators like Ibram X. Kendi, who popularized the latter term in his bestselling book *How to Be an Antiracist.* Rather, an underlying warrant of the essay is that many U.S. popular music lyrics, including Swift's, which do not ostensibly claim to speak on race, might be productively analyzed through the lens of cultural analysis suggested by DuBois, Murray, Morrison, Lott, or even a deconstructionist like Derrida. Ultimately, I claim that Swift's lyrics contain a limited and sometimes flawed commentary on U.S. racial citizenship, which has evolved over time, with a tendency towards a progressive, antiracist stance.

On the Whiteness of Country Music

When analyzing how Taylor Swift's lyrics might trade in metaphors or rhetoric about race, one might first consider her early career status as a musician marketed directly to a country music audience. Though the history is complicated, country music has been associated, since its origins, with the U.S. South and a specific image and conception of racial whiteness. As documented in Karl Hagstrom Miller's book *Segregating Sound,* the very idea of country music as a genre developed as a byproduct of the segmentation of musical markets based on race. Prior to the Second World War and for some time after, the popular music industry specifically marketed so-called "race records" to distinct racial groups, especially African Americans. The country music industry, centered in Nashville, Tennessee, emerged in part to provide recordings to an audience segment, white Southerners, who were overlooked both by the producers of race records and by the more cosmopolitan, New York-based pop music industry that was beginning to dominate sales charts and the radio. At least one commentator, Geoff Mann, has gone so far as to argue that country music "sounds white" because the genre and the industry surrounding it continued to supply its audience with a culturally acceptable way of imagining and celebrating whiteness and by extension white racial supremacy after the Civil Rights Movement, when such ways of representing race became unacceptable in the wider, mainstream commercial culture. Simultaneously, that wider culture was becoming more homogenized into the shape of familiar 1950s conformity. Interestingly, in this context, since her political turn, Swift has often expressed her intent not to "go back to the 1950s" culturally.

Due to her age and relatively sheltered upbringing, when Taylor Swift debuted as a professional musician, it would have been difficult for her to appreciate this longer history and her place within its shifting dynamics. Nevertheless, her early music arguably plays into cultural stereotypes of racial whiteness as they were articulated in mainstream country music at that time. Specifically, much of the early marketing and content of Swift's music celebrates her innocence and purity, values that are associated with a small-town life that is assumed to be racially homogenous, and in songs like

"Love Story" and "White Horse," with the actual color white. In these songs, symbolism surrounding the color white, associated with marriage and chivalry, is detached from a racial context, but it arguably provides these early lyrics with a racial subtext that is uncomfortable to hear in a musical genre that has often communicated to its audience in straightforwardly racist ways, reproducing stereotypes and indeed promoting white supremacist ideology directly in isolated but prominent instances. As is familiar to her fans, Swift's public image during this time was, appropriately, that of a young, innocent, small-town girl destined for big things, an image reinforced both by her lyrics and her styling. This image was only loosely related to Swift's actual biography: raised in suburban Pennsylvania by stage parents who took the extreme step of moving to Nashville to further their daughter's career.

Swift's breakthrough song "Tim McGraw" appeared as the leadoff track on her self-titled debut album and was that album's first single. In the song, Swift expresses the hope that every time her ex-boyfriend hears the country singer Tim McGraw, he thinks of her. In the song, Swift mentions signifiers of small-town, rural life, including "backroads," "blue jeans," and a "Chevy truck." She even goes so far as to mention "Georgia stars," though at the time the song was written, Swift lived in Tennessee. Indeed, it is worthwhile to keep in mind when listening to Swift's early country songs that she wrote them as an outsider, having only lived in the U.S. South for a few years before she started to become popular. As noted by the journalist Malcolm Gladwell, this trajectory is rare for country artists, most of whom originate in the U.S. Bible Belt, specifically the states of Tennessee, Texas, Kentucky, Alabama, Arkansas, and Virginia.[3] Notably, these are also states that (with the exception of Kentucky) joined the Confederacy during the Civil War.

Especially when entering this musical tradition as an outsider, Swift is expressing a cultural preference for a genre that deservedly or not is associated with the values of the Bible Belt, the Confederacy, and indeed white supremacy, no matter how resentful some country performers may be of that legacy. For instance, the subjects of her song, Tim McGraw and his wife Faith Hill, are notable as two Nashville celebrities who have been outspoken, like Swift, about their liberal politics and support for the Democratic party. However, McGraw's own debut hit "Indian Outlaw" (1994) is one of the most racially offensive songs produced by a country artist ever.[4] In it, he uncritically repeats stereotypes about Native Americans living in "wigwams" and smoking "peace pipes." The lyrics in the song are cruel and dehumanizing; he ostensibly romanticizes Native Americans as outlaws and maybe even in some weird way is claiming to feel kinship with Native Americans, but the general effect of the song is irredeemable and unserious. Surely, Swift did not have this song in mind when she mentioned McGraw in her own song, as he is much more familiar to country audiences for his emotional love songs like "Don't Take the Girl" (1994) and "Just to See You Smile" (1997). However, it is likely that she would have at least been aware of the song, as it was still playing on

---

[3] Gladwell obtains this result through a simple review of "best country song" lists.
[4] This song and the others by McGraw mentioned below appear on his album *Greatest Hits*.

country radio at the time of her debut. As mentioned in a contemporary report in the *LA Times* (Hochman), when "Indian Outlaw" was released in 1994, some Native American groups accused McGraw of not only profiting from the song's harmful stereotypes and cliches but indeed leaning into the controversy surrounding them to bolster his outlaw image. This is a decent indication of the context that surrounded Swift's debut as a country artist.

The Wider Cultural Context Surrounding Swift's Early and Middle Career

With her second record *Fearless* (2008), Swift solidified her status as a critically and commercially successful recording artist and started to give hints at the steps she would take to move away from the country music genre. From the beginning of her career, the marketing surrounding her music had always been multifaceted, not only targeting country fans but also the teen market that had reestablished itself in the previous decade with the success of artists like Britney Spears, Christina Aguilera, The Backstreet Boys, and NSYNC. Early in her career, among these stars, Swift was associated most closely with the musician and television personality Miley Cyrus, whose father Billy Ray Cyrus had scored a country crossover hit in 1992 with the song "Achy Breaky Heart." For instance, Swift appeared in a cameo in the film spinoff of the younger Cyrus's television show, *Hannah Montana: The Movie* (dir. Peter Chelsom, 2009). As late as 2010, Swift included an interview clip of Cyrus as part of her stage show (in Vena, n.p.).

It was around this time that Swift experienced a public humiliation when the rap star Ye (better known as Kanye West) interrupted her acceptance speech for an MTV Video Music Award in late 2009. Though it is arguably chauvinistic to think of Ye's unwanted and unwarranted interference with Swift's career as being definitive, it is represented in this way in Swift's Netflix documentary *Miss Americana*, the content of which Swift almost definitely had a hand in determining. In other words, she acknowledges the role that Ye played in the formation of her public image during this critical stage of her career, despite the fact that she neither welcomed nor approved of this attention.

Unwittingly, Swift's involvement with Ye placed her at the center of discussions concerning race in the U.S., if for no other reason than the fact that it reproduced racialized scripts for understanding conflicts between Black men and white women, scripts that both artists arguably embraced in later recordings and performances related to the incident. For instance, at the next year's MTV Video Music Awards, the "scene of the crime" so to speak, Swift performed her new song "Innocent" from her 2010 album *Speak Now*. This album is notable as Swift's only album on which she wrote all of the songs herself, an impressive feat given the album's length, complexity, and generic grounding in the contemporary country genre that relies on professional songwriters as a way of bolstering star talents. In her performance of "Innocent" at the VMAs, Swift regrettably drew on plantation imagery that seemed almost directly lifted from the set of *Gone with the Wind* (dir. Victor Fleming, 1939), which, along with *Birth of a Nation* (dir. D.W. Griffith, 1916), is one of U.S. visual culture's foremost racist epics.[5]

Elsewhere on *Speak Now*, Swift surreptitiously castigates Ye in lyrics that seem naive but betray a subdued violence that verges on the macabre. For instance, the track "Mean" is one of the songs on the album that fits best in the country genre, given its rather prominent use of banjo (an instrument of partial African origin) as musical accompaniment. In the song, Swift sings about a bully, maybe even a relative who makes her "feel like nothing." In the chorus she even goes so far as to assert that "one day" she will be "big enough" so the bully "can't hit" her. Certainly, these lyrics are partially symbolic, and it is likely that Swift was imagining herself in a male role when singing the song, but it is nevertheless chilling to imagine the physically slight Swift being hit by anyone, especially a male relative, which seems to be what the song implies. Given that many commentators have noted that the song sounds like a retort to the controversy set off by West indicates the deep feelings the incident triggered in Swift, which she echoes in interviews in *Miss Americana*, both from the time of the incident and the filming of the documentary.

The image of the white woman imperiled by the Black bully has been difficult for Swift to shake off. As she has made the self-conscious transition from country singer-songwriter to pop artist, the racial politics of her music have repeatedly come under criticism. Most notably, on her career-defining album *1989*, Swift found it difficult to integrate sounds and lyrical tropes from other genres without evading accusations of cultural appropriation. The videos produced to promote *1989* did not allay these concerns and indeed might have worsened them. Notably, in the video for her song "Shake It Off," one of Swift's biggest hits and arguably her definitive pop song, Swift appeared alongside Black women dancers performing in a hip-hop style. The basic concept of the video is that Swift fails to perform a number of dance styles, from hip-hop to ballet, and in general, the cast of the video is racially diverse. However, the dancers in the hip-hop sequence of the video are all Black and noticeably more physically imposing than the dancers in other parts of the video, something that the video accentuates in a cringeworthy shot of Swift singing while positioned underneath a Black dancer's spread legs, looking up at her thighs.

Though the point of the video is to highlight Swift's charming awkwardness in that performance setting, it intentionally contrasts her delicacy and lack of coordination with the Black women whose movements are presented as sexualized and raunchy. Specifically, at the time, there was a moral panic around the dance move called "twerking," which conservative commentators viewed as a kind of moral degeneracy, especially due to its popularity among young people on social media. Only recently, Cyrus, the teen performer whom Swift had praised and emulated, had caused a stir of her own when she was caught performing the move during another infamous MTV VMA performance. In Swift's video, her inability to twerk is played for laughs, but in the context of her conflict with Ye and her earlier association with the country music

---

[5] I have discussed this performance in more detail in a previous article, "The Innocent and the Runaway."

genre, it came off to some viewers like a demeaning contrast was being drawn between her purity as a performer and the raunchiness of the Black dancers.

The video for another *1989* song "Wildest Dreams" featured Swift on an African safari, though in the video no Black people are seen. In the entertainment press of the time, the director of the video, Joseph Kahn, who is Korean-American, defended the decision not to include Black actors in the video set in Africa by stating that it just was not something that he or the crew thought was necessary given the concept behind the video, which was merely meant to evoke the romance of the video's natural setting.[6] These videos were released in the early stages of activism surrounding police brutality against Black people and the popularization of the Black Lives Matter hashtag (#BLM). For the most part, Swift's transition from country to pop was praised. Based on sales numbers, she retained her old audience and presumably added many new fans, but this increased exposure almost certainly made Swift more susceptible to criticism and raised audience expectations with regard to her views on social issues in a media environment that was becoming increasingly politicized.

Notably, during this time, Swift embarked on a couple of collaborations with rap artists Kendrick Lamar and Future, and she even tried rapping herself on the track with Future and Ed Sheeran from her 2017 album *reputation* entitled "End Game." Since that time, several critics have noticed the increased prevalence of what seem to be rap-inspired lyrics in Swift's songs, with regard to their lyrical tropes, imagery, and what hip-hop fans might call her lyrical flow, which is sometimes more like spoken word than melodic pop. Even "Shake It Off" contains a schoolyard-style rap section and the lyrics, "Can't stop, won't stop," in the chorus—a phrase repeated in many hip-hop songs and in the title of a popular book about the genre by the author Jeff Chang.

Taylor Swift's Progressive Turn

Especially since Swift came out in support of the U.S. Senate and House candidates Phil Bredesen and Jim Cooper in the 2018 federal election, she has been able to evade, for the most part, further controversies with regard to her stances regarding racial prejudice and discrimination, though in many ways her views on these issues are unresolved. To be clear, it is not completely reasonable that Swift address any and all social issues, and if she feels she has nothing to add to discussions on race, her silence may be more thoughtful than noncommittal. On the other hand, Swift's career has coincided almost exactly with a period of intense dialogue around race in the U.S. that many hope will result in more serious efforts on the part of the nation's political leaders to address racial injustices in meaningful ways. It stands to reason that the most prominent pop star in the U.S., who comments freely on other social issues, such as LGBTQ rights and violence against women, would have a position on racial matters,

---

[6]	The controversy was discussed in a *Hollywood Reporter* article, "'Wildest Dreams' Director Defends Taylor Swift's Music Video Against 'Whitewashing' Allegations."

especially given the prominent role played by Black, Asian, and Latino people in the contemporary pop music industry that Swift attempted to court after her move away from the country genre on *1989*. For her part, Swift did post a Tweet in support of the protests against police violence in the summer of 2020, but other than that fairly rote rehearsal of liberal piety, Swift has stayed silent on the racism that she once perceived in a figure like Marsha Blackburn, the current Senator from Tennessee who defeated Bredesen and whom in *Miss Americana* Swift describes directly as a "racist."

Interestingly, it is on Swift's least successful album commercially, 2019's *Lover*, where she addresses issues surrounding racial inequality and difference in a way that seems at all direct, though when she does so her engagement is arguably more complex than the straightforward statements of antiracist solidarity she has posted on Twitter. The album *Lover* was intriguingly framed around the concept that Swift is a lover not a fighter and not a hater either, the specific antithesis to being a lover that she invoked in the lyrics to "Shake It Off"—"the haters gonna hate, hate, hate," etc. She reiterated this contrast in marketing materials surrounding the release of *Lover*. In the lyric book for the album, for instance, she writes, "I've decided that in this life, I want to be defined by the things I love—not the things I hate, the things I'm afraid of, or the things that haunt me in the middle of the night. Those things may be struggles, but they're not my identity." Swift's thought here is noble, and despite the fact that *Lover* has been her least successful album commercially to this point, the message has almost certainly resonated with her fanbase, which has continued to expand and become more passionate.

Arguably, *Lover* contains Swift's most succinct political messaging. Though it would be a stretch to assert that it comments on racial politics directly, certain tracks at least insinuate Swift's feelings about racial difference. A case in point is the *Lover* track "The Man." The *Miss Americana* documentary captures the recording and composition of this song at an early stage. The documentary itself is named after another *Lover* track, "Miss Americana and the Heartbreak Prince," in which Swift again addresses her rivalry with Ye, who is there conflated with Donald Trump, whom Ye politically supported, as an example of toxic masculinity. The implication is subtle, but one of Ye's most acclaimed albums is *808s & Heartbreak* from 2008—hence his epithet "heartbreak prince." Listening to playback of the instrumental track for "The Man," Swift and her producer Joel Little, who is credited as a co-writer, collaborate on lyrics and melodies to go with the synthesized beat they have created for the song.

The central concept of the song is familiar. As a woman performer, Swift is imagining what it would be like to be a man. The pathos in the song is arguably enhanced by Swift's life narrative, which she seems to assume will be familiar to her intended listener: the beginning of her career as a teen idol in a country music genre that values tradition; her transition to pop music, which to some extent involved her sexualization; her famous romances with several celebrities; her conflict with Ye; the accusations of cultural appropriation; her simmering feud with alpha-male music executives Scooter Braun and Scott Borchetta. She tags her attitude toward all these controversies and conflicts with her refrain in the chorus: "If I was a man, then I'd be the man." Based on its representation in *Miss Americana*, it almost seems as though we get to see Swift at exactly the moment she came up with this line. She stands up straight as she sings it and gestures with her hands in a kind of celebratory dance. It is a simple line, but perhaps one that signifies more than Swift intended.

In this context, it is hard to overlook the etymology of the contrast Swift establishes here by imagining herself as "the man" and not just "a man." As noted in the *Dictionary of American Regional English*, the usage of the pronoun "the" in front of the word "man" in this way has a very specific etymological origin that the *Dictionary* traces back to the U.S. South: "Man . . . with *the*: **a** A man who is in a position of power, esp over the speaker; the boss . . . **b** By ext: the White man in general; White society." Among the etymological examples given, one is taken from James Baldwin's novel *Another Country*, where it is used to refer to a band leader. Notably, Baldwin also titled his horrific short story about a lynching in a small Southern town "Going to Meet the Man." It is almost certain that when Swift calls herself "the man," she does not intend for listeners to hear that as an admission that she has designs on the power of "the White man in general," but based on lyrics elsewhere in the song and how she talks about the song in *Miss Americana*, there are indications that such an idea might not have been completely outside her frame of reference. Notably, elsewhere in the song she wonders:

> What's it like to brag about raking in dollars
> And getting bitches and models
> And it's all good if you're bad
> And it's okay if you're mad?
> If I was out flashing my dollars
> I'd be a bitch, not a baller.

Swift's lyrics here clearly reference cliches and tropes common to rap songs and what in this case, derogatively perhaps, might be called "hip-hop culture." This is a culture to which Swift knows she does not have an authentic connection, even if she has often expressed her admiration for rap and rappers.

There is another and somewhat related usage of the word "man" within Black vernacular English that is also mentioned in the *Dictionary of American Regional English*: "**3** A male friend, esp a close and trusted one. *esp freq among male Black speakers.*" It may not be as much of a stretch to imagine that this is really the meaning of "man" Swift has in mind when she calls herself "the man," and here one could detect inklings of the dialectic of "love and theft" that Eric Lott first identified in the misappropriations of Black culture by white performers that characterized blackface minstrelsy in the antebellum era in the U.S. Throughout her transition to pop star, Swift has sometimes awkwardly acknowledged the role of Black performers in that tradition. She has spoken out on racial issues, however vaguely, and she has collaborated with Black artists. *Miss Americana* highlights her friendship with YouTube celebrity Todrick Hall, a Black man and outspoken gay activist, as well as the making of the video for her song "You Need to Calm Down," which was specifically intended as a protest in support of GLAAD and featured appearances by Hall and other queer Black celebrities RuPaul, Laverne Cox, and Karamo Brown. At one point in the documentary, Hall is even depicted painting Swift's nails, clearly an innocent act of affection on his part but also an act of subservience that both of them seem to acknowledge when they joke about his becoming a manicurist (as opposed to the well paid and highly visible celebrity that he actually is).

When discussing the concept behind "The Man," Swift opines at one point about why "they," presumably men in general but perhaps just Black men specifically, get to call women "bitches" and boast about sleeping with models. In the documentary, no framing is given for these comments, but they evidence an "us versus them" othering that drifts in between references to men and women, and to Black and white. This is about where Swift's affective relationship towards issues of racial inequality lies. She is conscious of such issues and concerned. She seems to want to understand Black perspectives (other ethnic groups do not seem to register), but through some confluence of circumstances—her upbringing, her adult experiences as a highly privileged celebrity, her unfortunate and very public conflict with a Black man who has subsequently revealed himself to be an irascible bigot— Swift cannot quite seem to liberate herself from the narrow imaginary of her childhood transition from white suburban Pennsylvania to white suburban Tennessee, from Union North to Confederate South, from fleshpot to Bible Belt, no matter how much she has attempted to answer for or directly repair the trauma of that historical legacy.

Coda: Stare Into the Darkness

Reflecting on the arc of Taylor Swift's short but impressive stint as the U.S's foremost popular musician, it is hard not to notice the role that color has played in her lyrical imagination—from the white knights and horses of her early singles to the red passion of her physical and lyrical maturation, to the rainbow colors of *Lover*, and to her "late night" album, 2022's *Midnights*, with its dark tones of scarlet, maroon, and lavender, as well as the sublime whiteness of "snow on the beach." As she discusses in *Miss Americana*, Swift is known for generating mood boards to accompany her lyrical ideas, an idea borrowed from the fashion industry and the therapeutic language of self-actualization, in which predominant colors, like musical timbres, guide her conceptualization.

The song "Lavender Haze" from *Midnights* is framed around the image of Swift staring "up at the ceiling" with someone, presumably a lover, in what might be a post-coital moment. The gender of the lover is not mentioned, and in fan communities, the invocation of the color "lavender," a symbol of gay pride, has been given a queer reading. She feels social pressure to conform to "1950s shit." Clearly, this term is an allusion to the social context of gender discrimination during that period, but given Swift's more recent association with queer Black figures like Hall, RuPaul, Cox, and Brown, it does not seem too farfetched to assert that she might also want the listener to think, at this point, about the social context of Jim Crow. Notably, a 1950s-style mise-en-scène was deployed in Swift's video in which these celebrities appeared. At this stage in her career, Swift has clearly transcended the trappings of Jim Crow-era country and plantation nostalgia that permeated some of her early work, and as she matures, along with U.S. society, it has sounded as though she has become more aware of her status as a white celebrity, artist, and citizen struggling to communicate, in a perhaps improving but still segregated republic, across the color line.

Works Cited

Baldwin, James. *Another Country*. Dial: New York, 1962.

Baldwin, James. "Going to Meet the Man." *Going to Meet the Man*. Dial: New York, 1965. 227–249.

Birth of a Nation. Directed by D.W. Griffith. D.W. Griffith Corp. 1915.

Chang, Jeff. *Can't Stop, Won't Stop: A History of the Hip-Hop Generation*. Picador: New York, 2005.

Cullen, Shaun. "The Innocent and the Runaway: Kanye West, Taylor Swift, and the Cultural Politics of Racial Melodrama." *Journal of Popular Music Studies*, vol. 28, no. 1. (2016): 33–50.

Cyrus, Billy Ray. "Achy Breaky Heart." Written by Don Von Tress. Polygram, 1991.

Derrida, Jacques. *Specters of Marx: The State of the Debt, the Work of Mourning, and the New International*. Routledge: New York, 1994.

DuBois, W.E.B. *The Souls of Black Folk*. A.C. McClurg: Chicago, 1903.

Dylan, Bob. *Love and Theft*. Columbia, 2001.

Garcia-Márquez, Gabriel. "Nobel Lecture: The Solitude of Latin America." *NobelPrize.org*, Nobel Prize Outreach AB 2023.

Gladwell, Malcolm. "The King of Tears." *Revisionist History* Podcast. 15 August 2023.

Gone with the Wind. Dir. Victor Fleming. MGM, 1939.

Hannah Montana: The Movie. Dir. Peter Chelsom. Disney, 2009.

Hochman, Steve. "Country Hit 'Indian Outlaw' Hits a Nerve." *LA Times*, March 24, 1994.

Kendi, Ibram X. *How to Be an Antiracist*. One World: New York, 2019.

Lott, Eric. *Black Mirror: The Cultural Contradictions of American Racism*. Harvard University Press: Cambridge, 2017.

Lott, Eric. *Love and Theft: Blackface Minstrelsy and the American Working Class*. Oxford University Press: Oxford, 1993.

"man, n." *Dictionary of American Regional English*, vol. 6. Harvard University Press: Cambridge, 2013. Accessed online August 15, 2023.

Mann, Geoff. "Why Does Country Music Sound White? Race and the Voice of Nostalgia," *Ethnic and Racial Studies*, vol. 31. (2008): 73–100.

McGraw, Tim. *Greatest Hits*. Curb, 2000.

Miller, Karl Hagstrom. *Segregating Sound: Inventing Folk and Pop in the Age of Jim Crow*. Duke University Press: Durham, 2010.

Miss Americana. Dir. Lana Wilson, Netflix. 2020.

Morrison, Toni. *Playing in the Dark: Whiteness and the Literary Imagination*. Harvard University Press: Cambridge, 1992.

Murray, Albert. *The Omni-Americans: Some Alternatives to the Folklore of White Supremacy*. Library of America: New York, 2020.

Swift, Taylor. "Taylor Swift - Eminem's 'Lose Yourself' and Uncle Kracker's 'Smile' Grand Rapids, MI." *YouTube*, 29 July 2011.

Swift, Taylor and T-Pain. "Thug Story." *vimeo*.

Vena, Jocelyn. "Taylor Swift Brings Fearless Tour To Madison Square Garden." *MTV.com*. 28 August 2019.

"Wildest Dreams' Director Defends Taylor Swift's Music Video Against 'Whitewashing' Allegations." Hollywood Reporter, September 2, 2015.

Ye (Kanye West). *808s & Heartbreak*. Roc-A-Fella. 2008.

Part Three

Time, Curious Time: (Re-)Writing Memory

12

"Time, curious time": Time, Memory, and Agency in Taylor Swift

Miranda Steege

There are many Taylor Swifts. One need only recall the end of the music video for "Look What You Made Me Do," in which an array of Swifts, each dressed in an iconic costume from the songwriter's past, argue with each other, or consider the lyrics of "mirrorball," in which Swift writes, "I can change everything about me to fit in." In this essay, I will focus on two Swifts, which I am calling "Swift-as-speaker" and "Swift-as-creator." Swift-as-speaker is the intradiegetic Swift, the speaker of the lyrics of each song, who is bounded by the story the song itself tells. This is not the "real" Taylor Swift but rather the persona she crafts within each song and throughout her oeuvre. Swift-as-creator is the extradiagetic Swift, the songwriter who creates the lyrics and story. Swift-as-creator is also the professional Swift who participates in the production and distribution of her albums. Swift, of course, has had many collaborators in her songwriting, and she is by no means solely responsible for how her music and brand are marketed and sold. Swift-as-creator is, therefore, not the "real" Taylor Swift but rather an artistic and professional entity.

This essay discusses the balance of agency and power between these two Swifts, specifically in relation to a major theme of her work: time and memory. I will argue that Swift's oeuvre is structured by a complex, essentially contradictory theory of time and memory. As depicted within the songs themselves, time is active and agential; Swift-as-speaker appears at the mercy of memories which either freeze her in past moments or speed her journey into an unknown future. On the other hand, Swift-as-creator crafts her depictions of being controlled by time in a way that allows her to take control of her own personal and professional narrative as a female singer-songwriter and businesswoman. This move is strengthened by her professional strategies of gaining agency over her career and persona, particularly her reclamation of her earlier works via re-recordings. Swift-as-creator uses time and memory to her own ends, even as Swift-as-speaker finds herself under their sway.

Theorizing Swift as split between speaker and creator echoes work that has been done on many literary authors, especially poets, who frequently occupy the role of both speaker and creator in similar ways. Scholarship on nineteenth-century women poets is particularly helpful here because of the tendency of these writers to use this split persona to navigate the complicated Victorian landscape of gender, power, and authorship—a landscape not entirely dissimilar from that Swift has faced in her own historical moment. For example, Isobel Armstrong's writing on the "expressive tradition" of Victorian women's poetry and Sarah Paul's work on narration as strategic female self-centering in Elizabeth Barrett Browning offer insights into how Swift's portrayal of herself as at the mercy of forces beyond her control paradoxically gives her more agency over her work and career.

I will, for the most part, stick closely to Swift's lyrics in this essay, demonstrating how they construct their own theory of time and memory that is, I argue, relatively consistent across Swift's oeuvre. While Swift's skills, perspective, and aesthetics have certainly evolved over her career so far, her investment in the capacity of time and memory to preoccupy, overwhelm, and even reshape lives remains a throughline from her earliest works to her most recent. Ultimately, I argue that Swift-as-creator is able to manipulate time and memory enough to gain a substantial—but still incomplete—agency over her own personal and professional narrative, and that this is a specifically gendered strategy combatting cultural skepticism around the talent and acumen of women artists.

Swift-as-Speaker: At the Mercy of Time and Memory

Swift-as-speaker frequently finds herself in the grip of memories she cannot control, tossed about between past, present, and future. Within Swift's lyrics, time itself has agency. Rather than simply passing her by, it actively shapes her life. In "invisible string," time is "curious" and "mystical": strange, peculiar, an object of fascination with a life of its own. It is responsible for her state of wellbeing, hurting and then healing her, and it dictates her emotional landscape, giving her first "the blues" and then "purple-pink skies." Time can keep her stuck in place; she is "paralyzed" by it in "All Too Well," and in "right where you left me," she gets "frozen" in the moment of a bad breakup. In other instances, time hurries her along faster than she would like. In "Nothing New," she can "feel time moving" as she worries about losing relevance, while a summer love affair slips away into "a moment in time" in "august." In "Never Grow Up" and "Innocent," she looks wistfully back to a simpler youth.

Time is intimately linked to memory, which is its primary tool for enacting its agency on Swift-as-speaker. Memory is what stops her from moving forward into the future, letting go of the past, or living in the present. In "Red," persistent images of a former relationship make it impossible for her to move on. "Cornelia Street" describes a potential future in which she can never walk past the place she shares with her current lover because the memories of their time together will be too strong. Even when memory's effects are more benign, Swift-as-speaker is unable to control them; in "New Year's Day," for example, she urges herself and her lover to "hold onto the memories," but the possibility of growing apart from him still looms over the song. Meanwhile, in "Back to December," her continued attempts to return to the moment of a breakup to make a different choice cannot in fact repair the broken relationship. Memory gets her in its grip and casts her back and forth in time, challenging her ability to control how she reacts to current situations and flooding her with unasked-for emotions. Time is peculiarly elastic in many of Swift's songs, which frequently shift between past, present, and future perspectives. It does not move in one direction, making its control over her more total and less predictable. Swift's songs have a tendency not merely to dwell on memories of the past but to envision future moments in which Swift-as-speaker will be doomed to relive her memories of the present situation. These potential future memories hold great power. Sometimes they enable her to hang onto precious time that has slipped away, but more often, they cause her imagined future self pain and grief. The frequent shifts of tenses and perspectives in Swift's lyrics trap Swift-as-speaker in slippery and often complicated temporal loops, thrusting her in and out of memories that exert a powerful sway over her.

This treatment of time and memory is present even in Swift's earliest works. The fact that she was still in her mid-to-late teens when she co-wrote and released her first two albums does not stop her from engaging heavily in nostalgia and reflecting at length on the past. "Tim McGraw," her very first single, thematizes the power of memory and the bittersweet passage of time. The lyrics urge a former lover to return to specific memories of their relationship when he hears her favorite song: moonlight on the lake, faded jeans, a head on a chest, dancing all night. The McGraw song referred to in the title has the power to evoke the past so strongly it can transport the former lover to a different time and place. Yet as much as Swift wants to control her ex's experience of time and memory, she cannot fully do so. The phrase "I hope" repeats throughout the song—"I hope it takes you back to that place," she sings to him: "I hope you think of me."

A number of other early songs engage with temporality in similar ways. Take, for example, "Love Story": while the majority of the song is a seemingly simple tale of forbidden love from the perspective of its teenaged singer, its first line frames the entire story as a series of memories. The line, "We were both young when I first saw you," seems to suggest the narrator is looking back on the story from some future moment. The music video adds another layer of temporal distance between the song's narrator and the story of what happened to her by showing a contemporary high-school-aged Swift experience a sudden flashback when she sees a boy sitting on the grass; suddenly, she and the boy are wearing vaguely historical clothes and playing out their love story in some sort of mythical past. The music video suggests that this past is capable of springing up at any moment and sweeping Swift-as-speaker away.

"Mine" also turns a seemingly straightforward, chronological recollection of a relationship into a back-and-forth journey between different memories and moments in time. Swift-as-speaker looks back on how this relationship unfolded—the first meeting, the fights, the landmark moments. Yet she does not remain in the static position of someone recalling these moments at will. Instead, a visceral experience of the early days of their relationship continually thrusts itself upon her because whenever she looks at her lover, "it's like the first time." Additionally, her memories play an active role in the relationship, strengthening it when it falters by reminding her of how she felt sitting by the water at the moment she began to truly believe in their future. The lover also experiences these memories. Just after the bridge, the chorus repeats, but from his perspective instead of hers; he is now the one remembering their history. The music video emphasizes the important role of memory in their relationship by putting Swift in a clearing surrounded by photos of moments they've shared hanging from trees. It also adds another layer of memory by showing the current-day Swift having flashbacks to her own parents' fighting when she was a child—persistent memories that impede her ability to trust her lover. It is only the more recent memories of him that finally exorcise these earlier, less pleasant memories. The final few shots of the video return to the first moment they meet and then show Swift in the clearing of photographs, singing, "I can see it now."

Although the temporal elasticity in "Mine" is mostly beneficial, time's ability to bend and loop at will causes difficulties for Swift-as-speaker in other songs. Often, Swift-as-speaker loses her grounding in the present moment when she is gripped by the conviction that her future will be haunted by memories of that moment after her present relationships and priorities have shifted or ended. Take "Long Live," a song about finally succeeding within a music industry that, according to the lyrics, has previously viewed her as an upstart outsider. The song opens on a moment of triumph as the crowd cheers her on. Yet its first words indicate that Swift-as-speaker is unable to live in the present: she begins by telling herself to "remember this moment." This introduces the song's peculiar narrative framing: the entire thing is a plea to herself, her colleagues, and her listeners to remember the present moment. "Long live," a phrase repeated in the chorus, is equal parts command and supplication. "Long live" evokes the superstitious linguistic magic of its most common usage, "Long live the king." If one wishes it hard enough, says it enough times, surely, hopefully, the object of the statement will indeed live on even after its death. This rhetorical move is present, too, in the phrase, "May these memories break our fall," a lexical construction in which the imperative "may" echoes statements that also function as repeated invocations of gravitas, whose speaking holds its own power—"May the Lord be with you," "May the force be with you." Swift is calling on her future memories of the present moment to aid her in some as-yet-unspecified time of need.

Whether she has the power to do so, however, seems uncertain. While Swift-as-speaker is trying to crystallize this triumphant moment in her memory, she is not entirely confident that the passing of time won't erase it. In the bridge, she speaks directly to someone who has helped her get to this moment and is sharing in her triumph. She asks them to promise to stand by her "forever" but immediately acknowledges her lack of control over the future, giving them an alternative: if "fate" separates them, this passes the story on to their future children. Inexplicably, the person's children will not already recognize the very famous Taylor Swift but must be told her name when their parent points her out in old photographs. This suggests an almost unlimited power on the part of time to erase memories and reshape lives. The song's final lyrics are an apparently declarative "We will be remembered"—as if, perhaps, Swift-as-speaker has finally gained confidence in her ability to secure her future legacy. However, after so much lyrical energy spent on trying to ensure that the moment will live on in people's memories, this assertion reads less like an absolute statement and more like a defiant hope.

"Cornelia Street" is perhaps the most potent example of Swift-as-speaker's lack of control over time and her susceptibility to the power of memory. Like "Wildest Dreams," the song frames a current relationship through the lens of potential future memories. Unlike the earlier song, however, Swift-as-speaker is not resigned to the relationship's eventual end. She repeatedly states that she hopes she will never lose her lover, and her fear that she will makes her vulnerable to the strange elasticity of time and memory. The song takes place when the relationship is several years old, but it barely lingers at all in the present moment. The speaker moves between two other periods: one, the memories she recalls from the early days of the relationship, and two, an imagined future in which those memories will cause her heartbreak if she and her lover ever break up. There is only one point in the song in which Swift-as-speaker is truly in the present moment: "You hold my hand on the street / Walk me back to that apartment." But the lyrics immediately shift back to memory: "Years ago / We were just inside." It is as if the relationship is so important to Swift that she cannot simply live in the present, needing to immortalize it in her memory even if doing so will cause her tremendous pain in the event of a split from her lover. Indeed, she sings that she is "terrified" of him ever walking away. Her lack of control over time and memory is frightening enough that she is unable to enjoy what she has in the moment. The present is forever overshadowed by the past, the future, and future memories of the past.

Swift-as-Creator: Manipulating Time and Memory

When viewed as the subject of her own lyrics, Swift is frequently powerless over the waves of memory and shifts in temporality that shape her life. Yet Swift-as-creator has a much firmer grasp on them, using their elasticity and power to her own advantage. In fact, many of her songs can be read as attempts to gain control of time and memory—to put them in an order that tells her preferred story about her life and career. Within the lyrics, she is at the mercy of time; as a songwriter, however, she gets to narrate, centering her own voice so that even when she appears helpless, sad, or angry, she is still in control of how listeners understand her experiences. Her skill at evoking memories through tiny details does more than give power to memory; it also shows off her own ability to make memory work for her. This strategy of giving herself agency as a creator is, I will argue, partly a response to gendered assumptions that female artists, especially younger ones, are easily exploited, do not earn their praise, and are valuable for their authentic expressions of emotion rather than their skill at their craft.

It is helpful, here, to consider Swift within a longer tradition of female writers who have made similar decisions about their self-presentation both within and external to their works. We may, for example, understand Swift's separation of the largely helpless Swift-as-speaker and the more agential Swift-as-creator as a twenty-first-century version of the strategy Sarah Paul reads in Elizabeth Barrett Browning's *Sonnets from the Portuguese*: a counterintuitive attempt to use a display of helplessness and teary emotion that allows the writer to claim the traditionally masculine form of the love sonnet—or, in Swift's case, the love song—for herself. Paul reads the "cringing posture of the female narrator … her fears of inadequacy, her self-pity and self-hatred, her frequent references to tears and ashes, pale cheeks, and trembling hearts" as Barrett Browning's strategy to combat the gendered expectations for the woman within the love poem. Paul writes that it is "an agenda whose chief purpose is to forestall *covertly* (that is without alienating her audience) that reduction of the female to the status of disempowered icon that had marked previous efforts in the genre" (78). By refusing the idealized image of woman as adored object of desire and instead occupying the position of unworthy lover, Barrett Browning allows her speaker full human complexity.

Swift's music, particularly early in her career, has often been described in ways similar to the Victorian conventions around white, middle-class, female writing: emotional, sentimental, with authenticity of feeling taking precedence over craft. Isobel Armstrong notes the qualities "attributed to [Victorian] women's poetry—conventional piety, didactic feeling, emotions, sentiment" (295). Swift's early critics often emphasized similar qualities. For example, Jody Rosen's 2008 *Rolling Stone* review of Swift's second album claims that "For *Fearless* to feel any more like it was literally ripped from a suburban girl's diary, it would have to come with drawings of rainbows and unicorns in the liner notes." Roger Holland's 2006 review of Swift's debut album says it "rings with … authenticity." These descriptions suggest that, as a teenage girl, Swift's gift is more purity of emotion than songwriting skill. Holland also calls attention to her attractiveness in sexualized ways at the same time as emphasizing her youth and exploitability: "Sixteen years old, blonde, willowy, and undeniably gorgeous, Swift is every marketing man's wet dream girl." As Swift matured, she became increasingly aware of this gendered response to her music and persona. Several songs address the issue directly; most notably, "The Man" suggests that if she were male, people would praise her work ethic and business savvy rather than focusing on her appearance and manners. Yet Swift-as-creator's presentation of Swift-as-speaker in her lyrics does at least as much work to counter gendered limitations and expectations as anything Swift has explicitly stated about gender.

In Nate Sloan's analysis of the "work" of Swift's songwriting, he identifies both craft and agency as affective meanings Swift assigns to the concept of work (13). I would argue that the two are inextricably aligned within her songwriting; craft is the way she exercises agency over the stories she tells in her songs. Take "seven," for example, which depicts an idyllic Pennsylvania childhood that is likely inspired by the real Swift's. It is a carefully constructed recounting of specific memories that reframe Swift's current fame as a bittersweet victory; it asks listeners to see from her perspective all the things she has lost by becoming a major celebrity. Swift suggests she was at her best at age seven, when she was allowed to "scream ferociously" whenever she wanted. She gains listeners' sympathy by evoking images from childhood memories that are both specific to her and relatable to many: sweet tea, a swing, a friend's braids. Her inability to picture the friend's face is an example of Swift-as-speaker's lack of control over memory but also of Swift-as-creator's ability to deploy images of her own helplessness, almost paradoxically, to take control of her life story. The sense of wistful nostalgia she evokes through these lost moments suggests that the way the media depicts her life— glamorous, beautiful, and full of drama—is not entirely accurate. Even the speaker's inability to access those lost moments plays into the song's power to shape Swift's self-narrative.

Just as Swift-as-speaker has been portrayed as at the mercy of time and memory since the beginning of her career, so too has Swift-as-creator been utilizing her depictions of these phenomena to gain agency over her personal and professional narratives since her earliest days in the spotlight. Again, her first single, "Tim McGraw," is instructive here. As noted above, this song speaks to the power of memory to shift time by pulling her back into a prior moment. However, Swift's statements about the song's genesis suggest that Swift-as-creator has much more agency than Swift-as-speaker. In an interview with *CMT*, she claims she wrote the song in high school while *anticipating* a breakup with an older boyfriend who would be going to college soon (Morris). The song takes place three years after the relationship it describes; Swift-as-speaker cannot change what happened or do more than hope her ex still remembers her. But Swift-as-creator uses the song to take control over the story of a breakup that has not yet happened and that she cannot prevent. "Tim McGraw" frames this relationship as a perfect summer romance; Swift-as-speaker is likable and relatable. Before the real-life relationship has even ended, therefore, Swift-as-creator shapes how she will be perceived after it does.

One of Swift-as-creator's most potent manipulations of time and memory extends beyond song lyrics into the world of the music industry. In 2019, Swift publicly expressed frustration with her former record label, Big Machine Records, and its executive Scott Borchetta for refusing to sell her the masters to her first six albums without requiring her to produce a new album in exchange for the masters of each previous one (Grady). This meant that Big Machine and Borchetta would continue to own the rights to make, sell, or distribute copies of much of Swift's music. Further exacerbating the tension was the subsequent sale of the Big Machine Label Group to Scooter Braun, meaning that Braun, whom Swift accused of "incessant, manipulative bullying," now owned her masters without her prior knowledge or consent (taylorswift). Braun, she wrote, has "stripped me of my life's work [. . .] Essentially, my musical legacy is about to lie in the hands of someone who tried to dismantle it" (taylorswift).

Swift has made a number of moves to try to regain agency over this legacy, one of which is crafting songs about the situation that utilize time and memory to tell her side of the story and even to suggest that her professional antagonists are themselves subject to the power of memory over their own lives and feelings. For example, "my tears ricochet" can be read as an account of Swift's falling out with Borchetta. She suggests as much in an interview with *NME*, explaining that she was particularly affected by the film *Marriage Story*'s portrayal of divorce because "all of a sudden it felt like something I had been through. I think that happens any time you've been in a 15-year relationship and it ends in a messy, upsetting way." That description that lines up with her professional relationship with the former record label executive (Gallagher). The song is written from the perspective of someone witnessing her own funeral, at which a person who was formerly important to the deceased manipulates the narrative to gain sympathy from the mourners despite the fact that he is responsible for the speaker's death. Swift-as-speaker is characteristically helpless to turn back time or rewrite her memories of the relationship; she is a spirit who cannot find rest. Yet Swift-as-creator is not nearly so helpless. She gets to tell this story the way she wants to; she frames herself as the victim of the situation. She allows Swift-as-speaker to be the sole narrator, and she uses this voice to depict the song's antagonist as a pretender, a manipulator, and a thief. In fact, she goes further: she imagines this antagonist is haunted by his deeds—that he replays her "stolen lullabies," that he misses her, and that killing her has killed him too. If this character is a stand-in for Borchetta, this means Swift is suggesting he is suffering for his actions, not just financially, but emotionally. She crafts a version of Borchetta that may or may not resemble the real person, but that affords her some emotional satisfaction and agency over her own story. In this iteration of the story of their fallout, Swift-as-speaker's grief has the capacity to wound her deeply, but Swift-as-creator turns that grief into a weapon, one that "ricochets" like a bullet, damaging not just her but Borchetta as well in a very precise trajectory that appears planned to hit where it hurts most.

These lyrics recall Paul's description of Elizabeth Barrett Browning's speaker in *Sonnets From the Portuguese* as emotional, teary, and inadequate. Paul writes that Browning's strategy of presenting her narrator this way offers an outlet for a fuller range of self-expression: "the reader . . . begins to notice that for a self-effacing person, the speaker takes an unusual number of opportunities to display herself overtly, in all her grief and infirmity, in the text" (80). In "my tears ricochet," Swift-as-speaker deploys the image of herself as helpless ghost to express her anger at her professional mistreatment by powerful men. As in many of her most heartbroken, sorrowful songs, she appears the victim within the lyrics, but they are her words, sung in her voice.

They are also the foundation of her professional success. And in pursuit of this success, Swift has gone far beyond song lyrics in her response to the situation around ownership of her masters. She has taken the rather extraordinary step of re-recording and re-releasing several of her older albums—four by the end of 2023, presumably with more to come. This means fans, radio stations, and anyone licensing her music can swap out the re-recordings for the originals. These re-recordings are a bid for control over Swift's music from her first six albums.

The re-recordings are undoubtedly a response to Borchetta's and Braun's actions, and they clearly offer Swift agency in her professional life. Yet they also effect a peculiar change on the songs themselves, creating a dialogue between the present-day Swift and her younger self. Although she sings the same lyrics she wrote years before, the time gap creates a greater distance between Swift-as-creator and Swift-as speaker. The Swift who has artistic control over these re-recordings is older and wiser than the persona she takes on in the lyrics. This feels particularly evident in *Fearless (Taylor's Version)*, with its stories of high school, young love, and the disillusionment that follows the first experiences of heartbreak and betrayal. "Fifteen," for example, already creates a gap between Swift-as-speaker, who is caught up in first dates and first days of school, and Swift-as-creator, who sings from a place of greater maturity, urging her younger self to remember that "In your life, you'll do things greater than dating the boy on the football team / But I didn't know it at fifteen." But the re-recordings take Swift-as-creator much further into her own future, looking back from a vantage point not of a few years but of more than a decade—a decade during which she has certainly done much "greater things" than either the Swift described in the song or the Swift who originally wrote it. Listeners are compelled to reflect on Swift's journey while listening, noting how much more power she has gained over time.

The re-recordings also play with the elastic nature of time by including not only the songs on the original albums but new recordings of songs "from the vaults"—that is, songs that were supposedly intended for those albums as well but didn't make the cut. When she released *Fearless (Taylor's Version)*, she told *Cosmopolitan* that it included "Songs I absolutely adored but were held back for different reasons (don't want too many breakup songs, don't want too many down-tempo songs, can't fit that many songs on a physical cd)" (Bowenbank). With increased creative control and commercial appeal, Swift suggests that she can now include whatever songs she wants. In *Red (Taylor's Version)*, this meant doubling the length of the album and offering a ten-minute extended version of "All Too Well." Swift positions these albums as more authentic—more hers, not just commercially, but artistically as well.

The "from the vault" songs also give listeners a new glimpse into Swift's past—one that is carefully mediated by her present self. "Nothing New," a track on *Red (Taylor's Version)* that was ostensibly written by Swift during the original process of making *Red* but not released until much later, is an example of how Swift-as-creator uses the re-recordings of older songs to reshape listeners' and fans' own memories of the singer-songwriter. "Nothing New" speaks to the younger Swift's fears of becoming obsolete. Although she is currently enjoying fame and celebrity, Swift-as-speaker is fixated on the idea that once she is no longer shiny and new, interest in her work will fade. The song gives her age as twenty-two, which is how old she was when *Red* was originally released. This younger Swift imagines a sort of "fever dream" in which, on some future day, she will meet the next big female pop star, who will possess the "radiance" only seventeen-year-olds have. This star will tell Swift she is following the map Swift laid out for her success; Swift will be publicly happy for her but privately devastated. Had Swift released the song on the original *Red*, this vision would have been merely speculation—yet another example of Swift-as-speaker being unable to live in the present moment because she is afraid time will eventually destroy it. But because she released it at the age of thirty-one, Swift-as-speaker's fears of irrelevance are undercut by Swift-as-creator's knowledge of her continued success. Her lyrics about meeting a younger version of herself are still emotionally affecting, but they also appear remarkably prescient, given that 2021 saw the rise of a teenaged pop star much like the one described in "Nothing New": Olivia Rodrigo, whose album *SOUR* was nominated alongside Swift's *evermore* at the 2022 Grammys. At the time, Rodrigo publicly declared her love for Swift, citing her as a major inspiration. In March 2021, she told SiriusXM, "I feel so lucky that I just was born at the right time to be able to look up to somebody like her [...] Her support and genuine compassion and excitement for me [has] just been so, so surreal" (Viswanath).

Swift's listeners may, therefore, be impressed with Swift-as-creator's ability to predict the future, while also noting a major difference that gives her much more agency than the younger version of herself depicted in "Nothing New": Swift has not, as the song fears, lost her popularity or acclaim. From her current much less vulnerable vantage point—having, in fact, recently received a Grammy for Album of the Year for *folklore* in 2021—Swift was able to release this song about fearing her imminent decline knowing that decline never took place. The popularity of *Red (Taylor's Version)* only enhanced this sense of security in her ability to control her career, given its immense success—it debuted at Number 1 on the Billboard 200 chart—despite the fact that it is composed largely of preexisting songs (Caulfield). Indeed, Swift has rarely been more in control of her own narrative than when releasing older songs about moments when she felt that time would erase her and memories of her would fade.

"All Too Well (Ten-Minute Version)" exemplifies this phenomenon. Most listeners of *Red (Taylor's Version)* are aware that the real-life relationship that inspired the song is firmly in her past. Although she is singing lyrics that suggest she is stuck within the memories of this time, her present-day self has actually been able to move on; at the time *Red (Taylor's Version)* was released, she had been in a steady relationship since late 2016 or early 2017 (Santino). As with "Nothing New," Swift shares this very vulnerable picture of herself from a place of relative agency.

Furthermore, the addition of new lyrics greatly enhances Swift's control over the narrative of the breakup. The ten-minute version paints a more negative picture of the ex-lover than the original. Whereas the latter does suggest the breakup was probably the lover's fault and calls him "cruel," the former also contains extended examples of the lover's mistreatment of Swift-as-speaker and the subsequent emotional fallout. In "All Too Well (Ten-Minute Version)," Swift-as-speaker appears in a more vulnerable light, a young person taken advantage of by an older lover. She shares more painful memories in this version, including the lover's missing her twenty-first birthday and her crying at a party. He keeps her a secret, refuses to say he's in love until the relationship is already on the decline, and treats her like a "never-needy, ever-lovely jewel" whose "shine" reflects on him. These additional memories spill out from gaps between the original lyrics, overwhelming both her and the listener. Swift-as-speaker is even more at the mercy of time and memory than in the original song, but in exchange, Swift-as-creator gains increased narrative control over the story of the relationship.

Additionally, the repeated phrase, "I remember it all too well," is not only an expression of helplessness in the face of all-consuming memory; it is also a defiant claim to Swift's own version of the relationship. Swift-as-speaker is still trapped in the vivid moments from the relationship that replay endlessly in her head, stuck in an ever-looping past. But the phrase "I remember," while suggesting an inability to forget, also seems to accumulate narrative authority as it is repeated, so that Swift's claims that the love affair was indeed "rare," "real," and "sacred"—despite the ex's refusal to take it seriously—impart a sense of control over her own story. She is not making things up or misremembering how the ex treated her. The newer version's extended outro gives her even more control over the narrative. It loops for a minute and a half before fading out, offering short summations of each memory the song depicts intercut with the phrase, "You remember it all too well." This phrase always overlaps with the phrase that follows it, so that rather than, for example, "You remember it all too well / It was rare," The listener hears "You remember it all too / It was rare," with "well" overlapping the next word. In short, it sounds like she is saying, "You remember it all too"—as if to say, *I remember it, but so do you.* In her version of this story, she is not the only one at the mercy of shifting time, which throws up memories of their relationship whether she wants them or not; the ex-lover is caught by time, too, whether or not he admits it.

Time's Double Bind

Through control over her craft and her commercial output, Swift stakes a claim over her personal and professional personas. As Sloan argues, "Taylor Swift uses the work of songwriting to create a sense of self in an industry dependent on fracturing her identity into myriad, saleable parts" (23). However helpless in the face of time and memory the subjects of her songs seem to be, Swift-as-creator approaches these subjects from a place of agency.

That is to say—mostly from a place of agency. While Swift's legacy appears far sturdier than it did in 2011, the year *Red* was originally released, the 2020 Netflix documentary *Miss Americana* suggests that Swift is still preoccupied with the possibility of losing the public's interest. She tells the viewer, "As I'm reaching 30, I'm like, I want to work really hard . . . while society is still tolerating me being successful." Even with the success of subsequent albums, Swift remains sensitive to the possibility that the public's tastes and attitudes will change—possibly, as she suggests, due to a combination of misogyny and ageism.

Yet perhaps even more important than the possibility of Swift-as-creator's eventual decline in undercutting her hard-won control over time and memory is the fact that most listeners' primary experience of her is as Swift-as-speaker. Many fans keep track of her professional and personal moves as much as they can. Yet Swift's music is still the main type of mediation between her and the public. Fans sing along to her lyrics at concerts, at parties, in the car and in the shower; they tattoo them on their arms and plaster them on laptops and water bottles. The persona Swift crafts through her songs— the Swift-as-speaker brought into being by the interaction between Swift-as-creator and her listeners—is the one most people connect with on a deep, emotional level. They know best the Swift who is at the mercy of time and memory. Ultimately, however much control Swift is able to exercise over her own story in the face of gendered assumptions, however much she is able to turn painful memories and fears of time passing her by into exquisitely crafted lyrics, the emotional resonance of her songs lies in their expression of frustration, anxiety, and stubborn hope in the face of time and memory's power. Playing with time offers Swift a partial, never-quite-satisfying agency over both her personal life and her artistic legacy.

Works Cited

Armstrong, Isobel. "'A Music of Thine Own': Women's Poetry – An Expressive Tradition?" *Victorian Poetry: Poetry, Poetics and Politics* (2nd ed.). Routledge: London, 2019, 293–348.

Bowenbank, Starr. "Taylor Swift's 'You All Over Me' Is Alllll About Trying (and Failing) to Get Over Your Dreaded Ex." *Cosmopolitan*, 26 Mar. 2021.

Caulfield, Keith. "Taylor Swift Scores 10th No. 1 Album on Billboard 200 Chart With 'Red (Taylor's Version).'" *Billboard*, 21 Nov. 2021.

Gallagher, Alex. "Taylor Swift wrote early 'My Tears Ricochet' lyrics after watching 'Marriage Story.'" *NME*, 9 Dec. 2020.

Grady, Constance. "The Taylor Swift/Scooter Braun controversy, explained." *Vox*, 1 July 2019.

Holland, Roger. "Taylor Swift: *Taylor Swift*." *PopMatters*, 9 November 2006.

Miss Americana. Dir. Lana Wilson. Tremolo Productions, 2020. *Netflix*.

Morris, Edward. "When She Thinks 'Tim McGraw,' Taylor Swift Savors Payoff." *CMT*, 1 Dec. 2006.

Paul, Sarah. "Strategic Self-Centering and the Female Narrator: Elizabeth Barrett Browning's 'Sonnets from the Portuguese.'" *Victorian Popular Culture*, special issue of *Browning Institute Studies*, vol. 17. (1989): 75–91.

Rosen, Jody. "Fearless." *Rolling Stone*, 13 November 2008.

Santino, Catherine. "Taylor Swift and Joe Alwyn's Relationship Timeline." *People*, 31 Aug. 2022.

Sloan, Nate. "Taylor Swift and the Work of Songwriting." *Contemporary Music Review*, vol. 40, no. 1. (2021): 11–26.

taylorswift. "For years I asked . . ." Tumblr, 30 June 2019.

Viswanath, Jake. "Olivia Rodrigo Sampled A Taylor Swift Song On Her New Album & Here's Why." *Bustle*, 1 June 2021.

13

"Say you'll remember me … all too well": Taylor Swift's Memory Work

Maggie Laurel Boyd

In her guide to *Living a Feminist Life*, Sara Ahmed proclaims, "to share a memory is to put a body into words" (23). She arrives at this proclamation after recalling an assault, noting how her bodily reactions testify to her experience, despite her assaulter's disregard. She suggests that our bodies absorb such experiences, and that such experiences accumulate to comprise our bodies. In her framework, attending to our memories helps us more fully attune, or re-tune, ourselves to our bodies and thus how we encounter the world and how the world encounters us. Memory work is radically embodied and necessarily narrated, as it entails finding language for sensory and sensational experience—a quest not unfamiliar to Taylor Swift, who sings that she has "spent my whole life trying to put [love] into words," indicating that her discography seeks to describe what love feels like ("You Are In Love"). At the end of the song "Daylight," Swift insists that "you are what you love." Taken together, these two lyrics imply that Swift's attempts to put love into words also function as attempts to put her self into words.[1] And, in intimating that narrating what she loves will also reveal who she is, Swift links her selfhood with bodily affect. I suggest that from the beginning of her career into her re-recordings, Swift's songwriting represents an effort to put her body into words and to position her body within the public eye, and that relies on sharing her memory. In this paper, I show how Swift has consistently substantiated the power of her own memory, presenting it as constantly under revision—that is, not necessarily stable—but also always under her control—that is, firmly a facet of her power.

Swift therefore participates in an understanding of memory in which memory affirms experience even though—and perhaps because—it is so mercurial, so malleable. As I note throughout, this understanding appears in feminist theory, memory scholarship, and literature. I do not suggest that Swift has studied these works or that these scholars see themselves as speaking to Swift's writing. Instead, I identify Swift's

---

[1] Though the real Taylor Swift is not necessarily the speaker of her songs, for the sake of convenience and consistency, I adopt "Swift" as shorthand to refer to the persona developed in her work. I focus on her own portrayal of that persona, rather than press's and fans' perceptions, as I am primarily interested in how Swift presents and plays with memory, and the implications thereof.

overlap with this literary and theoretical tradition to argue that her lyrics have an analytical depth worth exploring *and* to depict how an exemplar of pop culture processes and performs that tradition. Swift's approximately 110 million monthly listeners offer one index of her music's cultural force ("Taylor Swift"). Examining her engagement with memory in that music can thus reveal much about our collective conceptualization of memory, selfhood, and the links between them. Ultimately, memory functions as a resource for embodying and empowering the self, which I parse into (1) constructing the self, (2) authorizing the self, and (3) re-imagining the self.

"think of me": Memory to Construct the Self

Throughout her oeuvre, Swift uses her memory as a tool toward constructing the self-image that she most wants to promote. In the article accompanying her selection as 2023 Time Person of the Year, Sam Lansky emphasizes that Swift has become *the* master narrator of her story, wondering, "haven't we all become selective autobiographers in the digital age as we curate our lives?" Swift excels at such autobiography because she so effectively curates her memories in her music. At times, she crafts an idealized self, but even then, she reveals that such self-construction requires a deliberate arrangement of memories. For example, in "Wildest Dreams,"[2] she instructs her lover to remember her "standing in a nice dress / staring at the sunset, babe / red lips and rosy cheeks." She offers a romanticized vision of her identity, a still snapshot of perfect beauty, perhaps to offset the coming break-up. In the bridge she predicts a moment when, someday, after this man leaves, "I bet these memories / follow you around." Such language suggests that her memory will haunt him, evoking Eavan Boland's poem "Daughter," where she defines memory as "the ghost of the body" (line 14). Swift conveys this ghostliness, presenting her memories as mobile and almost agentic and explicitly summoning them to control how her body lingers in his, and the world's, imagination.

We might say that Swift plays the long game; this man might be able to leave her, but she gets the final verdict by carefully positioning how she will feature in his memories. Her ability to orient herself in their shared memory—or, to put her body into words—supersedes both her and her lover's ability to orient themselves in the relationship at all. It matters less how they relate to each other, and more how they will remember one another. And Swift is the one who decides the latter. Moreover, remembering her in this manner is her one condition for their entire affair. Rather than seeming self-sacrificial, though, the fact that memory is the only cost she imposes on this relationship reveals her awareness of memory's power and her ability to wield it.

The assertion in "Wildest Dreams" is reminiscent of her debut single "Tim McGraw." With her refrain of, "when you think Tim McGraw / I hope you think of me," she turns

---

[2]   Whenever possible, I cite the re-recorded songs that Swift has termed "Taylor's Version[s]."

a mega-famous musician into a signifier of herself, using this reference to elicit specific moments shared only by the "you" and "me" of the song. This maneuver taps into memory's personal nature, often seen as its primary difference from history.[3] She also describes her gratitude that "you" did not see her mourning the break-up, thus leaving intact the rose-colored memories on the lake and in the truck. As in "Wildest Dreams," with "Tim McGraw," Swift insists her lover adopt a memory of herself that is idyllic and static, focused largely on her appearance: her "little black dress," "old faded blue jeans," and shining blue eyes. It is fundamentally an image that Swift seeks to transpose, and fundamentally that of her body.

But this is the memory Swift details to her lover, not to her audience—she gives her listeners further insights, including that she spent September crying. Even as Swift composes one image of herself, she simultaneously offers another one in which she is *not* composed. From her first album, then, Swift has incorporated her memory as a source of evidence while also drawing attention to how she curates it. In "The Evidence of Experience," Joan Scott worries that the recent trend toward relying on experience to address erasures in the historical archive might "constitute subjects as fixed and autonomous" rather than ever-changing and inter-dependent (782). This perception of experience seeks to stabilize something that Scott emphasizes is fundamentally unstable. Although Swift hardly fulfills Scott's injunction that we inspect, if not entirely deconstruct, the premises upon which we claim subjectivity,[4] it remains notable that Swift illustrates her chosen evidence of experience—her memories—as manipulable. This framing might even proffer one way to be clear that experience is still the product of construction and interpretation, as Scott desires (Scott 779, 791, 795). Exhibiting her emotional turmoil elsewhere in "Tim McGraw" does not undermine the memory she presents in the chorus; instead, it brings her audience into this careful construction. Listeners glean insight into not just Swift's body *in* the past but also her embodied experience *of* the past.

Such work is most apparent in her masterpiece "All Too Well [10 Minute Version],"[5] which presents her as very decomposed—indeed, as "not fine at all." As in these other examples, Swift taps into her memory to re-instate her perception as the reigning narrative of events and thus reclaim her sense of self. Unlike "Wildest Dreams" or "Tim

---

[3]   Geoffrey Cubitt summarizes the scholarly conversation on memory's relationship to history as presuming that history presents "a particular kind of critical encounter" with the past, whereas memory presents "a more intimate or continuous connection between past experience and present consciousness" (28, 30). Such a demarcation establishes history as a specialist and quasi-objective domain unlike memory, with its accessible, subjective connotations. Critics continue to parse differences between these terms and the relationship to the past that each denotes, but for my purposes, I emphasize that memory is commonly considered a space of intimacy, individuality, and interiority.

[4]   Scott is exceedingly clear that any evidence, including experience, is always political, an awareness that Swift has seemed to lack—at least publicly, and certainly in 2006 (Scott 797).

[5]   I should note I do not chronicle change over time; "All Too Well [10 Minute Version]" was first written before "Wildest Dreams" was released. I do not argue that Swift's use of her memory had any teleological trajectory but rather a consistently careful construction.

McGraw," though, "All Too Well [10 Minute Version]" centers the young girl left distraught more than the one dressed in her best outfits. Of this lover, she asks, "the idea you had of me, who was she?" and answers for him: "A never-needy ever-lovely jewel." But Swift counters this view in which she is only an eternally beautiful object, offering instead a version of herself as a complex human devastated by loss, left "weeping in a party bathroom." In all these instances, whether to document her loveliness or her lovelornness, Swift uses memory as her primary tool in her enterprise of self-construction. She has made this enterprise an incredibly successful economic one as well, in her willingness to bring her listeners into that creative process.

"I was there": Memory to Authorize the Self

In presenting memory as fundamentally embodied and embodying, Swift also accesses its potential to substantiate her claims, showing how her agency is and has been forged in the realm of memory making. Rosi Braidotti, another feminist theorist, elaborates that "Temporally speaking, a body is a portion of living memory that endures by undergoing constant internal modifications following the encounter with other bodies and forces" (57). If the body is not just *like* a memory—changeable and personal—but an actual piece of memory—corporeal and palpable—then just as putting a body into words entails sharing memory, so too does putting words to a body. And Swift pursues both. Returning to "All Too Well [10 Minute Version]," Swift sings again and again, "I was there / I remember it all too well." Her insistence that she remembers this relationship in all its configurations—reciting these lines right after recalling trips upstate, to his mom's house, and to their kitchen with equal vividness—locates her power to narrate experiences in her ability to recall them. And each of these memories that she lists to construe this relationship accentuate sensory experience, highlighting the chill of the air or the light reflecting from the snow. The song conveys the memory of this relationship primarily through such distinct, tangible images. As the song fades out, Swift even repeats, "wind in my hair, I was there, I was there / down the stairs, I was there, I was there." She captures the exhilarating feeling of the relationship in the sensation of a crisp wind lifting strands of hair and the ever-increasing hurtle toward its collapse in the sensation of a midnight scurry down the stairs. The symbol of the scarf—which winds through the song alongside her refrains and haunts the "you" just as these memories haunt the "I"—further exemplifies the materiality of this song. With such materiality, she suggests that her capacity to remember is rooted in her bodily presence. And as she roots her memory in her body, Swift simultaneously roots her authority in her memory. Because she was there, she can remember it, and because she can remember it, she can speak of it.

The song thus suggests memory more effectively expresses an experience than something said in the moment. Mark Freeman comes to a similar conclusion in his study of memoirs, advising that we consider memory not a distortion of a reality—given that reality is "always already permeated by narrative," even in the present—but an opportunity for revelation (272–4). He thus understands memory's mediated nature as possibility-making. I suggest Swift accesses this opportunity, as she intervenes in her memories of this relationship to identify what (and who) went wrong. In her Pulitzer Prize-winning *The Optimist's Daughter*, Eudora Welty attributes to memory a unique potential for such intervention. Reflecting on her father's corpse, the protagonist decides, "The past is like him, impervious, and can never be awakened. It is memory that is the somnambulist. It will come back in its wounds from across the world, like Phil [her late husband], calling us by our names and demanding its rightful tears. It will never be impervious. The memory can be hurt, time and again—but in that may lie its final mercy. As long as it's vulnerable to the living moment, it lives for us" (179). Framed as a righteous return, memory, with its volatility, carries a power that the past's solidity precludes. Welty implies that because memory is alive, it is vulnerable; because it is vulnerable, it is open to meaning; because it is open to meaning, it can be a tool in and site of transformation.

Certainly, that transformation has been the case for "All Too Well"—Swift has been quoted as saying that the song was once "very hard" to perform but is now less about a gut-wrenching heartbreak and really "100 percent about us and for you," by which she means her fans (Zoladz). But it is not just the experience *of* the song that has shifted; it is also the experience *in* the song that shifts. Soon after its re-release, Lindsay Zoladz writes that it has always been "a song about the weaponization of memory," including painfully specific details "to assert, in the face of an unfeeling and perhaps manipulatively disbelieving ex, that this experience really happened" and, ultimately, "to find retroactive equilibrium in a relationship that was based on a power imbalance that she was not at first able to perceive." The song becomes a space in which to re evaluate these emotions and to reclaim selfhood, to—as Welty describes—seize memory's vulnerability in order to revise its meaning, probe its wounds in order to find its mercy.

Although Swift's description of her lover as making her miserable every time she thinks of him might seem to indicate that her memory has betrayed her and is out of her control, the song serves to reverse that relationship. Perhaps she cannot rid herself of her memory, but she can wield it to reveal precisely how she was hurt. Indeed, her insistence on remembering functions as an accusation; she might forgive, but she will not forget how she has been treated. If Swift remembers this past *too* well for her own comfort, she puts it to good use.

Importantly, Swift does not need her memory to appear coherent or impermeable to find it authoritative; instead, she characterizes it as "flashbacks and echoes" ("Red"). That her memory appears in fragments reflects an established trend in memory scholarship that understands memory to be fundamentally fragmentary. For example, Wulf Kansteiner refers to memory as "multimedia collages," and Freeman similarly imagines memory as a "richly textured, multivocal text"; both accounts indicate memory's piecemeal structure and imply its constructed, even creative nature (Kansteiner 190; Freeman 263). But scholars are clear, too, that this distance from a comprehensive, chronological perspective on the past hardly diminishes its potency. Kansteiner admits, "There is no natural, direct connection between the real and the remembered," and on the same wavelength, Paul Ricoeur's conception of memory as work—both exertion and cultural production—highlights how it is not a transparent repository of the past but an act of transforming many liminal experiences into words (Kansteiner 190; Ricoeur 129). Memory remains negotiated territory, but it also provides crucial insight into the lived experience of the past. And charting that territory means claiming the truth-value of one's own lived experience.

Memory's capacity to chart and claim lived experience operates as a significant source of specifically feminist power. In Ahmed's understanding, "feminist work is often memory work" because our memories contain vital insight into how we exist and have existed in the world (22). If feminism is a theoretical lens, then in Ahmed's terms, memory is the actual glass through which feminists view experience; it is the evidence that clarifies analysis. And yet Ahmed is clear, too, that memory is hardly a stable register of the past. Instead, she depicts her methodology as allowing a memory "to acquire a certain crispness" and then gathering those "memories like things" to find new connections and derive a bigger picture (22). Ahmed even defines "feminism as memory making" (241). Swift might similarly define her songwriting as memory making.

As a woman and self-identified feminist,[6] Swift might also see her songwriting as a feminist act that thereby overlaps with Ahmed's technique. At times, it does, as when Ahmed argues that feminist memory keeps us accountable to our history even if it prevents reconciliation, akin to Swift's singing on "mad woman," "They say, 'move on,' but you know I won't" (Ahmed 262–3). And at other times, it doesn't, as when Ahmed asserts that feminists seek to overturn an unjust system rather than participate in it, but Taylor Swift sings on "The Man" that she should be deemed the ultimate patriarch in such a system (Ahmed 263). It is true that Swift, as an immensely successful woman, struggles against sexist discourse, and it thus makes sense that she finds in her songs the perfect space and in her memories the perfect material to confront such a discourse (Aguirre). And it is also true that Swift's feminism has its limits, even regarding her memory making. Given that her memories are rooted in her bodily reality, they are inevitably informed by her position as an enormously wealthy white woman and a cultural icon. Because of her standing, the discussion about Swift can be thunderous, but also because of her standing, her voice can ring that much louder.

Swift has increasingly vocalized her experience in her music rather than in other forums, like social media posts or interviews. The claims she makes—whether they resemble Ahmed's and other feminist theorists' or not—appear then mostly in her songs, where she stages—literally—her memory to assert power against the rhetoric that seeks to define her. Memory making is thus the site of Swift's power, too, giving her a way to attest to her experience.

---

[6] This self-identification came eight years into her career, when she was 25. At first, she avoided claiming the label feminist, but eventually decided, "I've been taking a feminist stance without actually saying so"—and actually saying the opposite (quoted in Thomas). As Emily Thomas points out, Swift's shift reflected the shift in the general attitude toward feminism. Since then, Swift has become more vocal about her feminism, but her belated acceptance of the topic shows that her politics have always had their limits.

Swift also asserts her agency in choosing *not* to make memories, in choosing to forget—as she sings in the aptly-named track "I Forgot That You Existed." By disregarding this person, Swift shows that she can dismiss the power they had over her, including the harm they caused and any lessons they taught her. Instead, her memory of this person and their role in her life is "just a blur," a void that Swift calls "magical," "nice," and "peaceful." Her dismissal might be surprising after the *reputation* era, when Swift reassesses past tensions with Kanye West alongside the anxiety of a budding relationship; she ends the album insisting, "hold on to the memories / they will hold on to you" on a song entitled "New Year's Day." This day might typically symbolize new beginnings, but for Swift there is no possible clean slate. In addition to this refrain about memory's grip, the song centers around cleaning up from the night before. It wrestles with the repercussions of the past while reminding us that anything new—a new day, year, era—carries remnants of earlier times. Letting go of that past does not seem possible or even desirable, given that here this reciprocal relationship with memory carries a mournful tone, especially as it is overlaid with her fear that someday her lover will become a stranger. And yet by her next album, *Lover*, she writes playfully about her ability to *not* hold on to memories and find the freedom therein. If holding on to the memories means they will hold on to you, then it requires a careful choice to keep them close or to move on. Sometimes that choice is magical, sometimes it is melancholy. But it remains an act of agency, creating a space in which Swift can—again and again—generate her own narrative.

"I've got me": Memory to Re-Imagine the Self

Importantly, Swift continually rewrites that narrative, refusing to let her life story settle into a stable entity. Swift has famously devised new endings for canonical texts,[7] particularly on *Fearless*, where she rejects preordained scripts in songs like "Love Story" and "White Horse," with the former envisioning happy endings for *Romeo and Juliet* and *The Scarlet Letter* and the latter envisioning a literal departure from a fairytale world (Roznovsky). Swift hardly just revises Shakespeare or the Brothers Grimm, though—she also revises her own body of work. Her second single, "Teardrops On My Guitar," originally describes unrequited love. But 14 years later, after a battle over her master recordings, Swift re-signifies those teardrops as stemming from losing her "stolen lullabies" ("my tears ricochet"). On "my tears ricochet," Swift determines that if she spends her time "screaming at the sky," this harm has also reverberated back to its source: "you had to kill me, but it killed you just the same." The teardrops that launched her career have ricocheted, leading to this moment where she now yearns not for her

---

[7] Kansteiner focuses on collective memory construction, but this play with inherited narratives via memory shows how Swift might fit into his category of so-called memory makers, or those who "selectively adopt or manipulate" the "intellectual or cultural traditions that frame all of our representations of the past" (Kansteiner 180).

friend but for her art. In another and even more obvious twist, Swift moves from reminiscing about how "loving you was red" to deciding "it's golden" ("Red," "Daylight"). Such addenda suggest Swift's willingness to rearrange her own images, to continue reassessing her past and reinforming her future as she perceives and plays with her memories. As a result, memory permits her the ability to re-imagine who she has been and who she will become.

Ever-conscious of her own performances, when she sings on "gold rush" about turning "your life into folklore"—a wink at her previous album—she also encapsulates her ongoing project to turn *her* life into folklore, which means endowing her experiences with a mythic quality and taking them seriously as material for that mythmaking. Folklorist Elaine Lawless suggests that folklore "reside[s] in our memory and/or in the act of narrative performance," both of which provide avenues for "for freeing the imagination" because of their creative, dynamic quality. Swift combines memory with narrative with performance, creating a space in which she can continually re-imagine her self. By putting her body into words, she has given herself lasting form in our cultural consciousness. Her work re-recording her first six albums indicates her ability to (re)inscribe her memories onto that cultural consciousness, functioning now even more explicitly as a remembering voice, removed from but no less protective of her past. As Bekah Waalkes writes, *Red (Taylor's Version)* "thematize[s] returning to the archive," an effort that conveys how "the work of memory is never really done—that there's always more to find." Swift continues working and reworking her memory, mining this material to not just make sense of her past but also to make sense of her future.

In the last song Swift released before beginning to release these re-recordings, the final bonus track on *evermore* entitled "it's time to go," Swift ostensibly addresses her former label executive. Although most of the song is in the second person, phrased as happening to someone else, Swift switches to the first person for one section. This point-of-view shift draws attention to this verse and signals that it centers on her experience. She describes leaving her label after fifteen years of work and little support, and then she declares, "He's got my past frozen behind glass / but I've got me." She affirms here her own power to re-sing, and re-sign, the past. Her capacity to keep making meaning and selfhood from her memories appears as the defining feature of her identity. Swift may have lamented about the sale of her recordings—"I was either investing in my past or my and other artists' future, and I chose the future"—but we can rest assured her future will give her an opportunity to reinvest in and re-imagine, yet again, her past (Aguirre). And given that her subsequent album, *Midnights*, tells "the stories of 13 sleepless nights scattered throughout my life," she has already begun that work (@taylorswift).

Indeed, in her tenth album, Swift overtly presents a changing perspective on the memories that have long constituted her music. As she explores the many shades of a relationship in "Maroon"—invoking burgundy, wine, blood, scarlet, rust, rose, ruby and, of course, maroon—Swift notably never mentions red, which was the title of another second track and of her 2012 album. In "Maroon," she still sings about dancing in New York, but now the memories she once designated as red have become darker and deeper. In the bridge, she resentfully proclaims, "and I wake with your memory over me / that's a real fucking legacy to leave." Although she calls it "your" memory, she really refers to *her* memories of "you," suggesting that her memories dictate this legacy and now demarcate this person. These lines yet again depict memory as tangible, a presence that exists on top of her, like a blanket that starts to smother her in the night. This tangibility is a through-line of the song; she continually seeks and situates this legacy in physical traces, like a wine stain on her shirt, a blush on her cheeks, and bruises on her neck. To conceptualize how this relationship faded, she uses the metaphor of phonelines rusting to materialize the way they lost contact. She uses lips as synecdoche not just for the entire person she once loved but also for the sense of belonging that she once felt in the relationship and the meaningful connection that they sustained before those lines of communication corroded. In these images, Swift continues to carefully construct her memories in vivid details and simultaneously draws our attention to how they shift under inspection and after introspection.

This effort to inspect her memories and to inflect them with new meaning serves as *Midnights*'s central project. For example, "Question ...?" interpolates the "I remember" from "Out Of The Woods," framing the song as a set of memories. "Out Of The Woods" uses that same "I remember" as a refrain and the hook to the chorus to illuminate how her present perspective reshapes her sense of this relationship; she can both recall her fragile hope that their relationship would make it and realize now that it was always doomed. This song is full of echoes, both in its rampant repetition and its sonic qualities, culminating in an actual echoing effect at the end, which substantiate for the listener the way that these memories resound through her mind. It makes sense, then, that they reverberate yet again in "Question ...?," which, like its predecessor, uses its chorus to ask questions but, this time, designs those questions to probe the other's perceptions. While "Out Of The Woods" wonders, "do you remember?" as the song ends, it remains rhetorical, with the song centered on Swift's images of their time together. "Question ...?" returns to her memories but this time invites a dialogue, asking not just *do* you remember, but *what* do you remember—being kissed, leaving your lover's house, fighting for her? And yet, she hardly cedes power; not only are these leading questions, but Swift also frames this whole song with that opening echo from "Out Of The Woods," a reminder that *she* remembers. She might bring another person into this arena, but she does not yield the stage to them. She can re-open old stories to discern, and perhaps devise, new meanings, without ceding any power over her source-text, her memory.

Like "Maroon" and "Question ...?," "Would've Could've Should've" stands out on *Midnights* for its blatant interaction with an earlier song: "Dear John." Swift again repopulates this memory to reexamine it with the insight that she has gained over time—a reconfiguration enabled by her consistent rendering of memory as constantly varying and no less substantive for being so. In "Dear John," each refrain laments, "I should've known" that she would end up crying, and the song ends accusing, "you should've known" that she would write a song about him. Swift returns to these "shoulds" in "Would've Could've Should've," clear here that her memory is no source of pleasure, repeating that even as an adult, these "memories feel like weapons." She endows her memory with a painful tangibility, a presence that keeps the tomb as well as the wound open and so prevents any resolution, whether of dying or of healing. These memories are both splintered and splinters—that is, fragmented and sharp-edged objects, resembling the stained glass that Swift feels her mind to be. Swift bears those weapons in this song, much as she does in "Dear John." And in sharing those memories, she creates space to shift their meaning once again; her willingness to keep revising her memory allows her to keep re-relating to it in new terms.

This process functions as the topic of "You're On Your Own, Kid," in which Swift recapitulates her life story with devastating scrutiny, narrating her realization that fulfilling feminine ideals—a perfect hostess, a perfect body, a perfect love story—would not save her. This song re-evaluates and ultimately rejects these metrics by which she has measured her self-worth. Over the course of the song, Swift depicts an interpretive shift; "on your own" begins the song by signaling her isolation but ends the song by signaling her independence, as a source of possibility rather than peril. When she looks back, she celebrates how "something different bloomed / writing in my room," as well as how "I saw something they can't take away"—with the "something" in both cases seemingly referring to her self. Her art enables her to grow, and then to keep going. Whereas she once sought ownership over the "he" who does not love her and the body that is not "better," she now centers owning her self—a self that continues to blossom as she continues to put her body into words.

Four years into a career that has now spanned decades, on her third album—notably entirely self-written—Swift addresses her co-performers and her audience with the closing song "Long Live," which vows in each chorus and in the final line, "we will be remembered." She commits to constructing a memory that contains everyone involved: her crew, her band, her audiences. Sara Ahmed teaches us that "How a world is shaped is memory" (263). Swift's memory has shaped many world tours and has even permitted "us" the chance to "rule the world." If Taylor Swift will be remembered, it will be on her own terms.

Works Cited

Aguirre, Abby. "Taylor Swift on Sexism, Scrutiny, and Standing Up for Herself." *Vogue*, 8 August 2019.

Ahmed, Sara. *Living a Feminist Life*. Duke University Press: Durham, 2017.

Boland, Eavan. "Daughter." *New Collected Poems*. Norton: New York, 2009. 263.

Braidotti, Rosi. "Becoming Woman: or Sexual Difference Revisited." *Theory, Culture & Society*. vol. 20, no. 3. (2003): 43–64. *Sage Premier*.

Cubitt, Geoffrey. "History and Memory: An Imagined Relationship." *History and Memory*. Manchester University Press: Manchester, 2007. 26–65. *ProQuest Ebook Central*.

Freeman, Mark. "Telling Stories: Memory and Narrative." *Memory: Histories, Theories, Debates*. eds. Susannah Radstone and Bill Schwarz, Fordham University Press: New York, 2010. 263–78.

Kansteiner, Wulf. "Finding Meaning in Memory: A Methodological Critique of Collective Memory Studies." *History and Theory* vol. 41, no. 2. (May 2002): 179–97.

Lawless, Elaine J. "Folklore as a Map of the World: Rejecting 'Home' as a Failure of the Imagination (American Folklore Society Presidential Address, October 2009)." *Journal of American Folklore* vol. 124, no. 493. (2011): n.p. *Gale Academic OneFile.*

Ricoeur, Paul. "Personal Memory, Collective Memory." *Memory, History, Forgetting,* University of Chicago: Chicago, 2004. 93–132. *ACLS Humanities Ebook.*

Roznovsky, Lindsey. "Taylor Swift's Fascination with Fairy Tales Comes Through on New Album." *Country Music Today,* 10 November 2008.

Scott, Joan W. "The Evidence of Experience." *Critical Inquiry* vol. 17, no. 4. (Summer 1991) 773–97.

"Taylor Swift." *Spotify.*

@taylorswift. "Midnights, the stories of 13 sleepless nights scattered throughout my life, will be out October 21. Meet me at midnight." *Instagram,* 29 August 2022.

Thomas, Emily. "Taylor Swift Reveals She Has Been A Feminist All This Time." *The Huffington Post,* 24 August 2014.

Waalkes, Bekah. "A Book for Every Era of Taylor Swift." *Electric Literature,* 21 November 2022.

Welty, Eudora. *The Optimist's Daughter.* Vintage, 1990. Originally published in 1972.

Zoladz, Lindsay. "Taylor Swift's 'All Too Well' and the Weaponization of Memory," *New York Times,* 15 November 2021.

14

"Scrap[s] of you": Fabrics of Memory in *folklore* and *evermore*

Claire Hurley

The eternal, in any case, is far more the ruffle of a dress than some idea.
                                        Walter Benjamin, *Arcades Project* N3,2 463

She'll patch up your tapestry that I shred.
                                        Taylor Swift, "champagne problems"

In the opening remarks to her commencement address at New York University's graduation ceremony in May, 2022, Taylor Swift pronounced, "We are each a patchwork quilt of those who have loved us." Patchworking, or the process of sewing together separate pieces of used fabric to form a new material, becomes a central allegory for memory in Swift's later oeuvre, especially in her critically acclaimed records *folklore* and *evermore*. Throughout the sister albums, Swift weaves together a homespun poetics that is drafted through fabrics and fabrication. The infamous "scarf" from the earlier track "All Too Well" is joined by a host of other garments: the "sweatshirt" and "Levi's" of the eponymous "cardigan," the "Eagles t-shirt hanging from the door" in "gold rush," and "All [the] closets" left by Swift's grandmother in "marjorie." Alongside full garments, the songs also catalogue "scraps"—remnants of past relationships—indexed as an important site of remembrance. The fabrics bear these memories within their weave, and it is the materiality of these textiles, their physical presence in the world, which Swift uses to reconstruct women's historical memory. As she explains in her introduction to *folklore*, "Picking up a pen was my way of escaping into fantasy, history, and memory."

The act of remembering has been a principal concern for Swift since her earliest work, and in the opening credits for *All Too Well: The Short Film*, she cites Pablo Neruda: "Love is short, forgetting is so long" (Neruda 43). Yet Swift's pandemic albums mark a major departure, as she turns away from confessional lyricism and toward collective storytelling. Swift's collective utterance emerges through her use of *fabrication*—her invention of characters and storylines, which shifts her poetics into the realm of the fictional. In the accompanying essay for *folklore*, Swift articulates that fabrication—stitching together reality, myth, and invention—is at the heart of the project, as she incorporates "fairytales and parables. Gossip and legends." "A tale that becomes folklore," Swift affirms, "is one that is passed down and whispered around ... Now it's up to you to pass them down." Swift recalls that the hegemony of the patriarchy is upheld through limiting female knowledge—controlling women by restricting the stories they tell and how they circulate. Therefore, this chapter will explore how, in "pass[ing] down" a patchwork of women's tales across these albums, Swift fabricates an imaginative archive of female experience, using garments and scraps to weave imaginative forms of female memory. In fabricating remembrance in this way, I argue, Swift attempts to "patch" the holes and counter the erasure of women's historical memory in a patriarchal world, revealing the provisionality of memory itself—as a "patchwork" that must be continuously remade.

"cardigan"

The song "cardigan" is an excellent introduction to how Swift chronicles the role of material fabrics in memorialization. In this track, the marks of heartbreak are invisible, and it is their abstraction that Swift contends with. Struggling with the absence of her partner, the speaker is "chasing shadows in the grocery line" as she is haunted by loss. This sentiment is a familiar one. Throughout the albums *Speak Now* and *Red*, there is a fascination with exploring the phantoms of past romantic entanglements. In her writing for the musical *Cats*, Swift even identifies memory itself as spectral: "And the memories were lost long ago / but at least you have beautiful ghosts." During the opening song to *folklore*, "the 1," the narrator discloses: "I thought I saw you at the bus stop / I didn't though." Using the familiar environments of the grocery store and the bus stop establishes how this haunting is routine and ubiquitous, which Swift expresses in the line, "The smell of smoke would hang around this long" ("cardigan"). Like smoke, it is precisely the immateriality of romantic memory that is the problem.

Swift articulates the violence of this yearning through the dichotomy of marks and markings, invoking both presence and absence. The memory lingers "like a tattoo kiss," which as an image appears as both a permanent mark ("tattoo") and fleeting touch ("kiss"). The mental wounds inflicted are also given corporeal form using bodily markings: "You drew stars around my scars / But now I'm bleedin'." But these marks are not only visited upon the body but also materialized and, crucially, *conserved* by fabrics, as he "marked me like a bloodstain." Like the "blood-soaked gown" of *Midnights*'s "You're On Your Own, Kid," the emotional "bleedin'" of the speaker has been transferred onto cloth, which preserves the stain of suffering. In Swift's lyrics, the bloodstained clothing records—and retains—the potency of grief. This idea can be traced back to *1989*'s "Clean," with the "wine-stained dress / I can't wear anymore." Evolving again in *Midnights*'s "Maroon," as Swift dwells on a past relationship during a sleepless night, the line, "The burgundy on my t-shirt / When you splashed your wine into me," captures the exact moment that is preserved by the wine stain, forever immortalized in cloth. As a vessel to conserve trauma, then, Swift uses fabrics and clothing to remember—and retain—the suffering of women.

Throughout "cardigan," romantic presences are felt and held through items of clothing, as visible remnants of psychic traumas. The track opens with a closet of memories: a "vintage tee," "high heels," "sweatshirt" and "Levi's" document the teleology of the relationship. However, as listeners we are not offered the links between the garments and their associations. Instead, Swift operates through parataxis, as the opening line, "Vintage tee, brand new phone," exposes the speaker as a millennial (think early 2000s indie culture) but eliminates the connection between these objects. This artistic strategy is reminiscent of Walter Benjamin, who in the *Arcades Project* stated, "I needn't *say* anything. Merely show. I shall purloin no valuables, appropriate no ingenious formulations. But show the rags, the refuse—these I will not inventory but allow, in the only way possible, to come into their own: by making use of them" (N1a, 6 460).

In a Benjaminian fashion, Swift exhibits rather than explains. She constructs a patchwork of clothing, makeup, and images with no prejudice toward their preconceived value. The eponymous "old cardigan" is given the same weight and power as her poetic imagery or her prosaicisms. Through this anti-hierarchical patchworking, Swift emphasizes that the preservation of both high and low culture is essential to women's memory.

This idea is furthered through Swift's central idiom in the song: "Sensual politics" ("cardigan"). A play on the title of Kate Millett's feminist treatise *Sexual Politics*, the phrase infers the same meaning as Millett, that sex is always political, but also opens up new potentialities, namely that sexual desire, possession, and abandonment can be understood through the politics of the "sensual"—the physical or material, instead of the purely intellectual. Thus, Swift's "sensual politics" becomes an organizing system for understanding patriarchal modes of dominance, and her "cardigan" is a key symbol. In her introduction to *folklore*, Swift cites the cardigan, explaining that it "still bears the scent of loss twenty years later." The fabric of the cardigan memorializes the "sensual politics" of the relationship—by bearing, or wrapping within it, the grief of heartbreak. During the chorus, the speaker describes herself as discarded and vulnerable, "like I was an old cardigan / Under someone's bed." Distinct from the paratactic imagery in the first verse, we are told that the "old cardigan" is a figurative stand-in for the lyric "I." But simile is a weaker device than metaphor, which reveals the speaker to be hiding within this conceit—or purposefully obscuring herself from view.

Playing hide and seek is a common trope in Swift's oeuvre, as she often teases her audience with her identity as a celebrity, honest lyric confession, and forms of forgery. Her penchant for simile and metaphor plays into these switches of register, as she hides herself within imagery. As George Lakoff suggests in *Metaphors We Live By*: "[T]he very systematicity that allows us to comprehend one aspect of a concept in terms of another... will necessarily hide other aspects of a concept...a metaphorical concept can keep us from focusing on other aspects of the concept that are inconsistent with that metaphor" (10).

Swift is heavily invested in understanding how such systems of meaning are constructed, and particularly how meanings can be concealed. Thus, the simile of the cardigan is carefully fashioned by Swift to "hide" and then later unravel the "sensual politics" of the song. Within the song's game of hide and seek, the cardigan itself, once rejected and ignored, becomes the only trustworthy physical remnant of the relationship. Like a historic relic, the cardigan "bear[s]" the traces of the past, but it remains buried, until it is rediscovered by the speaker.[1]

In the video for "cardigan," the meaning of the garment shifts at the end of the track, as it becomes a warm and consoling shawl for Swift, who wraps it around herself for comfort. By withholding the cardigan's full meaning in the song lyrics and only revealing its full symbolic potential in the accompanying visuals, Swift is employing a devious feminist strategy. Rather than openly disclosing the depths of female experience from the outset, she prefers to uncover—and develop—garments of female memory. The cardigan's change in meaning demonstrates that female memories and narratives can be multi-layered and, crucially, can be transformed. No longer redundant, the cardigan becomes a potent female symbol of warmth and care. The lyrics repeat, "I knew you'd come back to me," as it is in the act of return—and retrieval by Swift herself in the video—that the garment's meaning transforms.

As American poet Adrienne Rich explores in her poem "Diving into the Wreck," women can revive and rework "the book of myths" by "go[ing] down" into the wreck of female history to better understand the contemporary moment (128). Like Rich, Swift is invested in exploring "the thing itself and not the myth" by opening the gap between male signification and female meaning (Rich 128). By reclaiming and transforming symbols such as the cardigan, locating "the wreck and not the story of the wreck," Swift exposes the provisionality of female symbolic meanings (Rich 128). While the cardigan is revealed as holding transformative potential, the speaker's understanding of masculinity remains unwavering throughout the song, captured in the refrain, "I knew you." Here, male hegemony is registered as stable and constant. As such, "cardigan" is a song about undervalued female epistemologies—the all-important intuitive and deep-seated knowledge of young women in relationships. "I knew you," the speaker repeats thirteen times across the track in various formulations. In *Sexual Politics*, Millett recognizes that women do not have the language to express their oppression and so remain "in their subordinate position [through] the fairly systematic ignorance patriarchy imposes upon women" (59). But in her twenty-first-century context, Swift twists this logic to show how alternative models of knowledge *can* be circulated by women. The speaker demonstrates her broad comprehension of patriarchal oppression by linking James's toxic masculinity to her own father's behavior: "leaving like a father" ("cardigan"). Although a "systematic" understanding of patriarchal culture may still be elusive, Swift locates embodied female knowledge inside clothing. It is through the rediscovery of the cardigan that the speaker can finally conceptualize and vocalize her prior romantic experience. Her knowing is materialized through the cardigan, as a garment that represents the importance of holding onto female memory. By utilizing everyday clothing, Swift finds new ways to understand, express, and pass on her feminist knowledge. Thus, in the song "cardigan," Swift presents a hermeneutics of textiles—ways of knowing and interpreting the world through fabrics.

---

[1]   Tracing the evidence of past relationships is also explored in *Midnights*'s "Hits Different," where Swift proclaims, "I find the artifacts / cried over a hat," demonstrating the affective impact of clothing's totemic remembrance.

Fabrics of Knowledge

Another song which foregrounds the epistemology of fabrics is "marjorie." Written in honor of her grandmother, an opera singer who died when Swift was thirteen, the song contends with the loss of a family member. Swift discloses, "One [tale] starring my grandmother, Marjorie, who still visits me sometimes . . . if only in my dreams." The song plays with prescribed knowledge forms, "know[ing] better," and memories "so alive" that they reincarnate the dead. The opening lines are spoken as if by Marjorie herself, as she passes down feminist wisdom: "Never be so kind, you forget to be clever." However, this aphorism is entirely invented by Swift, who tells us she is having an imagined conversation with her grandmother "in my head." Much of the song exists in this imaginative mental space, which consists of memories, dialogue, and spiritual communion. Swift repeats several incantations; she says, "what died didn't stay dead," which she chants like a necromantic resurrection spell.

But it is in the bridge that Swift turns away from the metaphysical and towards the materiality of her grief. In the lyric, "Should've kept every grocery store receipt," we witness an archival desire in Swift—to collect and preserve fragments of memory. Like the cardigan, Swift seeks to accumulate and archive relics of the everyday. Despite claiming that "every scrap of you would be taken from me," there are in fact remnants of Marjorie—in the clothing she bequeathed to Swift. As Benjamin claims, "the eternal, in any case, is far more the ruffle of a dress than some idea" (N3,2 463). Here Benjamin, like Swift, signals toward his most potently material philosophy: it is the tangible artifact that will endure rather than the grand conception. What endures of Marjorie are her dresses, which counteract her absence through their material presence. In the bridge, Marjorie's garments transform into symbols of hope—"All your closets of backlogged dreams"—as the clothing holds within it the aspirations of her grandmother. However, these hopes are "backlogged"—delayed and never realized—as Swift recognizes the social barriers in place for women of Marjorie's generation.

Thus, the grief recorded in the song is twofold, as Swift laments her grandmother's death and mourns the unrealized dreams of women throughout history. This lacuna of knowledge was acknowledged by Swift, as she explained to Zane Lowe: "I'd open up my grandmother's closet and she had beautiful dresses from the sixties. I wish I had asked her where she wore every single one of them." Here, Swift reveals that she has the material remnants, but their narrative is missing. Therefore, it is how these "scraps" and material fragments are chronicled by Swift herself that is key. As Benjamin articulates, it is "the ruffle of a dress" that can materialize history—the uneven "ruffle" here conveying texture and, crucially, movement or teleology. As the song closes, Swift changes the narrative and defies pre-existent knowledge by claiming, "I know better / But you're still around." In visiting what has been "left" behind, namely Marjorie's clothing, Swift is able to reconjure and reconstruct her grandmother's presence through storytelling.

Swift infers the necessity of uneven, rather than smooth, female narrativization in the following track, "closure." The song stands as a testament against the idea of forced endings, as she explores how patriarchal dominance attempts to force resolution. "I don't need your closure," sings Swift, signalling her refusal to be neatly enclosed, as well as gesturing towards her broader feminist project of re-visiting female stories. Again, she turns to the materiality of textiles, and particularly their uneven surface, to convey this act of feminist resistance in the second verse: "I can feel you smoothing me over." Rather than accept the compression of male passive-aggression, Swift identifies herself as a "wrinkle"—a crumpled fabric that has been creased from wear or folding. As Sara Ahmed asserts in her conception of the "Feminist killjoy," "Feminists do kill joy in a certain sense […] our failure to be happy is read as sabotaging the happiness of others" (4). In her refusal to be "smooth[ed]" over and her assertion that "I'm fine with my spite," Swift repudiates the fantasy of female forgiveness. Fans have pointed out that the song seems to reference Swift's antagonistic relationship with her former producer, Scott Borchetta, who sold the rights to her masters in 2019. In an interview with CBS Sunday Morning in August of that year, Swift commented: "You know, people go on and on about, like, you have to forgive and forget to move past something … No, you don't. You don't have to forgive and you don't have to forget." This phrasing mirrors the image of the wrinkled fabric, as the crumpled material does not forget—it displays the creases as an indentation of the past.

Like the "bloodstain" from "cardigan," the structure of fabric holds its damage and serves as an instructive allegory for trauma. As Swift intimates later, "Staying friends / Would iron it out so nice." Refusing to be flattened into submission, Swift employs the rough textures of fabric as evidence of the brutality of her treatment. As another form of "sensual politics," then, the textuality of fabrics provides an important space for narrativization, as the structure of the textile retains the tale of its past. The image of the "wrinkle" represents this teleology, as it embodies the processes of aging.[2] The "wrinkle" is also reminiscent of her *Red* track "All Too Well" and the line, "I'm a crumpled-up piece of paper lying here." Thus the "wrinkle" becomes an important texture of memory in Swift's oeuvre, as the "crumpled" paper, like the wrinkled fabric, registers and retains its scrupled contours—the sensual haptics of being bent and dented. But as an allegory for feminist resistance, Swift herself becomes the "wrinkle" within patriarchal culture, memorializing oppression and denying its erasure.

Fabrics as Narratives

Throughout *folklore* and *evermore* Swift is fascinated by the ways in which fabrics—such as knit—can hold meanings and narratives. In "seven," a youthful narrator says to her friend, "pack your dolls and a sweater," as protection from the elements for their imaginative adventure. As Rachel Handler flippantly surmises, *folklore* is a "haunted album about knitwear." *evermore* extends this fascination; in "tolerate it," a song which chronicles a one-sided marriage, the narrator asks, "Where's that man who'd put blankets over my barbed wire?" Encasing warmth is highly valued by Swift, who plays with the

---

[2] The "wrinkle" also appears in her *Midnights* track "Hits Different" with the line, "a wrinkle in time / like the crease by your eyes."

tropes of being held and wrapped up within relationships. Again "All Too Well" is an important reference point, as that "scarf" acts as a key totem of remembrance, signifying the enveloping swaddle of lost love. At the Toronto Film Festival, Swift acknowledged that the scarf is a "metaphor," symbolizing entwined romantic memory as the knitwear is passed "between us," just as the memories are shared. Whilst the speaker may remember the ill-fated romance "all too well," her partner "keep[s]" the remnants of the relationship "in [a] drawer" hidden away, unable to "rid" himself of their shared history. Although concealed and neglected, the "scarf," like memory itself, is retained, as demonstrated in the concluding line: "you remember it all."

In *folklore*, the "cardigan" becomes a fresh invocation of such shared memory, and the merchandise sold alongside the album even included a cream "oversized chunky knit" cardigan (originally sold for $49), like the one worn by Swift in the video. In a complementary image for *folklore*, Swift wears a specific kind of knitwear—the Aran knit. Rosalind Jana explains that the knitwear has a "complex history and mythology": "Traditionally made from undyed *báinín*—sheep's wool, typically cream-coloured—it often incorporates patterns including cable, basket and diamond stitch. These patterns are said to be imbued with different symbolic meanings ranging from luck with fishing to hopes for future wealth."

In Swift's roll-neck version, her sleeves are decorated with "raised diamond stitches," and it has "cable stitches of varying sizes running down the body" (Power). Such patterns, claims Heinz Kiewe in *The Sacred History of Knitting*, can be traced back to Celtic knotwork, "a tradition dating back more than 1,000 years" (Jana). These designs in knitwork reveal how women participated in private forms of narrativization, even when they were excluded from public historical documentation. Women would knit symbols into the construction of woollen garments, materializing memory into the very fabric itself. The Aran knit, widely used on the coast for seafaring, has particular associations with death and memorialization, as the myth goes that "fishermen who were drowned at sea could be identified by the unique patterning and stitching of their Aran sweaters" (Jana). Thus, in weaving entirely unique designs, the history of the Aran knit attests to women's handmade identities and their methods for conservation. As Jana contends, the Aran knit is "a perfect example of the mingling of history, folklore, and deep social significance." Swift's knitted cardigan embodies this arcane history within its weave, referencing the creativity of forgotten female ancestry.

Alongside knitwear, Swift also invokes a wide range of woven textiles in *folklore* and *evermore*. Her visual aesthetic choices for the albums signal her obsession with fabric patterning and weaving; she wears lace, gingham, check, flannel, stripes, and tartan in various marketing materials—each recognized for its distinctive interlacing of woven fibers to construct an interlocked design. On the cover of *evermore* and in *the long pond studio sessions*, Swift wears tartan—or plaid—revising the earlier image of her "plaid shirt days" in "All Too Well." Tartan, which is often incorrectly branded as plaid, "refers to the pattern of interlocking stripes, running in both the warp and weft in the cloth" (Tartan Museum). This act of weaving, or the process of composing fabric by patterns of criss-crossed, interlocking vertical and horizontal threads, becomes another delicate form of craftwork invoked across the albums. Swift uses the allegory of weaving to explore the interlinking of individuals in relationships, as she expresses in *Lover*'s "Daylight": "All of you, all of me (Intertwined)." In *evermore*'s "happiness," she extends this enmeshing further, as the protagonist describes the interweaving of bodies through sex, imploring: "I pulled your body into mine / Every goddamn night." Here the act of pulling, of weaving one body into another, has been repudiated, leaving a gaping hole in the relationship.

Along with the relational allegory, Swift weaves particular language, imagery, and intertextuality across the two albums. In the *long pond studio sessions* interview, Swift acknowledges that when writing the song "hoax," there was no singular experience that she was pulling from, but rather she was entwining multiple lines of inquiry. Imagery appears and subsides throughout the albums, with shifting visions of seascapes, forests, and cabin-like interiors woven throughout. Musical collaborator Aaron Dessner especially commends the song "epiphany" for "the way that you weaved that together, where there is remembrance and bearing witness to your family's history, but then recognition of the heroes of today" (*long pond*). Here, Dessner articulates that Swift's method of weaving is crucially a method of narrativization, linking seemingly disparate elements to formulate new material. As recognized by Dessner, Swift's various writerly strands—including the confessional, fictional, and historical—are woven together for the purpose of this construction. Rather than relying on a singular thread of meaning-making, Swift handles complex, multifarious strands of women's memory to fabricate new modes of storytelling.

The song "seven" combines strands of dreamlike fictionality and wistful remembrance in its depiction of girlhood. Its chorus opens with a collective chant, "Cross your heart won't tell no other," as secretive patterns are communicated between the young pair, the overlapping "cross" reflecting the most rudimentary design. Woven shapes are also found in the hairstyles of the girls—"Your braids like a pattern"—as these motifs of nostalgia are entangled through time. Braids, or hair plaiting, is another key image, as *evermore*'s album cover shows Swift, back to the camera, with a long French plait down her tartan-covered back. Like the tartan fabric, it is the pattern of the plait—the intertwining of separate elements to form a new design—that is privileged by Swift. Memories may be faint in "seven," as the protagonist can't "recall" the face of her young companion, but beyond purely visual memory, Swift insists that "sensual" or affective memories are more enduring. "The love lasts so long," insists the speaker, who can remember "sweet tea in the summer" and the pattern of the "braids." As a coda for female genealogy, Swift is implying that such patterns are "passed on" through the female lineage—mother to child, girl to girl. As Kat Tenbarge claims, in "seven," "Swift captures that feeling of being a queer child perfectly." There is a queerness to this patterning, since, as in weaving, hands are needed to make the "cross" and particularly the "braids," which require an intimate manual process. As a methodology for how women pass down and share meaning, the patterns in the song become haptic codes for female love and care. Swift tells us that these shapes are "passed on like folk songs": as a form of "folk" memory, the dreamlike recollection of these patterns is carried forward and re-shared. This patterning acts as a shared cipher of female communication in "seven" but also as a code for imaginative transformation, as the "braids" lead like a ladder to "the moon and to Saturn." Thus, in tracing the patterns of girlhood, Swift also reworks them, memorializing the love shared between young girls and "pass[ing]" that on herself through music.

Weaving Memory

So far, this chapter has moved from a large- to a small-scale fabrication—considering the garment ("cardigan"), the surface of fabrics ("wrinkle"), the knit and weave of fabrication, and lastly basic patterning. Here, I turn to the most essential structure of fabrics—the strands with which it is composed—which Swift features in her track "invisible string." The song records the attempt to locate a thread of narrative meaning in sifting through memories.[3] The track opens with the sound of prominent guitar plucking, and as Dessner discloses in the *long pond studio sessions*, he used a particular instrument which "deadens the strings so it sounds really old." This type of finger-plucking grasps each string individually, which is reminiscent of the way that thread is woven onto a loom. The lyrics also cite fabrics, as Swift opens with a "teal" colored "shirt" as one of the first signifiers of memory. As with "cardigan," Swift employs patchworking here, listing a range of disparate "clues" to formulate a picture of fates intertwined. The three verses of the song cover different ways to read these "signs" of meaning, firstly through color ("green" grass is compared to the "teal" shirt), then through sound (Swift's track "Bad Blood" is set against the voice of a "waitress"), and finally through a form of "sensual politics," as the materials cited evoke textuality. Throughout Swift's oeuvre, we are told that signs and signifiers are unreliable indicators of the world. "Time," notes the protagonist, "gave me no signs," indicating that experience was unreadable, and Swift questions, "Were there clues I didn't see?" Like in "seven," sight is not the most valued sense here, but instead Swift treasures touch—the strings of the guitar and the textures in the final verse. The "cold steel" and the crunchy "gold" leaves suggest that the material textuality of memory is a more reliable source than sight or sound.

In addition to a temporal shift through the song, there is also an imaginative transference, as the leaves turn from "green" to "gold." As such, Swift isn't in fact locating "clues" or "signs" in the song but inventing the connections between them. As Derrida writes in *Archive Fever*, "The archontic principle of the archive is also a principle of consignation, that is, of gathering together" (3). Like the archive, memory also works through this process of assemblage and re-assemblage. The "green" leaves become "gold" once Swift has gathered and transcribed that meaning upon them. As a patchwork of memory, the specific signs themselves become almost irrelevant. What's really at stake, then, is the active process of creation through memory—the narrative thread that weaves these "clues" together. The "invisible string" of the song does not exist, but what is real is Swift's artistic rendering of it. Instead of reading the "signs," Swift invents—or fabricates—her own version of their entwined history. To spin a yarn is both to spin fibers into cloth and to tell a story, most often a fanciful or imaginative tale. Thus, the track reminds us that all memory is an act of creation—a fabrication of "scraps" of material, endlessly reconstituted. Swift fashions a patchwork of images and

---

[3]   This is later reflected in the video for "willow," where Swift follows a golden thread through fantastical worlds, leading her to play a game of cat's cradle in which the golden string is looped and patterned between the two children.

objects in the song, from the "teal" shirt to the "dive bar," stitching them together to construct a new composition. As such, Swift herself entwines the "invisible string" between memories, crafting meaning through the narrative thread that she herself has woven.

Across the sister albums, Swift stitches "scraps" of memory together—not just from her own experience but as a collective patchwork of forgotten women's histories. As Katja May argues, "Practices of needlework and their narrative renderings .... are essentially political because of needlework's strong connection with contested understandings of femininity, women's work, protest and the political" (18). As a form of fabrication, patchworking combines all the elements previously discussed—weaving, patterning, threading, stitching—to fashion a new material. Patchworking uses discarded fabrics, cuts them up, reworks them, and finally pieces them together in a new configuration. As Swift herself recalls, "*evermore* was the first time I didn't discard everything," since she re-shaped and re-used the "scraps" from *folklore*. As an allegory for collective female remembrance, piecing together bits of "fantasy, history, and memory," the patchwork embodies Swift's narrative method in *folklore* and *evermore*. Where there are holes in women's experience, Swift seeks to patch over and mend that loss. As she writes in "champagne problems," "she'll patch up your tapestry that I shred." Here Swift identifies patriarchal history as a "tapestry"— meticulous, ornate, and widely appreciated for its artistry—while female history is a "patch[work]": mismatched, asymmetric, and full of gaps constantly needing mending. But Swift's lyrics also suggest that women need to "patch" over the rich "tapestry" of male-dominated history with female memory, reconstituting the image with new stitchwork, creating a revised picture. This new vision of wholeness speaks to a shared feminist history; as May argues, "making is a way of connecting not only materials, but also bodies, in ways that generate new openings for Feminist solidarity" (58). As Swift acknowledges, "There was something different with *folklore*. In making it, I felt less like I was departing and more like I was returning." In her practice of patching women's stories and reconstituting female genealogies, Swift engages in a "process of redress ... for the reworking of dominant narratives" (May 21). In recovering and reworking materials, Swift refashions female memory for the twenty-first century, but it is not just the final garment—or artifact—that Swift invests in. Rather, it is the *process* of making and re-making—its provisionality—that Swift's work encompasses.

Conclusion: Patchworking Diversity

Like a "patchwork quilt," Swift enacts forms of contingency, as her songs can be revised and embroidered over. This can be most readily observed in *Taylor's Versions*, the re-recording of her studio albums, including, at the time of this publication, *Fearless, Red, Speak Now*, and *1989*. Therefore, I want to conclude by attending to an aspect of memory that Swift has yet to address: racialized memory. The "patchwork" of stories that Swift assembles in *folklore* and *evermore* must be acknowledged for their whiteness, as she heralds a range of white literary figures including J. M. Barrie, Charlotte Brontë, and Emily Dickinson. Her musical canon is also white, as the albums pull from folk, pop, indie, and country traditions. In "Why Does Country Music Sound White?," Geoff Mann argues that the roots of country music celebrate a specifically white form of historical memory: "[T]here is [a] way in which the nostalgia that suffuses country music might be plainly white. For example, in Merle Haggard's 1981 hit 'Are the Good Times Really Over For Good?', the good times— 'back before Elvis'—are also back before *Brown* v. *Board of Education*, not to mention the Civil Rights movement" (88).

Nostalgia for a rural past "is a white idiom, not a black one," claims Kathleen Stewart, as this desire to re-capture the past sidesteps the "violence and tragedy" of racialized America (106). Thus, in her act of retrieval—in memorializing and revising past stories— Swift is in fact reinforcing a white historical methodology. George Yancy describes this process of cleaving to a white ontology as "a process of suturing":

(from Latin sutura, meaning a "seam" or a "sewing together") [it] is the process whereby whites install forms of closure, forms of protection from counter-white axiological and embodied iterations, epistemic fissure, and white normative disruption. The process of suturing involves an effort—though I'm sure that for whites it is not recognized as an effort or as a site of active maintenance—to be "invulnerable," "untouched," "patched," "mended together," "complete," "whole." (xv)

To "suture" whiteness indicates a form of wholeness, which pieces together "narrative authority," thereby occluding racialized "alterity" (Yancy xv). In Swift's overlapping patchwork of "history, fantasy and memory," there is little space for racialized perspectives (Swift *f* 2020). So, whilst the characters of her stories may not be directly identified as white, their very lack of racialization indicates a universalized white hegemony (DiAngelo 9). As May argues, "to be sutured" is to be "oriented towards whiteness as the default mode for conceiving the self" (107). Thus, in order to attend to white privilege and acknowledge racialized positionings, Yancy conceptualizes a process of becoming "un-sutured" from whiteness: "To be un-sutured, which is linked to losing one's way, is dispositional and aspirational. As such, being un-sutured involves a continuous process of renewal and commitment . . . and having the capacity, even if it waxes and wanes, to avoid narrative closure" (xvi).

Swift's poetics, as I have argued through this chapter, demonstrate this capacity for "un-suturing." Through her fabrics of memory, Swift materializes forgotten histories, fabricates new narratives, and, most importantly, reveals the contingency of memory itself—as a "patchwork" that must be continuously reproduced. As May argues, "practices of needlework can be a catalyst for processes of un-suturing," and therefore through Swift's practice of reworking the fabrics of memory, there is the possibility of pulling apart the seams of white authority (107). As she herself acknowledges in her introduction to *evermore*, "I have no idea what will come next. I have no idea about a lot of things these days." In 2023's *Speak Now (Taylor's Version)*, Swift even rewrote the lyrics to "Better Than Revenge" to correct her prior slut-shaming iteration. Therefore, to attend to the dominance of white-supremacist historicization, Swift should develop racial literacy to craft new *intersectional* iterations of female memory. Swift's "patchwork quilt" of remembrance must be open to fresh forms of relation, to a radical diversity of experience that can defy the closure of white hegemony. To "patch" minoritized perspectives into her fabrics of memory, Swift must first be ready to "shred" the "tapestry" of her own whiteness.

Works Cited

Ahmed, Sara. *Living A Feminist Life*. Duke University Press: Durham, 2017.

Benjamin, Walter. *The Arcades Project*. Belknap Press: Cambridge, 1999.

Derrida, Jacques. *Archive Fever*. University of Chicago Press: Chicago, 2017.

DiAngelo, Robin. *What Does It Mean to Be White? Developing White Racial Literacy*. Peter Lang: New York, 2012.

Handler, Rachel. "Taylor Swift's Freaky Folklore Movie Mood Board." *Vulture*, 28 July 2020.

Jana, Rosalind. "Taylor Swift Is Bringing Centuries-Old Knitting Traditions Back into Demand—Here's How." *Vogue India*, 12 Aug. 2020.

Lakoff, George. *Metaphors We Live By*. University of Chicago Press: Chicago, 2017.

Mann, Geoff. "Why Does Country Music Sound White? Race and the Voice of Nostalgia." *Ethnic and Racial Studies*, vol. 31, no. 1. (2008): 73–100.

May, Katja. "Everyday Textures: Practices Of Needlework, Meaning-Making And Socio-Political Transformation." University of Kent: Kent, 2020.

Millett, Kate. *Sexual Politics*. Columbia University Press: New York, 2016.

Neruda, Pablo. *Twenty Love Poems and a Song of Despair*. Jonathan Cape, 2004.

Power, Bairbre. "Taylor-Made: Boost for the Irish Craft Industry as Pop Star Wears Aran Jumper to Promote New Album." *Independent Online*, 25 July 2020.

Rich, Adrienne. *Diving into the Wreck: Poems 1971-1972*. W. W. Norton: New York, 2013.

Stewart, Kathleen. *A Space on the Side of the Road: Cultural Poetics in an "Other" America*. Princeton University Press: Princeton, 1996.

Swift, Taylor. "All Too Well: The Short Film." *YouTube*, uploaded by Taylor Swift, 13 Nov. 2021.

Swift, Taylor. "Beautiful Ghosts for the Motion Picture Cats." *YouTube*, uploaded by Taylor Swift, 15 Nov. 2019.

Swift, Taylor. "Folklore Essay." *Twitter*, 24 Jun. 2020.

Swift, Taylor. *folklore: the long pond studio sessions*. Disney +, 25 Nov. 2020.

Swift, Taylor. "I Have No Idea What Will Come Next." *Twitter*, 11 Dec. 2020.

Swift, Taylor. "In Conversation with Taylor Swift." *YouTube*, uploaded by TIFF Originals, 16 Sept. 2022.

Swift, Taylor. "NYU's 2022 Commencement Speaker Taylor Swift." *YouTube*, uploaded by New York University, 26 May 2022.

Swift, Taylor. "Taylor Swift On 'Lover' And Haters." *YouTube*, uploaded by CBS Sunday Morning, Aug 25. 2019.

Swift, Taylor. "Taylor Swift's Songwriting Process On 'evermore.'" *YouTube*, uploaded by Apple Music, 16 Dec. 2020.

Tenbarge, Kat. "As a Woman Who Loves Women, Taylor Swift's 'folklore' Lyrics Resonated Deeply with My Queer Experiences." *Insider*, 1 Aug. 2020.

"Tartan Terminology." *The Scottish Tartans Museum and Heritage Center, Inc.* 5 Mar. 2019.

Yancy, George. *White Self-Criticality Beyond Anti-Racism: How Does it Feel to be a White Problem?* Lexington Books: Lanham, 2014.

15

"The corner I haunt": Trauma, Time, and Space in Taylor Swift's Post-Hiatus Oeuvre

Carolin Isabel Steiner

"I just wanted to say I am sorry to anyone who ever wasn't believed because I don't know what turn my life would have taken if somebody—if people didn't believe me when I said that something had happened to me." These are the words Taylor Swift used to mark the anniversary of her court case against radio DJ David Mueller, who had been found guilty of sexually assaulting her (*Miss Americana*). Spoken in front of a sold-out stadium in Tampa, Florida, this declaration on August 14, 2018, marks a pivotal point in Swift's post-hiatus discography: not only one at which she chose to speak her own trauma as a sexual assault survivor but also one at which she signaled that her work as a songwriter should be understood within this context. In this article, I take Swift up on her invitation to contextualize her work accordingly and propose a reading through a traumatic lens of the contrast between her post- and pre-hiatus oeuvre. "Hiatus" here is referring to the period between 2016 and 2017, when, amidst controversies about her not distancing herself from the alt-right movement,[1] the aforementioned sexual assault lawsuit, and an uncomfortably public feud with Kanye West, Swift removed herself from the public eye. "Every domino fell," she said in an interview with Laura Snapes for the *Guardian*. "It became really terrifying for anyone to even know where I was. And I felt completely incapable of doing or saying anything publicly, at all." A year later, she emerged and released her sixth studio album, *reputation*, a record shaped by notions of revenge, justice, and self-sufficiency. (The recurring and highly-marketed symbol for her *reputation* era was a snake, the emoji Kanye West fans spammed her social media presence with during the 2016 feud.)[2] I argue that this faultline between her fifth and sixth records, *1989* and *reputation*, is where a substantial change in Swift's narrative identity has taken place, which manifests itself in the emergence of traumatic manifestations in her post-hiatus work.

---

[1] Due to her perceived apoliticality, right-wing actors decided to frame Swift as an "aryan princess," which the media decided warranted a public rebuttal on her part.
[2] The music video for "Look What You Made Me Do" featured Swift in a diamond-filled bathtub with a single dollar bill floating amidst the diamonds—she had countersued Mueller for a single dollar (cf. Weaver).

The discussion about what qualifies as a traumatic event has long been ongoing, often criticized for its disregard for female lived realities by omitting experiences of everyday violence in favor of events which were perceived to be outside the scope of expected human existence. Sexual assault is, however, very much an experience that members of many groups can expect to encounter during their lifetimes. In this article, I therefore follow Lothe and refer to trauma as a potentially polytemporal phenomenon, which manifests in "the lasting effect(s) of a deeply distressing or disturbing event" (153). Such an approach does not define Taylor Swift's personal relationship to trauma or any traumatic events she may have experienced; rather, it acknowledges Swift as an artist who has not only endured potentially traumatizing events but also framed herself as a survivor, and it focuses on examining her body of work rather than her as a person through the lens of trauma studies.

In the context of trauma studies, it is necessary to position Swift's writing in a framework suitable to carefully situating her oeuvre and its (non-?) relation to her biography. Her writing explodes a wide variety of genres by blurring the lines between fiction, testimonial, auto-fiction, and the meta-fiction surrounding the autobiography of her delicately crafted public persona. There are many applicable genres, but for the purpose of this essay, I broadly position Swift's work as life-writing: somewhere at the intersection of her lived experiences and the meta-fiction contributing to her public image, therefore accepting that her words move fluently between boundaries of the *real* and *fictive* in an ongoing negotiation of lived experience, commodification, and public persona.[3] At the core of this, I want to emphasize that narrative serves an important device for creating and remediating identity, in what McAdams and McLean call *Narrative Identity*. They describe the phenomenon as "a person's internalized and evolving life story, integrating the reconstructed past and imagined future to provide life with some degree of unity and purpose" (1). Rather than situating her oeuvre according to fictionality or autobiographicality, I instead focus on the narrative identity Swift has created.

With this in mind, I propose a reading of Swift's work along two specific axes: firstly, in the context of temporality and the breaking and reinterpreting of time in her post-hiatus work, as "the breaking up of the unifying thread of temporality" is "an essential dimension of psychological trauma" (Stolorow 158); and secondly, focusing on spatial dimensions and her constructions of home and familiarity as markers of girlhood and safety, whose disruption becomes clear in her later work.

---

[3] Swift's writing neatly slots into the *testimonio* genre in places ("Testimonial literature highlights the possibilities for solidarity and affiliation among critics, interviewers, and the subject who 'speaks'" [Kaplan 210]); however, given that testimonial literature is, at its core, interrogating post- and neo-colonial contexts and lives, I have deliberately chosen to exclude Swift's writing and refrain from using *testimonio* as a framework.

Storytelling and Silence: Literary Trauma Theory

"The relationship between trauma and narrative is close but problematic," Jakob Lothe has notably argued in his foundational work on said relationship (152). The field of trauma studies is based on the underlying belief that traumatic events are not ingrained in conscious memory in a way that allows regular access and recall of the traumatic memory, instead being situated at the threshold of the conscious and sub-conscious. Traumatic memories tend to be subjects of flashbacks, dreams, and other acts of uncontrolled recall after a certain latency period, a reproduction and reinterpretation of the traumatic event which may culminate in the narrativization of a survivor's trauma (Kurvet-Käosaar 306).

A key part of traditional trauma theory is the concept of *unspeakability*: as the memory of the traumatic event is not fully accessible to the survivor, they are incapable of articulating the gravity and entire scope of an event. They are stuck in a linguistic gap between the *speakable* and the experienced, a denotative hesitancy that leads to compulsive repetition of the traumatic event (Caruth 4). As Lothe, previously having pointed out the tense relationship between trauma and narrative, summarizes:

> On the one hand, a person who experiences an event in his or her life as traumatic, and who feels a need to tell others about the experience, may choose, and be able, to do so. On the other hand, a different person who experiences the same event may not feel the same need, or be able, to talk or write about it. While our memory of a traumatic event may prompt narration, it may also thwart narration. Moreover, although a person who tries to tell about a traumatic event may find the narrative activity helpful, narration inevitably takes him or her back to the event, thus perhaps making the person remember what he or she wants to forget. (152)

Life-writing offers a "space of interrogation" for the limits of how traumatic events can be mediated through narrative (Kurvet-Käosaar 305). While there has been a surge of autobiographical writing interrogating and engaging with "suffering, violence and injustice in common everyday life" in the last decades of the twentieth century, life-writing is constrained by the boundaries set through publishers and readerly expectations, limiting the ways in which the life-writer can articulate and express their experiences (Kurvet-Käosaar 305-7).[4] Therefore, representing traumatic experiences may require a departure from the realm of the autobiographical and the creation of

---

[4] Kurvet-Käosaar points to a "vogue" of consuming and publishing trauma for pleasure and profit, and while I wish to dismiss this notion, I would like to emphasize that participation in the discourse of traumatic events can facilitate community resilience and provide survivors with tangible mental health benefits (cf. Steiner; Garcia and Rimé; Rimé et al.; Kennedy-Moore and Watson; Berry and Pennebaker). Luckhurst counters this as well: "Whilst often dismissed as symptomatic of a mass culture of narcissism, the success of the trauma memoir is merely further evidence of the affective transmissibility of trauma I've tracked across virtually every arena of discourse, whether scientific or cultural, professional or amateur, high or low" (119).

personal distance by carving out "fictional textual spaces that might be more suitable" for the narration within aforementioned constraints (Kurvet-Käosaar 307). The limits imposed by the genre conventions of life-writing run perpendicular to the more general challenges survivors face when narrating their experiences.[5] Lothe writes that "the decision to narrate [...] can enable a [...] survivor to come to terms with aspects of his or her traumatic experience," emphasizing that the resistance of such experience to narrativization is part of this process. Therefore, while trauma may manifest through various narrative techniques such as dissociation, flashback, repetition, and recurrent use of images, the absences thereof may speak just as loudly. As Meretoja puts it, "[t]he interplay between storytelling and silence is woven into their fabric so intimately that one does not exist without the other" (305).

Thus, in such a reading, silence and narrative must be seen as two sides of the same coin. A storyteller, therefore, may express traumatic events and their effects not only through what they say (and indeed how they say it) but also in what they do not say (and, therefore, how they do not say it). Such dictates apply not only to authors and poets, for whom we have long used well established techniques of analysis, but also songwriters and popular musicians—those who speak (or do not speak) not only to the grand collective traumas of our age, such as Anthropocene climate change, war, profound inequality, and global crises, but also the traumas at a micro or community level: the perils of coming of age, interpersonal relationships and their breakdown, grief, and abuse. Moreover, these traumata, while often anchored in discrete events, are not static points. Rather, their effects develop and change across time, necessitating a dynamic temporal approach to their depiction and, as a result, to the analysis of their depiction.

Still Twenty-Three: Breaking Time, Shifting Time

Since her debut in 2006 and continuing across a discography that spans nearly two decades, Taylor Swift has used temporal dimensions in her storytelling in ever-evolving ways, which complement and challenge the uses of narration and silence. Swift's pre-hiatus discography shows temporal markers following intra-textual chronologies, creating narrative arcs within individual songs.[6] As Sloan points out, this is primarily rooted in genre conventions; country music, a genre Swift drew extensively on in her earlier works, tends to focus not on momentary snapshots like pop music but instead observes the flow of time (6). At the center of this is what Neal terms the Time-Shift paradigm: "a combination of poetic devices, formal structures, and stylistically

---

[5] Most of the literature on life-writing and trauma studies (as well as a good portion of trauma studies in general) have focused on Holocaust survivors. While the points made stood the test of time and continue to be relevant in a broader context, I have chosen to omit the word "Holocaust survivor" from relevant quotes, instead speaking about "survivors" in order to avoid drawing accidental inferences to comparable gravities of different traumata to the Holocaust.

[6] Notably, *1989* is the first record on which Swift starts to deviate from these temporal patterns; it therefore occupies a threshold position.

normative harmonic elements that together project the segmentation of and passage of time" (42). One of the countless examples of the Time-Shift paradigm in Swift's discography is "Tim McGraw," the opener of Swift's self-titled debut album. The song starts with a snapshot of the narrator's relationship with "a boy in a Chevy truck / that had the tendency of getting stuck / on backroads at night." The first chorus reveals that the relationship has since ended, with the narrator hoping that her former lover still thinks of her whenever he listens to Tim McGraw, and Swift intersperses more snapshots of their relationship: "I hope you think of my favorite song / the one we danced to all night long ..." The second verse places the narrator in the grieving stages of a lost relationship: the immediate sadness, but ultimately her moving on and remembering the relationship as "a letter you never read / from three summers back." The pre-chorus softens the hope asserted in the first chorus; during the first chorus, the narrator hopes she will be remembered, whereas the second chorus is softened in the pre-chorus, with the narrator stating, "And lookin' back on all that, it's nice to believe ...," before segueing into the chorus. The narrative arc closes in the bridge, with the narrator back on her lover's street at least three years after their relationship, leaving the previously unread letter on his doorstep. At the same time, the narrator reveals that the chorus had been lines from aforementioned letter all along, thus placing her current self at a temporal distance from the words she wrote at least three years prior: "And there's a letter left on your doorstep / and the first thing that you'll read / is, 'When you think Tim McGraw ...'" The insertion of the word "is" in the first chorus line shifts the chorus into the past in the form of a letterhead, allowing the listener to have witnessed the progression of the narrator's relationship from honeymoon phase to closure.[7]

While the Time-Shift paradigm still occasionally resurfaces in Swift's post-hiatus work (such as in "Getaway Car," when the narrator reveals that she ends up leaving her lover in a motel and robbing him blind), the focus of her writing slowly shifts to moments in time: short periods chronicled in one song, snapshots and singular changes in relationships rather than overarching, complete histories. "Gorgeous," for instance, tells the story of the narrator's pining for someone during a single evening, while "Dancing With Our Hands Tied" looks back on a relationship doomed to fail.

The further into the post-hiatus discography she moves, the more Swift explodes temporal conventions; as she goes, she breaks and reassembles time, re-interprets memories, reconstructs past happenings. In "The Archer," this works both on a sonic and lyrical level. The narrator skips through time, lingering on the threshold of the present before predicting that the addressee could be the one to stay; she poses the question, "Who could stay?," while an ever-increasing beat accompanies her like the sonic manifestation of anxiety. Even though it becomes faster and more prominent, it never drops, leaving both the listener and the narrator in a threshold state of temporal dislocation. This culminates in songs like "exile," where the narrator is incapable of placing herself in time, not sure whether she is experiencing *déjà vu* or has previously

[7] For more examples of this, see Neal's analysis of Swift's earlier works.

encountered the situation; "I think I've seen this film before," she reflects. In "Hits Different," the narrator places a lover from her past into the present by wondering whether she's hearing his key in the door or just hallucinating, implying that "they" are about to "take her away."

"exile," a duet between Swift and Justin Vernon of Bon Iver, finds two former lovers negotiating their emotions after a break-up. Not only is Swift recalling déjà vu in the chorus, but the song further outlines the diverging perceptions and dislocations of time between Swift as narrator and her partner. Vernon's narrator voices his disappointment at how swiftly his lover has moved on, as it only takes her "five whole minutes / to pack us up and leave me with it." Swift's narrator, on the other hand, has perceived the end of the relationship as a long time coming: "Second, third, and hundredth chances / balancin' on breaking branches / those eyes add insult to injury." These diverging perceptions climax in a call-and-response section in the bridge, with Vernon's narrator postulating, "You never gave a warning sign," while Swift as narrator answers, "I gave so many signs." Similar temporal disjunction is at the core of "Maroon"—"I wake with your memory over me / that's a real fucking legacy," Swift writes—as well as "right where you left me." In the latter, Swift's narrator, having been dumped at a restaurant, ceases to flow with time, unlike the people around her. "Friends break up, friends get married / strangers get born, strangers get buried," she sings, "but I'm right where you left me." Stuck at "23 inside her fantasy," she considers whether her former lover has a family by now, and she imagines shattered time as broken glass while declaring herself a revenant devoid of the agency to rejoin the temporality she watches from the corner table: "Help, I'm still at the restaurant, still sitting in a corner I haunt / [. . .]/ right when I felt the moment stop / glass shattered on the white cloth / everybody moved on, I, I stayed there / [. . .]/ You left me no choice to stay here forever." Both "exile" and "right where you left me" exemplify the move from Time-Shift paradigms to momentary snapshots in time—snapshots that Swift, as in the case of "right where you left me," expands to narrative spaces beholden to exploded time. Choosing not to point to the moment *when* she was left but rather *where* she was left, Swift as narrator figures herself post-hiatus as an extradiegetic haunter, exiled from a world where time flows in a linear fashion and forced to watch from the liminal temporal space she is trapped in.

Between Home and Exile: Space and Displacement

While Swift's pre-hiatus discography anchored her firmly in familiar contexts and a vaguely defined Americana of slamming screen doors, trucks, and muddy backroads (that gave way to a subsequent identification with New York), her post-hiatus work is dominated by displacement and positions *home* as a contested space. Kaplan writes that "[t]raditionally, Western autobiographical writing has participated in the literary construction of 'home'; a process of generalizing the particular, fabricating a narrative space of familiarity and crafting a narrative that links the individual to the universal" (212). Narratives seen in Swift's earlier work, such as "The Best Day," create an idealized version of childhood, chiefly anchoring her sense of self in the familiarity of home. The song details the narrator's comfortable and loving relationship with her parents—"I grew up in a pretty house / and I had space to run and I / had the best days with you," she writes—in a manner consistent with her images of idealistic, if not always unproblematic, domesticity. "Fifteen," too, is similar; Swift takes the mundane and often unseen experiences of teenage girls and frames them in the context of her own coming-of-age: "You sit in class next to a red-head named Abigail / and soon enough you're best friends." The spatial politics of her earlier works are clearly shaped by a sense of optimism, of reveling in the safety of the familiar but also by the curiosity of conquering new places within a lyrical universe of a generalized Americana. As Fogarty and Arnold put it, "Taylor Swift is a monument to the idea that there once was a place called America. She recalls an old American dream—of high school popularity contests, apple pies, dreamy boys next door, and a very old, very white, Christian nation" (1).

Post-hiatus, Swift harshly breaks with this narrative space; displacement, disillusionment, and dissociation surface at the forefront of her textual spaces. Home, a concept always intrinsically tied to personal relationships, is dismantled on several fronts. For one, the sense of safety, the girlhood sketched out in earlier works, is threatened by mortality. In "marjorie," Swift reminisces about her late grandmother, reflecting on the lost time she cannot grasp anymore. I "[s]hould've kept every grocery store receipt," she writes, "'cause every scrap of you would be taken from me." In "Soon You'll Get Better," Swift as narrator engages with her mother's breast cancer and subsequent brain tumor diagnosis while refusing to acknowledge the gravity of the situation: "I know delusion when I see it in the mirror / you like the nicer nurses, you make the best of a bad deal / I just pretend it isn't real." Leaving the child-like naivety of her earlier textual spaces behind, Swift as narrator revisits her own childhood as well. "seven" finds Swift reinterpreting childhood memories, retelling the story of a friendship with a nameless girl whose abusive household she had witnessed: "And I've been meaning to tell you / I think your house is haunted / Your dad is always mad and that must be why." She imagines having tried to mitigate the situation for her friend, singing, "And I think you should come live with / me and we can be pirates / then you won't have to cry / or hide in the closet."

At the same time, Swift reconstructs homelands in relationships, from "Death by Thousand Cuts"—"Our songs, our films, united we stand / our country, guess it was a lawless land"—to "exile," in which she says, "You're not my homeland anymore ... You were my town / now I'm in exile, seein' you out." In these songs and others, Swift emphasizes the falling apart of landscapes and returns to haunted, inescapable grounds; eventually, each narrator becomes a ghost herself, fusing with the places she is cursed to haunt, a phenomenon neatly illustrated in "Carolina." "Oh, Carolina creeks / running through my veins," Swift writes, "And you didn't see me here / No, they never did see me."[8]

---

[8] "Carolina" and "right where you left me" occupy a more complex position in Swift's work in terms of life-writing. The former was written for the film soundtrack to the 2022 movie adaption of "Where the Crawdads Sing," while the latter was inspired by a Netflix show. They subsequently can be understood as less autobiographical than her other work.

This fusing of self and space is evident in the portrayal of Swift's own corporeality in the latter part of her work. Deploying imagery of wounding and scarring, Swift confronts the most intimate sites of hurt; thoughts of suicide appear in "this is me trying" ("Pulled the car off the road to the lookout / could've followed my fears all the way down"), while disordered eating figures in "You're On Your Own, Kid": "I hosted parties and starved my body / like I'd be saved by the perfect kiss." When she reckons with a problematic relationship in "Would've, Could've, Should've," Swift writes that "[t]he wound won't close / I keep on waiting for a sign." The fusing of space and self as well as the structural vulnerability of space itself are explored in "ivy," in which the speaker's illicit lover is described as the ivy penetrating the walls of a house with which she narratively fuses: "My house of stone, your ivy grows / and now I'm covered in you." The threat to the narrator is verbalized in the statement that her husband, should he find out about the affair, would "burn this house to the ground," thus destroying both plant and home.

Moreover, Swift positions the unspoken present in relation to previously inflicted hurt. In "hoax," the narrator accuses her lover of hurting her, but she does not reveal what they have done. She sings, "You know it still hurts underneath my scars / from when they pulled me apart / but what you did was just as dark," thus referring to the self-fragmenting events that sparked her hiatus in the first place; in addition, she identifies the place to which her self-perception was so intrinsically tied—"You know I left a part of me back in New York"—in order to position the hurt as both still unspeakable and a return to previous injury. At the same time, she fragments her identity in the spatialized form of the time before and during her hiatus, with pre-hiatus "Welcome to New York" positively locating her in the city, post-hiatus "False God" fusing her disillusioned self with the city, and "hoax" treating her departure from city at the cost of her sense of self. Since Swift the narrator relates processes and sites of trauma that Swift the songwriter has very publicly experienced, it therefore seems germane to approach this period in her work through trauma. Reading through this lens, the disorientation and dislocation in her post-hiatus work becomes palpable; the absence of linearity and order becomes its very own sense-making process, inviting listeners to *perceive* Swift's expression of the traumatic without Swift having to *speak* it explicitly.

Ghostly Scenes: The Revenant in Swift's Machine

Haunting also dominates the latter part of Swift's work; constant returns to the past and themes dealt with in earlier writing return with violent force and newfound clarity. When Swift had previously played with the language of haunting, such as in her pre-hiatus song "Haunted," she had operated within the confines of linear time. It is only in the post-hiatus oeuvre that the polytemporal spectrality of trauma asserts itself, and in precisely the moments that Swift as narrator finds herself frozen in time, returning to the figurative crash sites to reexperience her wounds. While she had reflected on an at best unhealthy and at worst emotionally abusive relationship in "Dear John"—"Or maybe it's you and your sick need / to give love then take it away"—the extent of the damage done becomes apparent only more than a decade later in "Would've, Could've, Should've."[9] Swift clearly connects both songs through references to age; in "Dear John," she asks, "Don't you think nineteen's too young / to be played by your dark, twisted games / when I loved you so?," while declaring in "Would've, Could've, Should've" that "I damn sure never would've danced with the devil / at nineteen." She thus suggests that the closure previously offered in "Dear John"—"But I took your matches / Before fire could catch me," she had written—had provided a false sense of safety. In the later song, she reckons with the ramifications of an identity-shattering, fragmenting event—"God rest my soul, I miss who I used to be"—in a way that equates the past relationship with a physical wound that refuses to heal. After a decade of attempting to overcome the damage done, she returns to the girlhood she lost to the relationship, hinting that her former partner has fragmented and seized the agency that belonged to a past iteration of herself: "Give me back my girlhood, it was mine first."

Revenants in themselves, her re-recordings occupy a liminal space between Taylor past and Taylor present. Swift's highly publicized endeavor to regain control of her masters by rerecording previous records allows her to reinterpret while also forcing her to revisit her past, to allow herself to haunt her pre-hiatus discography. Her vault songs—that is, songs originally written earlier but initially released with the rerecorded albums—break the natural flow of time by forcing her oeuvre and her listeners into previous eras. Most prominently, the ten-minute version of "All Too Well," released almost a decade after the original song's release, expands on the previous version. While the original was a heartbreak anthem, Swift's 2021 revisitation turned the piece into a political statement. Once more, a relationship with a noticeable age gap is at the center of a song—"And I was never good at tellin' jokes, but the punch line goes / 'I'll get older, but your lovers stay my age'"—but 2021 Taylor calls out her former lover for dating her despite having perceived their age gap as a dealbreaker: "You said if we had been closer in age, maybe it would've been fine / and that made me want to die."

To read Swift's post-hiatus work as a narrative, autofictional *cri de coeur* is to glimpse the previously unspoken, to recognize latently emergent reproductions of traumatic events through her narrators. The aforementioned commentary about the problems with dating significantly older men is just one example. Relying on flashbacks and images of night terrors,[10] Swift reworks the language of trauma in her oeuvre, sometimes even explicitly. Written in response to the COVID-19 pandemic, "epiphany," a song about both war trauma and medical trauma, engages with the incomprehensibility of trauma; "[o]nly twenty minutes to sleep," Swift writes, "but you dream of some

---

[9] It is worth pointing out that "Dear John" was written about fellow singer-songwriter John Mayer, who was 32 years old when dating Swift, 19 years old at the time (cf. *Rolling Stone*).
[10] Consider lines such as "I can't let this go, I fight with you in my sleep" ("Would've, Could've, Should've"); "Misery like the war of words I shouted in my sleep" ("long story short"); and "Cursed you as I sleep-talked" ("The Great War").

epiphany / just one single glimpse of relief / to make some sense of what you've seen." Indeed, much of Swift's later work echoes Jean-Michel Ganteau's description of traumatic narration: "[T]he narrator gropes her way through fantasies and fragmented memories of her past, unearthing piece after painful, meaningful piece, the better to relapse into tormenting doubt the next instant." Having shared the "stained glass windows" in her mind, Swift's post-hiatus oeuvre remains a testament to the hauntings of her discography.

Coda: Haunted?

That evening in Tampa, in hindsight, was much more than a statement. It was, in many ways, a caesura in which Swift definitively banished the persona of the silent and superficial all-American girl next door. In the years following, Swift instead delivered a depth of critical reflection previously unprecedented in her work, blurring the lines between the private and the political. While Swift has always toed the line of privacy and yet performing the private in her public life, post-hiatus Swift instead engages with deep-cut topics and intimate glimpses into her artistic work with the traumatic— ironically while rolling back her public performances of the private, with her six-year-relationship yielding no more than a handful of paparazzi photos. Leaving behind her carefully cultivated image as a press darling, the public sees Swift shedding her apoliticality in favor of a positioning herself as a democrat, a feminist, and a witness to the harm caused to marginalized groups in the wake of the Trump election (cf. *Miss Americana*). All of this operates within the narrative trauma-based discourse within her work; Swift's position as a global superstar itself underlies her disrupted sense of safety and her struggles to express her politicality in the wake of safety concerns. (Swift has had to face a large number of stalkers over the years.) To examine the ways in which Swift approaches trauma (chiefly through her artistic output) is to see Swift explode time itself. The very circumstances of her post-hiatus trajectory provide both artist and listeners with opportunities to engage with traumas past and present, while also providing opportunities to examine those past traumas in retrospect, with the benefit of distance. Swift's "open tombs" hence remain not only the open crypt of experience but also a public testament to the fact that the past is, in fact, not written in stone. It is open to reinterpretation and recall, even if that reinterpretation comes in the form of a cathartic "*Fuck the Patriarchy* key chain on the ground"—skipping town entirely optional.

Works Cited

Berry, Diane S., and James W. Pennebaker. "Nonverbal and Verbal Emotional Expression and Health." *Psychotherapy and Psychosomatics*, vol. 59, no. 1. (1993), 11–19.
Caruth, Cathy. *Unclaimed Experience: Trauma, Narrative, and History*. Johns Hopkins University Press: Baltimore, 1996.

Fogarty, Mary, and Gina Arnold. "Are You Ready for It? Re-Evaluating Taylor Swift." *Contemporary Music Review*, vol. 40, no. 1. (January 2021): 1–10.

Garcia, David, and Bernard Rimé. "Collective Emotions and Social Resilience in the Digital Traces After a Terrorist Attack." *Psychological Science*, vol. 30, no. 4. (April 2019): 617–28.

Kaplan, Caren. "Resisting Autobiography: Out-Law Genres and Transnational Feminist Subjects." *Women, Autobiography, Theory: A Reader*, eds. Sidonie Smith and Julia Watson, 1st ed., The University of Wisconsin Press: Wisconsin, 1998, 208–16.

Kennedy-Moore, Eileen, and Jeanne C. Watson. "How and When Does Emotional Expression Help?" *Review of General Psychology*, vol. 5, (no. 3. (September 2001): 187–212.

Kurvet-Käosaar, Leena. "Trauma and Life-Writing." *The Routledge Companion to Literature and Trauma*, eds. Colin Davis and Hanna Meretoja. Routledge: London, 2020. 305–16.

Lothe, Jakob. "Narrative." *The Routledge Companion to Literature and Trauma*, eds. Colin Davis and Hanna Meretoja. Routledge: London, 2020. 152–61.

Luckhurst, Roger. *The Trauma Question*. Routledge, 2008.

McAdams, Dan P., and Kate C. McLean. "Narrative Identity." *Current Directions in Psychological Science*, vol. 22, no. 3. (2013): 233–38.

Meretoja, Hanna. *The Ethics of Storytelling: Narrative Hermeneutics, History, and the Possible*. Oxford University Press: Oxford, 2018.

Miss Americana. Dir. Lana Wilson, Netflix, 2020,

Neal, Jocelyn R. "Narrative Paradigms, Musical Signifiers, and Form as Function in Country Music." *Music Theory Spectrum*, vol. 29, no. 1. (April 2007): 41–72.

Rimé, Bernard, et al. "Social Sharing of Emotion, Post-Traumatic Growth, and Emotional Climate: Follow-up of Spanish Citizen's Response to the Collective Trauma of March 11th Terrorist Attacks in Madrid." *European Journal of Social Psychology*, vol. 40, no. 6. (2010): 1029–45. *Wiley Online Library*.

Rolling Stone. "John Mayer: Taylor Swift's 'Dear John' Song 'Humiliated Me.'" *rollingstone.com*, 2012.

Sloan, Nate. "Taylor Swift and the Work of Songwriting." *Contemporary Music Review*, vol. 40, no. 1. (January 2021): 11–26.

Snapes, Laura. "Taylor Swift: 'I Was Literally about to Break.'" *The Guardian*, 24 Aug. 2019.

Steiner, Carolin Isabel. "A Wound Has No Voice: Silence, Emotions, and Community Resilience in the Wake of Collective SARS-Cov-2 Trauma." *NextGen Scientific Review*, vol. 1, 2023.

Stolorow, Robert D. "Trauma and Temporality." *Psychoanalytic Psychology*, vol. 20, no. 1. (2003): 158–61.

Weaver, Hillary. "Taylor Swift Has Finally Been Sent the Symbolic Dollar She Won in Court." *Vanity Fair*, 2017.

Part Four

This Ain't a Fairy Tale: Considering Craft, Genre, and Mediation

16

Show, Don't Tell? How Taylor Swift Complicates a Writing Cliché

Samantha Bañal

While working as a writing consultant at the University of Miami, I kept fielding the same concern: "My professor wants me to 'show, don't tell.' What do they mean?" Then, another student would arrive with explicit instructions to use only active verbs in a short personal introduction and, once again, to show, not tell. Similarly, as a high school Dual Enrollment teacher, I frequently advise my students after they find a YouTube video or TikTok that extols the "show, don't tell" approach for their college application essays. Students, understandably, get frustrated with this cliché that has become shorthand for complex skills in rhetoric and composition. Rather than delve into why active verbs work better than passive ones or the deleterious effect that only "telling" your argument can have on a paper's authority, professors outside the traditional writing programs and other well-meaning advisors often revert to this phrase and expect young writers to produce a "show, don't tell" essay. As student after student expressed their vexation to me as their teacher or tutor, I began to ask a question in return: "Do you listen to Taylor Swift?"

Before getting into Swift and what she could add to this conversation, I should first address where the "show, don't tell" adage comes from and why it continues to hold value well over a century after its emergence. Sources disagree on who first uttered this phrase, but most place its origin within the playwriting form, where it grew more from necessity than choice. A modern playwright cannot tell the audience what is going on because that would require deconstructing the fourth (and invisible) wall that descends from the proscenium arch. Twentieth-century approaches to drama effectively silenced a play's "tells"—those extended soliloquies that populate many of Shakespeare's plays, for instance. Many credit playwright and short story pioneer Anton Chekhov with this advance, citing a letter to his brother in which he urged the importance of evocation through specific details instead of a generalized declaration (Yarmolinsky 14). This approach to prose descriptions impacted short fiction well into the first half of the twentieth century, as it crossed the Atlantic and informed, for example, Ernest Hemingway's approach to writing. The "show, don't tell" idea slowly became dogma and now permeates academic spaces as diverse as creative writing programs, journalism schools, and legal writing seminars. Now, it is often the only piece of "writing advice" most professors offer because of its simplicity and reliability in encouraging audience participation. Taylor Swift agrees in an essay for *Elle* magazine: "The writing I love the most places you into that story, that room, that rain soaked kiss. You can smell the air, hear the sounds, and feel your heart race as the character does."

To recreate this style that Swift unwittingly describes, a quick Google search yields countless blog posts and videos that detail the essential features of the "show, don't tell" approach. In 1996, journalists James Tankard and Laura Hendrickson decided to clarify the "show, don't tell" rule, outline its main features, and test their effectiveness for writers and readers. Their "show, don't tell" commandments include specificity, concrete language, appealing to the senses, dialogue, figures of speech, active or narrative terms, and strong verbs (Tankard 37–9). Yet students are rarely offered this checklist and must intuit what "show, don't tell" means. While a university-level writer might understand concepts like vivid verbs and active voice, the other guidelines often fall by the wayside. Furthermore, in their overview of "show, don't tell" methods, Tankard and Hendrickson also include critiques like Carol-Lynn Marazzo's, which "remind us that abandoning *telling* for the sake of exclusively *showing* can cause a reader to feel 'distanced'" (37). This often produces essays that pack a narrative punch but offer little in the way of argumentation and especially voice, that ineffable quality that evades writers who jump to "showing" without first wading in the waters of "telling" who they are, where they come from, and how their specific perspective emerged. This distance pervades the "show, don't tell" approach and can create treacherous gaps between writer and reader, as an overreliance on "show" writing often trusts readers to assume more than they understand.

To clarify these approaches further, "show" writing relies upon narrative more than argumentation, according to popular understandings, while "tell" writing directly addresses the reader and clearly delineates a stance. Most traditional composition classes prioritize the latter over the former, as the continued emphasis on argumentative writing and thesis statements reveals. Students at either advanced high school levels or their first year at university still labor under old models like the three-point paragraph, third-person perspective, a five-paragraph structure, and other self-effacements. Transforming them into writers for diverse spaces necessitates an introduction to basic principles in purpose, audience, and genre. What are you writing for, whom are you writing to, and what writing category does your work fall under? Young writers accustomed to only directing their work toward a teacher and for a grade must learn to broaden their scope. Most challenging, this pedagogical turn pushes students to create their own goals and voices as writers while adapting to the multitudinous writing genres they utilize in a hypertextual media landscape. Whether they are "creating content" or submitting a research proposal, writers must do so in spaces that did not exist less than a decade ago, forcing them to inhabit unfamiliar voices and utilize new forms on a constantly shifting basis.

The "show, don't tell" rule arguably retains its validity within these specific contexts and across audiences. Still, overall, a far more productive conversation would instead focus on interdisciplinary examples that have blurred the lines between these two seemingly opposed methods. For instance, American songwriters, especially in the blues and folk traditions, have consistently displayed the power of mixing show and tell. Taylor Swift's oeuvre is the latest, potent example to clarify this double-edged maxim of writing instruction. In a classroom, discussions of Swift's work punctuated with direct applications to writing craft allow young students to connect abstract, rhetorical concepts to a familiar, approachable writer. Through a brief overview of Swift's work, students can understand the necessity of sharing personal truths, the importance of streamlined "showing," the pitfalls of inauthentic "telling," and the powerful possibilities when the two mix. Thus, an analysis of Swift's work from a writing perspective offers a new path around this tired cliché and provides a means to teach students how and when to show or tell.

Like many successful popular artists, Taylor Swift spent the beginning of her career searching for purpose and audience within an established genre. Since then, she has continued to shapeshift to dizzying effect, as her Eras Tour celebrates. Her greatest weapon throughout has been her ability to expand her audience through sharing stories or telling truths. To create a distinct voice within a genre, a writer must take a set of rules and slightly bend them to their purpose and targeted audience. When Swift emerged as a powerful country voice, she was an outsider who personally experienced few of those country music stereotypes: working-class concerns, rural life, and middle-American masculinity. Swift's version of country music combatted this seeming lack by focusing on the larger narrative rather than the details. Grown from the rich tradition of American folk and blues, country music is still an intrinsically "show" genre and has since remained faithful to the story form. These stories often stoke nostalgia or inspire escapism. To realize this genre's purpose, songwriters utilize what Nate Sloan calls the Time-Shift paradigm, where "the lyrical material of the chorus shifts over each appearance, creating a large-scale narrative structure of transformation and deliverance" (15). Instead of being told what caused a relationship's decline, the listener experiences these memories along with the singer and shares their loss. Swift managed to identify these genre touchstones and wrapped her songwriting approach in their mantle. This Time-Shift paradigm comes to her disposal at the highest points of her career and embeds into her songs' structure an integral tenet of the "show, don't tell" approach: conveying meaning through inference and connection rather than through a stultifying account of events.

Once she mastered this overarching structure, Swift opened it wide to welcome a broader fan base, particularly young women, by utilizing detailed appeals to the senses. Contrary to what most students believe, a story does not automatically lead to "show" writing; that story must be conveyed through subtle, often implied ideas. Classic country imagery like rusty hinges, slamming doors, and the smell of clover in spring permeates Swift's work, but already in the early transition to *Fearless*, we see her creating narratives that fully embrace *her* chosen audience rather than that of the country music genre en masse. For example, she refuses the simple, trite complaint that her rival for a man's affection is just another "cool girl." Instead, Swift achieves the same results through details: "She wears short skirts, I wear t-shirts / She's cheer captain, and I'm on the bleachers" ("You Belong With Me"). Without directly telling us, we understand the dichotomy between Swift's speaker and her romantic rival: the quirky girl versus the cool girl. Then, in another massive hit off *Fearless*, she describes "a balcony in summer air" and beckons her listeners to see "the lights … the party … the ball gowns," evoking the scene rather than closely delineating it ("Love Story"). The distinction between the shows and tells here seems small, which paradoxically grants them their power. The shows are so *showy* that they almost seem like tells, but they always shrink from crossing that threshold and lend Swift's speakers a subjective ambiguity that she's now become famous for both on and off her records. Swift continues this prioritization of metaphor and imagery over direct expression in "Red," the titular song off her crossover album.

"Red" demonstrates her expertise in the subtle Time-Shift, country paradigm while also previewing the passionate declarations that would distinguish her writing within pop music. In "Red," the speaker transitions between different aspects of a relationship, including the details of "loving him" to the pain of "losing him" and finally "remembering him." However, rather than directly tell this pain to her listeners, she instead illustrates the pain through colorful imagery conveyed in about every other line. These comparisons run the gamut from the conventional "losing him was blue like I'd never known" to the metaphorical "loving him was red" but then transition to more specific, Swiftian comparisons. For instance, she frames the song with "Loving him is like driving a new Maserati down a dead-end street," which is both evocative and surprising, moving past cliché and into territory that belongs only to Swift. Despite this "show, don't tell" tour de force, the song includes a bridge where she also explains:

> Remembering him comes in flashbacks and echoes.
> Tell myself it's time now, gotta let go,
> But moving on from him is impossible
> When I still see it all in my head
> In burning red.

Discarding metaphor and simile, the speaker now explains her thought process with the distance of time and the structural remove that her bridge offers. She gives herself a pep talk while also confessing to her listeners that she is struggling to move on, which clarifies the song's message without undoing the elusive "showy" qualities of the song's main verses. Additionally, this bridge marries a key feature of the Time-Shift paradigm with a powerful self-declaration. "Red" is a fantastic place to start for students who understand the pros and cons of show and tell on paper but have trouble executing these ideas in their writing. In one song, they see a writer move back and forth between these two modes, which perform in microcosm the show *and* tell songwriting technique that also undergirds the album *Red*'s crossover power.

In her *Pitchfork* review of its recent reissue, Olivia Horn calls *Red* "the clear nexus between where Swift's career started and where it was heading" and says that the album "revealed the extent of her pop ambition." *Red* also revealed Swift's willingness to put aside the "showy," overtly narrative style of her country albums and successfully transition to pop. Nate Sloan deftly traces Swift's evolution during this period and connects her resignation from country with her movement away from its extended narrative structure. Thus, rather than "show" through dialogue or sensory language, pop music (especially the pop chorus) focuses on sending a clear message. "The pop form does not work for a narrative journey," Sloan explains, "but for three minutes of sustained emotional tension" (16). The most significant examples of these extended moments of emotional tension also often align with self-affirmations, especially from women artists throughout the decades. These declarations hold powerful teaching potential because, while Gen Z students seem savvier than ever with regard to self-declaration, they still hesitate before beginning personal essays, an intimate yet increasingly ubiquitous form that centers first-person "telling."

Red is a "tell" album that begins with "State of Grace," "Red," "Treacherous," and "I Knew You Were Trouble," all of which—except for "Red"—create a veritable barrage of direct addresses. Her country songs roped listeners into the narrative through a shared sense of nostalgia, but her pop songs utilize clear and direct tells to make listeners feel what she feels or wants her subject to feel in that extended ever-present moment. To achieve this goal, pop songwriting essentials like hooks and bridges take center stage on *Red* and offer Swift spaces to reveal the power in "telling," despite the dogma claiming that a "tell" can only weaken a writer's aims. A good hook or bridge is as essential to the pop song as a good thesis or argumentative transition in a student's paper, so this pop maneuver serves as a direct, teachable moment for students still unsure how to "tell" without losing argumentative nuance. *Red*'s opening songs offer a great lesson here. In its first verses and pre-chorus, "State of Grace" appears to follow the country playbook, "showing" through description and metaphor, but then the chorus is riddled with "This is … ," "Love is … ," and "These are … " anaphora. The first chorus arrives relatively late for a pop song but is repeated right before the song ends, acting almost as a conclusion. She performs the same maneuver throughout "Treacherous" with its "is treacherous … reckless … dangerous" epistrophes in each chorus. Swift understands the risks in relying solely on "showing" and assuming an audience is getting the message, so she swaps in simple and repetitive declarations to keep their perception in check.

Returning to a student's concerns in this regard, argumentative writing often requires emphasis and clarification through simple statements aimed directly at the reader. In her theoretical analysis of the "show, don't tell" rule, Jan Zwicky observes, "Poets occasionally tell for summary emphasis … but even then, we often feel that we are being shown something beyond what is told—as though what appears to be an instance of telling is nonetheless some kind of showing" (897). This summative telling occurs throughout *Red*, where Swift pins down her metaphorical meaning and offers clear takeaways for listeners. Thus, Swift executes these overt "tell" maneuvers but bends them to build her personal narrative, especially during such a transitional moment in her career. While many pop artists rely on aesthetic presentations—music videos, social media, clothing design, and performance—to build their pop personae, Swift instead folds these narratives into her songs. She reveals how "telling" a personal truth enough times can create a persona; whether that persona aligns with Swift herself is another question and arguably *the* core question for the most significant modern pop artists from Madonna to Beyoncé.

Transferring these lessons to a classroom, however, often proves difficult or shocking because these pop figures seem extraterrestrial to most students. Indeed, what could a first-year college student learn and execute from the works of creators so disconnected from "real life"? Yet, whether it is Taylor Swift or the favorite artist of their choice, students should realize that audiences only believe what they are repeatedly told and what is proven through evidence, both of which often arrive as "tells." How to take ownership of their voice and how to develop their writing persona are among the most beneficial lessons a writing teacher can offer a student. To bring this lesson home, consider the biggest hit off *Red*: "We Are Never Getting Back Together." The title itself is a tell, a declarative statement. Before the listener even presses play, they know Swift's stance. That is not enough for Swift, though. As a preamble to the anthemic chorus, she exclaims, "I'm telling you, I'm telling you," and then the chorus asserts, "We are never, ever, ever getting back together." While we hope young writers declare who they are and find their voice, they often capitulate and use generalized fillers or adopt a trend to gain easy access to a high grade, an internet following, or a career. Swift's personal declarations can thus act as craft models and inspiration. As Swift moved away from country music and into the maelstrom of pop music with its various angels and demons, her stance as a woman who "tells her truth" became both her greatest asset and her Achilles heel. Likewise, students often struggle to discern when to utilize a "tell," as Swift does throughout *Red*, and when to pull back on these direct statements.

These telling declarations highlight the correlative importance for student writers of thesis statements, conclusion sentences, and forecasting statements. Nevertheless, these writing tools can be overused, transforming a poignant rhetorical device into an unwieldy sledgehammer. While Jan Zwicky concedes the importance of telling for summative or argumentative effect, she also warns, "Telling of the problematic kind involves an airless explicitness; it does not just connect the dots, it obliterates them with a felt marker" (898). When Swift exclaims her subject position or calls out an ex-lover on *Red*, she does so with passion and zero apologies, but she ensures that her audiences understand the reason behind the "tell." These declarative hooks and refrains complete her overarching narrative rather than replace her commitment to description, imagery, and metaphor. She continues this careful balancing act on her post-crossover hit *1989*, but in the wake of that massive success, *reputation* and *Lover* featured certain stylistic faults that led to a comparatively lukewarm critical reception. There are many reasons for this shift, both personal and professional, that have arguably lessened in the passing years, as both albums have gained a special devotion amongst younger fans especially. Students can observe her compositional mistakes in these albums and emerge better writers, as Swift herself does in *folklore* and *evermore*. Meanwhile, they can also learn the importance of resilience and how the writing process is not always linear.

The weaknesses in *reputation* and *Lover* can be traced mainly to inauthenticity or a pop musician's momentary narcissism. Every star has an album or two about fame's downsides. These albums can work if the artist owns that their personal experiences are inherently foreign to most listeners (as Lady Gaga does on *The Fame* and *Fame Monster*, for instance). Swift does not quite pull this off with *reputation*. Without delving into the do's and don'ts of pop stardom, *reputation* suffers from "telling" either too loudly or too often while also wrapping these callouts in musical styles that reflect the bevy of producers Swift invited into the studio, rather than her personal, cultivated style. *Lover* fared better amongst critics who noted its tonal and thematic shifts away from *reputation*. Unlike *reputation*'s musical styles that are often wildly outside Swift's wheelhouse, *Lover* marks a return to *Red*'s aesthetic and contains numerous songs that pay homage to her fans and express her acceptance of good, contented love, which reflects her career-long commitment to raw intimacy. Unfortunately, *Lover* also highlights those aspects of her life and persona that still refuse definition, particularly her politics. Acknowledging these career-long critiques that only grow more pronounced as her fame does, Swift responded with what Spencer Kornhaber called "the Pride posturing of *Lover*," most likely referencing "You Need to Calm Down" and its accompanying rainbow-themed music video. Together, Swift's often self-serving feminism and cloying neoliberalism distract from *Lover*'s strengths and instead emphasize the ways she has benefited from the industry's prioritization of some stories and voices over others.

Though she would have us think otherwise, as a rich, straight, white woman with an unparalleled social platform, Swift's voice instantly commands greater credibility than those of countless artists who want or need to tell their stories. We cannot deny that her shows and tells are deftly crafted. However, we also cannot deny that women of color—who have arguably cultivated similar oeuvres that portray their relationships with various people or declare their personal views—are often relegated to the fringes of pop culture. Only Rihanna and Beyoncé have matched Taylor Swift in successfully revealing their private lives while maintaining their top status in the music industry. Meanwhile, Swift has opened the door for a new generation of white female artists to share their stories without facing the media repercussions that still shut out most artists of color working outside conventional forms. Thus, we reveal further critiques of the "show, don't tell" method, particularly how it prioritizes white, patriarchal, and heteronormative voices over the marginalized who indeed *must* tell their truth, *must* get political because their lives are constantly under scrutiny and attack. A writing approach focused on dismantling the "show, don't tell" dogma through a close look at Swift's work must also engage with how BIPOC musicians from Tina Turner to Janelle Monae have always beggared claims that it is better to show than to tell.

Taylor Swift has tried to obfuscate the privileges inherent to her subject position, but they never quite succeed because "telling" is doomed when paired with inauthenticity. No matter how good the "tells" on *Lover*—and there are great ones like "Lover" itself with its profuse confessions and promises—they often feel vapid because they rely on a tone-deaf white feminism or exploit queer neoliberal politics. In his overview of her work's feminism, Myles McNutt argues, "Swift's celebrity has been defined by these types of half-measures, wherein acts that reinforce her feminism ultimately fail to manifest as a reorientation of her larger celebrity brand toward explicitly feminist causes" (87). The half-measures McNutt has in mind include her Album of the Year acceptance speech for *1989* and her albums' bonus materials that usually highlight her creative authority but also reveal a dependence upon men in the production room or during the writing process. The lesson here for students would focus again on relying upon their own voice and authority, not someone else's. Even a great writer like Swift gets hamstrung by her inability (or her refusal) to consider her subject position and accept its limitations. What matters is that she returns to the careful balance of personal show and tell that made her a songwriting prodigy and continues contributing to her most recent, critically acclaimed work. She moved away from telling someone else's stories and either returned to her own or created entirely new fictions.

folklore and *evermore* emerged during the height of the pandemic and while many still languished under strict quarantine rules, grief, or general overwhelm in 2020. In Amanda Petrusich's review of *folklore* for *The New Yorker*, she identifies Swift's storytelling as "a kind of sense-making process, a real and useful chance to order the world." While critics noticed this understanding of her audience's needs, others connected these albums to the surprisingly impersonal narrative Swift created. "Swift said in announcing the album," Chris Willman writes of the *evermore* debut, "that she was moving further into fiction songwriting." Both albums were written in but not necessarily out of the collective pandemic crisis, but their shared commitment to fictional storytelling binds them inextricably together in listeners' minds. As a result, they highlight the value of showing over telling, but, in more nuanced ways, they exemplify the importance of an authentic tell even when shrouded in careful fiction. Rather than continue excavating the well-trodden dig of personal perspective, Taylor Swift and her cowriters turned to the narrative form almost exclusively and created fully realized characters and detailed plot lines. In his overview of the popular song at the beginning of the new millennium, Keith Negus argues that the pop song structure often includes characters, whether closely matched with the speaker or entirely fictional beings, that fall into types like the happy housewife, the outlaw, or the fallen woman (618). These common stereotypes reemerge in Swift's *folklore*, but with a distinct twist: they are often younger, trapped in evocative settings, and their stories continue across the album rather than exist in one song.

Taylor Swift no doubt possessed a clear goal for each of her previous albums as she wove her track listings together, but she places that cohesive style front and center on *folklore* and *evermore*. Swift's co-writer Aaron Dessner perhaps explains this shift best: "She had a vision, and it was connecting back in some way to the folk tradition, but obviously not entirely sonically. It's more about the narrative aspect of it" (Gerber). To cultivate these narratives, Swift no longer devotes merely a verse or two to show or tell, but instead she assigns an entire song to one, the other, or a mixture. At times, there is a clear, narrative "showing" in songs like "exile," with its introspective dialogue between two characters, or the imagery in "cowboy like me," which hearkens back to her country albums. Yet, she then follows these moments with a personal "tell" like "marjorie" or "the last great american dynasty," tributes to her grandmother and her home's former owner, respectively. This shift in scale and scope can help young writers begin to put their body of work into perspective. Students embarking on their academic and professional lives often see their work discretely—separate papers for separate classes for separate grades—but to create voice, authority, and style, students can do no better than to consider their work as a connected narrative. Whether to develop a personal brand or to cultivate a specific perspective, young writers should curate their portfolio and reinforce the bridges that hold it together, whether those bridges are imagined or built upon personal truths.

Taylor Swift, the subject of relentless scrutiny for her work's personal connections, no doubt desired and deserved a moment to play within fiction. Our students often have the opposite problem. Young writers usually freeze when confronted with a moment to share their story or provide their (well researched and analyzed, but still subjective) perspective on an important subject. Sheldon George's brilliant, practical article on the personal essay, "The Performed Self in College Writing," helps shed some light on this issue. He pinpoints how students shrink from the personal because they fear the quagmire of appearing deceitful when sharing stories rather than just giving information. George argues, "By suggesting to them the ways that the narratives we each tell of our past are perspectival, rather than factual, I encourage students to manipulate more actively the discursive narratives of their past" (325). Swift has taken this advice throughout her career, arguably weaving her personal life into a narrative on album after album, as we have been reminded with the extended reissue of "All Too Well" and the release of *Midnights*, a scrapbook of past loves and songwriting inspirations. This further validates the idea that a writing course that emphasizes personal narrative naturally leads writers to a more authentic, evocative style than they might have achieved had they tried to share their perspectives with the barest facts and most meager tells.

Yet, students should also remember that the mixture of show and tell will get them the furthest mileage. While critics admitted Swift's devotion to the narrative form with *folklore* and *evermore*, Chris Willman also observes, "Swift never settles into fiction-writer mode for too long a stretch before coming back to something plainly diaristic." What makes these albums work is not their seeming devotion to show over tell or vice versa; they are her most successful creations because she never stays in one place for too long. The Time-Shift paradigm returns, for instance, in songs like "tolerate it" and "the last great american dynasty." She utilizes a "show" linchpin like dialogue on "betty," while evocative details litter both albums but perhaps find their fullest, most nostalgic form in a pop masterpiece like "august." On the other hand, she creates clear "tells" throughout both albums, but especially on songs like "illicit affairs," "this is me trying," and "willow," each with their yearning declarations. All her engines are firing on these two albums as she bares her career-cultivated skills for a hungry audience. She flickers between perspectives and styles from show to tell while also developing new methods to "tell" her truth that do not fall into an oppositional "show" category.

Finally, Swift further enhances the tension between fact and fiction, public and personal, by refusing clear conclusions and nonchalantly accepting the inevitable autobiographical connections. In their overview of the "show, don't tell" method, James Tankard and Laura Hendrickson argue, ". . . writing that involves *telling* typically involves presenting conclusions, while writing that involves *showing* presents observed details and allows readers to draw their own conclusions" (40). Their shared commitment to ambiguity grants *folklore* and *evermore* their evocative power. Spencer Kornhaber's rave review of *folklore* for *The Atlantic* emphasizes this great strength. He first takes "epiphany" and admits that "a song like this doesn't seem like it should work" because of Swift's privilege, the clichéd war metaphor, and its long-distance connection between her grandfather's fighting in the Second World War and herself living through the pandemic. Nevertheless, the song works because she does not pin the meaning down or try to tell it to her listeners. "Swift doesn't describe the epiphany," Kornhaber explains; "we have to dream it for ourselves." Here, I argue Swift goes further than showing or telling; she does neither and instead performs the narrative equivalent of fading to black.

Swift threads this ambiguity through both albums and especially on *evermore*. In her *Rolling Stone* review, Claire Shaffer remarks, "If Swift seems hesitant to give her characters happy endings, or endings in general, it may be because she's still figuring out her own chapter right on the page." This refusal of finality may be the most powerful lesson she can offer writers. Swift was not and is not afraid to put something on the page, record it, and release it even when what she expresses may not be "complete" or "figured out" or "polished." It is no coincidence that these two albums were released as Swift continued re-releasing her back catlogue. Right now, Swift's authority is a work in progress, characterized by returns, open endings, and an acceptance that she does not have all the answers or cannot be everything to everyone. In our current social landscape, where students feel an enormous pressure to say the right words, share the most perfect takes, and hold their breath while their audience reacts, Swift's current commitment to ambiguity, fiction, and revision offers a different route towards cultivating a body of work and, ultimately, an authentic voice.

Placing Taylor Swift within the American songwriting tradition from country to pop and singling her out as a pro in "show" and "tell" naturally begs the question: Why Taylor? Throughout this essay, I have emphasized the details of Swift's skill while also understanding her broader aims, especially in these last few years as she revises her discography through the Taylor's Version projects and reviews her life in music through the Eras Tour and a memoir-style album like *Midnights*. When I first approached Swift's songs as a model for the "show, don't tell" method, I saw her as a poster girl for the "show" idea, leaning on narrative for poetic power over anthemic "tells" like many of her pop peers. Indeed, she seemed to embody the strength that Tankard and Hendrickson identified in "show" writing: "*show* language should make writing more credible or believable. *Show* language could be expected to be more believable because *telling* often presents the writer's conclusions without supporting detail" (41). This explains why Swift shows so much in her autobiographical anthems, those same songs that Swift claims create the most connection between herself and her audience. One need only look at the uproar around "All Too Well"'s re-release and short film to see her power at work.

Released while the fervor over *folklore* and *evermore* still simmered, "All Too Well" proves that Swift has always been doing the hard, thoughtful craft work that reaches its fullest potential on her latest albums. Regarding "All Too Well" and Swift's overarching impact back in 2013, Judy Rosen argued, "You could call Swift a generational bard: She merges the pleasure of old-fashioned song craft with millennial social-media oversharing." Over a decade later, she need not rely solely on personal narrative, but she will not shrink from it if personal narrative possesses irresistible pop potential, as it has with her singles off *Midnights*. Once again, perhaps Swift's greatest songwriting gift— and the one most applicable to our current plugged-in students—is her ability to discern the best course for the moment, audience, and form. And yet, more than these craft-centered considerations, my students draw me to Taylor Swift's work and its classroom potential. I have taught literature and writing courses at the university and high school levels for over a dozen years. During that time, I have noticed various pop artists fall in and out of favor when I encourage my students to connect our classroom discussion or practices to contemporary creators. In the past five years, however, Swift has emerged as the clear frontrunner in my students' minds when I ask them to find evidence of our in-class work in another writer's output. Young students almost intuitively understand that she consistently displays writing savvy, and they enjoy hunting for evidence that substantiates their intuition.

I have used Taylor Swift to teach everything from pastoral poetry to practical writing skills. Much of this power comes from her commitment to "show" language because such language naturally begs for close reading. Jan Zwicky also notes this connection: "The literary writer's ability to show is, thus, developed in response to a more widespread capacity, one that humans share with many other species: the ability to read" (899). We want to read into these stories; we gravitate to their narrative qualities, to their details, and even to a deft use of "tells" to ensure we get the message. Finally, as Zwicky continues, "When we 'get it', we see how things fit, there is a release of psychic tension. This is one definition of pleasure" (899). I see the sense of accomplishment, the epiphanies, and the pleasure when my students work out a Taylor Swift song or realize its potential for imparting knowledge. When addressing her commitment to her personal "tells," Swift argues, "The glimpse into the artist's story invites us to connect it to our own, and in the best-case scenario, allows us the ability to assign that song to our memories." Not to end on a disagreement with Taylor, but there is another best-case scenario that I have witnessed play out in my classrooms: students, through Swift's work, can realize the power of sharing their truth, telling their stories, and displaying their skills in various forms and genres. While Swift has much at her disposal to amplify her voice and ensure it is heard above her detractors, her core skills in show and tell remain her most vital and teachable attributes.

Works Cited

George, Sheldon. "The Performed Self in College Writing: From Personal Narratives to Analytic and Research Essays." *Pedagogy*, vol. 12, no. 2. (2012): 319–41.
Gerber, Brady. "The Story Behind Every Song on Taylor Swift's *folklore*." *Vulture*, 27 July 2020.
Horn, Olivia. "Red (Taylor's Version) Album Review." *Pitchfork*, 15 Nov. 2021.
Kornhaber, Spencer. "Taylor Swift is No Longer Living in the Present." *The Atlantic*, 28 July 2020.

McNutt, Myles. "From "Mine" to "Ours": Gendered Hierarchies of Authorship and the Limits of Taylor Swift's Paratextual Feminism." *Communication, Culture and Critique*, vol. 13, no. 1. (2020): 72–91.

Negus, Keith. "Authorship and the Popular Song." *Music & Letters*, vol. 92, no. 4. (2011): 607–29.

Petrusich, Amanda. "Taylor Swift's Intimate 'Indie' Album, 'Folklore.'" *The New Yorker*, 24 July 2020.

Rosen, Jody. "Platinum Underdog: Why Taylor Swift is the Biggest Pop Star in the World." *Vulture*, 17 Nov. 2013.

Shaffer, Claire. "Taylor Swift Deepens Her Goth-Folk Vision on the Excellent 'Evermore.'" *Rolling Stone*, 11 Dec. 2020.

Sloan, Nate. "Taylor Swift and the Work of Songwriting." *Contemporary music review*, vol. 40, no. 1. (2021): 11–26.

Swift, Taylor. "For Taylor Swift, Pop is Personal." *Elle*, 28 Feb. 2019.

Tankard, James, and Laura Hendrickson. "Specificity, Imagery in Writing: Testing the Effects of 'Show, Don't Tell.'" *Newspaper Research Journal*, vol. 17, no. 1. (1996): 35–48.

Willman, Chris. "Taylor Swift Has Her Second Great Album of 2020 With 'Evermore': Album Review." *Variety*, 10 Dec. 2020, https://variety.com/2020/music/reviews/taylor-swift-evermore-album-review-1234851525/

Yarmolinsky, Avrahm. *The Unknown Chekhov: Stories and Other Writings Hitherto Untranslated by Anton Chekhov*. Noonday Press: New York, 1954.

Zwicky, Jan. "Show, Don't Tell." *Theoria*, vol. 87, no. 4. (2021) 897–912.

17

"I never knew I could feel that much": Taylor Swift's Recuperative Aesthetics of Excess

Anastasia Klimchynskaya

Taylor Swift has frequently been accused of emotional excess. This is, in itself, unsurprising, for her oeuvre has unflinchingly explored the depth and complexity of the vast spectrum of human emotional states, from love and heartbreak to rage and despair, and female emotion has historically been considered excessive simply by its very existence. Swift herself has extensively commented on such gendered double standards, pointing out, in particular, that there is a "different vocabulary for men and women in the music industry ... A man is allowed to 'react'; a woman can only 'over-react'" ("Taylor Swift on 'Lover' and haters"). Never one to let others have the last word, however, Swift has, over her successful but tumultuous career, shown herself to be master of appropriating, subverting, and re-signifying existing assumptions and narratives, particularly ones imbricated within larger power dynamics. With this in mind, I argue that insofar as Taylor Swift has a particular aesthetic quality that defines her oeuvre, it is excess, by which I mean a too much-ness, a conscious going beyond the boundaries of what is collectively and culturally understood and accepted as normal, reasonable, or appropriate when it comes to feeling, behavior, or self-expression. Considering Swift's career in three phases—her early country period, her pop music phase and concomitant global superstardom, and the pandemic era—I suggest that throughout all three, Swift has embraced and deployed different forms of an aesthetic of excess. Moving, respectively, from the unaffected excesses of the romance genre, with its idealism and emotionality, in her country albums, to the exaggerations of parody and satire in her pop music, to, finally, a confident linguistic capaciousness that transcends genre boundaries with the indie/alternative sound of *folklore, evermore,* and *Midnights,* I suggest that Swift has utilized excess in order to both validate the notion of unbounded female emotion and interrogate the gendered assumptions that make this recuperative act necessary in the first place.

In the Beginning: Swift's Country Period

Since the beginning of her career, Taylor Swift has been not only a singer but a songwriter, and one of the defining features of her craft is that she writes her own songs, based largely on personal experiences but also drawing from those of friends and family. It is no coincidence, therefore, that she made her debut in country music, a genre known particularly for its storytelling and therefore, as Nathan Hubbard has pointed out, a natural home for a young girl with an acoustic guitar interested in singing her own songs (Hubbard and Princiotti). And yet, country music was and remains a genre known for its male and conservative leanings, and despite the success of artists such as Shania Twain, Faith Hill, Carrie Underwood, Dolly Parton, and the Dixie Chicks, Swift was one of "only a handful of new female voices to break out at country radio in a decade that was almost completely dominated by males" (Malec). Perhaps unsurprisingly, then, Swift's early albums, *Taylor Swift* and *Fearless*, provoked a confused response from critics, for Swift explored the tried-and-true themes such as falling in love, heartbreak, and betrayal—all commonplaces in country music—not only from a female but from a *teenage* female perspective. Writing about the highs and lows of her own life, Swift aptly "capture[d] the experience of being a teenage girl" (Hubbard and Princiotti).

But if female emotion is considered excessive in itself, this is doubly true of teenage female emotion. And yet it is precisely what these albums embrace, and make a statement in themselves by doing so. Through an apt symbiosis between lyrics and music, form and content, they unapologetically give expression to the world-consuming way in which one experiences emotions in their teens *and* implicate the listener in this experience. "The Way I Loved You," for example, begins by describing a seemingly perfect relationship ("he is sensible and so incredible"), but the music crescendos only as the song reaches its chorus, which reminisces about a previous, imperfect, tempestuous, but significantly more meaningful relationship: "screaming and fighting and kissing in the rain / and it's 2AM and I'm cursing your name." The emotional excesses and passion of the bygone relationship, its "screaming and fighting," are not only described lyrically but signaled musically, inviting the listener, too, to sing and scream out loud and therefore share in that heightened emotion. "Love Story," Swift's retelling of *Romeo and Juliet*, is similarly infectious: in telling this tale of star-crossed lovers, Swift allows much of the music to fall away during the bridge between verses to describe a moment of despair as the heroine thinks her Romeo has abandoned her; "I got tired of waiting," she laments. But as she reaches the chorus, where her story breaks with Shakespeare's to give the lovers a happy ending in which Romeo "pulled out a ring and said 'Marry me, Juliet,'" Swift increases the dynamics of the song and changes the key to signal the twist to the well-known tale. Again lyrics and music function in tandem, the sonic contrast between the calmer bridge and the rapturous chorus making the ecstasy of the unforeseen happy ending palpable and implicating the listener in this visceral emotion. In other words, the song is not only effective but *affective*, allowing no escape from the depth of feeling and making a cool, distanced, and "objective" stance quasi-impossible. And with *Fearless*'s groundbreaking success (including a Grammy for Best Album in 2009), Swift's ability to give voice to "a generation that hadn't had a voice in early 2000s music" (Hubbard and Princiotti)—young women—reshaped the landscape of popular music.

Fearless was followed by *Speak Now*, Swift's entirely self-written third album and one in which the first hallmarks of a *recuperative* aesthetic of excess emerge, as Swift foregrounds the expression of "excessive" female emotion as a political act. In the world of popular music, a musician's album is often referred to as an "era," defined visually, sonically, and lyrically by a particular set of genres, themes, and aesthetics, and *Speak Now* is one of Swift's most cohesive and distinct eras; through lyrics, music videos, promotional materials, and tour set pieces, it constructs an elaborate and visually distinct world characterized by the imagery and conventions of fairytale, fantasy, and romance. Her lyrics repeatedly emphasize the storybook nature of the album: "the story of us looks a lot like a tragedy now" ("The Story of Us"); praying that "this was the very first page / not where the storyline ends" ("Enchanted"); "you held your head like a hero / on a history book page" ("Long Live"). Many of the songs on the album evoke fantasy worlds, with their princesses, castles, spells, and curses, through titles such as "Enchanted," "Haunted," "Castles Crumbling," and "Long Live." In "The Story of Us," she casts a relationship falling apart as a potential battle, though "I would lay my armor down / If you said you'd rather love than fight"—a possibility seemingly foreclosed by a "twist of fate." "Long Live" translates Swift's road to fame and professional triumphs into the language of the fairytale or the epic, singing to her fans, "I had the time of my life fighting dragons with you," while "Timeless" imagines variations of Swift's existing romance in other times and places, evoking the trope of the arranged marriage common to historical romances: "In the fifteen hundreds off in a foreign land / And I was forced to marry another man / You still would've been mine." Visually, too, this era is marked by a palette of pinks and purples that sees Swift donning elaborate princess gowns for performances and promotional materials.

In other words, *Speak Now* exists in the literary mode of romance. Rosalind Williams has neatly delineated the modes of myth, romance, and realism, defining myth as centering divine and supernatural possibilities, realism as focusing on prosaic reality, and romance as existing in "the middle range between human and supernatural" (29), at once believable and larger-than-life. Most famously exemplified by medieval Arthurian romances and *chansons de geste* (French songs of great deeds by mythologized national heroes), it is, historically, a mode in which men have figured as heroes. Swift's *Speak Now* is similarly larger-than-life—for example, "When Emma Falls in Love" describes its eponymous character as being "like if Cleopatra grew up in a small town," evoking one of the most mythologized women in history as an analogy for a young woman in small-town America. And the album liberally draws from what Williams has aptly termed romance's "familiar machinery" of dragons, wizards, knights, curses, enchanted castles, and damsels in distress. Yet in doing so, it centers the female experience—it is Swift, in her princess gown, who is fighting dragons ("I had the best time fighting dragons with you," "Long Live")—and transforms these commonplaces into allegories of the heightened emotional states and experiences of a young woman. "Long Live" alternates straightforward descriptions of a sold-out concert ("crowds in stands," "confetti" falling to the ground) with fairytale imagery ("we were the kings and the queens") to convey the superlative ecstasy Swift experiences: "And I was screaming, 'Long live all the magic we made'/And bring on all the pretenders, I'm not afraid."

"Castles Crumbling" sees the downfall of that success, with Swift watching her "reign end" as crowds that used to "chant [her] name" scream at the palace gates, while "Haunted" evokes the curses and haunted castles of a Gothic tale as Swift describes how it's "getting dark and it's all too quiet," but the haunting here is a past relationship, looming like a specter: "can't breathe whenever you're gone / can't turn back now, I'm haunted."

In other words, *Speak Now* constructs a world whose fairytale geography is built out of the emotional experiences Swift so passionately and authentically expressed on *Fearless*. In this, it evokes the conceit of the *Carte du Pays du Tendre* ("Map of the Land of the Tender"), an allegorical map of the stages of a relationship, originating in seventeenth-century French literary salons (typically founded and hosted by aristocratic women). The true path through this landscape leads from a new acquaintance to affection, passing through love letters, punctuality, and sensibility, and avoiding indifference and enmity. The salonnieres's map, it must be noted, counselled the avoidance of emotional excess, such as passion; nevertheless, as Pamela Cheek writes, "in this geography of sentiment the personal is indeed political . . . placing the female prerogative at the center of civilization" by privileging "the private amorous contract contingent on woman's inclination" (45). Indeed, *Speak Now* is thematically similar to *Fearless*, centering a young woman's experiences of love, heartbreak, crushes, and breakups and constructing an alternate world whose geography and characteristics are formed out of those experiences. The central fantasy of his album, then, is its imagining of a world in which female emotional surplus is not only tolerated but celebrated.

This conceit of an emotional landscape would continue throughout Swift's oeuvre. Lamenting the loss of a "great love" on "Death by a Thousand Cuts," for example, Swift sings, "Our songs, our films, united we stand / Our country, guess it was a lawless land." The lovers' shared experiences, including the town they grew up in together, have become a "lawless land," a physical space whose map they appear to have lost. New York City, in particular, figures as a significant location in the Swiftian mythology and her oeuvre. On *Lover*, the metropolis becomes an allegory for a long-term but highly private relationship between Swift and her partner of six years—the map of their inner lives. "False God," for example, sees Swift accusing him of "Staring out the window like I'm not your favorite town / I'm New York City," and continues the metaphor by singing, "I'm the West Village / I still do it for you," while in the closing track "Daylight," she confesses, "My love was as cruel as the cities I lived in." But the most famous instance is of course "Cornelia Street," where Swift resided during the beginning of her relationship with Alwyn, and which to this day is a site of pilgrimage for Swifties visiting New York. "And if this ever ends / I'd never walk Cornelia Street again," Swift sings, such that Cornelia Street becomes a feeling rather than a place ("sacred new beginnings / that became my religion"); while the street itself is only one block long, its metaphorical significance is vast: if the relationship ends, the *emotional state* of nascent, shared love cannot be recovered. In Swift's capable hands, then, one of the world's most important metropolises becomes a young woman's *Carte du Tendre*, mapping her inner state and the course of her relationship.

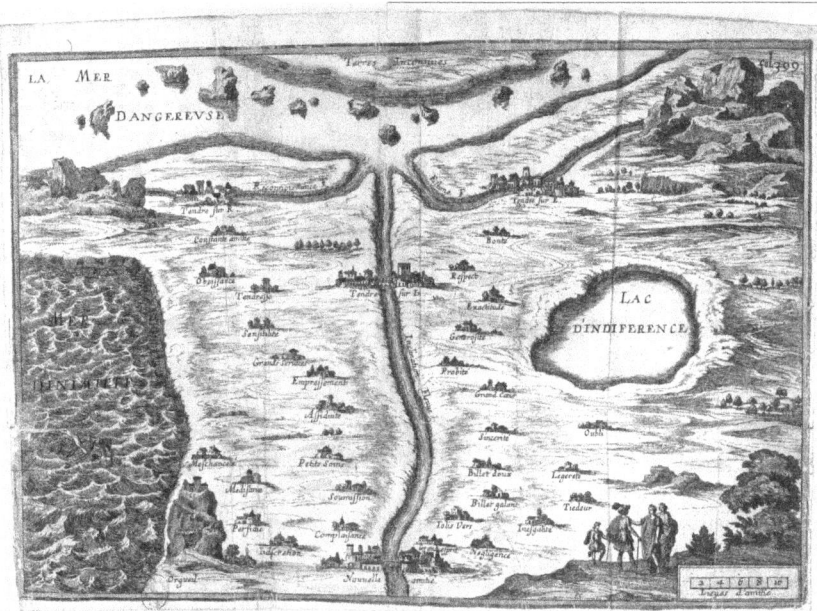

Clélie, Roman History, first part by Madeleine de Scudéry, François Chauveau, Paris, Augustin Courbé, 1654. BnF, Reserve of rare books, RES-Y2-1496 © National Library of France

Pop and Popularity: *1989* and *reputation*

The release of Swift's fifth album, *1989*, heralded a set of significant transformations in both her personal and professional lives. Relocating from Nashville to New York City and moving from her teens to her twenties, she transitioned from being a teenage girl dreaming about "living in a big old city" in "Mean" (*Speak Now*) to a young woman living in that very city, celebrated on *1989*'s opening track "Welcome to New York." At the same time, Swift moved from country to pop music and, with this album, truly broke into the mainstream, leading to a heightened scrutiny of her private and romantic life. Prior to this, Swift's public image had been that of a blonde-haired America's sweetheart, but as she now grew up and shed her small-town Americana roots, media coverage overwhelmingly tended to portray her as promiscuous and emotionally volatile. As Swift reflected in an interview with *Vogue*, "I went out on a normal amount of dates in my early 20s, and I got absolutely slaughtered for it" (Gay), which, as she has frequently pointed out, would not have happened to a man her age engaging in the same behavior.

The songwriting of this era therefore sees Swift once again deploy excess to highlight such gendered double standards and the politicization of her private life. "Blank Space," which *Billboard* would name one of the most important songs of the 2010s, here offers a key example. Its conceit is at once simple and striking: Swift parodies her media image by inhabiting the persona that was ascribed to her. As she herself explained:

> But then my second reaction ended up being, hey that's actually kind of a really interesting character they're writing about. "She jet sets around the world collecting men, and she can get any of them, but she's so clingy that they leave and she cries, and then she gets another one in her web and she traps them and locks them in her mansion and then she's crying in her marble bathtub surrounded by pearls." ("Taylor performs 'Blank Space' at The GRAMMY Museum")

The root of caricature and satire lies in hyperbole, which allows for the absurdities of an existing reality to be revealed through exaggeration. By unabashedly embracing the persona of her media image—"I'm a nightmare dressed like a daydream," goes an iconic line—Swift demonstrates to what extent that image is already a caricature, a hyperbole of her lived reality based in outdated gendered assumptions. Though she was, at the time, engaging in unremarkable behaviors such as having relationships and sharing those experiences in her art, those behaviors were portrayed as excessive by virtue of merely existing, and in embodying this manipulative ("love's a game, wanna play?") and emotionally volatile ("we'll take this way too far") persona, Swift aptly renders visible the gap between her real life and the exaggerated portrayal of it. In this way, "Blank Space" makes visible how female emotion is, by definition, seen as excess—how, as she herself has said in an interview with Barbara Walters, "If a guy shares his experience in writing, he's brave. If a woman shares her experience in writing she's over-sharing, or she's over-emotional, or she might be crazy, or 'Watch out she'll write a song about you.'"

The song's music video further drives this point home, deploying a *visual* aesthetic of excess in support of the song's musical and lyrical project. Specifically, it represents emotional excess as *material* excess, making literally tangible the way in which Swift's media image is exaggerated. Leaving behind her classic country aesthetic of unruly blonde curls, Swift here transforms into an elegant, perfectly coiffed aristocratic woman, riding with her lover(s) through the vast, manicured grounds of a lavish estate. In fact, the video was filmed at Oheka Castle, an extravagant mansion on Long Island that served as inspiration for Scott Fitzgerald's *The Great Gatsby*, a classic about, among other things, the hollowness of wealth that Swift would namecheck on *reputation*. Here, however, the extravagances of material wealth are the emotional excesses of the song made literal: Swift's alter ego, clad in couture and gems, looks the very image of a madwoman as she weeps hysterically, mascara running ("screaming, crying, perfect storm"); incapable of containing herself, she destroys a vintage car with a golf club in anger. The song's famous "long list of ex-lovers," meanwhile, is realized as a hallway of paintings of these lovers in her lavish mansion, each one ripped to shreds by Swift wielding a knife—for this madwoman will "leave you breathless / or with a nasty scar." Material and emotional excess are married, both clearly beyond the pale of the "normal," thus making palpable what Swift's emotional excesses *would* look like if they existed and thus revealing to what extent the media image she here embraces is an exaggeration.

Swift's *reputation* extends this logic to an entire album. After the success of *1989*, Swift found herself maligned in the media and on social media following the release of an edited phone call and a series of disparaging tweets by Kim Kardashian. Disappearing from the public eye for over a year, Swift took this time to write *reputation*, a "concept album" throughout which she takes on a darker persona, one uninhibited by conventional notions of morality, conscience, propriety, or emotional restraint; the "nightmare dressed like a daydream" of "Blank Space" morphs into the "actress starring in your bad dreams" ("Look What You Made Me Do"). In particular, "I Did Something Bad" sees Swift confessing, against a background of violin strings, "I play 'em like a violin/And I make it look, oh, so easy," recalling the woman of "Blank Space" for whom "love's a game." "Getaway Car" describes leaving a relationship that had run its course for another man in terms of double-crossing a partner in crime: "We were jet-set, Bonnie and Clyde (oh-oh) / Until I switched to the other side, to the other side," Swift sings, likening her relationship to the partnership between two of the most famous outlaws in American culture and confessing that she "put the money in a bag and I stole the keys." And even in "Don't Blame Me," a love song about the blossoming relationship happening quietly behind the headline-grabbing events of Swift's life, she echoes "Blank Space" in admitting, "I've been breakin' hearts a long time / and toyin' with them older guys."

The album's *pièce de résistance*, however, is unequivocally "Look What You Made Me Do," *reputation*'s first single, whose jarring sonic landscape signals that "the old Taylor can't come to the phone." The new Taylor is a darker one, driven by anger and a thirst for revenge; as she confesses, "the world moves on, another day another drama/But not for me, not for me, all I think about is karma." She is righteously and excessively furious, indulging in her madness. In "The Man," Swift would later imagine how much more acceptable that behavior would be if she were male: "it's all good if you're bad / and it's okay if you're mad." "Mad" here carries connotations of both anger and insanity; the latter, in particular, is a word with a gendered literary and cultural history within Western culture. Lord Byron, one of the greatest of the Romantic poets, was famously "mad, bad, and dangerous to know," a prime example of the cultural trope that conflates madness with genius within men. In women, by contrast, madness has often been a way to invalidate justified emotion by characterizing its very existence as exceeding reasonable boundaries. Literature is full of such madwomen, from Medea in Greek myth to Bertha Mason in *Jane Eyre*, compelling and horrifying at once, and "Look What You Made Me Do" consciously evokes such associations. Swift here is mad in both senses of the word, consumed with anger and deranged in her behavior—in the music video, she crashes an expensive car into an electric pole, lounges in a bathtub of diamonds, and sets money on fire. Obsessed with revenge, she reiterates, "I've got a list of names / and yours is in red underlined," recalling the persona of "Blank Space" bragging, "I've got a blank space, baby, and I'll write your name." Her behavior is, in every sense, "too much," her anger unacceptable (as Swift would later sing when she returned to the topic on *folklore*, "no one likes a madwoman"). Yet at this moment in time, she has already become the villain of the cultural narrative; as she sings in "Delicate," "my reputation's never been worse." If there is nothing left to lose, if she has already been cast as the madwoman, why not be it, indulging in all the excesses (read: freedoms) that the role offers her rather than tiptoeing the constraining lines of respectability?

This logic extends not only to *reputation*'s continued engagement with Swift's media image but to that other familiar Swiftian topic: a love story. As we have seen, Swift has been villainized more than once for writing love songs and breakup songs; such confessions were always parsed as excessive. At the same time, Swift's image up until this point had been a relatively "clean" one, with no explicit references in her music to drinking, drugs, or sex. But with "the death of her reputation," as Swift calls it in a poem that accompanied the Target version of the album, "she felt truly alive," no longer stifled by living up to that reputation. And so, *reputation* offers Swift the freedom to express emotions that have, for more than a decade, been cast as excessive in terms of a different set of excesses: drinking and drugs. Seen through the lens of the album, her life seems to take on the character of one of Jay Gatsby's parties ("Feeling so Gatsby for that whole year," she claims in "This Is Why We Can't Have Nice Things"). "Don't blame me / my drug is my baby / I'll be using for the rest of my life," Swift sings on "Don't Blame Me," likening being in love to a drug high, "the trip of my life." She here sings of the same subject as she has on her many other albums, and the madness of passion, the "screaming and fighting" and "feeling insane" of "The Way I Loved You," is cast in similar terms: "don't blame me / love made me crazy" ("Don't Blame Me"). The emotional core (love, heartbreak) has not changed, but it has come to be voiced by a different and darker persona—a person a that it is easier to stomach having those emotions, indulging in them with a touch of madness and sharing them so publicly.

The Pandemic Era: *folklore, evermore,* and *Midnights*

Swift has always had an undeniable way with words and a knack for a well-turned phrase that subverts expectations and twists familiar metaphors: "I struck a match and blew your mind" ("Getaway Car") is but one example.[1] She makes use of "conceits"— extended and logically complex metaphors—in the vein of metaphysical poets such as John Donne, as, for example, when a getaway car after a heist becomes a metaphor for a relationship that falls apart as Swift leaves one lover for another ("Getaway Car"). She invests quotidian and unremarkable objects with oversized signification, such as the scarf in "All Too Well," which maps the start, development, and end of a relationship. But as we have seen previously, these turns of phrase and moments of linguistic brilliance have, thus far, worked hand in hand with the sounds and visuals of her albums. But the advent of the COVID-19 pandemic precluded many such possibilities. Studio visits were replaced by voice notes recorded on Swift's iPhone and sent to collaborators, and elaborate music videos were replaced by much simpler ones, with Swift styling herself. Visually and sonically, these albums are pared down, the percussive, almost overproduced tracks of *reputation* and *Lover* replaced by simpler, calmer melodies.

---

[1] For an in-depth consideration of such subversions, see Margrét Ann Thors's essay in this collection.

At the same time, these albums are marked by a kind of *linguistic* excess that supports a whole-hearted, unrestrained escape into the imagination. As Swift wrote in the introductory note to the album, "In isolation my imagination has run wild and this album is the result, a collection of songs and stories that flowed like a stream of consciousness." This lack of restraint in indulging in the imagination recalls the moral panic surrounding women readers of the novel following its rise in the eighteenth century. These anxieties centered "on the genre's peculiar emotional power over women and the disruption of their domestic lives" (Gallagher 277). The concern was that women would relate too deeply to fictional characters and inhabit a made-up world too extensively, losing sight of real-life attachments and obligations due to a runaway imagination and a sense of reason too limited to control such excess. In other words, it was a set of gendered anxieties that "the lines between fantasy and reality blur," as Swift describes *folklore*. And in fact, the album and its twin make a number of overt references to such novels, particularly those penned by women authors, including *Jane Eyre*, whose madwoman in the attic lurks between the lines of "madwoman," and Daphne de Maurier's *Rebecca*, which inspired "tolerate it."

In other words, with *folklore*'s runaway imagination—it is Swift's first album to center primarily on other people's stories, whether imagined, historical, or present-day—Swift again "indulges" in a gendered form of excess. And it is specifically *linguistic* excess that facilitates this imaginative escape. As Swift described the creative process of *folklore* in a conversation with Paul McCartney:

> I was reading, you know, books like *Rebecca*, by Daphne du Maurier, which I highly recommend, and books that dealt with times past, a world that doesn't exist anymore. I was also using words I always wanted to use—kind of bigger, flowerier, prettier words, like "epiphany," in songs. I always thought, "Well, that'll never track on pop radio," but when I was making this record, I thought, "What tracks? Nothing makes sense anymore. If there's chaos everywhere, why don't I just use the damn word I want to use in the song?" (Doyle)

What Swift articulates here is the discovery of an artistic and linguistic freedom, with her lyrics newly unconstrained by pop's commercial requirements. But Swift breaks another set of rules, too: commonplace adages about "good writing," which dictate, in particular, that metaphors should not be mixed and that "brevity is the soul of wit." The freedom of the imagination to "run wild" beyond reasonable boundaries is enabled by her lyrics' linguistic excesses, their violations of the dictate that "less is more." Here, more is more.

Thus, for example, in "willow," the lead single from *evermore*, Swift likens herself to "the water when your ship rolled in that night / Rough on the surface but you cut through like a knife," before piling on the similes—in addition to the beloved's being "like a knife," Swift herself is "lost in your current like a priceless wine." In this abundance of metaphor, crammed into the space of one verse, she herself has transformed from the water to debris in a flowing current. What's more, there is perhaps even a play on words between current/currant, possibly an evocation of *currant* wine (wine lost in shipwrecks is often priceless due to the way it undergoes aging), while in the chorus that follows shortly after, simile makes way for metaphor once again: "life was a willow, and it bent right to your wind." In short, with metaphor upon metaphor and simile upon simile, Swift boldly eschews dictates about being concise and mixing metaphors, inundating the listener with image upon image and sensation upon sensation: a nighttime river with a powerful current, ships sailing in, shipwrecks, knives, currant wine, and willows in the wind.

Swift's wealth of physical detail, as my colleague Betsy Winakur Tontiplaphol has pointed out in this volume, has long been a defining feature of her artistic style. Eschewing a "spontaneous overflow of powerful feelings," in "Swift's lyric world, precisely observed details abound." It is tangible, material, and full of sense memory; "the songs' emotionality is *cultivated* through Swift's careful place-making and scene-setting," her use of sensual detail and minute observations. In "willow," too, Swift's overabundance of language conjures up vivid imagery suffused with nostalgia (a distant world of shipwrecks and moonlight on the water) and sense memory (a willow rustling in the wind, currant wine). And yet none of these—shipwrecks, willows, or currant wines—are quite "real." Metaphors and similes, by definition, evoke images in the mind's eye in order to add texture and depth to an imagined world even though they are not themselves *part of* that world. And so, as Swift's language runs free on *folklore* and *evermore*, it conjures up image after image after image but not in order to painstakingly and systematically construct a fictional world in the conventional sense, a Westeros or Narnia. Preoccupied with tried-and-true Swiftian topics—love, longing, devotion—she builds a world out glimpses of bygone moments, ephemeral relationships, and intriguing scenarios (teenagers kissing on the High Line, a divorcée throwing parties at a mansion by the sea, seven-year-olds on swing sets in Pennsylvania), mingling them with vivid metaphors—time sipped away like a bottle of wine, mirrorballs, ricocheting tears, cardigans, and old films—to color in a world of abstractions (feelings and emotions) with sense memory. It's this mingling and linguistic richness that create a world that can be escaped to.

Swift had, arguably, experimented with some of these features on earlier albums, particularly *Red*, which possesses many of the seeds that would come to fruition on *folklore* and *evermore*. One of Swift's most experimental albums, *Red* famously did not win a Grammy due to its lack of sonic cohesion, alternating between country and pop as Swift toyed with new sounds and attempted to figure out how to transition genres and fit her developing songwriting into the commercial requirements and restraints of the music industry. It's perhaps unsurprising, then, to find on this album some of Swift's most intriguing experiments with new ways to turn a phrase, from "you double-crossed my mind" ("All Too Well") to "forgetting him was like trying to know someone you've never met" ("Red"). Yet the pressures Swift was clearly acting under in crafting *Red* were, as we have seen, not a concern during a pandemic, allowing her to fully develop an instinct that she had experimented with and add it to her repertoire.

This approach would see frequent use on *Midnights*, an album written and released after the lifting of many of the pandemic-era restrictions that had so profoundly marked the character of *folklore* and *evermore*, but which continues to engage with many of the same themes that Swift felt to be pressing a decade ago. Thus, for example, in "Mastermind," the concluding track of *Midnights*, Swift describes plotting to get together with a partner: "And the touch of a hand lit the fuse / Of a chain reaction of countermoves / To assess the equation of you / Checkmate, I couldn't lose." As in "willow," different metaphors pile up: lighting a fuse, a chemical chain reaction, a mathematical equation, a game of chess (a common metaphor for courtship in early modern literature). But rather than worldbuilding, the priority here is a recuperative act akin to that of "Blank Space," as Swift continues to return to her media image and the gendered double standards of the music industry. In particular, in addition to promiscuity and infidelity, Swift has frequently been accused of being manipulative and inauthentic, and in an interview with *CBS Sunday Morning*, Swift offered multiple examples of the different vocabulary applied to men and women in the music industry: "a man does something, it's strategic. A woman does something, it's calculated." And in "Mastermind," Swift is indeed calculating, hyperbolically so; as she had taken on the role of a madwoman in "Blank Space," the overabundance of metaphors and adjectives associated with plotting and scheming—"cryptic and Machiavellian," "mastermind," approaching a relationship like a chess game, setting a long chain of events into motion—allow her to similarly inhabit the caricature-like persona of a calculating woman. Like her darker alter ego on *reputation*, who flees a relationship as if it were a heist, she "schem[es] like a criminal," setting in motion a series of events until she catches her beloved in a relationship. But here, too, Swift subverts expectations, just as she did when she changed Romeo's and Juliet's ending in "Love Story." For while the persona of "Blank Space" could have no happy ending, her lies and "clinginess" driving men away, this mastermind gets her happy ending with a lover who "knew the entire time." Despite her gender, she is strategic rather than calculated.

As of this writing, *Midnights* is Swift's most recent album. She has often lamented the way women in the music industry must constantly reinvent themselves, noting that the female artists she knows "have reinvented themselves twenty times more than the male artists. They have to or else you're out of a job. Constantly having to reinvent, constantly finding new facets of yourself that people find to be shiny" (*Miss Americana*). Swift's own variations on an aesthetic of excess, too, are also reinventions, ways to remain in dialogue with the narratives told about her and, in so doing, to remain "shiny," exciting, and relevant. And yet, such narratives are also crucially recuperative, a trenchant interrogation of the zeitgeist, and though Swift is at the top of her career and celebrating it with a retrospective Eras Tour, it's unlikely she'll cease creating. As time, curious time, moves forward, then, it will be fascinating to see how she will reinvent herself yet again, the ways in which she will again challenge gendered assumptions, and how excess will figure in that work. In the meantime, Swift continues to break record after record. Her female fans have grown up, but they stream her music as they once purchased her CDs, remaining loyal because she has allowed them something unique: indulging in our emotional states, living in our inner worlds, and embracing and celebrating feeling deeply and passionately. She has written the cultural landscape in doing so, and built a career of it to boot. A mastermind, indeed.

Works Cited

Doyle, Patrick. "Musicians on Musicians: Taylor Swift and Paul McCartney." *Rolling Stone.*

Cheek, Pamela. *Sexual Antipodes: Enlightenment Globalization and the Placing of Sex.* Stanford University Press: California, 2003.

Gallagher, Catherine. *Nobody's Story: The Vanishing Acts of Women Writers in the Marketplace, 1670-1920.* University of California Press: California, 1994.

Gay, Jason. "Taylor Swift As You've Never Seen Her Before." *Vogue.* 14 April 2016.

Hubbard, Nathan, host, and Princiotti, Norah, hosts. "Fearless." *Every Single Album: Taylor Swift. The Ringer.*

Malec, Jim. "Taylor Swift: The Garden in the Machine." *American Songwriter.* 23 July 2020.

Miss Americana. Directed by Lana Wilson, Netflix, 2020.

"Taylor performs 'Blank Space' at The GRAMMY Museum." *YouTube*, uploaded by Taylor Swift, 7 January 2016.

"Taylor Swift on 'Lover' and haters." *CBS Sunday Morning.* CBS, 25 August 2019. Television.

Tontiplaphol, Betsy. "Baby, We're the Late Romantics: Taylor Swift and Biedermeier Romanticism."

Walters, Barbara. "Barbara Walters Presents: The 10 Most Fascinating People of 2014." ABC, 14 December 2014. Television.

Williams, Rosalind. *The Triumph of Human Empire.* University of Chicago Press: Chicago, 2013.

18

"Making the stone stony": The Paradox of Defamiliarization and Hyperfamiliarity in Taylor Swift's Songwriting

Margrét Ann Thors

"Taylor Swift considers herself, above all else, a songwriter," writes Joe Coscarelli of *The New York Times*. A quick glance at the headlines, however, makes clear that in the public consciousness, Swift is foremost a celebrity, not a songwriter. A 2014 *Rolling Stone* feature states that beyond Swift's numerous accolades—multiple platinum best-selling albums, multiple Grammy wins—she is a "billion-time gossip-blog subject" (Eells). Undue attention has been paid to Swift's personal life and public persona, not least because she is a young woman. Her outfits and relationships and social cliques have been rigorously dissected and commented upon, often at the expense of more serious analysis of the art and craft of her songwriting. As a celebrity, Swift has made upwards of a billion dollars, but as an artist she has been trivialized, dismissed, or diminished. This essay seeks to correct that through a radically different approach to her work: a Formalist reading of Swift's oeuvre.

I use Russian formalist Viktor Shklovsky's concept of defamiliarization—also known as *ostranenie*, or "making strange"—as a lens through which to analyze Swift's lyrics. Defamiliarization, according to Shklovsky, is the purpose of art: it prompts the audience to see the familiar through fresh eyes. To do so, artists use poetic language, which Shklovsky distinguishes from practical, everyday language. As I will argue, Swift's lyrics are uniquely literary in that they often use everyday language but in clever, fresh ways, and often to subversive or provocative ends. In the spirit of the Russian Formalist movement to which Shklovsky was central, I focus exclusively on Swift's songwriting, conducting a close reading of lyrics from every stage of her career—though, admittedly, skewing toward her later works, from *Red* onward, which arguably reflect greater maturity and artistic craft.

One of the (many) paradoxes Swift embodies is that her lyrics are simultaneously hyper-familiar (*she's describing my life!*) and de-familiar. In this essay, I introduce three literary techniques Swift uses to defamiliarize while remaining hyper-familiar and hyper-relatable: (a) complicating clichés and idioms, (b) playing with oxymoron, paradox, and juxtaposition of opposites, and (c) manipulating syntax to deliver a surprise.

I argue that while the content of Swift's lyrics tends to be hyper-familiar (break-ups, arguments and reconciliations, longing) the way she warps and plays with language renders the lyrics fresh, exciting, and "strange" and gives listeners a new lens through which to critique gender stereotypes, conceptualize love, and understand their own lives.

Defamiliarization

For Shklovsky, defamiliarization is not *an* artistic technique; it is *the* artistic technique. He argues that in the everyday world, our senses dull; we become habituated to what's around us and no longer perceive its essence. We wind up passively perceiving labels, or what Shklovsky calls the "sacks" around objects, rather than their true nature. But art, he says, can, and indeed *must*, if it is to be called art, help us recover our ability to perceive the essence of the world around us. "Art exists that one may recover the sensation of life," he explains; "it exists to make one feel things, to make the stone stony" (20). In other words, art forces its audience out of habituation and into active perception. Engaging with art can therefore be a way to recover the sensation of childhood, when the world was new and had not yet been categorized, labeled, and taken for granted.

Swift expresses a similar longing in her song "seven" from the album *folklore*: "Please picture me in the weeds before I learned civility; I used to scream ferociously any time I wanted." For Shklovsky, art is a way to access the world before we "learned civility," or became so accustomed to life that we no longer really experience it. Art "exists to [. . .] make the stone stony" (20) in that it forces us to see the stone with fresh, unburdened eyes. It uses language to render the stone—an object so familiar—*strange*, and in so doing, it prompts us to examine the stone as though we have never seen it before. "Art," says Shklovsky, "removes objects from the automatism of perception" (21), compelling us to engage actively with the text and, through it, the world.

Pop music is not typically associated with defamiliarizing or making the world strange. The *Cambridge Companion to Pop and Rock*, for instance, describes pop as appealing to a wide listenership and largely devoid of formal artistic qualities. According to this definition, pop exists not to challenge the status quo or incite activism but to "raise spirits and aspirations" and generate revenue (Connelly and Krueger 667). There is nothing inherently defamiliarizing about pop; in fact, its familiarity is part of what makes it, well, popular. But Swift has always put her own spin on genre. Her country music roots, pop reinvention, and more recent forays into folk and electronic music make it difficult to box her into a single category. Across genres and albums, she has brought with her an "emotional yet uncommonly inventive [. . .] style," according to *Rolling Stone*, who included her in their 2015 list of the 100 greatest songwriters of all time. It is that "uncommonly inventive" style that makes the familiar strange and showcases Swift's artistry.

Text as Art, or Taylor as Text?

A Formalist approach to literary analysis ignores everything but the text. But Swift's songs have always been analyzed with respect to her life; entire websites are devoted to speculating about which songs are about which of her ex-boyfriends. Such biographical readings are not (necessarily) flawed or unproductive. But when the art is conflated with the artist, especially when the artist is a ubiquitous public figure, tabloid spin can overshadow the form and content of the work. As one *Rolling Stone* feature puts it, "Taylor Swift the celebrity is such a magnet for attention, she can distract from Taylor Swift the artist" (Sheffield). A Formalist approach to Swift's lyrics can counterbalance the highly biographical mainstream critique of her work and persona.

This is not to say there is no argument to be made for biographical readings of her lyrics. In fact, one of the ways Swift defamiliarizes is via tongue-in-cheek references to her own life; in "Delicate," for instance, she writes, "This ain't for the best; my reputation's never been worse, so you must like me for me"—"for the best" and "like me for me" are clichéd phrases listeners have heard before, but they take on new meaning in the context of this song which, like the whole *reputation* album, tackles Swift's public image head-on, taking ownership of the fact that her "reputation's never been worse." Something similar happens in her *1989* vault track "Slut!," in which she seizes the epithet that has been thrown at her for the past decade and a half. She writes, "Got lovesick all over my bed," conflating (a) the disorienting, "sick" feeling of being in love with (b) her supposedly promiscuous image, while also (c) gesturing at the discomfort many people feel at the thought of a young woman being sexually liberated, as though there is perhaps something sickening about Swift's being "lovesick" and sleeping around. Sometimes appreciating the full extent of Swift's defamiliarization entails considering what audiences know of her public and personal life—aspects Shklovsky and the Formalists would not take into account. For the purposes of this essay, however, I focus primarily on Swift's lyrics themselves.

Technique A: Complicating Idioms and Reinventing Clichés

When the word "cliché" first entered common discourse, it was used to describe the clicking sound made by a stereotype, a printing plate used to create many versions of the same design. A cliché was a time-saver, a shortcut. Writers are warned to steer clear of clichés; they're so familiar and overused that readers tend to zoom past them without conscious thought or reflection. However, Swift frequently reclaims and makes strange clichés as well as idioms—sets of words whose meaning can be derived from the whole phrase, but not from its individual parts (e.g. "under the weather"). Often Swift's lyrics turn familiar phrases on their heads, tack on an addendum, or undermine the conventional meaning, thereby forcing us to really *see* both the language and the experience being described.

This technique is at work in much of her songwriting, particularly from *Red* onwards. The line, "The damsels are depressed" ("Miss Americana and the Heartbreak

Prince"), for instance, reimagines the phrase, "damsel in distress." What is powerful about such a reworking of cliché is that the new line both stands on its own and calls to mind the original line. Consciously or unconsciously, listeners hold both lines in their minds simultaneously, and the presence of one deepens and complicates the meaning of the other. In this example, Swift provides a feminist rereading not just of the phrase, but of the archetype it represents. The damsels in Swift's line are not "in distress" and awaiting a prince to rescue them; rather, they are "depressed," and there is an implication that the patriarchal nature of society might play into that depression, especially since the next line reads, "Boys will be boys, then where are the wise men?" Again, Swift takes a familiar line—"boys will be boys"—and forces listeners to actively think it through; if we shrug off boys' bad behavior, then what kind of men will they grow into? Her invocation of "the wise men," which harkens both to the Biblical Magi and to stereotypes about men's supposedly superior rationality, is also laced with feminist sarcasm and critique, especially when viewed alongside songs like "The Man" on *Lover* ("I'm so sick of running as fast as I can / Wondering if I'd get there quicker / If I was a man") and "Now That We Don't Talk" from the *1989* vault ("[...] with important men who think important thoughts").

Similarly, in "All Too Well" on the rerecorded *Red* album, Swift writes, "From when your Brooklyn broke my skin and bones / I'm a soldier who's returning half her weight." Like the "damsels are depressed" line, here she imbues a familiar phrase, "skin and bones," with multiple layers of meaning. First, there is the literalization of skin and bones being "broke[n]" by the ordeal they have been through. There is also the image of a war-beaten soldier returning home "half her weight," nothing but "skin and bones," which drives home the toll this relationship has taken on the speaker and provides fresh imagery to capture the familiar experience of heartbreak. Swift often uses metaphors of battle to describe the experience of love and loss; in "You're Losing Me," she writes, "Fighting in only your army, front lines don't you ignore me." In "The Archer," the refrain is, "I've been the archer, I've been the prey." In "The Great War," she extends the battle metaphor throughout the whole song, noting the "knuckles bruised like violets," "all that bloodshed, crimson clover," and "bombs" and "burning embers" as the lovers "fight" and try to "draw up good faith treaties." Such interplay between love and war is not itself unique. But Swift casts this dichotomy in new light, using idioms like "skin and bones" to conjure, at once, the physicality, violence, and damage to self-image wrought by heartbreak.

Figurative language about war is not Swift's only approach to making the familiar topics of love and heartbreak strange. Clichés about time recur in many of her songs, for instance, the "Sad Beautiful Tragic" line, "And time is taking its sweet time erasing you," and the "invisible string" line, "Time, mystical time, cutting me open, then healing me fine." In the first line, she personifies time and attaches to it the idiom of "taking [one's] sweet time" to suggest that even time itself sometimes slows down and makes it hard to move on. In the second line, she plays with the cliché "time heals all wounds," indicating that in this case, it was time that both caused the wound and, in time, healed it. The "All Too Well" line, "Time won't fly, it's like I'm paralyzed by it," toys with the cliché "time flies"—and in turn echoes the sentiment of the "Sad Beautiful

Tragic" line: time is moving slowly, it refuses to "fly" as it is supposed to, and so she is "paralyzed" and unable to move on. Swift uses clichés to access and give voice to very familiar, very human concerns: What if time *doesn't* heal this wound? What if time takes too long to mend this heartbreak? What if the idiom or cliché we have taken for granted no longer holds true?

Swift frequently takes phrases listeners recognize, phrases we are so familiar with as to gloss over, and makes them new again. Often, she does so in quick succession, mashing together reimaginings of different clichés and idioms. In "Lover," the titular track on her 2019 album, she writes, "My heart's been borrowed and yours has been blue / All's well that ends well to end up with you." Here, she references the "something borrowed, something blue" tradition said to bring luck to a bride on her wedding day and pairs it with the idiom, courtesy of Shakespeare, "all's well that ends well." She imbues the "something borrowed, something blue" saying with new meaning by using it to describe the hearts of the lovers: hers has been borrowed (and ultimately returned) by others, and his has been battered. But ultimately, "all's well that ends well" because— the next phrase explains—the lovers end up together.

Again in "All Too Well" (10-Minute Version), Swift returns to the "all's well that ends well" line, but in a markedly different tone and context: "They say that all's well that ends well, but I'm in a new hell every time you double-cross my mind." Unlike the story in "Lover," this one hasn't ended well; the speaker is in a "new hell." Her former lover doesn't just "cross her mind," as the saying goes; he *double*-crosses it. This clever line suggests that the speaker is not only thinking about her ex constantly but also that the ex betrayed—"double-crossed"—her. It would be difficult to pack so much meaning into a compressed space without drawing on familiar phrases. Swift does not need to reinvent the wheel every line but rather needs to alter the language just enough to make us pay attention and derive new understandings.

In "this is me trying," she writes, "I was so ahead of the curve, the curve became a sphere, fell behind all my classmates, and I ended up here." Here, she makes the idiom literal: she follows the character along the (physical) arc of the curve until it brings her back to where she started—except that now, she is behind everyone else. This not only helps listeners visualize the trajectory on which the speaker is moving but also calls into question life paths: Are they linear? Spherical? What does it mean to wind up where you started, but now behind everyone you once outpaced? In "End Game," she writes, "I bury hatchets, but I keep maps of where I put 'em," thereby twisting the idiom "bury the hatchet," i.e. forgive and forget, into evidence of her "bad girl" reputation: she knows where to go to dig up the past when she needs to. Again, she makes the idiom concrete and physical, giving listeners a new lens through which to understand what it means to forgive but not forget. In the first single on *Midnights*, "Anti-Hero," Swift writes, "I'll stare directly at the sun but never in the mirror." To stare at the sun is, metaphorically, idiomatically, to look at the piercing light of truth, strong enough to make your eyes water, strong enough to damage your vision. The speaker has the guts to look there, and yet she avoids her own reflection, indicating her reluctance to face the truth about herself, that she is "the problem."

Technique B: Playing with Oxymoron, Paradox, and Juxtaposition of Opposites

Oxymoron, paradox, and juxtaposition are literary techniques that force dissimilar objects or concepts together to render fresh, unexpected insights. While the boundaries between them can be slippery, there are important differences that distinguish them from one another. Oxymoron is a figure of speech that combines two seemingly contradictory elements that, when viewed together, make sense; for instance, a "jumbo shrimp" or "open secret." Closely related, paradox is a statement that contradicts itself yet still seems true; for instance, "I know that I know nothing." Finally, juxtaposition places two contradictory words, characters, or concepts together to better illuminate their similarities and differences; for instance, "That's one *small step* for man, one *giant leap* for mankind." Contradictory combinations, mash-ups of opposites, and paradoxical truths are unexpected and, at first glance, confounding. They force us to wake up and see the world anew.

Oxymoron

The word "oxymoron" is itself an oxymoron: it combines the Greek word *oxus*, meaning "sharp," with the Greek word *mōros*, meaning "foolish"—a clever fool. From Shakespeare's *Romeo and Juliet* ("Parting is such sweet sorrow"; "O brawling love, O loving hate"), to W. B. Yeats's "Easter 1916" ("terrible beauty"), to John Legend's hit "All of Me" ("perfect imperfections"), oxymorons abound in literature and lyrics.

On the surface, oxymorons often seem like empty contradictions; one cannot be "perfectly imperfect," and a feather cannot be heavy as lead. But often upon deeper reflection, oxymorons capture important truths. In "The Story of Us," Swift writes, "I'd tell you I miss you, but I don't know how; I've never heard silence quite this loud," gesturing to the familiar oxymoron "deafening silence." Strictly speaking, silence cannot be deafening, but characterizing it at such underscores how all-encompassing and unbearable the silence is; the lover's absence is a palpable, painful presence. In "Sparks Fly," she writes, "Just keep on keeping your eyes on me, it's just wrong enough to make it feel right." This line mashes together "wrong" and "right" and suggests the farther you go to either extreme, the closer you come to its opposite—a sentiment that perhaps anticipates the *1989* hit "Blank Space," which I will discuss below.

In "Wildest Dreams," Swift writes, "He's so tall and handsome as hell; he's so bad, but he does it so well." The phrase "handsome as hell" is oxymoronic, as is the "so bad [...] so well"; these contradicting characterizations suggest an alluring villain and a dangerous love. Even the title of "my tears ricochet" is an oxymoron; tears don't ricochet, but bullets do. By turning tears into weapons, projectiles, the speaker suggests that the wrongs against her—that which made her cry—will be avenged. Her anguish ricochets back to those who inflicted pain upon her; her tears are dangerous to others, not just herself. Here, as in other songs, Swift reimagines topics that are often belittled, feminized, and seen as weaknesses (tears, heartbreak) as, instead, unlikely emblems of strength.

Paradox

While oxymoron usually refers to contradictions at the level of diction and syntax, paradox is an opposition between ideas or themes. In "Last Kiss," Swift plays with the poles of knowing and not knowing: "All that I know is I don't know how to be something you miss." The paradoxical phrase "all that I know is I don't know" (which then takes on new meaning once Swift sings the word "how . . .") underscores how adrift the speaker feels in the wake of this heartbreak; she is unsure of how to live in this new reality. On the titular track of *Red*, Swift again turns to paradox to capture the feeling of heartbreak: "Forgetting him was like trying to know somebody you've never met." This is a paradox, and that is the point: Swift is emphasizing how difficult—impossible, even—it is to forget this ex-love.

In "All Too Well," she writes, "And I know it's long gone and that magic's not here no more / And I might be okay but I'm not fine at all." We usually think of "okay" and "fine" as synonyms, and so it's paradoxical for the speaker to be "okay" but "not fine at all"; the paradox snaps us awake, out of what Shklovsky calls the "automatism of perception" (21), and prompts us to question the subtle differences between these words and what they might mean for the speaker. Does she tell everyone she is okay, but inside she is falling apart? Does she mean to suggest that in the ex-lover's eyes, she is okay, as in decent, but not fine, as in superior quality? That the line generates such questions indicates that listeners cannot take the language or what it represents for granted.

In "Look What You Made Me Do," Swift writes, "But I got smarter, I got harder in the nick of time; honey, I rose up from the dead, I do it all the time." It is a paradox to rise up from the dead "all the time." Here, the paradox emphasizes just what it takes for the speaker to resurrect herself—her reputation—and also underscores the many deaths the speaker experiences: she (or her reputation) is constantly being killed, and so she's rising from the dead "all the time." Metaphorically, this is what Swift has done her entire career, and it is why her decade-and-a-half reign at the top of the music charts can be divided into such distinct "eras." As Swift herself remarks in the 2020 documentary *Miss Americana*, "The female artists that I know of have reinvented themselves twenty times more than the male artists. They have to or else you're out of a job" (Wilson). Perhaps Swift's most acute reinvention occurred in the wake of her very public 2016–2017 feud with Kanye West and his then-wife Kim Kardashian, out of which Swift emerged not as the America's sweetheart fans had come to know and expect but as an edgier, grungier, darker, and more vengeful iteration of herself (Ordoñez). As she says in the opening track of *reputation*, "The old Taylor can't come to the phone right now [. . .] Because she's dead." The paradox of rising from the dead all the time serves not just as a strange way to think about the impact of media scrutiny and public scandals on Swift's career but also as a prism through which to question and critique the immense pressure female artists face to remain fresh, relevant, and in Swift's words, "shiny" (Wilson).

Juxtaposition

Swift's songwriting is full of juxtaposition—of colors, weather patterns, right and wrong, good and bad, love and loss. In "I Almost Do," Swift writes, "I bet it never ever occurred to you that I can't say hello to you and risk another goodbye," highlighting the speaker's fear of letting a lost love back into her life only to invariably lose him again. In "Blank Space," she uses the conceit of a blank space, a Mad Lib of sorts, to cheekily tackle the promiscuous reputation that has been thrust upon her; "Darling, I'm a nightmare dressed like a daydream," she writes, emphasizing the contrast that gets taken up again in "Style" between her "good girl faith" and "tight little skirt." "Blank Space" also contains the iconic line, "I can make the bad guys good for a weekend," playing up the unhinged extremes around which the song revolves. Even the line, "So it's gonna be forever, or it's gonna go down in flames," juxtaposes two possible—and contradictory—outcomes, emphasizing the highly charged nature of this relationship: it's all or nothing. The speaker is fire and ice, Mary and Madonna, nightmare and daydream; she is, in Swift's words, "crazy, but seductive, but glamorous, but nuts, but manipulative" (Klosterman).

The titular track on *Red* is replete with contrasts and juxtapositions, most notably between colors: "Losing him was blue, like I'd never known; missing him was dark gray, all alone / [. . .] But loving him was red." Losing and missing are ascribed dark, doleful colors, but "loving him" is the color of passion, excitement, fire: red. Later, in "Getaway Car," Swift writes, "The ties were black, the lies were white, in shades of gray and candlelight"—a clever line that both juxtaposes "black" and "white" and plays with their connotations. "The ties were black" indicates this was a fancy black-tie affair, where people told white lies, and where they entered a morally gray area, doing devious deeds in the (gray) shadows. In "Treacherous," she writes, "And all we are is skin and bone, trained to get along, forever going with the flow, but you're friction." The last word packs a punch because it is juxtaposed with "the flow"; as the speaker's love interest stands out from the crowd, so does this unexpected word.

In "happiness," she writes, "I was dancing when the music stopped," to indicate that she was still in love when the relationship ended. In "I Wish You Would," she describes her and her lover as "a crooked love in a straight line down," implying that the love is at once singular and doomed. In "The Archer," she asks rhetorically, "Who could ever leave me, darling, but who could stay?" The speaker of this song is caught between diametric opposites—archer and prey, leaving and staying—and seems not to know how to escape from this ping-pong of extremes, hence her plea: "help me hold on to you."

Ultimately, Swift's use of oxymoron, paradox, and juxtaposition serves to describe hyper-familiar experiences in strange, unfamiliar ways. The dissonance between words, characters, or ideas perks up our attention and helps us to, in Shklovsky's words, "recover the sensation of life" (20).

Technique C: Manipulating Syntax to Deliver a Surprise

In this third technique, Swift uses a particular syntactical setup to deliver a surprise and, in the process, defamiliarize. Many of Swift's most memorable lines, particularly the clever zingers, employ the following sentence structure: independent clause + comma + conjunction (especially "but") + independent clause. We have seen this structure elsewhere in this essay, most notably in the previous section about oxymoron, paradox, and juxtaposition. In "All Too Well," for instance, the lines, "I'd like to be my old self again, but I'm still trying to find it," and, "I know it's long gone and that magic's not here no more / and I might be okay, but I'm not fine at all," employ this syntactical structure, as do lines such as, "He's so bad, but he does it so well" ("Wildest Dreams"), "I like shiny things, but I would marry you with paper rings" ("Paper Rings"), and "Who could ever leave me, darling, but who could stay?" ("The Archer"). The surprise is signaled by the conjunction and comes to fruition in the latter half of the sentence. As we see in the examples above, because the surprise entails undermining or recasting what preceded it, there is an inherent link between this syntax and juxtaposition. Take, for instance, this line from "cardigan": "You drew stars around my scars, but now I'm bleeding." The first half of the sentence sounds whimsical and endearing and works on both literal and metaphorical levels. The close rhyming between "stars" and "scars," words that differ by only a letter, adds to the rose-tinted feel of this line. But then comes the second half of the sentence, signaled by the "but"; what follows will contradict, or at least complicate, what came before. We learn the speaker either has fresh wounds (presumably caused by the "you" addressed in the song) or that the process of drawing stars around the speaker's scars caused those healed wounds to reopen. We must rethink our understanding of the line in light of the clause that follows the conjunction.

In "All Too Well," Swift writes, "I was never good at telling jokes, but the punchline goes: I'll get older, but your lovers stay my age." Here we see a doubling of this syntactical format, which might explain why the line packs such a punch. The first clause, "I was never good at telling jokes," is undermined by the second, which sets up the punchline of a joke: I'll get older, the joke goes, but you'll continue dating twenty-year-olds. The punchline hinges on the "but" and what follows it, as do the figurative punchlines of many of Swift's lyrics. Consider, as another example, these lines from "Dear John": "I lived in your chess game, but you changed the rules every day"; the first clause is the set up and the second is the figurative punchline.

This syntactical arrangement isn't limited to sentences that use "but" as the conjunction. In "I Did Something Bad," Swift writes, "They're burning all the witches even if you aren't one, so light me up." Here, the fulcrum point of the lyric is "so," and the punchline is the speaker's dare: "light me up," by which she means, "I'm not scared of your witch hunt." Similarly, in "Daylight," Swift uses "so" to unite two halves of a zinger lyric: "Luck of the draw only draws the unlucky, so I became the butt of the joke." In the span of a single lyric, we move from "luck of the draw," with its positive connotations, to a reversal of the idiom (the claim that "luck of the draw *only draws the unlucky*"), to a personalization: "I became the butt of the joke." In "my tears ricochet," Swift writes, "We gather here, we line up weeping in a sunlit room / and if I'm on fire, you'll be made of ashes too." The sentence hinges on the "and," which unites these clauses and forces an unexpected connection. As with the lines from "cardigan," here the image conjured by "weeping in a sunlit room" is quickly undermined, or recast, by the subsequent clause. There is nothing menacing about the "weeping" or "sunlit room" of the first clause, but the second half swiftly changes tone and issues a threat: if I burn, you'll go down with me. Such unexpected leaps in tone and register keep listeners on their toes and out of the trance of passive, automatic thought.

In these and many other instances, Swift uses syntax to interrupt passive, habitual perception; the conjunction veers the tone and sentiment into a different direction and forces us to pay attention.

Conclusion

As Nate Sloan points out, Swift "has positioned 'hard work' as a key feature of her persona since childhood; she has repeatedly emphasized that great songwriting doesn't 'just happen.' Rather, it takes time, effort, art, and craft. In Swift's words, 'I wanted to say to people, You realize writing songs is an art and a craft and not, like, an easy thing to do? Or to do well?'" (Aguirre 512 in Sloan 17). I bring this up as a reminder that if Swift is, as *Rolling Stone* and many others argue (or in some cases, reluctantly admit), one of the greatest songwriters of all time, then it's worth conducting close readings of her lyrics as literature and analyzing the artistic techniques she uses. Mainstream critiques of Swift and her work will undoubtedly continue to focus on her celebrity, but scholars and music critics must also carve out space for analysis not (only) of her private and public life, but of her texts.

This essay's close reading of Swift's lyrics as literature enables us to draw a few conclusions about her songwriting. First, Swift has been making clever use of clichés, idioms, oxymorons, paradoxes, juxtapositions, and syntax since her earliest albums. That said, she appears to take full ownership of these techniques from *Red* onward. Perhaps these techniques are part of what makes Swift's later albums feel more mature and realized than her opening acts. Second, some of Swift's most beloved songs of all time (for example, "All Too Well") are among the richest in these defamiliarizing techniques. Put differently, many of Swift's most loved and critically acclaimed songs are also her most literary and defamiliarizing. Finally, it's possible to foreground Swift's lyrics and analyze them without respect to her ex-boyfriends. While it can be fun to speculate about who the intended "you" is in any given song, and while knowing who or what a song is about can sometimes add layers of meaning, critics have too often let Swift's celebrity overshadow her art. An approach like that of the Russian Formalists, which focuses solely on the text without regard for context or personality, may be too extreme writ large, but in the case of Swift's songwriting it serves as a necessary counterbalance.

Works Cited

Aguirre, Abby. "Taylor Swift on Sexism, Scrutiny, and Standing Up for Herself." *Vogue*, 8 August 2019. Qtd. in Sloan, Nate. "Taylor Swift and the Work of Songwriting." *Contemporary Music Review*, vol. 40, no. 1, 11–26.

Connelly, Marie and Alan B. Krueger. "Rockonomics: The Economics of Popular Music." eds. Ginsburg, Victor A. and David Throsby. *Handbook of the Economics of Art and Culture*. Elsevier, 2006. 667–719.

Coscarelli, Joe. "How Taylor Swift Writes a Love Song." *The New York Times*. 24 December 2019.

Eells, Josh. "The Reinvention of Taylor Swift." *Rolling Stone*. 8 September 2014.

Frith, Simon; Straw, Will, and John Street, eds. *The Cambridge Companion to Pop and Rock*. Cambridge University Press: Cambridge, 2011.

Klosterman, Chuck. "Taylor Swift on 'Bad Blood,' Kanye West, and How People Interpret Her Lyrics." *GQ*. 15 October 2015.

Ordoñez, Olivia. "'I'm Still Trying Everything to Keep You Looking at Me'": Taylor Swift and the Autotheoretical Construction of Public Selves. *Feminist Studies*, vol. 49, no. 2–3. 2023: 394–420.

Sheffield, Rob. "All 206 of Taylor Swift's Songs, Ranked." *Rolling Stone*. 26 October 2021.

Shklovsky, Viktor. "Art as Technique." In *Modern Criticism and Theory: A Reader*, ed. Nigel Wood and David Lodge. Routledge: London, 2013. 15–30.

Sloan, Nate. "Taylor Swift and the Work of Songwriting." *Contemporary Music Review*, vol. 40, no. 1. (2021): 11–26.

"The 100 Greatest Songwriters of All Time." *Rolling Stone*. August 2015.

Wilson, Lana. *Miss Americana*. Netflix, 2020.

19

"This is me trying": Autofiction and Taylor Swift

Maria Juko

Coming from an artist known for the autobiographical influences on her songwriting, the first line of Taylor Swift's opener "the 1" on her eighth studio album, *folklore*, "I'm doing good, I'm on some new shit," raised questions. By the first chorus, Swift sings "[a]nd if you wanted me, you really should've showed." Swift dropped the album on July 24, 2020, amidst the first lockdown due to the Covid-19 pandemic. At the time, Swift was in a relationship with Joe Alwyn, and her fans, known as "Swifties," were confounded to hear the first verse and immediately started to look for its subject—but could find none (see for example "ALBUM REACTION: Folklore—Taylor Swift," *Chats and Reacts*'s YouTube video). A look at Swift's written prologue for *folklore* offers explanations: "I found myself not only writing my own stories, but also writing about or from the perspective of people I've never met, people I've known, or those I wish I hadn't." Introducing the records with a "prologue," Swift foregrounds the notion that these albums form narratives of their own rather than being purely autobiographical.

Taylor Swift has always been considered a superb lyricist, but particularly on *folklore* and *evermore*, both released in 2020, she establishes herself as a maturing artist that tries to navigate past successes and disappointments and a hopeful, albeit uncertain, future. Although she also includes her first trilogy of pure fiction on *folklore* ("cardigan," "betty," and "august" all narrate a teenage love triangle from different perspectives) and perhaps a second one on *evermore* ("dorothea," "'tis the damn season," "goldrush"), both albums are strongly informed by biographical influences, such as *evermore*'s "marjorie," inspired by Swift's grandmother, Marjorie Finlay, an opera singer. These approaches to her songwriting allow for an argument that positions Swift as an author of autofiction, a combination of autobiography and fiction. Fittingly, *Pitchfork*'s Jill Mapes observes in their review of *folklore* that "[a]fter years as pop's most reliable first-person essayist, Swift channels her distinct style into what are essentially works of fiction and autofiction." Indeed, Taylor Swift's two albums echo Christian Lorentzen's observation that "in autofiction there tends to be emphasis on the narrator's or protagonist's or authorial alter ego's status as a writer or artist and that the book's creation is inscribed in the book itself." Replace book with song here and Swift as protagonist/writer could be the subject of this quote. My point is this: Autofiction allows Swift to become more of an alter ego than a direct translation of herself.

It should be noted that understandings of the term autofiction differ, particularly on the level of fictionality. For one, Nina Bouraroui explains that "[a]utofiction doesn't arise from the urge to invent, to create a fictional other and tell a tale according to the rules of a particular form. [...] It may not be the absolute truth the author is telling," but the subject's experience retold. Bouraroui reads autofiction as a thinly veiled rendering of the author's account and mentions genre-defining works, such as Hervé Guibert's 1990 *To the Friend Who Did Not Save My Life*, in which he chronicles his life after being diagnosed with AIDS, and Annie Ernaux's 1990 *Simple Passion*, inspired by a passionate love affair. The titles Bouraroui lists deal with illness, disability, sexuality, and trauma rooted in the respective authors' singular experiences. Pointing to the different meanings of "autofiction" in their edited collection on the genre, Alexandra Effe and Hannie Lawlor argue for a dynamic definition, loosely understood as "something to do with the self and with fiction" (1). Meanwhile, Effe and Alison Gibbons in that same collection suggest that "[a]utofictional writing refers to the intentional production of a text both as autobiographical and as fictional, and the complementary intention that the text be recognized as such" (66). They suggest that "The author aims to represent their self, or a dimension of their self, while also purposefully taking creative liberties in the act of self-narration. This is what we call an act of *autofictionalization*" (66; emphasis in original). As they go on:

> Autofictional writing is thus distinct from lying and misremembering [...] and aims at something in addition to self-representation. Potential goals of the intentional act of autofictionalization include those associated with fictional modes in general [...] includ[ing also] creative, explorative thinking in the pursuit of self-understanding, self-performance and self-creation, and readerly positioning (with the aim, for example, of anticipating objections or of inviting reader engagement). (66)

Effe and Gibson understand autofiction to be not a factually true retelling but a story that allows for creative interpretation on the author's part. I claim this second notion of autofiction for my reading of Swift's *folklore* and *evermore*. By considering Taylor Swift in light of theories of autofiction, this chapter shows that the genre enables Swift's artistic engagement with her own experiences. Unlike other genres, such as biography or life-writing, autofiction allows Swift to include her experiences in a more fictional setting without baring herself explicitly. Fans gain from this a sense of universality, able to relate to more of Swift's songs, but her craft also encourages fans to connect to Swift's struggles as a female artist growing up in the twenty-first century. While autofiction makes it possible for Swift to disassociate herself from the story, it also invites fans and critics to trace connections between songs and Swift's real life, thereby generating renewed interest in her music and life.

It seems that particularly this last observation motivated Swift's decision to change her writing approach. Since the beginning of her career, Swift's songs have been scrutinized and analyzed meticulously; even the prestigious *Rolling Stone* magazine examined the connections between her lyrics and her real-life dating history (Spanos). An autofictional approach to songwriting enables Swift to disassociate herself from the contents and make herself less vulnerable to media scrutiny. This is reflected in interviews she gave to promote the album in 2020, in which she notes that the "diaristic" form of writing was not "sustainable for her" (Apple Music interview, "Taylor Swift's Songwriting Process on 'evermore'"). Unlike her previous records, the lyrical "I" is no longer a direct translation of Taylor Swift, the artist, as the written prologue declares: "A tale that becomes folklore is one that is passed down and whispered around. […] The lines between fantasy and reality blur and the boundaries between truth and fiction become almost indiscernible." In effect, it is in the written prologue for *folklore* that Swift announces a shift in her storytelling. However, as Alison James notes about these kind of disclaimers, "[w]hen foregrounded in this way, the signpost of fictionality becomes a signpost of *fictionalization*, only accentuating the referential uncertainty surrounding the first-person narrator […] encouraging an autofictional reading, regardless of the author's stated intention" (53). Building on these theoretical deliberations, I assert that Swift develops from an autobiographical into an (auto)fictional writer on these two stand-out albums.

At the same time, this fictionalization invites more speculation on the connections to her personal life, allowing the media and fans to question the entanglement between fact and fiction. Considering Swift's songwriting, Emily Yahr notes in her article "2022: The year in review (Taylor's version)":

> People make jokes about the Taylor Swift Cinematic Universe, but it's not even really a joke. Since her debut country album in 2006, Swift has carefully and steadily built her own mythology, embedding puzzles and hints about the true meaning of her work in album notes and sprinkling clues about her life in social media posts and videos. Her use of symbols and imagery has only grown over time, […] her fans seem as if they are practically speaking another language with abbreviations, coded catchphrases and references that only they understand.

What articles such as Yahr's point out is that fans are conditioned to trace connections between Swift's texts and real-life events. Fostering a community of amateur sleuths, Taylor Swift invites fans to speculate and figure out her plans and upcoming song titles and albums, often integrating secret messages into her album art, booklets, and posts on social media. For her album *Midnights*, she created a mini-series, *Midnight Mayhems with Me*, on her TikTok account in which she announced each song track's title. Interestingly, Effe and Gibbons argue on autofiction that:

> [the] rootedness in reality is likely to create personal relevance which, empirical studies suggest, is linked to higher emotional involvement—that is, to an affective effect. […] Such contemplation will also mean more critical, […] more creative, engagements with the text, including the ways in which readers relate to autofictions and what changes they themselves might put into action in their lives. (77)

In similar fashion, fan engagement, "personal relevance," is a crucial part of the Taylor Swift (marketing) machine that relies on fans to dissect every song. In interviews to promote *folklore* and *evermore*, Swift established that there is an element of fiction attached to most of the songs but that she still finds herself in them, alluding to the autofictional mode (Apple Music interview). Her extended selection of songs from *folklore* and *evermore* for her extremely successful Eras Tour playlist suggests that for her, these songs are also incredibly meaningful.

At this point, the story of Swift's success has become a tale itself, for *she* is folklore by now—tales and rumors whispered among friends and haters. For one, all song titles on *folklore* and *evermore* are stylized in lowercase letters, signalling that there is no definitive beginning to these stories; rather, they are a collection of tales. The *OED* defines "folklore" as "[t]he traditional beliefs, legends, and customs, current among the common people; the study of these," and "recently in extended use: popular fantasy or belief." Therefore, the title of the album *folklore* hints at the fictional component of Taylor Swift's stories. This is a notable change from her earlier album titles, which had an autobiographical component attached to each of them: for example, *Taylor Swift* was self-titled; *1989* is her birth year; and *Lover* dealt with her relationship with Alwyn and, more so, self-love. On *folklore*, her personal stories are present in all of the songs, but more than her biographical notes, Taylor Swift homes in on her lyrical abilities. As the term "folklore" implies, fictional characters are infused with feelings that Swift had explored on earlier records, and fact and fiction merge in her storytelling—just as in folklore, where stories are frequently conveyed in an oral storytelling mode. Even earlier examples of autofiction exist, such as "Love Story" on *Fearless*, where Swift uses the timeless dramatic relationship between star-crossed lovers Romeo and Juliet for her meditation on teenage love. In contrast, literary references made on 2020's *evermore* and *folklore* become more central. In "the lakes" she alludes to Romantic poet Wordsworth ("what are my words worth"), "mad woman" could be a reference to Charlotte Brontë's *Jane Eyre* (the "mad" Bertha Mason is imprisoned by her husband Rochester), and "the last great american dynasty" is inspired by philanthropist Rebekah West Harkness, whose house Swift bought (Sager); these intertextual references in her lyrics could spawn a chapter on their own.

Swift's ninth studio album *evermore* was released only five months after *folklore*. Again, song titles are styled in lowercase, signalling a continuation of *folklore* in style and theme; as Swift describes it in her written prologue for *evermore*, "it feels like we were standing on the edge of the folklorian woods and had a choice: to turn and go back or to travel further into the forest of music. We chose to wander deeper in." The *OED* defines "evermore" as "for all future time" and "something that lasts for evermore; unending time; eternity." The title hints at the stories that have become folklore, but Swift questions the idea of eternity. In line with *folklore*, *evermore* is similarly rooted in its reflection on interpersonal relationships. Yet the fictional character to her lyrics is still present, with titles such as "cowboy like me." Focusing on a pair of scammers falling for each other, the song is reminiscent of *reputation*'s "Getaway Car" in alluding to criminals and lovers Bonnie and Clyde.

Swift announces in her prologue that *folklore* is a product of isolation—"[i]n isolation my imagination has run wild"—and *evermore* is its continuation. Through the lens of autofiction, Swift's two pandemic records emerge as singular experiences in her artwork. The albums are marked by a sense of introspection, as Swift reflects on her self-image and her relationship with fans, as well as the media. Taken together, these themes reveal *folklore* to be a deeply personal meditation on her status as a superstar during a time in which fan reactions were limited to the online sphere. The following record *evermore* borrows some of these themes but also dives deeper into dramatic relationships, with Swift not necessarily equated with the lyrical "I" but including call-backs to earlier records and themes that the artist explored in the past.

Introspection vs. Media Scrutiny

Songs such as "exile" and "this is me trying" position the lyrical "I" in more dramatic relationships, including call-backs to Swift's experiences, particularly her relationship with the media and her craft. Effe and Gibbons note that "[t]he autofictional mode, in sum, allows [artists] to develop new perspectives on [...] the world, and to, momentarily at least, transform [their] (experience of) self" (68). Rather than arguing that this incorporation of fictional elements limits Swift's songwriting, I assert that it enriches her themes and homes in on her skills to tell a story. Expanding her horizons by extrapolating ideas from fiction, Swift's approach to her story-writing is not new, but this integration of experiences other than her own was certainly a way of reconnecting with her story-writing skills. It was also a way of dealing with some of the criticism of her overwhelmingly autobiographical writing. This culminated in her third win for Album of the Year at the 52nd Grammy Awards in 2021. No other female artist had achieved such a feat before her. The change in her approach and inspiration, not just musically but also in terms of writing, paid off.

For one, "exile" combines aspects of a dramatic romantic relationship with Swift's "self-exposed exile from the public eye following her harrowing 2016" (Sager), which she also discusses in the 2020 documentary *Miss Americana*, directed by Lana Wilson: "When people fall out of love with you, there's nothing you can do to make them change their mind. They just don't love you anymore. I just wanted to disappear. Nobody physically saw me for a year, and that was what I thought they wanted." The song, a duet between Swift and Bon Iver, tells the story of a broken couple with each of the former partners disappointed in the other's inability to "see the signs." Is the song merely about a broken relationship, or could this also hint at Swift's disillusionment with the press and critics after seemingly losing their approval? Effe and Gibbon note that in autofiction, "[t]he author aims to represent their self, or a dimension of their self, while also purposefully taking creative liberties in the act of self-narration" (66). In "exile," Swift's persona comes across as indifferent; saying, "I'm not your problem anymore," implies a feeling of nonchalance in the lyrical "I" because the other side has given up on her already. Directly followed by the line, "So who am I offending now?," the lyrical "I" underlines this false indifference. Indeed, "You were my crown" signals the importance of that other person or people, perhaps her fans or critics. The line, "I think I've seen this film before," highlights the performative character of the spectacle surrounding this fictional couple's relationship or Swift's positioning of herself as the drama queen whose "crown" has been taken away from her. Finally, "[a]nd I didn't like the ending" speaks to a desire to rewrite a narrative that has been set into motion but cannot be changed anymore—storylines and relationships that have turned out a specific way without a chance to change them. The song "exile" can thus be read as a couple lamenting their past fallout or as a dialogue between an alter ego of Swift and the media, critics, and fans.

This working through her relationship with the media and her art also connects to her song "this is me trying," which I regard as the key example of autofiction on these two records. With *reputation* and *Lover* falling behind in terms of award recognition, Swift found herself with a new question: how would her art have to develop to reconnect with her critics? Despite the 2018 *reputation* tour having been a success, followed by a Netflix concert film, her *Lover* festival had to be cancelled due to the ongoing COVID-19 pandemic. The ninth track on *folklore*, "this is me trying," sounds like a worn-out tape, with Swift's soft-spoken lines perpetuating this sense of desperation and instability. The title is not just a plea for acknowledgement but also feels like an attempt by the speaker to convince herself that she is improving. After Swift's reemergence from her chosen exile, this is a thinly veiled confession of her anxieties. References to desperation, depression, alcoholism, suicidal thoughts, and, finally, a longing for affection are all mixed in this song, presenting a stark contrast to her overall more cheerful songs. This almost reflects Bouraroui's assertion that "[a]utofiction doesn't arise from the urge to invent, to create a fictional other and tell a tale according to the rules of a particular form. [...] It may not be the absolute truth the author is telling, but it is her truth as she lived and experienced it." Here, the speaker confesses that "[she's] been having a hard time adjusting," and she wonders what she can give and what she can do to please her audience and, more so, her critics. She talks about expectations, about giving up on believing in herself, and about her art becoming obsolete to her, explaining that "I had the shiniest wheels, now they're rusting." The next line, "I didn't know if you'd care if I came back," hints at her relationship to fans and/or critics, since she admits that she was not sure whether her return from her self-imposed exile would be a welcome one, though it is an exile that she seems to regret now. This is followed by four lines that chronicle her driving to the edge of a higher mountain, hinting perhaps at suicidal thoughts, but she ends up at the house of the addressee, readable as her fans or in general her audience. Twice she sings the titular lyrics, introduced in an almost casual manner: "I just wanted you to know." But this indifference feels stifled, as if the singer wants the addressee to realize that she is trying to change her life. Rather than a romantic relationship, her struggles with herself and with the music industry are at the center of the story.

This only manifests in the second verse with the line, "[t]hey told me all of my cages were mental," implying she was led to believe that she was not good enough. This negligence led to her "[getting] wasted like all my potential." Consider Jill Mapes, who notes in their review that "[a]t its best, Folklore asserts something that has been true from the start of Swift's career: Her biggest strength is her storytelling, her well-honed songwriting craft meeting the vivid whimsy of her imagination." But Swift here opens up about her anxiety about underperforming. Her level of fame, Swift implies, curtailed her creative prowess and included limitations, even and especially psychological ones.

The second verse continues this fear of being forgotten, suggesting that first "ahead of the curve, the curve became a sphere"; she fears that others took her place in the industry, that she "[f]ell behind all [her] classmates and [she] ended up here"—a metaphorical low point. Swift implicitly admits her dislike of the music industry's competition, of feeling pressured to deliver despite feeling anxious, and she hints also at the pressure she creates for herself. There is also a nod to her *reputation* era, when she expressed her anger at critics; "my words shoot to kill when I'm mad" is followed by an admission of regret. This confession is yet again followed by the act of sharing her anxieties with someone she does not know (without, however, resorting to strong alcohol), and it is followed again by her increasingly desperate announcement that she is trying to get better.

The bridge circles back to her desire to return to a time where she was less self-conscious; "[a]nd it's hard to be at a party when I feel like an open wound" is a line that refers to the permanent damage that she took from the last years in exile. When she confesses that "[i]t's hard to be anywhere these days when all I want is you," the "you" here could either be a lover or her fans. Swift ends the bridge with, "You're a flashback in a film reel on the one screen in my town"; similarly to the previous line, the "you" in this case could be a fictional lover to whom the lyrical "I" confesses their mistakes and insecurities. But the bridge could also be a "flashback" to an older version of Swift herself, to the days when she was lauded with praise. Now she feels the need to compare herself to the artists she believes have surpassed her. In "autofictional reading," Effe and Gibbons note, "[t]he factual schema leads readers to approach a text for information about the real world, the real author, and to evaluate the relevance of this information for themselves and their own lives" (65). What does Swift's confession mean to her fans? Swift's merging of personal experience and elements of fiction allows her to confess anxieties without exposing herself fully, behind a thinly veiled cover, leaving just enough breadcrumbs to encourage fans to reflect on the song's truth. Crafted in isolation, "this is me trying" is a deeply self-reflexive and confessional song that also allows listeners to discern the authenticity of Swift's concerns. It also makes it possible for them to connect their own anxieties with the lyrics, potentially realizing they are stifled in their lives as well.

Unsurprisingly, Swift is keenly interested in keeping in charge of her own music, which is why songs on *folklore* and *evermore* also center Swift's recent falling out with her former record label Big Machine and manager Scooter Braun. The sale of her catalogue in 2016 to Braun deeply affected Swift and made her ultimately decide to rerecord the six albums that she had released under contract with Big Machine. One of the most strikingly autofictional songs on *folklore*, "mad woman," is about a woman coming to haunt a past friend. This could be interpreted as a fictionalization of Swift's feud with Braun, as Swift equates her anger and subsequent vilification with people (even fellow women) believing her to be a "mad woman" and a "witch." Rather than feel insulted, she played with the notion of witch-hood and released a "lonely witch remix" of *evermore*'s "willow," reappropriating the insult as a form of female empowerment. In a similar fashion, on "my tears ricochet," a dead woman laments her relationship with a past friend, who, despite their riff, still attends her funeral, which could be interpreted as her former record company manager Steve Borchetta selling her records. Tellingly, Swift sings, "[a]nd when you can't sleep at night (you hear my stolen lullabies)," pointing towards Borchetta as the antagonist. Swift uses images of a graveyard, a funeral, and ghosts to represent her resentment of the situation that has transpired between her, Braun, and Borchetta. The gothic imagery in both songs helps her to work through these negative associations with the past, but by couching these mediations in fiction, she is also trying to distance and disassociate herself. All the while, it is also less clear whether she in fact is the ghost haunting or not, blurring the lines between fact and fiction. Again, this harks back to Effe's and Gibbons's suggestion that autofictional texts "include creative, explorative thinking in the pursuit of self-understanding, self-performance and self-creation, and readerly positioning (with the aim, for example, of anticipating objections or of inviting reader engagement)" (66). The autofictional approach to songwriting helps Swift to work through traumatic experiences that forced her to completely change her perspective on the music industry, palpable in these two songs. But there are just enough facts to discover so that fans, listeners, or critics can speculate on the connections between her writing and life. Swift uses autofictional writing to produce an almost immersive experience, and she directs listeners to level their critique at Braun and Borchetta.

A culmination of the mediation on fame is ostensibly given in "peace." Despite its title reflecting a happy ending, "peace" is a confession to the narrator's lover that their relationship will always be scrutinized: "But the rain is always gonna come if you're standing with me." Perhaps the song's title reflects Swift's having come to peace with the media's wanting to dissect her every move. So "peace" seems like a summary of her complicated relationship with the media, the attention she has received from the media, and how she can find a way to lead a normal life with a romantic partner, without losing herself or her love life. But we can only speculate if this is indeed about Taylor Swift and her private relationships. In a way, autofiction forces the reader to question the truthfulness of these words—when listeners know that Swift relies on her personal experiences, where does fiction begin and fact end (and the other way around)? At the same time as she criticizes, she also acknowledges that this will always be a part of her life. The song feels like a reckoning, a coming to terms with a never-ending life under the media lens.

The New Me

The lead single of *folklore*, "cardigan," and its accompanying music video were released on the same day as the album; the music video invokes themes of fantasy, with Swift wearing a long white nightgown and a long braid, climbing through a piano to fantastic worlds. Swift styles herself as a character from traditional folk tales, a Gretel or Rapunzel looking for the truth. The song is about trust broken, about wounds healing. The video shows a woman searching for herself, wandering through the world(s). In a way, the "cardigan" video demonstrates that Swift's own time of introspection led to this new style of music. This harks back to Swift's discussion of women artists in *Miss Americana:*

The female artists I know reinvented themselves twenty times more than the male artists, they have to or else you're out of a job. [...] "Be new to us, be young to us, but only in a new way and only the way we want. And reinvent yourself, but only in a way that we find to be equally comforting and also a challenge for you. Live out a narrative that we find to be interesting enough to entertain us, but not so crazy that it makes us uncomfortable." [...] As I'm reaching thirty, I want to work really hard, um, while society is still tolerating me being successful.

A clear contrast to her prior records, *folklore* includes a fictional (teenage) love triangle, following the betrayed lover who is confident that the cheating partner will finally return in "cardigan," the crushed lover who gives her all in "august," and the cheater who pleads for forgiveness in "betty." While these are not autofictional in the strict sense, Swift's past records have revealed that she went through teenage heartbreak herself and tapped into these memories for her writing. This speaks to her maturation as an artist (and as a woman) who now confidently manages to relate to all parties involved in the love triangle. Swift's trilogy of heartbreak, apologies, and hopefulness reveals her desire to expand her lyrical horizons by taking the perspectives of others to mediate her thoughts.

Echoing her prologue, Swift explores the perspective of a person complicit in "illicit affairs," putting herself for the first time into the role of the betraying party. The first two-thirds of the song read like a manual on how to conduct oneself as the wronging party; only late in the song does Swift switch to first-person narration. The lyrical "I" positions herself as the patronized party of this "illicit affair," telling the other person to not call them "kid" or "baby," perhaps signalling the involvement of an older partner. The song repeats the words "and," "don't," "look," and "you," with only one line starting with "I"; only in three instances in total is "I" used. Until the end, the lyrical "I" tries to put the blame off herself and disassociate herself from the "illicit" actions happening. Rather than taking responsibility, the lyrical "I" renders herself a helpless victim to the partner's "secret language." Owning that she "would ruin myself" for her lover, Swift, who was in a relationship then, seems to fuse truth and fiction. With "the road not taken looks real good now," *evermore*'s "'tis the damn season" also includes a call-back to *folklore*'s "illicit affairs," which includes the phrase, "take the road less traveled by." Both these iterations could be regarded as references to Robert Frost's 1916 poem "The Road Not Taken": "Two roads diverged in a wood, and I— / I took the one less traveled by, / And that has made all the difference." The lyrical "I" had to choose between two paths and chose not just the lonelier but also the more dangerous route. Perhaps it was also the one in which fewer voices could influence Swift, which turned out to be the right choice in the end, as the lyrical "I" states. This also underlines Swift's feminist character in the songs, as the lyrical "I" confesses her dislike of the confusion she would have to face when with this person. Even if not fully applicable, this aligns with Lauren Fournier's argument that autotheoretical art creates space for feminist practices. In effect, the autofictional character of her songs provides Swift with a layer of protection, as the lyrics cannot be simply called "diaristic" (Apple Music interview), yet it invites reflection about what these lyrics could mean. More so, Effe and Gibbon note that "[s]uch contemplation will also mean more critical, perhaps also more creative, engagements with the text, including the ways in which readers relate to autofictions and what changes they themselves might put into action in their lives" (77). At the same time, mediated through Swift's lyrics, fans might just be able to recognize their own relationships to be toxic.

Despite Swift's wish to disassociate herself from this autobiographical style of writing, fans and critics alike still look for connections between real life and lyrics (see "ALBUM REACTION: Folklore—Taylor Swift"). It should be noted that Swift, as a wealthy, white woman, is in a privileged position, as much as she is bothered by the media attention, to be able to move away from a purely autobiographical style of writing. Tellingly, Tope Folarin notes that "what nearly all writers of autofiction seem to have in common is that they're white": "Writers of color are sparingly featured in appraisals of autofiction. Indeed, the two writers of color who are consistently mentioned among the ranks of autofiction's practitioners—Teju Cole and Tao Lin— use characters whose lives and preoccupations are likely comprehensible to most members of the literary critic class." Folarin thus points to the overwhelmingly white production of autofiction, with Black or Asian-American writers seldom basing stories on their own experiences. These conditions align with Swift's general audience; Jenna Mahale observes that "[t]he typical Taylor Swift fan is unquestionably a straight, cis, white girl—the type of Swiftie that the predominantly white fandom is still most accepting of." In effect, Swift is powerful enough to rely on her predominantly white middle-class audience to embrace her new style of music. Swift's financial security and audience acceptance allow her to take for granted this acceptance, pointing thus also to the intersection of race, class, and form in Swift's change to autofiction. At the same time, fans are so conditioned to look for real-life connections in her lyrics that a change in her approach to songwriting does not immediately and necessarily translate in a change of perception by her fans.

In true Swiftian fashion, the fairy-tale character of the songs on *folklore* and *evermore* reflect on relationships and how relationships change a person, for better or worse. A pivotal working through the aftermath of a love story's ending, "happiness" reflects on what happens to a person who does not receive a "happily ever after." Swift explains the line, "I haven't met the new me yet," thus: "I was trying to sort of channel my friends who have gotten out of very, very long, impactful, life-altering relationships" (Apple Music interview). Herself having been in few long-term relationships, Swift tries to relate to her friends' experiences, mixed, however, with the confessional character we are used to. As a case in point, the line, "dress I wore at midnight," could be interpreted as a reference to Cinderella's dress, which was part of her wish from her fairy godmother—a contrast to the sultrier image of taking off a "dress" on *reputation*'s track of that title. Just like Cinderella, the lyrical "I" wishes for true love, another nod to the fairy-tale character of Swift's songs. Pointing to this notion, Swift writes in her prologue for *evermore*, "[i]t feels like we were standing on the edge of the folklorian woods and had a choice: to turn and go back or to travel further into the forest of this music. We chose to wander deeper in." In "happiness," the singer draws inspiration from her close friends but also reflects on her own change in style, her shift from country to pop to folk music. The "new me" thus also stands in for Swift's reigning in a new era, one of confidence and self-reflection. Folktales, fairy tales, and the idea of a happily ever after function as a through-line in almost all her songs. Swift keeps invoking images of the gothic and classic fairy tales but also of modern fairy tales, of modern dating stories. What becomes clear is how she perceives her life as a fairy tale that is far from perfect but very much real.

Coda

As a final observation, Swift's decision to rerecord her first six albums also returns her autobiographical storywriting to center stage. It will be thus interesting to follow her future records with the autofictional approach in mind: how will intermittent new recordings differ from her re-recordings and songs "from the vault"? Swift's next record, *Midnights*, was released on October 21, 2022, and, according to Swift, consists of "the stories of 13 sleepless nights scattered throughout my life" (Instagram), which leaves room for speculation about whether these songs were written in 2022 or before then. As Reddit user clandestine_duck writes, "the lighter on the album cover for *Midnights* is partly acknowledging that she's playing with fire by shifting the narrative back to her life." Indeed, *Midnights* marked Swift's return to the "diaristic" form of writing she had claimed could not "sustain" her (Apple Music interview).

This positions *folklore* and *evermore* as stark exceptions to an otherwise overwhelmingly autobiographic approach to song writing. Nevertheless, studying Swift's current and future records through the lens of autofiction can allow students and fans alike to approach the lyrics from a more intersecting point of view, generating fewer questions about a real-life fidelity but more potential for introspection and reflection as well as creative engagement with Swift's life. What images does Swift create by relying on certain emotions and events rooted in her own experience? And how can artists imitate this approach to writing to create a closer connection with readers? What points of access for comparison does she offer her attentive fans? To what extent does she invite fan engagement via her social media accounts? These are certainly questions that can provide a fair number of discussions for marketing, literature, and creative writing classes.

Works Cited

"ALBUM REACTION: Folklore—Taylor Swift," *YouTube*, uploaded by *Chats and Reacts*, 25 July 2020.
Bouraoui, Nina, "Top 10 books of autofiction." *The Guardian*, 16 Sept. 2020.
clandestine_duck, comment to "How do you guys feel about Midnights most likely being a personal album after folklore/evermore?" *Reddit*, no date, https://www.reddit.com/r/TaylorSwift/comments/x2fy35/comment/imjqvaj/?utm_source=share&utm_medium=web2x&context=3.

Effe, Alexandra and Alison Gibbons. "A Cognitive Perspective on Autofictional Writing, Texts, and Reading." *The Autofictional. Approaches, Affordances, Forms*, edited by Alexandra Effe and Hannie Lawlor. Palgrave: London, 2022. 61–82.

Effe, Alexandra and Hannie Lawlor. "Introduction: From Autofiction to the Autofictional." *The Autofictional. Approaches, Affordances, Forms*, eds. Alexandra Effe and Hannie Lawlor. Palgrave: London, 2022. 1–18.

"evermore, adv. and n." OED Online, www.oed.com, Oxford University Press, September 2022.

Folarin, Tope. "Can a Black Novelist Write Autofiction?" *New Republic*, 27 Oct. 2020.

"folklore, n." OED Online, www.oed.com, Oxford University Press, September 2022.

Frost, Robert. "The Road Not Taken." https://www.poetryfoundation.org/poems/44272/the-road-not-taken. *Poetry Foundation*. Originally published 1916.

Fournier, Lauren. *Autotheory as Feminist Practice in Art, Writing, and Criticism.* Massachusetts Institute of Technology, 2021.

James, Alison. "The Fictional in Autofiction." *The Autofictional. Approaches, Affordances, Forms*. eds. Alexandra Effe and Hannie Lawlor. Palgrave: London, 2022. 41–60.

Lorentzen, Christian. "Sheila Heti, Ben Lerner, Tao Lin: How 'Auto' Is 'Autofiction'?" *Vulture*, 11 May 2018.

Mahale, Jenna. "The Unbearable Whiteness of Taylor Swift's Fandom." *MIC*, 12 Jan. 2021.

Mapes, Jill. "Folklore. Taylor Swift." *Pitchfork*, 27 July 2020.

Miss Americana. Dir. Lana Wilson. Netflix, 2020.

Sager, Jessica. "We Broke Down All the Easter Eggs from Taylor Swift's Folklore So You Don't Have To." *Parade*, 11 March 2021.

Spanos, Brittany. "Ex-Factor: Taylor Swift's Best Songs About Former Boyfriends." *Rolling Stone*, 22 August 2016.

Taylor Swift: Reputation Stadium Tour. Directed by Paul Dugdale. *Netflix*, 2018.

"Taylor Swift's Songwriting Process on 'evermore' | Apple Music," *YouTube*, uploaded by Apple Music, 16 Dec. 2020.

Yahr, Emily. "2022: The year in review (Taylor's version)," *The Washington Post*, 26 Dec. 2022.

20

(Taylor's Version): Authenticity and Aura in Taylor Swift's Re-Recordings

Meghan Kuehnle

Introduction

Taylor Swift's narrative depends on a certain familiarity, a perceived proximity. She has maintained some semblance of the "girl next door" persona in her pop career, bolstering familiarity with her social media engagement, by inviting fans into her homes for "Secret Sessions," with mini early releases of her albums, and by referring to her fans in her Instagram posts as "you," and her albums as "ours." This cultivation of a parasocial relationship "the seemingly face-to-face relationship between spectator and performer"—is not particularly unusual among celebrities, but it is a move that Swift exemplifies and one that she has now harnessed in her mission to re-record her music and devalue the old masters (Horton and Wohl 215). Swift's re-recording mission depends on her fans' following her, maintaining their parasocial relationships, and on her selling the idea that the new, re-recorded "Taylor's Version" albums are more authentically "Taylor," closer to Swift herself. Swift, therefore, has engineered her re-recorded albums to sound remarkably similar to the originals, replacing and devaluing the original masters while adding unreleased songs that fill out the narrative and add to the canon of the original albums. While Walter Benjamin outlines a conception of authentic art that places ritualistic, original art in opposition to political, technologically reproduced art, Swift's re-recording project attempts to reapply aura and a sense of authenticity to her digitally reproduced music, marketing authenticity to listeners by promoting the re-recorded and revised albums as truer accounts of Swift's experiences and therefore closer to Swift herself.

Background

Swift's re-recording project started as one that was, foremost, financial and political. In 2019, Big Machines Records, the label for her first six albums, sold her masters to Scooter Braun, whom Swift claims subjected her to "incessant, manipulative bullying" ("For years"). Swift responded to this purchase by saying she had been "stripped ... of

[her] life's work" ("For years"). Swift's initial response to the sale of the masters intentionally invokes a gendered dynamic. She decries the men who are "controlling a woman who didn't want to be associated with them," and then she frames her response as a call to action in the larger music industry: "hopefully, young artists or kids with musical dreams will read this and learn about how to better protect themselves in a negotiation. You deserve to own the art you make" ("For years"). Despite Big Machine Records founder Scott Borchetta's protests that Swift had been offered a deal she had refused, Swift maintains that her music had been stolen and began discussions about re-recording her music to take control of her masters (Conscarelli).

Swift's masters were sold again in 2020 from Braun to Shamrock Holdings, and she explains that Braun's continued profit made a deal with Shamrock a "non-starter"; in the same response, she explains that she's "begun re-recording my older music and it has proven to be both exciting and creatively fulfilling" ("Been getting"). It is clear that Swift is committed to re-recording her masters and is confident that they will devalue the old masters, acknowledging this in a letter to Shamrock Holdings ("Been getting"). Swift's goal is to devalue the old masters and regain financial control of her music, but she takes pains to assert that this is also an artistic pursuit.

Swift, since these responses, has re-recorded and released *Fearless (Taylor's Version)*, *Red (Taylor's Version)*, *Speak Now (Taylor's Version)*, and *1989 (Taylor's Version)*, each of which quickly replaced the originals when searched on streaming services, the algorithm favoring the new version because of its more recent popularity (Towey). Swift's choice to delineate her new recordings by labeling them "(Taylor's Version)" is telling; she is placing a claim of ownership on her music (Battan). Swift clearly succeeded financially and in terms of popularity. Each re-recording broke a significant streaming record of its own, culminating in *Speak Now (Taylor's Version)* and *1989 (Taylor's Version)* consecutively breaking the Spotify record for most-streamed album in a single day (Caulfield; Kaufman; Peters; Towey). Swift is not the first artist to re-record her music to reclaim masters. Prince and Def Leppard re-recorded and released popular singles before coming to agreements with their respective labels, but Swift is unique in her commitment to her mission to re-record all six of her Big Machine albums despite negotiations and in her practice of updating albums with new songs upon their re-release (Conscarelli). Swift's re-recording mission is clearly political, speaking to the relationship between artist and music, and financial, claiming and profiting through ownership of her music, but it is also an artistic move. For her plan to succeed, the re-recordings must become the primary versions, deemed the most authentic versions according to fans.

Conceptualizing Authenticity

In "The Work of Art in the Age of Mechanical Reproduction," Walter Benjamin outlines a theory of authenticity that describes authentic art as having some "aura," a connection to its context. Benjamin writes that "what withers in the age of technological reproducibility of the work of art is the latter's aura . . . the technology of reproduction detaches the reproduced object from the sphere of tradition" (158). He explains that technologically reproduced art is sundered from this aura because it is detached entirely from its context, so it lacks authenticity. However, he claims that reproduced art is particularly suited to revolution, as it is more accessible to the general public, and that it lacks the sort of ritual value that authentic art has—"the unique value of the 'authentic' work of art always has its basis in ritual" (159). Benjamin differentiates between original art as ritualistic, contextualized in human practices surrounding artistic expression, and technologically reproduced art, which wields political power because of its availability to the masses. Technologically reproduced art lacks aura and therefore authenticity, so its ritual value is replaced with political potential. Swift, through her re-recordings, revises and reproduces art already designed for endless digital reproduction. In doing so, she attempts to reconstruct aura and a sense of authenticity, combining the ritual (for her fans) and the political (for the music industry) in her re-recorded masters.

Since the publication of Benjamin's article, technology has advanced from phonograph to vinyl, cassette to CD, mp3s to streaming. Now, music is designed to be digitally reproduced and endlessly streamed. Three general positions are held on the auratic status of recorded music: first, that recordings, though reproducible, "nevertheless can possess aura as forms of studio-perfected artistic productions"; second, that live musical events are "unique, aura-filled experiences"; and finally that aura "cannot apply to recorded music, consistent with Benjamin's argument" (Chapman 245). Philip Auslander explores the authenticity of live music, claiming that "all performance modes, live or mediatized, are now equal: none is perceived as auratic or authentic; the live performance is just one more reproduction of a given text or one more reproducible text" ("An Orchid," 50). He outlines the idea that in a "mediatized" culture, the recorded form used to be based on the live form, but it "eventually usurps the live form's position in the cultural economy. The live form then starts the replicate the mediatized form" (Auslander, *Liveness* 158). Listeners expect the live version to approximate the recordings, which take on a role closer to an "original." Auslander's discussions of the authenticity of live performances suggest that "live performances" are reproductions in themselves but that they still maintain some aura because of the cultural value attached to live events ("An Orchid" 166). Moreover, Auslander describes "a mass desire for proximity," a concept that clearly describes Swift's fans' desire to be close to Swift or anything Swift-related ("An Orchid" 162). Benjamin writes that "Every day the urge grows stronger to get hold of an object at very close range by way of its likeness, its reproduction" ("The Work of Art in the Age of Mechanical Reproduction" 32). These discussions of liveness and the cultural capital of liveness might be applied to Swift's re-recordings—though the re-recordings are not "live" versions, they still serve to represent her most current artistic expression and to offer fans perceived proximity.

While Auslander mostly accepts Benjamin's claim that reproduction leads to the destruction of aura and authenticity, others push back. Bolter et al. claim that "aura has not definitively decayed in the age of mechanical and now electronic reproduction. Popular music and film television indicate that our culture's desire for immediacy and therefore for auratic art remains strong"; instead there is a "permanent crisis of aura" (Bolter et al. 34, 36). Discussing the Wu-Tang Clan's push back against easy access to music by producing a single copy of their album to sell (reminiscent of Swift's own, admittedly wavering, push against streaming services), Ben Green counters that "people integrate music into their worlds in a variety of ways that extend and diversify its cultural significance," and "in this context music's aura does not necessarily wither. It becomes more multiple and multivalent, contingent and contested, but arguably this only extends its cult value, the power to enthrall and affect, both in the collectives it helps to define and in highly personal ways" (428, 438). Such an argument revises Benjamin's concept of aura, claiming that aura is developed through *new* traditions and through the development of cult value through reproduction, a concept that reflects back to Benjamin's connection of the auratic and the ritual. Likewise, Ahlers takes up Auslander's discussion of the aura of live music, arguing that aura persists through live performance and that marketing cultivates an auratic appeal for fans, suggesting that even if marketing cannot create an actual aura of art, it might produce something akin to an aura (Ahlers 123).

These discussions of aura acknowledge that if the concept of aura is to be applied to contemporary recorded and streamed music, it must be adapted. Andersson notes that "the radical fragmentation of what might be perceived as 'aura' appears to dovetail with a fragmentation of its technological, societal and, indeed, democratic context" (66). Andersson suggests that aura might still be applied to streamed music but that this aura is formed through the listener's unique relationship with the song: "an experience, a memory, or as a marker of a specific time in life, the song itself remains manifestly important" (63). There might be some aura to physical copies of music because of the choice that is made when choosing to purchase a CD or vinyl—it is this same choice that makes a listener's relationship with music significant even when streaming, the choice to spend money or time, or some "cognitive and aesthetic investment" (62). The key, here, is choice: "every listener can rest assured in the reflexive knowledge that their own path of choices—regardless of how arid, stale, and predictable the menu of options is—becomes a unique composite, not similar to any one else's play-list" (63). The listener, then, benefits from some perceived authenticity of their music or playlist, imagining or even constructing some aura around their choices. Swift leverages this investment in choice when marketing her re-recordings, the idea that listeners will choose her and will reflexively congratulate themselves for doing so, luxuriating in the knowledge that they have chosen "Taylor's Version," even if that version sounds remarkably similar to the original.

Swift's Re-Recordings as Financial and Political

Andersson's note that listeners' sense of the authenticity of a musical experience might be linked to their investment—whether financial, temporal, and social—is significant, since Swift (now a billionaire) herself clearly gauges her own success financially (Lansky 44). The music industry, of course, has long determined success based on sales (and now streams and views), and Swift is adept at creatively engineering profit and sales, selling special-edition albums to bridge "new and old industry structures" (Théberge 47). Beyond selling physical albums long after the form was considered dead, Swift has established advertising partnerships, brand collaborations, new ticket sales methods, new distribution methods for her Eras Tour concert film, and carefully constructed merchandise marketing schemes, including waves of limited-edition products. Swift stands out as a business-minded woman in the music industry and acknowledges this: "I'm sick of women not being able to say that they have strategic business minds—because male artists are allowed to" (Hiatt). Swift is proud of her financial success, particularly in comparison to men.

Describing the Netflix adaptation of Swift's *Reputation* World Tour, a recorded and produced "live" version of the concert, Arnold identifies that "*reputation* explicitly narrates a success story meant to argue that a young woman can achieve a level of financial success, stardom, and control previously known only to men" (29). However, Arnold claims that Swift's feminist messaging creates a tension; her conception of feminism and success as a woman are ultimately rooted in a "success" that is defined by men, one that is financial. Swift's re-recording project ultimately seems to reinforce this conflict. She frames the issue as one of artists' and women's rights, but the entire drama ultimately reduces to ownership. She wants to own her music, her art, but she specifically wants to take back financial control from men. Swift speaks to this in her *Time* Person of the Year interview, claiming, "What fuels a patriarchal society? Money, flow of revenue, the economy. So actually, if we're going to look at this in the most cynical way possible, feminine ideas becoming lucrative means that more female art will be made" (Lansky 54). Swift attempts to make sense of this tension, embracing this masculine conception of success, and though she names this as cynical, the idea that her success will flow down to other women is extremely optimistic. Swift, clearly, continues to care deeply about her financial power.

The possessive label of "Taylor's Version" on each re-recorded song lays claim to the music both financially and in the eye of the public, making clear that these versions are her songs, her stories. The business moves Swift makes align with Benjamin's conception of technologically reproduced art as political. However, the elements of ritual remain, particularly in Swift's re-recorded music. Fans ritualistically listen to her music, analyze lyrics and Easter eggs in community, make friendship bracelets to trade at concerts, and loudly support Swift in her re-recording mission. It is the illusion of proximity that Swift cultivates and the resulting sense of aura that allows fans to take on these ritual elements, to engage with technologically reproduced and re-recorded art as seemingly authentic even when this art is bound up in the financial and the political.

Cultivating Aura and Authenticity

Swift's re-recording narrative is ultimately a narrative of freedom—one born out of a desire for financial freedom and independence in her career. However, the narrative also depends on an idea that the re-recording and the financial freedom also come with "true" artistic freedom, the ability to tell *her* stories, offer *her* more authentic version. Of course, Swift's re-recording plan depends on listeners' acceptance of the idea that these versions are not only superior but also more authentic or truer versions of the albums. They depend, as Andersson explains, on the listeners' application of some semblance of aura to the music through choosing "Taylor's Version." Swift must construct re-recordings that both replace the originals and feel more authentic, warranting listeners' choice and therefore gaining the financial and cultural capital that accompanies replacing the originals.

Swift skillfully balances between closely replicating the original albums and adding value so that listeners are incentivized to choose "Taylor's Version." The songs that were on the original albums do, largely, sound extremely similar to the originals. Swift goes to great measures to ensure that the tracks are true to the originals, even inviting back many of the same instrumental musicians that played on the original albums to match the original album (Mylrea, "Taylor Swift—'Fearless [Taylor's Version]'"). Swift herself explains that "we really did go in and try to create a 'the same but better' version. We kept all the same parts that I initially dreamed up for these songs. But if there was any way that we could improve upon the sonic quality, we did" (Mier). Swift's dedication to closely recreating the original songs is key to her plan to devalue her old masters. Importantly, the quality is improved, mostly due to Swift's own vocals, more developed at 31 than they were at 18 or 22. Reviews of the re-recordings repeatedly recognize how the tracks remain similar while benefiting from Swift's improved vocals (Mylrea, "Taylor Swift—'Red [Taylor's Version]'"). The more the re-recordings mimic the originals, the more feasibly they can replace the original masters and the more easily listeners can seamlessly transition from old to new.

While Swift invited back original musicians, she also included some who weren't in the original recordings, most notably her touring band. In this move, Swift constructs a re-recording that is simultaneously true to the original, closely mimicking the original masters, but also closer to a "live" or concert version of the song, since "far more symbolic capital is attached to live events than to mediatized ones" (Auslander, *Liveness* 59). For Swift, live events are particularly important to her brand and her measures of success. Her tours have consecutively broken records for highest-grossing world tour, with her Eras Tour garnering a particularly high demand for tickets—evidence, Arnold ("Taylor Swift and the Other") claims, of fans' desire for an authentic Swift experience (McCluskey 48; Ygelsias). It is significant, then, that Swift should include both original recording instrumentalists and her touring band in the re-recordings. While the original instrumentalists help Swift to achieve the same sound as the original masters, aiming to replace them, her inclusion of the touring band incorporates the symbolic capital of "liveness" into the re-recordings, including some "aura" of her tours in the re-recordings. Thomas Levin explains that ultimately, "Adorno privileges the mediated over the 'unmediated' performance, arguing that the record is a better vehicle for opera than what he caustically describes as the 'supposed live performances' because it permits repeated audition. Listening to something a number of times, in turn, gives rise to a type of familiarity that is not a trivialization but is rather in the service of critical interrogation. In other words, a recording facilitates a close reading that is almost impossible with live performances" (42–3). By including her live touring band in her re-recordings, Swift offers her listeners the privilege and proximity of some semblance of the aura of live experience along with the ability to listen and re-listen, analyze and re-analyze, a ritual of Swift's fans. This listening experience contains more than the original, even if it sounds the same, bringing the listener closer to Swift through the illusion of "liveness." With this version, the listener gets it all—the original songs plus some of the sound of her tours, altogether forming a more authentic listening experience.

Developing Authenticity Through Revision

While her dedicated fanbase might automatically choose the re-recordings because of Swift's endorsement, reinforcing Andersson's claims about the aura of choice, a wider audience needs a reason to choose the re-recordings (or to return to listening to a decade-old album at all). To reintroduce already familiar albums while adding value, Swift adds "From the Vault" tracks to the re-recorded albums, unreleased songs she wrote alongside the original albums. The vault tracks are a key part of Swift's narrative that the "Taylor's Version" albums tell her story more authentically. These are the songs that didn't make the cut, songs that fill in previously undisclosed details and feelings from Swift's life at the time of writing the albums. And the vault songs play into the narrative that Swift's music, when controlled by Big Machine, was restricted, that fans weren't getting the full story. According to Swift, "Taylor's Version" is more authentic because it offers revisions to the album, adds details, stories, and emotions. And because Swift's music has always been narratively driven, this claim is compelling—the songs and stories do seem more real with new details. Swift uses these revisions to change narratives about relationships on *Red (Taylor's Version)* and *1989 (Taylor's Version)*, revealing complexity, and she revises her infamous lyrics on "Better Than Revenge" to align more closely with her more recent feminist (though distinctly white, marketable feminist) sentiments evident in songs like "The Man" and "mad woman," in interviews, and in her documentary *Miss Americana* (Kreps). While these revisions are present across the re-recordings, *Red (Taylor's Version)* exemplifies how the vault tracks change the album as a whole, allowing the listener closer access to Swift's feelings and experiences at the time of composition and shifting the narrative of the album altogether.

At first release in 2012, *Red* was clearly a breakup album. Though it includes highs and moments of hope, it is an album filled with romantic turmoil, detailing falling in love alongside break-ups. At the heart of the album is "All Too Well," the fabled fifth track, a spot Swift confirmed is reserved for her most emotionally vulnerable song on each album. And it is vulnerable—melancholic, the song details a relationship and its downfall, and ultimately mourns its loss (Aniftos). The song is one that ultimately mourns a relationship lost, and its power is in its poetic details, in Swift's descriptions of autumn leaves, refrigerator light, and a now infamous scarf ("All Too Well"). Though never a single, "All Too Well" became a fan favorite, something Swift acknowledged, telling fans that "you turned this song into something completely different for me," making clear how fans influence her relationship with her music and strengthening their sense of proximity (Braca; *Taylor Swift: Reputation Stadium Tour*).

Part of the allure of "All Too Well" was the knowledge that there was a much longer version than the original five minute, twenty-six second version. Swift revealed that "it took me a really long time to filter through everything I wanted to put in the song without it being a 10-minute song, which you can't put on an album" (Spellings). In the decade since Swift revealed that there was a longer version of the song, fans speculated about its contents, about whether they would actually hear the "true" version. On *Red (Taylor's Version)*, Swift finally delivered "All Too Well (10 Minute Version) (Taylor's Version) (From The Vault)" (at a certain point, the litany of parentheticals becomes comical). Despite its length, the ten-minute song became the center of the album's publicity, with Swift releasing a fifteen-minute short film set to the song (Spellings). It topped the charts, becoming the longest song to ever top *Billboard*'s Hot 100 (Trust). The popularity of "All Too Well (10 Minute Version)" is a product of fans' anticipation. Swift cultivates the idea that this song is the *true* original song, even more original and authentic than 2012's "All Too Well." This is the song that she originally wrote, cut down by Big Machine Records for the sake of commercial success, but which has returned, triumphant, beating all odds by topping the charts even at its full length. "All Too Well (10 Minute Version)" perpetuates Swift's narrative of her financial freedom and of re-recording as an expression of artistic freedom, all while maintaining her critical and financial success story, proving that her version was the best version—and the authentic version—all along.

"All Too Well (10 Minute Version)" is, truly, a revision of "All Too Well." While the original song is wistful, the tone of the expanded version changes entirely by the end. If the original describes a love lost, the ten-minute version describes a love betrayed, dishonored. Instead of a fairytale relationship gone wrong, it's now one that was out of balance all along; Swift sings, "You kept me like a secret, but I kept you like an oath." The new version has bite; Swift grimly jokes, "I'll get older, but your lovers stay my age," critical of her former lover's pattern of dating young women even after "You said if we had been closer in age, maybe it would've been fine." The original "All Too Well" was a story of tragedy, of lost love, revised to fit a twenty-two-year-old Swift's image, but this version reveals anger, criticality. Swift's message is clear: the true version of the story is one not only of heartbreak but also of bitter resentment. Only "Taylor's Version" features the true, authentic story.

A second vault track from *Red (Taylor's Version)* reveals another rift between the 2012 Swift narrative and what Swift reveals as her true experience on the re-recording. Despite *Red*'s focusing largely on romantic love and loss, a hit single, "22," stands apart from this romantic narrative and serves to characterize twenty-two-year-old Swift. The song describes a carefree Swift going out with friends, singing, "we're happy, free, confused and lonely at the same time ... Tonight's the night when we forget about the deadlines"; the refrain reminds listeners that, "Everything will be alright if / We just keep dancing like we're 22." Swift is an easygoing twenty-something, partying with her friends (innocently enough, of course). The poppy beat sets a breezy tone. To be twenty-two, in this song, is carefree, jubilant.

Swift revises this characterization of the twenty-two-year-old pop star ten years later, releasing the vault track "Nothing New," featuring Phoebe Bridgers. The lyrics reveal Swift's anxieties about fame and aging, even at twenty-two. Swift sings that girls are encouraged to have fun, but "Then they hunt and slay the ones who actually do it." This call to "go have fun" harkens back to the lyrics of "22," which describe Swift doing just that. Swift even more clearly makes a callback to "22," writing, "And I wake up in the middle of the night / It's like I can feel time moving / How can a person know everything at 18 but nothing at 22?" While "22" describes Swift's life as worry-free, "Nothing New" reveals her anxieties around aging, already feeling washed-up only four years after winning an Album of the Year Grammy Award at eighteen. And she asks, "will you still want me when I'm nothing new?" In "Nothing New," twenty-two-year-old Swift is painfully aware of the deadlines (both personal and professional) that the Swift in "22" brags about shirking. By adding "Nothing New" to *Red (Taylor's Version)*, Swift reveals a dissonant, complex narrative of herself at twenty-two. And she makes visible vulnerability that is not purely romantic, an addition to the album. The song develops a fuller characterization of Swift at twenty-two than the original *Red* did, and therefore, to listeners, seems to more authentically represent Swift, bringing them even closer to her experiences.

In "All Too Well (10 Minute Version)" and "Nothing New," Swift is either too young (according to her lover) or too old (according to the media and public). Only in "22" is she the perfect age, enjoying experiences appropriate to a twenty-two-year-old. Listeners to the to the original *Red* only get the "just right" narrative—they only hear "22." *Red (Taylor's Version)* revises the narrative of Swift's coming-of-age and young adulthood, adding in the pain of feeling simultaneously too young and too old. These revisions allow listeners to feel as if they're now hearing the true story, Swift's true experiences. This recognition promotes a feeling of closeness, invoking Benjamin's conception of a mass desire for proximity, and it reinforces the idea that this version of the album is more authentic, providing context (and therefore aura) through the additional tracks.

Notably, Swift released "Nothing New" only after she experienced continuing success, after proving that she can continue to produce increasingly record-breaking and highly acclaimed music. The song recounts her anxiety over failing to produce after *Fearless*, but Swift has won two more Album of the Year Grammy Awards since for *1989* and *folklore*, among many other Grammy accolades for a total of twelve Grammy awards and fifty-two nominations. Though the song is undeniably vulnerable, that vulnerability is tempered by the knowledge that Swift achieved enormous success and that despite spurts of negative media attention, she has continued to succeed into her thirties. The revision of *Red* to include uncertainty makes the album feel more authentic, but Swift manages her exposure, composing an image of authenticity with vulnerability that is retrospective, even safe, because the acute fears she expresses in the song have been disproven (even if the broader sentiment is a lasting one for Swift and women in entertainment, a point emphasized by her collaboration with another female artist).

Swift simultaneously recreates and revises. By re-recording aurally similar songs while adding vault tracks, she manages to reclaim ownership over her music by replacing and devaluing the old masters while revising the narrative of the original albums. The mimicry of the original songs is important—if Swift were to stylistically change these songs, they could exist alongside rather than replacing the originals, failing to achieve her financial and political goals. But the vault tracks allow her to add artistically to the album, revising her narrative to one that she markets as truer; she finally shares her authentic stories without the influence of her meddling record label and revises her own words in the case of "Better Than Revenge" to present updated values. Swift manages to capture her fans through loyalty, the streaming algorithm through similarity, and new or renewed listeners through added value and a revised narrative. And the revision of her albums' narratives contributes to her re-recording narrative, emphasizing that this music is hers and that she can now share the full version, the authentic version, because she is now artistically and financially free of Big Machine Records.

Challenges and Conclusions

All of Swift's choices on the re-recording project, from the aural similarities of the songs to the addition of the vault tracks, support her claim that these re-recorded albums, these songs, are more authentic than the originals. Swift draws on her fans' loyalty, but also on an idea of authenticity, an idea that she now has the artistic and financial freedom to share her full, true story, allowing listeners to become closer to the "real" Taylor. Swift cultivates a fantasy of true artistic freedom in her re-recordings, one born out of financial independence. Adorno and Horkheimer write that "Talented performers belong to the industry long before it displays them; otherwise they would not be so eager to fit in ... there is the agreement ... of all executive authorities not to produce or sanction anything that in any way differs from their own rules" (331). Swift produces a narrative that through her re-recordings, she is pushing back against the industry, that she is breaking away from artistic and political constraints through her break with Big Machine Records. In this narrative, her music is free; she no longer belongs to the industry. Of course, this narrative must be a fantasy. Swift is still beholden to the larger industry. Big Machine Records has simply been replaced with Republic Records (owned by Universal Music Group, the largest label in the world), and though Swift now owns her new masters with Republic Records, she is still just as much a part of the industry (or, "is the music industry" itself, according to Barbara Walters), even if she believes she has more artistic freedom and more freedom to share her politics. Swift claims that she is making moves that shift the industry towards artists' ownership and rights, writing, "hopefully, young artists and kids with musical dreams will read this and learn about how to better protect themselves in a negotiation. You deserve to own the art you make" ("For years"). Optimistically, Swift's plight and mission might help artists to negotiate more effectively and eventually change the industry. However, her choices have caused, in the meantime, immediate backlash for new artists. Swift's own new parent label, Universal Music Group, has already "been effectively doubling the amount of time that the contracts restrict an artist from rerecording their work" (Steele). Swift's own re-recording success has made the same savvy move more difficult for other artists; in this way, her move is politically counterproductive, even as she succeeds financially and artistically herself. While Swift promotes a message of artists' rights and a fantasy of financial independence, the backlash reinforces the structure of the industry.

For Swift, authentic music tells the whole story, appears unmediated and uncensored, and is a product of financial and artistic independence, of her particular brand of feminism. She establishes and sells this vision of authentic music through her new albums, which are specifically marketed as being more authentic versions of the original albums through their simultaneous replication of original songs and revision through vault tracks, allowing Swift to change the tone and narrative of the album as a whole while devaluing old tracks. While Benjamin argues that art is either authentic, auratic, and ritualistic, or reproduced and political, Swift's music, through her re-recordings, manages to exist between the two. The music is doubly reproduced through re-recording and technological streaming, political through her move against her old label and the music industry, and ritualistic for her cult following of fans, who might be convinced of the re-recordings' superior authenticity through their perceived increase in proximity to Swift herself. For Swift, to whom ownership seems to mean everything, the label of "Taylor's Version" declares authenticity, for what can be more authentic to fans (and to the artist herself) than her music, possessed by her? Swift's development of a new sense of authenticity through her re-recordings and the marketing campaigns around them raises new questions about the authenticity of digital music and the development of aura around it. Swift's re-recording models the cultivation of new ritual and political elements around her music, challenging the idea that art is either authentic or political. Swift, as usual, wants both.

Works Cited

Adorno, Theodor and Max Horkheimer. "The Culture Industry: Enlightenment as Mass Deception." *Global Literary Theory: An Anthology*, ed. Richard J. Lane, Routledge: London, 2013. 329–6.

Ahlers, Rob. "Benjamin's KISS: A Perspective on Music, Spectacle and Aura." *Journal of the International Association for Popular Music*, vol. 6, no. 1. (2016): 121–42.

Andersson, Jonas. "The metamorphosis of music-listening and the (alleged) obliteration of the aura." *Sounds of the Overground: Selected papers from a postgraduate colloquium on ubiquitous music and music in everyday life*, ed. Nedim Hassan and Holly Tessler, International Institute for Popular Culture: Turku, 2010. 58–71.

Aniftos, Rania. "Taylor Swift Unveils Vulnerable New Song 'The Archer': Listen." *Billboard*, 23 Jul. 2019.

Arnold, Gina. "I Don't Give a Damn About Your Bad Reputation: Taylor Swift, Beyoncé Knowles, and Performance." *Contemporary Music Review*, vol. 40, no. 1. (2021): 27–40.

Arnold, Gina. "Taylor Swift and the Other Side of Money." Taylor Swift: The Conference Era, 4 Nov. 2023, Indiana University: Bloomington, IN. Keynote Address.

"Artist—Taylor Swift." *Recording Academy Grammy Awards*, 2022.

Auslander, Philip. "An Orchid in the land of technology: Walter Benjamin and live performance." *Cultural Work: Understanding the cultural industries*. ed. Andrew Beck, Routledge: London, 2003. 161–98.

Auslander, Philip. *Liveness: Performance in a Mediatized Culture.* Routledge: London, 1999.

Battan, Carrie. "Taylor Swift Wins with 'Fearless (Taylor's Version)'." *The New Yorker*, 12 Apr. 2021.

Benjamin, Walter. "The Work of Art in the Age of Mechanical Reproduction." *Video Culture: A Critical Investigation*, ed. John G. Hanhardt. Peregrine Smith Books, 1986. 27–52.

Benjamin, Walter. "The Work of Art in the Age of its Technological Reproducibility (Second Version)." *Global Literary Theory: An Anthology*, ed. Richard J. Lane, Routledge: London, 2013. 155–63.

Bolter, Jay Davis, et al. "New Media and the Permanent Crisis of Aura." *Convergence: the International Journal of Research into New Media Technologies*, vol. 12, no. 1. (2006): 21–39.

Braca, Nina. "Taylor Swift's 'All Too Well': How the 'Red' Fan Favorite Became One of Her Biggest & Most Important Songs." *Billboard*, 10 Nov. 2021.

Caulfield, Keith. "Taylor Swift's Re-Recorded 'Fearless' Album Debuts at No. 1 on Billboard 200 Chart With Year's Biggest Week." *Billboard*, 18 Apr. 2021.

Chapman, Owen. "The Elusive Allure of 'Aura': Sample-Based Music and Benjamin's Practice of Quotation." *Canadian Journal of Communication*, vol. 36. (2011): 243–61.

Conscarelli, Joe. "Taylor Swift Says She Will Rerecord Her Old Music. Here's How." *The New York Times*, 27 Aug. 2019.

Green, Ben. "Having the sceptre: Wu-Tang Clan and the aura of music in the age of digital reproduction." *Popular Music*, vol. 36, no. 3. (2017): 427–40.

Horton, Donald and R. Richard Wohl. "Mass Communication and Para-Social Interaction: Observations on Intimacy at a Distance." *Psychiatry*, vol. 19. (1956): 215–29.

Hiatt, Brian. "Taylor Swift: The Rolling Stone Interview." *Rolling Stone*, 18 Sep. 2019.

Kaufman, Gil. "Taylor Swift's 'Speak Now (Taylor's Version)' Smashes 2 Spotify Records: Here's How She Reacted." *Billboard*, 13 Jul. 2023.

Kreps, Daniel. "Taylor Swift Talks Feminism, Misogyny in Maxim." *Rolling Stone*, 19 May 2015.

Lansky, Sam. "The Poet Laureate of Pop Culture." *Time*, 25 Dec. 2023.

Levin, Thomas Y. "Adorno on Music in the Age of Its Technological Reproducibility." *October*, vol. 55. (1990): 23–47.

McCluskey, Megan. "The Numbers (Taylor's Version)." *Time*, 25 Dec. 2023.

Mier, Tomás. "Taylor Swift Says She Went 'Line by Line' on Every Fearless Song to See What to 'Improve' on Re-Record." *People*, 9 Apr. 2021.

Miss Americana. Dir. Lana Wilson, performance by Taylor Swift, Tremolo Productions, 2020.

Mylrea, Hannah. "Taylor Swift—'Fearless (Taylor's Version)' review: a celebration of the star's breakout album." *New Musical Express*, 9 Apr. 2021.

Mylrea, Hannah. "Taylor Swift—'Red (Taylor's Version)' review: a retread of heartbreak." *New Musical Express*, 12 Nov. 2021.

Peters, Mitchell. "Taylor Swift Breaks Spotify Record for Most-Streamed Album in a Single Day With '1989 (Taylor's Version)'." *Billboard*, 28 Oct. 2023.

Spellings, Sarah. "Just Give In to the Exquisite Sappiness of 'All Too Well.'" *Vogue*, 12 Nov. 2021.

Steele, Anne. "As Taylor Swift Rerecorded Her 'Red' Album, Universal Reworked Contracts." *Wall Street Journal*, 12 Nov. 2021.

Swift, Taylor. Interview by Barbara Walters. *10 Most Fascinating People of 2014,* ABC News, 14 Dec. 2014.

Swift, Taylor [taylorswift]. "For years I asked, pleaded for a chance to own my work." *TaylorSwift.tumblr.com,* 30 Jun. 2019.

Swift, Taylor [taylorswift13]. "Been getting a lot of questions about the recent sale of my old masters. I hope this clears things up." *Twitter,* 16 Nov. 2020.

Taylor Swift: Reputation Stadium Tour. Directed by Paul Dugdale, performance by Taylor Swift, Taylor Swift Productions, 2018.

Théberge, Paul. "Love and Business: Taylor Swift as Celebrity, Businesswoman, and Advocate." *Contemporary Music Review,* vol. 40, no. 1. (2021): 41–59.

Towey, Hannah. "Taylor Swift's rerecorded 'Red' album broke 2 Spotify records in 1 day— here's why it's a big deal for the music industry." *Business Insider,* 15 Nov. 2021.

Trust, Gary. "Taylor Swift's 'All Too Well (Taylor's Version)' Soars In at No. 1 on Billboard Hot 100." *Billboard,* 22 Nov. 2021.

Ygelsias, Ana Moneoy. "Taylor Swift Breaks Own Tour Record With Sold-Out Reputation." *Recording Academy Grammy Awards,* 23 Aug. 2018.

Contributors

Samantha Bañal is a Cuban-American educator and independent scholar based in Miami. She graduated from the University of Florida, USA, with a Ph.D. in English, specializing in Victorian literature and queer aesthetics. She teaches dual enrollment literature and rhetoric courses to secondary school students while exploring the intersections between literary studies and pop culture in her personal research.

Maggie Laurel Boyd is a Ph.D. candidate and teaching fellow in the English Department and Writing Program at Boston University, USA. She also works as a writing fellow at BU's Educational Resource Center and in BU's Fellowships Office. She is currently writing a dissertation on healing in contemporary U.S. and Irish literature.

Shaun Cullen is an LA-based writer, researcher, and teacher. His work focuses on the interconnections among popular music, literature, and the avant-garde. He has published previously on Taylor Swift in the *Journal of Popular Music Studies*, and he recently taught game studies at Woodbury University and the University of Delaware (online), USA. He is currently at work on a book about rock music and the New Left.

Rita J. Dashwood is a literary scholar and historian of the eighteenth and nineteenth centuries. Her research focuses on women, property and cultural heritage, as well as the Romantic period's legacies in popular culture. She is a Research Foundation – Flanders (FWO) Senior Postdoctoral Fellow at Ghent University. She is the author of the monograph *Women and Property Ownership in Jane Austen* (Peter Lang, 2022) and the duograph *Reading the Romantic Ridiculous* (Routledge, 2024) with Dr Andrew McInnes, and she is writing her third book, *The Heiress: Women, Property and Economics, 1780–1900*.

Bridget Donnelly is Assistant Professor of English at Middle Tennessee State University, USA. Her research and teaching focus on eighteenth-century British literature, gothic and horror literature, gender and sexuality studies, and intersections among material culture, law, philosophy, and literature.

Erin Geary is a writer and critic from the New York City area. She hosts *Hivemind: A Pop Culture Podcast* and has written two collections of essays: *The Island* (2021) and *Hindsight* (2019). Her work has been published in *Doll Hospital Journal* and *English Leadership Quarterly*. She currently teaches high school.

Stephen Grandchamp is Assistant Professor of Digital Humanities and Literature at the University of Maine at Farmington, USA, where he is also the Director of the

Digital Humanities and Video Game Studies Lab. His research explores the intersection between traditional literary texts and contemporary media like popular music and video games.

Claire Hurley is Lecturer in American and Twentieth-Century Literature at the University of Kent, UK, specializing in experimental poetry, feminist theory, and radical politics. Alongside teaching modules such as "'Black Girl Magic': Contemporary Feminisms," she is also the president of Kent University and College Trade Union.

Maria Juko (M.Ed.) is currently reworking her dissertation for publication as an independent researcher and teacher in Potsdam. She researches women in the eighteenth and nineteenth centuries and examines adaptations of the period.

Ryanne Kap is a Chinese-Canadian writer and scholar from Strathroy, Ontario. Their creative writing has appeared in *Grain, Canthius, carte blanche, long con,* and elsewhere. They hold a B.A. in English and creative writing from the University of Toronto at Scarborough, Canada, and an MA in English from Western University, Canada. They are currently pursuing a Ph.D. in English and creative writing at the University of Calgary, Canada. Their research interests include adoption studies, pop culture studies, and Asian North American literature.

Devori Kimbro is Associate Lecturer in English at the University of Tennessee at Chattanooga, USA, where she teaches courses in both English and University Honors. She earned her Ph.D. in early modern literature from Arizona State University, USA, and has published several pieces on cultural and religious trauma in Renaissance England. Her work has appeared in *Prose Studies* and *The Sundial.*

Anastasia Klimchynskaya is Visiting Assistant Professor of English at Illinois Wesleyan University. She specializes in nineteenth-century literature in its intersections with science, technology, and the cultural imagination, and she has published widely on "popular" genres such as detective, gothic, and science fiction.

Meghan Dougherty Kuehnle is a doctoral candidate at The Ohio State University, USA, in the Department of Teaching and Learning, studying literacy education. Her research focuses on uncertainty and poetry instruction in secondary English Language Arts classrooms. Her additional research interests include writing instruction, ELA teacher education, narrative theory, and children's and young adult literature. She earned her B.A. at Boston College, USA, and her M.Ed. at The University of Notre Dame, USA, and has served as a high school English teacher.

Taylor McKee, Ph.D., is an Assistant Professor of Sport Management at Brock University, Canada. He has published on topics across history, sport studies, and media studies, including sport history, monuments and historical memory, and ethnomusicology.

Katherine Murray earned her B.A. in English at UCLA, USA, and her M.A. in Literature with a specialization in Critical Gender Studies at UC San Diego, USA. After graduating from UCLA, she au paired in Spain, then spent three years working in television development and tutoring high school students. She has taught undergraduates, high school students, middle schoolers, and elementary schoolers, and she has written extensively about domestic violence, toxic masculinity, and institutionalized sexism.

Brittany Reid, Ph.D., is Adjunct Professor of English at Brock University, Canada, and a Senior Research Analyst, Learning Solutions with McLean & Company. Her research explores Romanticism, theatre history, and sport studies.

Jennifer J. Smith is Professor and Chair of the English Department at North Central College, USA. She is the director of the Writing Center and coordinator of the First-Year Seminar in Writing. Her research and teaching focus on American literature and culture from the nineteenth century to the present. Her first book was *The American Short Story Cycle*, and her new book project is tentatively titled *Epistles in the Ether: Gender and New Media in Contemporary Literature*.

Miranda Steege works in queer theory, fan studies, and Victorian studies and teaches literature and writing at the University of Pittsburgh, USA. She completed her Ph.D. at UC Riverside, USA. Her writing has appeared in *Clues*.

Carolin Isabel Steiner is on staff at Wissenschaftliche Mitarbeiterin Coding Labs.

Margrét Ann Thors is a writer and Ph.D. candidate based in Reykjavík, Iceland. Originally from Fairfield County, Connecticut, she holds a B.A., M.A., and M.F.A. from Columbia University and currently teaches graduate and undergraduate courses in the English department at the University of Iceland. Her doctoral research is on literature and culture after 9/11. Her creative writing has been published in *Glamour*, *Creative Nonfiction*, *Ós Pressan*, *Storychord*, and other outlets.

Betsy Winakur Tontiplaphol is Chair and Professor in the Department of English at Trinity University in San Antonio, Texas, USA. Her specialty field is nineteenth-century British poetry, and she is the author of two monographs: *Poetics of Luxury in the Nineteenth Century: Keats, Tennyson, and Hopkins* (2011) and *The Pointe of the Pen: Nineteenth-Century Poetry and the Balletic Imagination* (2021). Her essays have appeared in several journals.

Index

Taylor Swift is abbreviated to TS in subheadings.

Songs appear in alphabetical order below the album titles in the entry Swift, Taylor.